◄ contents ►

FLCL

by Hajime Ueda
Story by Gainax

Volume 1

TOKYOPOP®

los angeles • tokyo • london • hamburg

FLCL Vol. 1
Written by GAINAX
Illustrated by Hajime Ueda

Translation - Roy Yoshimoto
English Adaptation - Stephanie Sheh
Retouch and Lettering - Tim Law
Cover Design - Gary Shum

Editor - Luis Reyes
Digital Imaging Manager - Chris Buford
Pre-Press Manager - Antonio DePietro
Production Managers - Jennifer Miller and Mutsumi Miyazaki
Art Director - Matt Alford
Managing Editor - Jill Freshney
VP of Production - Ron Klamert
President and C.O.O. - John Parker
Publisher and C.E.O. - Stuart Levy

A Manga

TOKYOPOP Inc.
5900 Wilshire Blvd. Suite 2000
Los Angeles, CA 90036

E-mail: info@TOKYOPOP.com
Come visit us online at www.TOKYOPOP.com

ISBN: 1-59182-396-X

First TOKYOPOP printing: September 2003
13 12 11 10 9 8 7 6 5
Printed in the USA

FLCL

INTRODUCTION TO FOOLY COOLY

Where do dreams end and reality begin? Video games, I suppose. Welcome to Mabase, a pleasant spot somewhere in the middle of Japan known for how much oddity passes unnoticed by its population. A giant factory sits at the edge of town puffing plumes of steam into the pallid sky, the frame of a burned out schoolhouse offers some curiosity to stirring children who need some kind of stimulation, and a local hero, a high school baseball player, has left to seek riches in America, leaving his little brother Naota to wallow in Mabase's ambient pallor. Unlike his brother, Naota isn't a star athlete, nor a colossal academic, nor a particularly attractive kid. However, Naota's life is about to become far more active than he has ever imagined when Haruko, an alien with a mean bass guitar, drops into his life.

どーとも
なってないねぇ

そこで
お友達が
エロ本の海に
沈んでると
ハナ血吹い

13

26

#2-a

34

36

39

40

42

43

Back to the
present...

#2-b

47

56

The City of
Devils…

If you falter in even the slightest degree, the City of Devils will overpower you and consume the Earth. Your battle is, therefore, endless. ✓

You slog away day and night to purge the city of demons, thereby stopping Endsville from destroying the world. ✓

You are an agent of Cantido, the God of the Black Flame. ✓

#2-c

63

Well, I'm through with cram school.

So I get bored. Naota, you wanna come too?

Hm?

You're really into this kind of crap, aren't you?

When they tore it down to redraw the district lines, weird things started happening. This old lady that lives up there has even gone crazy. We have to check it out after school!

Like a disembodied floating hand?

A ghost hand?

Sure, why not.

An' get me an issue of "Bomb"!

TV boy, if you're going shopping, make sure to get more snacks.

68

71

79

83

88

L'ange de la mort

2-d

Sunday

That's right. Lift those boxes. Since you don't have any nifty functions you can at least lend some muscle around the house.

Oh, you think he's all yours because you found him?

What a selfish attitude?

You're using him outside again? The neighbors have eyes, you know!

Nao, check the scorebook...

I found him?

Besides, who cares what people think? So there's a robot in the house. It just irds you out because it's shaped like a person and you don't like new people. It's all about...

92

93

94

95

100

You know her?

Huh?

Ni-na-mo?

...?

She's our class President.

Hmm...

It's cute, her looking down at you like that.

That's what she does. She's the mayor's daughter after all.

106

108

#2-e

When the old schoolhouse burned down...

...I was there, with my big bro.

Huh?

It's been a long time since I've seen a fire like this.

Did we miss the action?

Hey, Naota.

You guys...

Hold still!

I think I'm going to go to the hospital by myself...

Just color it like your hair.

HA HA HA HA HA

WHAT DID YOU DO?

SHUT UP!

Nah, he's smiling

He's mad?

Go to the hospital like this!

You can't understand how hard--

And being a fool is pure bliss.

To be a boy is to be a fool.

Ha. Ha. Ha. Ha. Ha.

Who's that?

......

118

The enemy's so close. We can't even see it.

Look out the window.

You said that last time.

And then I was attacked by --

What's wrong?

You want the truth?

I'm not a nurse.

"Guerrillas live among us."

Chairman Mao

You mean ...

... the feds?

Oh, is that the truth too?!

It'll just fall off eventually ... I think.

How long will this horn stay?

#3-a

If this
is my
life
flashing
before
my
eyes
...

...my
sound
and fury
signifies
nothing.

What's
that
scent?
It's not
Mamimi.
Who is it?

135

139

Mamimi's not answering.

Is she avoiding me?

...in the middle of the Cultural Fair.

According to my fabulous prediction, Sameji should be...

I didn't answer her, though.

Well, most students have class right now.

But she called me yesterday at this time.

142

145

153

155

157

162

166

THE
CREATIONIST
MOVEMENT
IN
MODERN
AMERICA

SOCIAL MOVEMENTS PAST AND PRESENT

Irwin T. Sanders, Editor

THE
CREATIONIST
MOVEMENT
IN
MODERN
AMERICA

Raymond A. Eve
Francis B. Harrold

Twayne Publishers • Boston
A Division of G. K. Hall & Co.

The Creationist Movement in Modern America
Raymond A. Eve and Francis B. Harrold

Copyright 1991 by G. K. Hall & Co.
All rights reserved.
Published by Twayne Publishers
A division of G. K. Hall & Co.
70 Lincoln Street
Boston, Massachusetts   02111

Copyediting supervised by Barbara Sutton.
Book production by Janet Z. Reynolds.
Typeset by Compset, Inc., Beverly, Massachusetts.

First published 1990.
10 9 8 7 6 5 4 3 2 1 (hc)
10 9 8 7 6 5 4 3 2   (pbk)

The paper used in this publication meets the minimum requirements
of American National Standard for Information Sciences—Permanence
of Paper for Printed Library Materials, ANSI Z39.48-1984. ∞™

Printed and bound in the United States of America.

Library of Congress Cataloging-in-Publication Data

Eve, Raymond A., 1946–
    The creationist movement in modern America / Raymond A. Eve,
Francis B. Harrold.
        p.   cm.—(Social movements past and present)
    Includes bibliographical references and index.
    ISBN 0-8057-9741-6 (alk. paper)
    ISBN 0-8057-9742-4 (pbk: alk. paper)
        1. Creationism. 2. Evolution. I. Harrold, Francis B., 1948–
II. Title. III. Series.
BS651.E84   1990
306.6'31765—dc20   90-40090
                                                                        CIP

To my parents, Ida and Arthur Eve,
and to Susan—R. A. E.

To my parents, Francis and Eileen Harrold,
and to Trudy—F. B. H.

Contents

About the Authors

Raymond A. Eve is associate professor of sociology at the University of Texas at Arlington. He received his Ph.D. in sociology from the University of North Carolina at Chapel Hill in 1975 with a specialization in social psychology and socialization and social control. He is member of Phi Beta Delta Honor Society for International Scholars. He has taught and published in the areas of criminology, delinquency, deviant behavior, sociology of the law, and computer applications in social sciences. He has also taught and published in the areas of socialization and social control, child development psychology, sociology of education, the social study of science, science education and pseudoscientific belief, and the analysis of collective behavior and social movements.

Francis B. Harrold is associate professor of anthropology at the University of Texas at Arlington. He received his Ph.D. in anthropology from the University of Chicago in 1978 with a specialization in Paleolithic (Old Stone Age) archaeology. Before coming to the University of Texas at Arlington in 1980, he taught at the University of Victoria (British Columbia). He has done field and museum research in France, Spain, and the United States and has published a number of articles on his archaeological research. His publications on creationism and other unconventional beliefs about the past include *Cult Archaeology and Creationism*, co-edited with Raymond Eve.

Preface

This is a book about an American social movement. The movement, creationism, is aimed at opposing the scientific theory of evolution. Creationists work to refute evolutionary theory and to restrict its promulgation, especially in public schools. They also seek to complement—or even to supplant—evolution in the schools with "scientific creationism," which argues that scientific evidence is actually consistent with the story of the divine creation of the universe and humankind as depicted in Genesis.

Creationism, with its elements of conservative Protestantism and "commonsense" philosophy, is a characteristically American phenomenon; it can be found elsewhere in the world, but it is most visible as a potent social and political force in the United States.

It is in several ways an unusual movement. For instance, it is ideological and phenomenological rather than economic in orientation. Creationists, unlike adherents of many other social movements, are not seeking to improve their job opportunities or their economic rights. Rather, they are attempting to have society grant their ideas on the origins and nature of mankind at least the same legitimacy that the scientific consensus accords to evolution. Creationism is unusual in another way; like the growing animal rights movement, it is the only modern social movement to directly oppose the prestigious scientific establishment with some success.

But despite its unique characteristics, the creationist movement nonetheless has a great deal in common with many other social movements, and like them, it can be described and understood from the perspective of the social sciences—especially by using the theory of social movements.

Thus, from a social scientific perspective we examine the history of the creationist movement in America, its ideology, the characteristics of its adherents, the organizations and changing tactics they use in their struggle against evolution, and the ways social movement theory can illuminate these subjects. We will also look a bit at the countermovement that has arisen among scientists and educators in response to the successes of creationists. Finally, we will venture some predictions about the future of the creationist movement.

Aside from the voluminous literature produced by creationists themselves, the great majority of the books about creationism are meant to refute or debunk it—to show that creationists are scientifically incorrect in their attacks on evolution. These treatments are often quite harsh in their characterization of creationists, whom they characterize variously as religious fanatics, anti-intellectuals, bigots, know-nothings, or even backwoods ignoramuses. Our approach is different. While we do not pretend to find the creationists' case scientifically valid, our primary focus is on understanding creationism *as a social movement.* We thus concentrate on who creationists are, how they see the world, and how they organize and agitate for their goals. Our own goal is a careful and fair analysis of a significant social movement.

No book is the exclusive product of the efforts of the author(s), and we wish to thank a number of people for aiding us. At Twayne Publishers, Irwin Sanders, Athenaide Dallett, Meghan Wander, and John Martin were dependable (and patient) sources of encouragement and constructive criticism. At the University of Texas at Arlington, the chairman of the department of sociology, anthropology, and social work, Dr. Ted Watkins, helped us in some very practical ways to bring this book to fruition. And discussions and correspondence with colleagues gave us much information and many insights during the long process of this book's gestation and writing. They include Anson Shupe, Theodore Greenstein, Jeffery Hanson, Kenneth Feder, Luanne Hudson, Eugenie Scott, William Bennetta, John Cole, Laurie Godfrey, Ron Hastings, and many others.

In closing, we particularly thank our wives, Susan Brown Eve and Trudy de Goede, for their tireless support and their willingness to proofread and eloquently critique the developing manuscript.

Chapter One

Creationism, Evolution, and Social Movements

There is no significant scientific doubt about the close evolutionary relationships among all primates or between apes and humans. The "missing links" that troubled Darwin and his followers are no longer missing. Today, not one but many such connecting links, intermediate between various branches of the primate family tree have been found as fossils. The linking fossils are intermediate in form and occur in geological deposits of intermediate age. They thus document the time and rate at which primate and human evolution occurred.

—The National Academy of Sciences (1984)

There is no evidence, either in the present world or in the world of the past, that Man has arisen from some "lower" creature. He stands alone as a separate and distinct created type, or basic morphological design, endowed with qualities that set him far above all other living creatures.

—Duane T. Gish, Institute for Creation Research (1985)

Introduction

These quotations represent the two extremes of a debate that has grown in intensity in recent years, a debate that focuses on the validity of the theory of evolution. The first quote represents mainstream scientific opinion, while the one from Duane Gish illustrates the view of a surprisingly large number of writers who claim that there is scientific evidence that the theory of evolution is bogus science. One might well wonder how such a state of affairs has come about; after all, we do not find public

1

arguments about whether atoms or gravity exist. Part of the answer
to this question lies in the fact that although the creation–
evolution debate centers on the understanding of a considerable amount
of scientific data and concepts, it is also affected far more by social and
psychological forces than most people believe.

There is widespread disagreement, most notably in the United States,
concerning whether the process of evolution produced mankind and the
earth's other species over a period of billions of years, or whether, as
represented in the Judeo-Christian Bible, all things were created by God
in six twenty-four-hour days only a few thousand years ago. Proponents
of both viewpoints have grown increasingly vocal and vehement in their
assertions that their opponents are at least deluded, if not downright
malicious.

Until recently, it appeared to most people that only the theory of evolution would receive support from twentieth-century scientists and that
it would be the only explanation of origins presented in public school
classrooms. But as the creation–evolution debate has grown over the
past two decades, it is increasingly common to hear claims that there is
much scientific evidence that supports the abrupt appearance of the earth
and all life-forms and that equal time should be allowed for both viewpoints in public school science classes.

The intense debate has generated considerable verbiage on both sides
of the issue, especially since the 1970s. Almost without exception, each
article and book involved has advocated either creationism or evolution
as the sole correct view of origins. These books and articles have mar-
shaled and interpreted the physical evidence judged relevant (for example, evidence relating to geological strata, fossil remains, and genetic
coding) with the intent of supporting one view or the other. There are a
few exceptions to this rule, in which authors have focused primarily on
the history of the conflict between the two groups (see, for example,
Nelkin 1982 and Larson 1985). Because this book is less about physical
science and more about *social* science, the focus is more on the social
actors and dynamics involved in the controversy and on its social, political, and educational implications, than on the physical science evidence
relevant to the debate.

A Spectrum of Views on Origins

Contradiction and ambiguity surround the terms used to describe and
categorize the various factions in the creation–evolution controversy.

For example, it is common to hear the term *the creationists* used as if it referred to a highly homogenous group of people. In reality, while all participants in the creationist movement share some aspects in common, deep divisions nonetheless exist among those, creating several different subcategories within the larger movement.

Ideologically, the creation–evolution controversy actually centers on at least five distinct issues:

1) *The origin of the universe.* Was the universe divinely created, or has it always existed, or did it come into existence without any supernatural cause?

2) *The age of the universe and of the earth.* Are they billions of years old, or only thousands?

3) *The origin of life.* Was life divinely created out of nothing, or did it result from chemical processes in the "primeval soup" of the early earth?

4) *Biological evolution.* Once it appeared, has life changed through a process of evolution (descent with modification), in which new species appeared while others became extinct, or have all the kinds of living things remained the same (with only minor changes within categories)?

5) *Human origins.* Did humanity evolve by a process like that posited for other life-forms, or were humans especially and distinctly created?

The various combinations of answers to these questions lead not to a simple creation–evolution dichotomy, but to a spectrum of beliefs and opinions within the overarching categories of "creationist" and "evolutionist."

At the naturalistic end of the continuum are a relatively small number of people who accept evolution and who do *not* accept any notion of divine or other supernatural involvement in the origins of the universe or humanity. Rather, they feel that only the laws of natural science can account for our origins. Their sentiments might be characterized by a statement like, "It's absolutely amazing what complex hydrocarbon molecule chains can do as a result of chance plus natural selection, given 20 billion years!" Such persons may be termed *nontheistic evolutionists.* They reject the belief that humans are the ultimate pinnacle of evolution and find fault with the associated assumption that evolution was guided by supernatural forces.

A second, much larger group of people also accept the theory of evolution over billions of years, but they believe the process was influenced or controlled by God, who is responsible for the universe's very exis-

tence. Those who hold these beliefs could in a sense be considered creationists since they clearly feel that the cosmos was divinely conceived
and is divinely directed. Nevertheless, they are usually referred to as
theistic evolutionists in the terminology that has grown up haphazardly
around this issue. Since this group is not usually referred to by the media
as belonging to "the creationists," the majority of Americans who believe
in the theory of evolution are left open to charges that since they do not
believe in a recent or abrupt creation they must be nonreligious. It is a
mistake, however, to assume that just because a person accepts the
theory of evolution, he or she cannot be a good Christian.

At the other end of the continuum are those commonly labeled creationists. Although creationism comes in subtly different varieties, we
can state as a general definition that creationism is the religiously inspired
rejection of the scientific theory of evolution in favor of traditional accounts of direct supernatural creation.

But there is also considerable diversity within this category. Subtypes
of strict creationists range from those who accept scientific findings that
the earth is very ancient (*old-earth creationists*) but who believe that
mankind was created recently, to those who follow a more literal reading
of Genesis 1 (*young-earth creationists*), who believe that God created the
entire universe in six twenty-four-hour days a few thousand years ago.
This latter group even tries to explain the geological and fossil records
by invoking the story of the great deluge of Noah and the animals on the
ark. Young-earth and old-earth creationists who do not simply dismiss
evolutionary theory altogether but argue that the scientific evidence actually shows that their beliefs are correct, are called *scientific creationists*. In recent years, the creationist movement has been increasingly
dominated by scientific creationist spokesmen and their arguments.

How Many Creationists Are There?

In the late 1970s a national public opinion poll taken by the George Gallup
organization found that 42 percent of a representative sample of the public believed that scripture is literally true. Another national poll taken in
1982 and reported in the *New York Times* in August of that year specifically found that 44 percent agreed that "God created man pretty much
in his present form within the last 10,000 years" (the creationist position
in its strictest form). Clearly, creationist beliefs are not confined to tiny
pockets of extremists but are the chosen position of nearly half of the
American public.

Creationism is not a uniquely American phenomenon, although its health is probably better in the United States than in any other country. In recent years, there has been a small but consistent creationist contingent in the United Kingdom, but it seems to have drawn its members almost entirely from the extreme fringes of British fundamentalism. The number of British strict creationists has been estimated at a few hundred thousand; after all, "In England, major debates about the scientific respectability of evolution were effectively over well before the end of the nineteenth century" (Barker 1985, 181). Michael Cavanaugh noted that creationism has been found "mainly in the United Kingdom and its former colonies (Australia, Canada, the Republic of South Africa, the United States, New Zealand) and to a lesser extent their foreign mission fields (India, Korea, Latin America, Nigeria). Its spread to continental Europe has been minor and recent" (Cavanaugh 1983). Barker (1985) says that creationism alone is taught in parts of Alberta and that at least one school board in British Columbia requires equal time for creationism and evolution.

Unlike the United States, Australia does not prohibit the teaching of religion in state-supported schools, and creationism seems to have blossomed there in recent years, with a magnitude second only to that of the United States. The Creation Science Foundation was established in Brisbane in 1980, has fourteen full-time employees, and publishes a glossy quarterly magazine, *Creation ex Nihilo,* and a newspaper, *Creation Science Prayer News* (Jones 1987, 326).

What Creationists Are *Not*

Creationist beliefs are so widespread that it would be a grievous mistake to assume, as many evolution advocates have, that those who *do* believe in creationism are either simpleminded or altogether uneducated. Many authors who decry creationism seem to feel that creationist beliefs are widespread due solely to ignorance or misinformation, and that accurate presentations of the scientific evidence for evolution will show creationists the error of their belief. We disagree. Our own research has shown that although creationist college students tend to have slightly lower grade-point averages and to read somewhat fewer books than others, these differences are actually quite small (Eve and Harrold 1986; Harrold and Eve 1987). There are many creationists who are of above-average intelligence and academic performance.

The creation–evolution debate involves much more than is commonly

perceived. Like participants in all social movements, the members of each camp find themselves immersed in group dynamics that tend to generate a certain view of reality from within their movement. Far from simply debating the scientific evidence, it appears that creationist and evolutionist groups structure their perceptions of reality in very different ways, based on very different cognitive principles and on different assumptions about the rules for knowing. Thus any social analysis of the movements involved will deal less with natural science and much more with the social psychology and worldviews of differing human groups. Important, too, to our perspective is an understanding of how these differences can lead the participants to interpret the meaning of even concrete evidence in ways that are heavily influenced by the social, political, economic, and historical forces to which each group is subject to different degrees and in different patterns.

The Creationist Movement and the Countermovement

The intensity of the creation–evolution conflict has given rise to social movements intended to advance the status of each argument, as well as to implement the logical consequences of each doctrine throughout many spheres of human activity. Like the other books in this series about various social movements—on civil rights (Blumberg 1984), feminist politics (Ferree and Hess 1985), and the antinuclear movement (Price 1989)—this book uses the social sciences to profile those involved in particular social movements—in this case, creationists. We will also use those portions of sociology and psychology concerned with the study of social movements to examine the creationist movement.

Newton's third law of physics generally says that for every action, there is an equal but opposite reaction. The rule is not as inviolate in social science as it is in physics, but there is a noticeable tendency for social movements to generate countermovements. The creationist movement is no exception; early successes have recently generated vigorous opposition. A considerable portion of this book is devoted to identifying the discriminating variables that influence whether an individual will be attracted to the creationist movement or to the proevolution countermovement.

Our scrutiny of both these movements may shed light upon their internal dynamics and also on their potential for ultimate success or failure in influencing social institutions and policies.

Studying Creationism Using Social Movement Theory

The study of social movements is usually considered a subarea within the study of collective behavior—the social-psychological study not of why *individuals* behave as they do but of why *social categories, aggregates,* or *groups* behave as they do. Why groups behave as they do is less widely understood than the psychology of individuals, and it is one of our purposes to show that group behavior in social movements can be analyzed more adequately using the principles of collective behavior.

One of the founders of the study of collective behavior, Herbert Blumer (1939), described two basic forms of collective behavior: *elementary forms* (such as riots, panics, sects, fads, and crazes), and *complex forms,* which are virtually synonymous with social movements. Both the elementary and the complex forms of collective behavior perform actions that are relatively spontaneous, unusual, even chaotic, and not yet institutionalized. (Sociologists speak of collections of roles for a traditional purpose as *institutions,* such as a banking institution or an educational institution.) But a social movement is somewhat more organized and longer lived than elementary forms.

The elementary and complex forms are both usually studied under the heading of collective behavior because under certain conditions elementary forms tend to develop into social movements. For example, the Christians of Roman times were clearly a fringe sect (an elementary form) but their church eventually evolved into a set of institutionalized and even mainstream religious organizations (complex forms).

What then distinguishes a social movement from elementary forms of collective behavior? True social movements tend to be more permanent than elementary forms. They have a definite specialization of tasks among their members, and at least the beginnings of a definite hierarchy based on the different statuses. They tend to have a relatively well-defined ideology and set of goals, as well as formal membership lists and more routinized channels for communication than elementary forms have.

Social movement organizations (or *SMOs*) are not to be confused with a social movement itself. An SMO is an organized group of persons who act to advance the purposes of a social movement. For example, there is a social movement against drunk driving that has become more visible in recent years, but it is the SMOs like Mothers Against Drunk Driving that give that social movement its tangible acting units.

Having defined the terms *social movement* and *social movement orga-*

nization, one of the tasks of this book will be to point out that creationists actually have several different social movement organizations to advance their movement. We will therefore try to identify and characterize creationists' main SMOs. We will also examine the proevolution social movement organizations. We will also investigate some of the dynamics between the creationist and evolutionist SMOs, the level of conflict between them, and the likely effects of their conflicts on our schools, churches, legislatures, and perhaps even the scientific competence and international prestige of the United States. We will also consider conflicts between the different social movement organizations *within* each social movement. These often have as much to do with the ultimate direction and success experienced by each movement as the tactics adopted by countermovements.

In any social movement, its members tend to develop a shared perception regarding the identity of the movement and its place in the larger world. Because the movement is an important reference group for most of its adherents, and because members interact a great deal with each other, the members tend to develop a shared *definition of the situation* (Turner and Killian 1987), or what Neil Smelser (1962) called *a set of generalized beliefs.* For SMO participants, generalized beliefs define both the nature of their movement and the situation in which the movement believes itself to be acting. The definition of the situation often includes elements such as a shared identity for movement participants; a definition of one or more social, political, or economic strains that the movement is intended to relieve; a definition of who or what is the source of the perceived strain; and a set of prescriptions for appropriate attitudes and actions that the members believe would lead to the reduction or removal of the strain. Creationist social movement organizations, and the corresponding countermovement organizations, do manifest these characteristics.

In Smelser's conceptualization of social movements, generalized beliefs are shared beliefs among the adherents of a social movement that operate to define for the members the source of the disequilibrium (or strain) that gave rise to the movement in the first place. Generalized beliefs also specify the tactics and goals that movement participants assume could remedy this disequilibrium. Turner and Killian (1987) criticized Smelser for overemphasizing social structural strains as the source of movements and for ignoring the diversity of motives and definitions of the situation among individuals in a social movement.

Nonetheless, creationists *do* share certain beliefs. Creationists do in fact appear to feel they have banded together in response to a strain, specifically the doctrines and policies of "secular humanists." Creationists see evolution as only one aspect of what they believe to be a creeping and fatal disease in modern society, the philosophy of secular humanism. *Secular humanism* is the belief that mankind should better its own condition as an organizing principle, even if this means that other values and beliefs are merely human products and are therefore open to debate and change. By contrast, most creationists stress that the purpose of human existence is to glorify God and to do his work according to principles set forth in a literal interpretation of the Bible. In their aversion to secular humanism, creationists have often drawn rather heavily on other conservative social movement organizations, especially those within the New Christian Right.

Those in the creationist movement also develop generalized beliefs about appropriate movement *goals* and acceptable tactics for their attainment. In order to be successful, all social movements must have a set of goals that symbolize the self-identity and that meet the material or emotional needs of movement adherents (and often of those who might be recruited to the movement in the future). Those in the creationist movements will find no shortage of a wide range of goals. As one specific goal, the creationist movement originally intended to replace evolution in the public schools with the teaching of Genesis. Having found this difficult, if not impossible, to achieve for various reasons, they shifted their goal from outlawing the teaching of evolution to achieving laws requiring equal time for the teaching of creationism in the schools (based on the assumption either that evolution is itself religion or that there is plenty of scientific evidence for creationism). Finding recently that this collective tactic, too, has been met with little success, the creationists have begun to shift from the courtroom to the grass-roots level, where they have begun to apply pressure to local school board members and local schoolteachers and principals to adopt textbooks with content more to their liking.

Some Implications of the Debate

One effect of the reanimation of creationism in the United States is seen in public school textbooks, especially biology textbooks. Recent studies have shown that coverage of the theory of evolution in high school biol-

ogy textbooks declined sharply in the 1970s and 1980s (Skoog 1979; Skoog 1984; Scott 1987).

Outside the creationist camp, evolution is widely regarded as the central concept in biology education. Gerald Skoog, a recent president of the National Science Teachers' Association, has said: "Evolution is the cornerstone of modern biology, and many courses in the public schools contain subject matter relating to such varied topics as the age of the earth, geology and relationships among living things. Any student who is deprived of instruction as to the prevailing scientific thought on these topics will be denied a significant part of science education."

The creation–evolution debate may hold enormous importance for the future of American science education in general, and biology education in particular, at a time when the United States' long-enjoyed world scientific leadership seems to have fallen into question.

The resolution of the debate will also undoubtedly affect how we define the proper spheres of science and religion. Many people who in the past several decades left what they saw as overly abstract, emotionally vacuous churches and turned toward the seemingly unlimited power of modern science have found that it, too, fails to supply them with a meaning for existence, a way to deal with stress or grief, and clear rules for living. Many of these people, not unlike those in some parts of the Moslem world, have begun to seek refuge by returning to a morally authoritative and emotionally robust form of religion. One extreme group of fundamentalist Christians, the Christian reconstructionists, would like to use the Bible as the indisputable guide to *all* human activity—for example, to supplement (or replace, if necessary) the Constitution and the Bill of Rights, or to guide the conduct of civil and criminal trials. They advocate, for example, the biblical idea that the delinquent child should be put to death for disobeying his or her parents, a policy that they see as unfortunately harsh but as mandated by the Bible and, therefore, not to be departed from. But most creationists would not favor such a degree of extremity.

The debate also highlights the question of who arbitrates what is valid knowledge in society. What, it might be asked, is the proper role of scientific authority and its associated establishment when it conflicts with popular opinion in a democratic society? Who should have the final authority over curriculum and textbook content? Should it be the scientific experts, or should it be the taxpayers (who would argue that in a democratic society it is their right to make these decisions for their own

communities)? Similarly, what is the proper relationship of the scientific establishment to creationists in a society that has a constitutional mandate to protect minority rights, including minority religious beliefs such as a desire to have prayer in schools or to prohibit abortion on demand?

Chapter Two

The Evolution of Creationism

No mention of religion, the only basis for morality; not a suggestion of
a sense of responsibility to God—nothing but cold, clammy materialism! Darwinism transforms the Bible into a story book and reduces
Christ to man's level. It gives him an ape for an ancestor on his mother's side at least and, as many evolutionists believe, on his Father's
side also.

    The instructor [of evolution] gives the student a new family tree
millions of years long . . . and then sets him adrift, with infinite capac-
ity for good or evil, but with no light to guide him, no compass to direct
him, and no chart of the sea of life!

                                   —William Jennings Bryan (1922)

To understand any modern social movement, we need to know something of its past as well as its present. No movement springs into existence suddenly, from no historical context. A movement makes sense
only against a background of social conditions, conflicts, and issues that
changed over time and gave rise to its present outlines.

    Today, when concepts such as evolution and the great age of the earth
are widely known and accepted, it may take a certain effort of imagination
to visualize a time when they were almost inconceivable. Creationist authors (like H. Morris 1984a, 25–28) enjoy pointing out that many of the
great scientists of the past, such as Newton and Kepler, were in modern
terminology creationists—that is, they never questioned the idea that the
universe was directly and divinely created, as described in Genesis. That
these scientists did not accept evolutionary theory does not particularly
help the creationist case, since of course they had no opportunity to

consider it. Similarly, say evolutionists, we do not think less of Einstein because Newton never accepted his general theory of relativity.

It is perfectly true that the scientific world generally accepted the biblical account of origins until the nineteenth century and abandoned it for other explanations only after a process of intellectual dispute. Charles Darwin's work was the most important, but not the only, element in this process. This history is beyond the scope of this book to discuss in detail (see Eiseley 1958 for a good general account, and Bowler 1989, J. R. Moore 1979, and Ruse 1979 for detailed studies). But in the coming of evolutionary thought to the United States and the conflict it engendered can be found the seeds of today's creationist movement.

Science and Religion before Darwin

The relationships between science and religion in the mid-nineteenth century, just before the arrival of Darwin's ideas in 1859, was very different from today's. Then as now, American science was practiced mostly in institutions of higher education, but on a very limited scale. The American colleges in which the few natural scientists of the day worked were what we would now describe as small, denominational liberal arts colleges (Hofstadter and Metzger 1955; Brubacher and Rudy 1976). Their main function was undergraduate education, and many professors were intellectual jacks-of-all-trades, teaching a variety of subjects. Graduate education was almost unknown, and faculty research was seldom encouraged. Despite such exceptions as paleontologist Louis Agassiz and botanist Asa Gray at Harvard, the level of scientific achievement in the United States was relatively low. Compared with Europe, the United States was scientifically a developing nation. Colleges saw their mission as being to transmit the wisdom of Western civilization rather than to produce new knowledge.

Religion was central to the cultural heritage of these same colleges; most were operated by Protestant denominations. On average, about a third of their faculty members were clergymen, and a similar proportion of their graduates went on to careers in the ministry (Hofstadter and Metzger 1955, 295, 297). Usually, religious exercises like chapel were compulsory, and a religious orientation permeated the curriculum—including the natural sciences.

The relation between religion and science in the American academic world was largely harmonious, and science was in the subordinate role.

Despite theological differences among denominations, the central doctrines of Protestant Christianity (including the authority of scripture) were almost universally accepted. In 1850, academics would have no more disagreed about whether colleges should produce good Christians than they would disagree today about whether education is better than ignorance. Scientists typically saw their rightful task as the systematic study of nature as God's visible handiwork. By studying the intricate and orderly design in the book of nature, one could learn through natural theology about its divine author. Natural science was thus complementary to the study of the book of scripture, perceived as God's direct word to humanity. Written by the same author, the two books could not contradict each other; God's truth was harmonious. Any contradictions were only apparent, not real, and were presumably due to a faulty reading of the book of nature. After all, nature was studied by fallible humans, while scripture came directly from God.

This relationship between science and religion was buttressed by various approaches to epistemology, or the underlying problem of how we know things (Kehoe 1985, 1987; Cavanaugh 1985; Marsden 1980, 1984), and to methodology. One of these approaches was the epistemological philosophy of Scottish Common Sense Realism, developed by Thomas Reid and other practical-minded Scottish thinkers of the late eighteenth century. They opposed the profound and disquieting skepticism of David Hume, who had argued that we can never really establish that relations of cause and effect exist in the external world. Instead, the Realists proposed that our ordinary common sense and perceptions do provide a direct and reliable guide to how the world works. Whatever arguments the skeptics might weave, it seemed to the Realists that we perceive the world as it really is and thus need not worry very much about whether we really do know what we think we know. Scottish Realism became popular among intellectuals in the United States. It was congenial to the stance taken by many Protestants that ordinary Christians could read and understand the Bible correctly themselves, without needing bishops and theologians to interpret it for them. It also resonated with that element in American culture that trusts practical horse sense and has little use for "eggheads" and speculation.

Buttressing the relationship between science and religion was the methodology typically associated with Scottish Realism, called Baconian after the sixteenth-century philosopher Francis Bacon. In this methodology, science was the collection and study of facts about the world. Baconian scientists distrusted words like *theory* and *hypothesis,* which

they associated with mere speculation without real study of the real world. Rather, science for the Baconians centered on the painstaking collection of facts about the natural world, in the belief that scientific conclusions would come naturally and self-evidently once one had carefully collected enough facts.

No serious challenges emerged to these ways of thinking until Darwin's time, although there had been a potentially threatening development in the science of geology, which came to America in the early nineteenth century. Geological evidence of the earth's history was potentially threatening to belief in Genesis because it seemed to indicate that the earth was very old. Although Genesis itself does not specify when creation occurred, traditional biblical interpretations had placed creation a few thousand years in the past. The most widely accepted date for creation, calculated by Archbishop Ussher of Ireland in the seventeenth century on the basis of inferences from internal evidence in the Bible, was 4004 B.C.

But geological interpretations were subsequently developed that seemed harmonious with the Bible. One harmonizing suggestion (the gap theory) was that there was room for an indefinite span of time between the first verse of Genesis ("In the beginning God created the heavens and the earth") and the subsequent verses describing the six days of creation. Another resolution was proposed by those who would today be called day-age creationists: that each of the six "days" of creation was actually of indefinite length, not simply twenty-four hours. Since the sun was not created until the fourth day, one could suggest that there could not have been solar days before then. Thus, the earth might be very old after all.

The dominant school of geological interpretation, however, was *catastrophism,* which attempted to reconcile the Bible with geological formations and the fossil record (with its many extinct creatures such as dinosaurs) by positing that a series of great cataclysms in the past had destroyed most life-forms. These catastrophes had been followed by the creation of new species to replace the old. The great flood described in Genesis, which only the inhabitants of Noah's ark survived, was simply the most recent of these catastrophes; the others occurred before man's creation.

Thus, the natural scientists of the early nineteenth century were generally able to reconcile the books of scripture and nature to their satisfaction, including the new "chapter" on geology. The only theological concession necessary was that certain information about the past (catas-

trophes before Noah's flood) must have been left out of Genesis, presumably because they are irrelevant to human salvation; but what
Genesis did say was widely accepted.

By 1850, in Europe, catastrophist geology was giving way to the *uni-
formitarian* approach of Charles Lyell and other geologists. His theory of
a very long earth history, of mostly gradual change, explained the geological and fossil record far better than catastrophism. But in the United
States, whose intellectual and scientific developments lagged behind Europe's, catastrophism still dominated.

A Scientific and Academic Revolution

The old relationship between science and religion in the United States
changed radically between 1850 (particularly after the Civil War) and
1900. This change, which among other things set the stage for modern
creationism, was due to several factors, most of them imported from
Europe.

One dramatic factor was the professionalization of scientists and academics (Brubacher and Rudy 1976; Hofstadter and Metzger 1955, 367–
412; Metzger 1987). Under the influence of German universities, American higher education began to develop the system of graduate education
that culminated in the Ph.D. degree, which had been almost unknown in
the United States before 1860. The number of graduate students in the
country grew from 198 in 1871 to 5,568 in 1900. When these graduate
students received their degrees, they typically became professors, but
their task was not only to teach, but to produce new knowledge
(research).

As American professors became more expert and began to think and
act as practicing scientists or historians, a shift also occurred in what
Hofstadter and Metzger (1955, 341) called their groups of reference.
That is, their primary loyalties gravitated from their particular colleges
and denominations to their professions. They became increasingly concerned with academic freedom—the right to write and teach, even about
unpopular ideas, without interference from authorities.

At the same time, academia became more secularized—that is, less
tied to religious doctrines and symbols. Nonsectarian colleges and state
universities grew in size and importance. Scientists and other academics
increasingly argued that the criterion for deciding whether to teach an
idea should be its truth or usefulness, not its consistency with religious
belief.

In the context of these widespread changes, other intellectual developments from overseas were of special importance for the creation–evolution issue.

The Higher Criticism The first was a new type of biblical analysis, the so-called higher criticism, which had originated primarily among scholars in Germany. Traditionally in Christendom, the Bible had been treated as a book totally unlike any other. But the new higher criticism used techniques of linguistic and historical analysis that had been developed for the study of ordinary historical documents and applied them to the Bible (Friedman 1987; Frye, ed., 1983). Scholars explored, for instance, the fact that Genesis contains *two* accounts of the creation of Adam and Eve. In chapter 1, God creates them together (with no specification as to how) after creating other forms of life, but in chapter 2, he forms Adam from dust and later forms Eve from Adam's rib, *before* creating plants and animals. Detailed analysis of content and style led the German scholars to conclude that the book of Genesis as we know it had been compiled several centuries before Christ by an author or editor who combined two somewhat different accounts of differing ages into a not-entirely-seamless whole. Furthermore, some stories in Genesis, such as Noah's flood, had striking similarities to much older stories recorded by ancient Mesopotamian scribes. Apparently, the ancient Hebrews had borrowed such stories from other peoples and modified them for their own religious purposes. Whether or not the Bible was divinely inspired (and many of these scholars did believe that it was), it had been written down by humans living in particular historical times, and it reflected their values, beliefs, knowledge and ignorance.[1]

Initially, the higher criticism came as a shock to Christianity, but it was eventually accepted by most theologians as a path to a greater understanding of scripture. Still, others denounced and rejected it as tampering with God's word. Dealing as it did with human affairs, higher criticism had little direct impact on the natural sciences, although it complemented developments in geology and other sciences by providing an independent critique of biblical literalism—another set of reasons for scientists and others to entertain some very nonbiblical ideas about the past.

Darwinism Even more important from our point of view was the impact on the natural sciences of the work of the English biologist Charles Darwin. In 1859, Darwin published one of the most influential books of modern times, *The Origin of Species*.[2] It was soon available in

the United States, where it created as searing a controversy as it had in England.

Darwin's theory, his evidence, his methods, and the arguments of his supporters and opponents are a vast and complex topic (see Bowler 1989; J. R. Moore 1979; Ruse 1979). Here we will touch only upon a few points useful for understanding today's creation–evolution controversy.

The idea of evolution—of descent with modification—was not new in 1859. Naturalists had proposed in the previous century (indeed, as far back as classical times) that species of animals and plants had not been fixed at the time of creation, as Genesis states, but could change over time.

Darwin, however, proposed the first really successful evolutionary theory by accomplishing two things. First, he amassed much evidence from all corners of biology (including embryology, comparative anatomy, and animal geography, as well as the fossil record) to make the best case yet that evolution had occurred and that it explained the diversity of living things. Evolution, in his view, is like a great tree, with some shoots (species) branching out into new species, some persisting little-changed, and some terminating in extinction.

Second, Darwin suggested a process in nature—natural selection— that could account for *how* evolution occurred, without having to rely on mystical or supernatural forces such as a supposed innate tendancy in living things toward progress. According to Darwin, species could change over time because some individuals had traits that better equipped them for their particular environments. These would out-survive and out-re-produce those less favorably equipped; as a result, the average charac-teristics of a species could, over time, change greatly.

Darwin exemplified the tendency in nineteenth-century science to ex-plain things in terms of naturalistic processes in the material world— which can be scientifically studied by observation, measurement, and so on—rather than in terms of supernatural forces, which cannot be so stud-ied. He also exemplified the replacement of Baconian science by a more modern science in which hypotheses and theories were not merely spec-ulations but explanations of nature that could be tested against observa-tions. (See Chapter 4 for more on modern conceptions of scientific theory.)

Despite the ensuing furor, American scientists rapidly accepted Dar-winism (Pfeifer 1974; Marsden 1984; Numbers 1986; J. R. Moore 1979). Because evolutionary theory made sense out of so much biological

knowledge that was otherwise puzzling (such as homology, or structural similarities among different life-forms, which could now be interpreted as indicating common ancestry), it quickly became the standard framework. Some dissenters found the theory too speculative, but even by 1880, an antievolutionist editor could name only two naturalists working in the United States who opposed evolutionary theory (Pfeifer 1974, 204).[3]

Outside the sciences, especially among religious intellectuals, Darwinism (i.e., evolutionary theory) encountered rougher going, and its triumph was less complete. Many, but not all, religious leaders opposed Darwinism on two grounds. First, they argued, the theory of evolution was scientifically incorrect. In the Baconian tradition, they cited Darwin's scientific opponents and made the case themselves (in an age when scientific matters were not deemed beyond the clergy's competence) that Darwinism was not a proved scientific conclusion but a mere theory.

Second, they vigorously opposed Darwinism because of what they believed would be its effects on religion and morality. If Darwin's ideas on how species originated were true, then Genesis was not totally factually correct. And what would happen to religious faith if the Bible could not be relied on for truth? What would happen to people's moral sense if they came to believe that humankind was descended from animals, not specially created by God? For many, the fact that evolutionary theory seemed to contradict cherished religious values was reason enough to dismiss it out of hand.

In intellectual circles the religious attack on the theory of evolution was pressed hardest from the 1860s to the 1880s, not the least in colleges. Several professors at denominational institutions were fired when they would not recant Darwinism. In 1886, for instance, James Woodrow of the Presbyterian Theological Seminary in South Carolina (and uncle of future president Woodrow Wilson) was dismissed for maintaining that evolution is compatible with Christianity (Wilson 1967, 58–70; Hofstadter and Metzger 1955, 328).

These religious objections reflected the traditional ideas of Baconian science and the unity of truth. Particularly noteworthy is their element of "doctrinal moralism," the notion that an idea or theory should not be adopted if it would have bad moral effects—or put another way, that presumed immoral outcomes (such as atheism and irreligion, in this case) dictate that a proposed theory could not be true (Hofstadter and Metzger 1955, 353). Such notions are still part of the creation–evolution controversy.

But the scientific acceptance of evolutionary theory and the success of

the higher criticism eventually led churchmen to revise their positions. Most of them relinquished claims of scriptural authority over the natural and physical sciences (Roszak 1987; Wilson 1967, 39–70). They took the position that religious and scientific knowledge are two different kinds of knowledge. Evolutionary theory, they said, is not a moral or religious doctrine; in turn, the Bible is not a science textbook but a source of moral and spiritual truth that was set down by men of a prescientific age and that reflects the limited knowledge of that age. Genesis, they concluded, does not give a scientific account of origins, but it does tell us that God's creative act began and sustains the universe—a notion not contradicted by Darwinian evolutionism.

Many conservative Christian theologians were unenthusiastic about the theory of evolution, but even they did not pronounce it anathema. Even some of the authors of *The Fundamentals,* the series of booklets published between 1910 and 1915 that gave fundamentalism its name, were relatively moderate in their treatment of Darwinism, accepting a possibly ancient age for the earth and limited forms of evolution (Marsden 1984; Numbers 1986). Thus, most religious intellectuals made their peace with evolution. Others who did not gradually became marginalized in the intellectual world (Marsden 1984).

During the intellectual conflict between traditional beliefs and the theory of evolution between 1859 and the 1880s, many notes were struck that still resound in today's creationist movement. But one difference stands out between late-nineteenth-century antievolutionism and that of later times: there was no strong feeling or agitation against evolution on the part of the general public. Antievolutionism was not a social movement: "The atmosphere which bred the anti-evolution laws of the 1920's and the Scopes trial in Dayton was not a problem for Woodrow and men like him in the 1880's, for the simple reason that most laymen had not heard enough about Darwinism to feel threatened by it" (Wilson 1967, 42).

No Gallup polls measured public opinion on Darwinism in the late nineteenth century, but indications are that most citizens of the time neither knew nor cared about the theory of evolution. Intellectual circles were very small in American society, and public education was far less available than it would be just a generation later.

The Antievolution Movement of the 1920s

A powerful antievolution movement did emerge in the 1920s, culminating in the passage of laws in several states against the teaching of evolution

in public schools. The sudden appearance of this movement may never be fully understood, but two factors clearly helped bring it about.

The first was the growth of public education, especially at the high school level (Larson 1985, 7–27). This process brought large numbers of people who were outside the colleges and seminaries face-to-face with evolution for the first time. Following the scientific trend, biology textbooks had by 1900 become thoroughly evolutionist. These texts were used in high schools, since biology was considered too complex a subject for younger children. Teaching the theory of evolution in biology courses was widely promoted by professional teaching textbooks and journals and was endorsed by the National Education Association in 1916. By that time, state systems of public education were supplying growing numbers of students who read the texts. U.S. high school enrollment in 1890 was about 360,000, or only 6.7 percent of the 14–17 age group; but by 1910, the figure had grown to over 1.1 million students (15.4 percent of the age group); it mushroomed to 2.5 million in 1920 (32.3 percent) and 4.8 million in 1930 (51.4 percent) (Tanner 1972, 37). For the first time in American history, many working-class and middle-class parents were sending their children to secondary school.

But as they did, they were often shocked to find that their children were receiving instruction (paid for with their own tax dollars!) that seemed to contradict their religious beliefs. These Americans knew little or nothing of the previous century's intellectual struggle over Darwinism; many perceived simply that an antireligious doctrine was being taught in the schools. It can be no coincidence that the antievolutionist movement arose in the midst of the fastest growth in high school enrollment in U.S. history.

The second factor that contributed to the emergence of the 1920s antievolution movement helped determine *when* it erupted. This factor was the "widespread sense of cultural crisis" (Marsden 1984, 104) that afflicted Americans, particularly conservative Christians, after World War I (see also Marsden 1980, 149–90; Numbers 1982, 1986).

Domestically, social attitudes toward behavior of which traditional Protestantism disapproved—like drinking, dancing, and gambling—were now more tolerant, because of great social and economic changes. Most Protestant denominations were themselves moving in the direction of liberalism or modernism, accepting these attitudinal changes and adapting themselves to the increasingly secular modern world. Such modernist Protestants saw religion as having to meet human needs in this world as well as in the next. They also tended to believe that religious ideas, even the Bible's revelation, should be subject to tests of reason and experi-

ence (Gatewood 1969). Modernism thus involved accommodation to biblical higher criticism and to evolution.

Furthermore, the millions of immigrants who had arrived over the previous decades, mostly from southern and eastern Europe, had increased
the influence and visibility of Catholics, Jews, and other non-Protestants
in American life. To many conservative Protestants, it seemed that their
beliefs, once the national consensus, were becoming a threatened minority viewpoint.

International developments, too, caused deep concern. The unexpected and dreadful carnage of the Great War had shaken the self-confi-
dence of Western civilization. People began to ask whether civilization
was in decline and whether these tribulations were signs of God's judgment. German militarism was widely blamed for the war, and many saw
it as a natural outcome of the acceptance of Darwinism. Some Germans
had even justified a "might-makes-right" philosophy by pointing to evolution's supposed demonstration that bloody struggle is "nature's way"
(Gould 1987a). Finally, the Bolshevik revolution in Russia (where evolution became official materialist dogma) and labor unrest at home led to
a "Red scare" just after the war. Some feared that the United States and
all other Christian nations were in danger of subversion by atheistic
revolutionaries.

William Jennings Bryan and the "Monkey Laws"   It was in
this atmosphere of crisis during the late 1910s and early 1920s that fundamentalism crystallized as a coalition of conservative evangelical Protestants resisting the changes associated with modernism (Marsden
1980). Fundamentalists provided the core of support for the antievolution
movement, but not all its supporters were fundamentalists.

Indeed, the most important instigator and leader of the movement,
William Jennings Bryan, was not strictly speaking a fundamentalist;
raised a Baptist, he had become a Presbyterian as a teenager. Bryan was
one of the best-known political figures in the land. Thrice a presidential
candidate and a former senator and secretary of state, he was a leader
of the Progressive political movement. He had long been an advocate of
the rights of farmers, workers, women, and children. He opposed mo-
nopoly capitalism and American entry into the Great War. Some have
seen his antievolutionism as an embarrassing retreat from his Progressive ideals, but it was actually consistent with his values (Gould 1987a;
Larson 1985; Numbers 1986).

Bryan and many others who wanted a just and humane society were

convinced that Darwinism would wreck that goal by sabotaging the moral development of students. It would remove the Christian basis for morality or, in his phrase, "replace the Golden Rule with the law of the jungle." He thought he could see two examples of such damage already—German militarism and robber-baron capitalism. Some capitalists opposed social welfare programs on the basis of social Darwinism, which in its extreme form contended that aiding the poor simply allowed "unfit" people to multiply, whereas letting them starve improved the human race by removing the stupid and lazy (Bowler 1989, 285–91). Social Darwinism in fact owed little to Darwin himself, who condemned it; it was mainly the work of his contemporary, social philosopher Herbert Spencer, who had confused evolution with a particular Lamarckian understanding of "progress." But Bryan and many others believed that this brutal ideology flowed naturally from evolutionary theory.

Bryan's antievolutionism also had Progressive roots in his faith that legislation could reform or prevent bad behavior. Just as righteous people had used the force of law to regulate child labor, to grant women the vote, and to combat the evils of liquor by prohibiting its sale by means of the Eighteenth Amendment, they should legislate a halt to the corruption of youth by Darwinism.

Finally, Bryan's position was Progressive in its unalloyed populism. For him, a democratic society's rules were to be made by the people and not by an elite, no matter how rich, powerful, or smart the elite was. He and his followers felt that the people themselves had a right to determine what was taught in public schools, whether biology professors liked it or not. "Those who pay the taxes," he said, "have a right to determine what is taught; the hand that writes the check book rules the school" (quoted in Larson 1985, 49).

Once tolerant of evolution, Byran had changed his mind by 1920. The next year, he learned of a bill that had been introduced into the Kentucky legislature to ban the teaching of evolution in public schools, and he seized the issue. To encourage more such bills, he wrote, spoke, and lobbied through his extensive political network, in concert with religious leaders like William Bell Riley, a Baptist pastor from Minneapolis. As a result of their combined efforts to rouse public opinion, antievolution bills were introduced into twenty state legislatures during the 1920s.

In four states (Arkansas, Mississippi, Oklahoma, and Tennessee), the bills became law between 1923 and 1928 (Larson 1985, 28–57). The Florida legislature passed a nonbinding resolution condemning the teaching of the theory of evolution as "improper and subversive." Elsewhere,

state educational bodies such as textbook commissions banned evolution from public school textbooks in Texas, North Carolina, and Louisiana. The California Board of Education ordered evolution to be presented "as a theory only." Even in states that adopted no such measures, parents, ministers, congregations, and other activists exerted considerable pressure at the local level on school boards, principals, and teachers. In cities, counties, and school districts from Portland, Oregon, to Paducah, Kentucky, teachers were forbidden to teach or discuss the theory of evolution; some were fired for doing so (Beale 1936, 227–40). As late as 1941, one-third of the teachers surveyed by Beale were "afraid to express acceptance of evolution" publicly (Beale 1941, 241), and in 1942, a survey of over three thousand secondary biology teachers found that fewer than half were teaching anything about evolution to their students (cited by Nelkin 1982, 33).

The public that supported the antievolution movement was large and varied. We have no exact indication of its size, but a nonscientific poll conducted in 1929 among seven hundred Protestant ministers gives us a clue. It asked the question, "Do you believe that the creation of the world occurred in the manner and time recorded in Genesis?" As few as 11 percent of the Episcopalian ministers but as many as 63 percent of the Baptists and 89 percent of the Lutherans answered yes (Numbers 1986). Another indication is found in Robert and Helen Lynd's famous *Middletown* study of Muncie, Indiana. Of the high school students in this small midwestern city in 1924, only 28 percent agreed that "the theory of evolution offers a more accurate account of the history of mankind than that afforded by a literal interpretation of the first chapters of the Bible." By the 1977 *Middletown III* restudy, that figure had risen to 50 percent (Caplow et al. 1983).

The scanty survey data available are consistent with Numbers's (1986) point that Bryan's supporters were not all stereotypical Bible Belt fundamentalists. Many antievolutionists were not fundamentalists; they included many northerners and urbanites. William Bell Riley of Minneapolis was perhaps the most prominent fundamentalist leader of the movement, and others hailed from other northern and western cities like New York, Los Angeles, and Philadelphia (Gatewood 1969, 37).

Although not all antievolutionists were poorly educated, the intellectual level of their campaign was below that of the original controversy a half-century earlier. Antievolutionists pressed their case mainly on grounds of doctrinal moralism and populism rather than science. The movement's thrust was not to promote debate on the merits of various views of

origins—it was to stop the teaching of evolution. There was no real attempt to convince scientists that they were wrong, but only to make them irrelevant in determining what was to be taught in public schools.

Interestingly, many antievolutionists (especially Lutherans) did not support Bryan, viewing his campaign as a risky entanglement of church and state. Nonetheless, rural, less educated, and fundamentalist people were most likely to oppose evolution; and it was in the South, where antievolutionism seems to have been strongest, that the only antievolution bills actually passed. Stark and Bainbridge (1985, 88–92) have argued that this was due less to a specifically southern Bible Belt mentality than to the disproportionate power of rural lawmakers in southern legislatures. Certainly, the rural, less industrialized, conservative South afforded Bryan his only concrete legal successes.

The Scopes Trial   The antievolution movement of the 1920s climaxed in the famous Scopes "monkey trial" of 1925. Much has been written on this trial (see especially Ginger 1958; de Camp 1968; and Larson 1985, 58–81), though today most people are acquainted with it through the fictionalized account in the play and film *Inherit the Wind*. Here we will stress only a few crucial aspects of the trial and its implications.

After the passage of the Tennessee antievolution law, the American Civil Liberties Union (ACLU) looked for a high school teacher who would volunteer for a court case to test the law. They believed that the law placed unconstitutional religious restrictions on academic freedom and the teaching of science. They expected to lose the case in Tennessee but hoped to be able to appeal to the U.S. Supreme Court and have the statute overturned there. John Scopes, a young teacher in Dayton, Tennessee, agreed to be the guinea pig. Dayton's city fathers approved beforehand of the arrangement, hoping that the national publicity would benefit the town economically.

The ACLU was assisted in defending Scopes by attorney Clarence Darrow, an agnostic and defender of unpopular causes, while William Jennings Bryan himself helped the prosecution. Both sides (especially Scopes's) brought expert witnesses, but most of them were not allowed to testify on the grounds that the truth or falsity of evolution was irrelevant to whether Scopes had broken the law by teaching it. Sensing an epic confrontation, the national press (which in those days meant mainly the northeastern press) came in droves, with the acid-tongued H. L. Mencken in the forefront. To use a modern term, the trial was a

media event. There were stirring speeches by Darrow on freedom of thought and teaching, and by Bryan on the right of the people to uphold traditional values. Darrow conducted a devastating cross-examination of Bryan, who testified as an expert on the Bible. All of this was breathlessly reported in newspapers and magazines and over the new medium of radio.

Despite the drama, the outcome was never in doubt. The jury duly found Scopes guilty of teaching evolution against the law, and the judge fined him $100. On appeal, the Tennessee Supreme Court upheld the state law as proper, saying that the people through their representatives could decide what was to be taught in their schools, and that Scopes, as the people's employee, had to follow their orders. But then the court threw out Scopes's conviction on a technicality (the fine had been improperly levied by the judge instead of the jury). The case was over, and the ACLU was denied its chance to appeal to the U.S. Supreme Court.

The Monkey Trial's Aftermath   In formal terms, the Scopes trial was a success for Bryan's cause, but this success exacted a price. The press had depicted antievolutionists largely as ignorant hillbillies resisting the progress of science and civilization. Mencken and others particularly ridiculed Bryan, who had seemed pompous and ill-informed under Darrow's cross-examination. When Bryan died, shortly after the trial, the movement lost a diminished leader.

The mainstream of educated Americans (including nearly all scientists, academics, and writers and many liberal churchmen) who were the antievolution movement's natural opponents thus had cause to celebrate a moral victory in the Scopes trial. The antievolution movement seemed to lose momentum after 1925. One antievolution measure was adopted by referendum in Arkansas as late as 1928, but most bills introduced in legislatures in the later 1920s failed. Apparently, some supporters had been embarrassed into silence by the monkey trial. Furthermore, it seemed that nearly all the states likely to take steps against evolution had done so by 1928. Bryan, whose nationwide prestige might have helped the movement outside the South, was gone. Finally, other issues began to distract movement supporters. Conservative Protestants opposed the 1928 presidential candidacy of a Catholic, Al Smith; then came the Great Depression.

By 1930, the creation–evolution controversy had lapsed into near-silence. The fundamentalists and other evangelicals who constituted the heart of the movement retreated from public battle into their enclaves—

seminaries and Bible colleges, religious publishing houses, church congregations, and interdenominational organizations—and were little noticed on the outside.

Proevolutionists took this silence for victory, but it was actually more of a truce. The "antis" had in fact gotten some of what they wanted. True, their beliefs no longer occupied center stage in American society, but the various state antievolution laws and regulations stayed on the books. And even though no one else was prosecuted for breaking these laws, they had a chilling effect on the teaching of the theory of evolution, not only in the South but all over the nation.

Quantitative measures of this effect are difficult to obtain; the high school biology texts of the period are the main source of evidence. Grabiner and Miller (1974) and Skoog (1979) have documented drastic cuts in the coverage of evolution in these books, beginning about 1926. The word *evolution* itself often disappeared or was replaced by euphemisms like *development*. Explanations of evolutionary theory and emphases on its central role in biology were generally reduced, qualified, or even removed in post-1925 textbooks, and biblical quotations or references were sometimes added. For instance, back in 1921 Moon's bestselling *Biology for Beginners* had stated in its preface that biology is "based on the fundamental idea of evolution" and averred that "both man and ape are descended from a common ancestor" (quoted in Larson 1985, 87; see also Bennetta 1986, 19; Scott 1987). By the 1926 edition, the word *evolution* had disappeared from the preface, as had Charles Darwin's portrait from the frontispiece. Evolution still played a significant role in this edition, but by the 1933 edition, the topic had been completely expunged. These changes were made not merely in special editions for southern states; students all over the country learned less about evolution from their textbooks.

This remarkable "self-censorship" (Grabiner and Miller 1974) by the New York–based publishing industry was due, not to religious conversion, but to simple economics. Publishers are in business to make money. Books containing too much evolution might be rejected where the topic was illegal or unpopular. It was easier on the balance sheet to issue a single nationwide edition of a book that contained material offensive to no one.

Almost none of these textbooks were written by university biologists; their authors were high school teachers or professional authors. This highlights a separation, then and now, between secondary and higher education. Most university scientists seem to have been uninvolved with

what was happening to high school biology instruction. By the same token, antievolutionists never fully extended their campaign to public universities. They seemed willing to tolerate evolution in the college curricula (which were then attended by only a tiny fraction of American youth) if they could fight it in the high schools.

The antievolutionists were partly successful, too, in a more symbolic sense. In any school with a reasonably consistent curriculum, students are taught what amounts to an authoritative view of reality. Regardless of whether children actually adopt this view of reality, there is symbolic value in one's view (like antievolutionism) being recognized as the official one by its institutionalization in the public school curriculum. This is an example of what Heinz (1983, 146) calls "labeling wars"—disputes over whose symbols will be recognized as officially correct and whose as deviant. Antievolutionists had been offended that what they saw as an atheistic creed was being taught as "official reality" in public schools. Where they succeeded in evicting or restricting evolution, they had put right the basic worldview that students were expected to learn. Their satisfaction is comparable to that of the Prohibitionists who knew that drinking went on after it became illegal but were nonetheless pleased because society had declared it reprehensible behavior deserving of punishment (Gusfield 1963). Antievolutionists, too, knew they could not ban evolution from society, but in some places they could get their version of reality reaffirmed as society's official one.

The antievolution movement of the 1920s can thus hardly be considered a simple failure. The truce that had been achieved between the opponents by 1930 persisted with little change until the 1960s.

The End of the Truce

After decades of latency, the creation–evolution dispute flared up again in the 1960s. In a way, this was because of the Russians. In 1957, the USSR launched Sputnik, the first artificial earth satellite, and Americans were shocked. They had always seen Russia as technologically backward, but now the Russians had surpassed the United States in space research. Something must be very wrong with American science.

In the wake of Sputnik, Congress allocated millions of federal dollars to support scientific research and training. The National Science Foundation (NSF) used $7 million of its allocation for the Biological Sciences Curriculum Study (BSCS), which developed a series of new high school biology textbooks (Nelkin 1982, 39–47; Larson 1985, 89–92, 95–97).

These books, developed by professional biologists, featured evolution as a cornerstone of modern biology in a prominent and straightforward way, without the evasions or euphemisms still common in other texts.

Appearing in 1963, the BSCS biology texts were widely adopted and were eventually used in nearly half the nation's high schools. Of high overall quality, they were backed by the NSF's prestige and endorsed by major educational organizations. Once again, many high school students were exposed to the theory of evolution in public schools.

An indirect effect of the adoption of the BSCS texts was the overturning of the antievolution laws that had been on the books since the 1920s. In 1965, when BSCS books were adopted in Little Rock, Arkansas, biology teacher Susan Epperson and the Arkansas Education Association filed suit against the state's antievolution law, under which the teaching of part of the book's material was illegal (Larson 1985, 98–119). The law was overturned, then reinstated at lower appeals levels, then in 1968 was finally thrown out by the U.S. Supreme Court on the grounds that it violated the First Amendment. The Court held that the law unconstitutionally served a sectarian religious purpose by imposing a religious restriction on the teaching of evolution. By 1970, all other state antievolution laws had also been voided or repealed. As Larson (1985) emphasizes, in the 1960s the justices saw evolutionism as generally accepted by society and as neutral in its implications for religion and morality. No longer did the argument that acceptance of evolution led to atheism and immorality seem to carry much weight.

Thus in the 1960s, antievolutionists suffered a double blow: the reemergence of evolution in the school curricula, and the removal of laws protecting their children from exposure to it. Their reaction to these developments gave rise to the modern creationist movement.

Chapter Three

Creationists and Creationism Today

> I'm having a hard time figuring out how much of this to believe being raised in a Christian home.
> —comment in a student evaluation of
> a college course on human evolution (1988)

> The Bible is the written Word of God, and because we believe it to be inspired thruout [*sic*], all of its assertions are historically and scientifically true in all of the original autographs. To a student of nature, this means that the account of origins in Genesis is a factual presentation of simple historical truths.
> —from the Creation Research Society's Statement of Belief (1963)

How Many Creationists Are There?

How many Americans reject the theory evolution? Are creationists a small and marginal minority, as some believe, or are they the actual majority of the public, as creationists have sometimes claimed? The truth lies somewhere between these extremes, but establishing exactly *where* it lies is not a straightforward matter.

The best, relatively objective information on this question comes from social surveys, but such data must be evaluated cautiously. It is well known that many factors can significantly affect people's reactions to an item in an opinion questionnaire, including exactly how the item is worded, what items precede it, and whether it arouses strong emotion. This problem is especially salient in the case of creationism and evolution. Many of the terms associated with the issue (such as *evolution* itself)

mean different things to different people—and it is apparent that many people do not clearly understand the modern theory of evolution that they say they oppose or support. Furthermore, creationists vary in just how much evolutionary theory they reject; they might unanimously oppose an item suggesting human evolution, for example, but split over one suggesting limited evolution unrelated to human origins.

With these caveats in mind, several studies can give us an indication of creationism's popularity, both among the general public and within particular segments of it. These include two fairly recent national probability samples of U.S. adults, with a margin of error of around 3 percent.

The first was conducted by the Gallup Organization in 1982 (*New York Times*, 29 August 1982, 22). Respondents were given several statements about human origins and asked which one they agreed with. Fully 44 percent agreed that "God created man pretty much in his present form within the last 10,000 years." Thirty-eight percent agreed that "Man has developed over millions of years from less advanced forms of life, but God guided this process, including man's creation." Only 9 percent thought that "Man has developed over millions of years from less advanced forms of life. God had no part in this process." In other words, 47 percent accepted that human evolution has occurred, with or without divine guidance. Finally, 9 percent had no opinion.

Further evidence of such views is found in a poll conducted by sociologist Jon Miller (1987a). Table 3.1 summarizes the portion of his study relevant here. Miller's respondents were presented with a statement favoring human evolution and were then asked whether they agreed or disagreed. The proportion of all respondents giving a negative (creationist) response (46 percent) almost exactly matches the proportion giving a creationist response in the Gallup poll. Similarly, the percentage of proevolutionary responses in Table 3.1 is close to the sum of the two proevolutionary responses in the other poll.

The data in Table 3.1 allow us to make some further observations. First, the higher the educational level of the respondents, the less likely they were to reject human evolution (see also Beckwith 1981–82; Reapsome 1980). This finding is consistent with others that link college education with more liberal religious and social attitudes (Funk and Willits 1987). Nonetheless, about one-quarter of those with graduate degrees are apparently creationists.

Second, women gave creationist responses distinctly more often than men. This result may well be related to men's greater average educa-

Table 3.1. Public Acceptance of Human Evolution

"Human beings as we know them today developed from earlier species of animals."

	Agree (%)	Disagree (%)	Not Sure (%)
All adults	47	46	7
Female	41	51	8
Male	53	41	6
High school dropouts	38	54	8
High school graduates	39	53	8
College graduates	63	32	5
Graduate degree	71	25	5

Note: Because of rounding off, not all percentages add up to exactly 100%.

Source: Nationally representative sample of 2,000 adults (Miller, 1987a)

tional level and to the greater average religiosity of women (see Rothenberg and Newport 1984, Table 3.1). In short, it appears that Americans are almost evenly split on the issue of whether humans evolved, with a small percentage unsure.

Creationism in the Classroom: Students   A number of studies have focused on college students's beliefs on evolution and creation. The two discussed here are not based on random samples and are therefore not necessarily nationally representative; but interestingly, they yielded similar results. Fuerst (1984) surveyed 2,387 students in biology classes at Ohio State University and found that overall, 63 percent accepted the modern theory of evolution. By course level, acceptance ranged from 50 percent in introductory classes to 86 percent in advanced undergraduate courses.

In another study, the authors (Harrold and Eve 1987) analyzed the responses of 979 students from five campuses in Texas, Connecticut, and California to two items. The first item is worded so that a creationist would disagree, the second so that a creationist would agree. (The data were gathered in cooperation with our colleagues Kenneth Feder of Central Connecticut State University and Luanne Hudson of the University of Southern California.) Table 3.2 shows the responses to two items, the second of which is essentially the same as the Gallup poll item discussed

Table 3.2. Acceptance of Evolution among College Students and High School Biology Teachers

"The theory of evolution correctly explains the development of life on earth."

	Agree (%)	Disagree (%)	Not Sure (%)
Texas students (N = 443)	46	40	14
California students (N = 367)	62	24	15
Connecticut students (N = 169)	58	19	23

"God created humanity pretty much in its present form in the last 10,000 years or so."

	Agree (%)	Disagree (%)	Not Sure (%)
Texas students	28	42	31
California students	19	59	23
Connecticut students	19	56	25
High school biology teachers (N = 190)	25	64	11

Note: Because of rounding off, not all percentages add up to exactly 100%.

Sources: Data gathered from students at five institutions in 1985 (Harrold and Eve 1987) and from an exploratory national study of biology teachers (Eve and Dunn 1990).

earlier. With the partial exception of the Texas students, the responses to the two items have similar patterns: with proevolutionist responses range from 46 to 62 percent on the first item, and from 42 to 59 percent on the second. The similarity in the responses to the two different questions is significant, because it suggests that the same students are opposed not only to *human* evolution specifically (the second item in Table 3.2) but also to evolutionary theory in general. Furthermore, it suggests that these students are not only rejecting evolution but are substituting for it the creation story in Genesis. In other words, they seem to be not only expressing antievolutionism (which could be atheistic, Hindu, or Buddhist in inspiration) but also affirming creationism.

The acceptance of evolution in the Connecticut and California samples (62 and 58 percent) parallels the 63 percent acceptance reported by Fuerst in Ohio. Students from the Bible Belt state of Texas are more likely than others to reject evolution. Creationist sentiment in the other samples, however, is certainly not low. Creationism is by no means an exclusively southern phenomenon.

The proportion of uncertain responses among students in Table 3.2, compared with Table 3.1, is relatively high. This presumably reflects the conflict and uncertainty some students feel as they grapple with these issues during the course of their college experience. Since increasing education is associated with decreasing belief in creationism, this result is what we might expect. Other studies of college students have produced results broadly similar to those described here (Zimmerman 1986; Almquist and Cronin 1988; Eve and Harrold 1986; Grose and Simpson 1982).

Though creationist belief is lower among the college students polled than among the general public, it is still apparent that one-fifth or more of the students in a typical college may reject evolution theory.

Creationism in the Classroom: Teachers and School Boards
Among high school biology teachers, Zimmerman (1987a) found that 78 percent of the 404 Ohio high school biology teachers who returned his mailed questionnaire accepted the modern theory of evolution. This is a large majority, but seen another way, over one-fifth of the responding biology teachers (in a state not usually considered part of the Bible Belt) either reject evolution or are not sure about it. Similar findings were reported by Tatina (1988) for high school biology teachers in South Dakota, and by Nickels and Drummond (1985) for those in Illinois. Furthermore, in a pilot study of biology teachers nationwide, Eve and Dunn (1989, 1990) reported even more striking findings; a quarter of their sample favored recent creation of humanity (see Table 3.2).

Among school board presidents, Zimmerman (n.d.) found that only 56 percent of 336 Ohio school board presidents accepted the modern theory of evolution. This group seems to reflect the attitude of the general public.

Scientists and Creationism Somewhat surprisingly, we have almost no statistical information on the views of those at the very center of this issue—scientists themselves. All parties to the creation–evolution dispute agree that the great majority of scientists accept the theory of evolution, but (as the Institute for Creation Research shows) there are obviously exceptions. The only relevant survey of which we are aware is a survey of readers of *Industrial Chemist* (9[2]:47, February 1988). Of 519 respondents to a brief questionnaire in the November 1987 issue, 23 percent answered no to the query, "Do you think it is possible that humans evolved in a continuous chain of developments from simple ele-

ments in a primordial soup, without supernatural intervention?" Forty-eight percent answered yes, and 29 percent replied "yes, but with supernatural intervention."

With due allowance for wording differences between surveys, the anti-evolutionary response here corresponds to those of other surveys among college-educated and college student respondents. Does this mean that creationism is as popular among scientists as it is among the general public?

For several reasons, it is not, despite creationist claims to the contrary (see Frazier 1988). *Industrial Chemist,* a trade magazine mailed free to forty thousand industrial chemists, sampled a population that is not representative of scientists in general. Many chemists in industry (like most of the high school biology teachers in Table 3.2) lack the graduate degrees that are usually accepted as demarcating scientists from others. Moreover, people in applied scientific fields outside academia are significantly more likely than others to have conservative religious beliefs (Vaughan et al. 1966); and there is a close connection between such beliefs and creationism. Finally, few industrial chemists work in areas that require familiarity with evolutionary theory or related subjects. Thus, even though we do not yet know specifically how many scientists oppose evolutionary theory, we can be sure that the data from this poll overestimate the true proportion.

In sum, there is a significant level of creationist belief, sometimes approaching 50 percent, in diverse sectors of American society. Even in well-educated segments of the population, such belief is not negligible. In a scientifically advanced nation, this state of affairs seems to call for an explanation. After all, we do not encounter widespread public disbelief in Einstein's theories of relativity or in the atomic theory of matter. Why evolution? The answer to this question lies in religious belief.

Who Are Creationists?

Overwhelmingly, American creationists are conservative Protestants who reject evolution on religious grounds. We are sure of this generalized statement for several reasons. First, opinion poll data show that similar percentages of people both reject the theory of evolution *and* accept the Genesis creation account. Second, nearly all organizations and individual activists publicly opposing evolution in this country frankly acknowledge the religious nature of their motivation.

Finally, other data link antievolutionism with conservative Protestant religious orientations. In Hunter's (1983) study of a national sample of over fifteen hundred adults, for instance, 82 percent of those classed as evangelicals agreed that "God created Adam and Eve, which was the start of human life," compared with 48 percent of both liberal Protestants and Catholics and 22 percent of secularists (those professing no religion). An interesting study (Eckberg and Nesterenko 1985) based on a telephone survey of 308 residents of Tulsa, Oklahoma found that acceptance of evolutionism among fundamentalists (apparently, those respondents who identified themselves with that term) was related not to education, income, or other social indicators but to degree of religiosity. For nonfundamentalists, by contrast, acceptance of evolutionism was strongly correlated with education. In other words, for most people, the higher their level of education, the more likely they are to accept evolution, but self-identified fundamentalists' (frequent) rejection of evolution is related not to how educated they are but to how religious they are. And in our study of college students, we found strong correlations (Pearson's r from 0.46 to 0.48) in all three samples between students' self-reported religious conservatism and a scale measuring creationist belief (Harrold and Eve 1987).

Problems in Categorizing Creationists   Creationists are characterized in the media and public discussion variously as Christians, fundamentalists, born-again Christians, Baptists, evangelicals, conservatives—and pejoratively as "Bible thumpers." Epithets aside, even the polite terms are often used imprecisely or incorrectly.

Curiously, the classification of creationists that probably comes first to mind for most people—denominational membership—is not a particularly reliable way to sort out creationists from others. True, denominations generally perceived as more conservative do tend to have more creationists than more liberal ones (Bainbridge and Stark 1980). Thus, there are more creationists among Baptists, Churches of Christ members, and Missouri Synod Lutherans than among Episcopalians, Presbyterians, and Methodists. But very few sizable denominations make the acceptance or rejection of creationism a doctrinal tenet, and most tolerate a considerable range of beliefs among their members. In consequence, some Baptists have no difficulty accepting evolution (such as John Buchanan, a Baptist minister who heads the anticreationist organization People for the American Way), and some Episcopalians are creationists.

A great deal of important variation in religious beliefs and practices in American Protestantism cuts across, rather than follows, denominational

lines. One axis of this variation that is important for understanding creationism is the cross-denominational phenomenon of conservative Protestantism called evangelicalism.

Evangelicals, Fundamentalists, and Pentecostals There is no consensus among students of religion, or even among evangelicals themselves, on exactly how to define evangelicalism, or on how to sort out unambiguously those who are evangelicals from those who are not (Marsden 1987; Barr 1982; Rothenberg and Newport 1984). Here we will follow Hunter's (1983) characterization, according to which an evangelical is a Protestant who accepts three propositions:

1) *Biblical Inerrancy* The Bible is regarded not as just a book of wisdom, but as God's absolutely authoritative word to man. Evangelicals differ as to just how straightforwardly Genesis and other biblical historical accounts must be understood, but they tend to accept such accounts literally unless they perceive a strong reason not to.

2) *The Divinity of Christ* Christ was not simply a wise teacher or an inspired prophet but was both man and God.

3) *Salvation through Christ Alone* Christ's atoning death on the cross, not one's good works on earth, constitutes man's only hope of an afterlife in heaven rather than in hell. For many evangelicals, this truth must be not only intellectually accepted but deeply experienced through acceptance of Christ as one's personal savior (the experience of being "born again").

Probably 40 to 50 million Americans fit this characterization (Marsden 1987), and their numbers have been growing steadily for several decades (Nelkin 1982, 59–63; Kelley 1972; Hadden and Shupe 1988). Some belong to totally or predominantly evangelical denominations (like the Southern Baptists); others to denominations split between evangelicals and "modernists" (like Presbyterian groups); others to denominations in which they are a small minority (like Episcopalians); and still others to nondenominational congregations and fellowships.

The broad category of evangelicalism includes two subcategories that are important for our study. The first is *fundamentalism,* or "militantly antimodernist Protestant evangelicalism" (Marsden 1980, 1987). Fundamentalists may be thought of as evangelicalism's hard-liners. Although they differ among themselves (sometimes passionately) as to what truly

constitutes fundamentalism, they share a belief that a number of doctrines are absolutely essential for salvation, including the sinful nature of man after Adam's Fall, the virgin birth of Christ, and the inerrancy of scripture. This last point is particularly relevant for our study of creationism. Fundamentalists generally hold that the Bible is always to be interpreted literally, except when its language is unmistakably figurative (for instance, in the Psalms).[1] As a fundamentalist minister once told anthropologist Alice Kehoe (1985, 165), "When the plain sense makes common sense, we seek no other sense."

Fundamentalists have a strong tendency to hold highly particularistic beliefs (Maguire 1987); that is, they are certain that their beliefs are right and necessary for salvation, while those of others are simply wrong. To most fundamentalists, Jews, Catholics, and liberal Protestants are doomed to hell, no matter how sincere they are in their religious commitments, unless they change their ways. This explains the great emphasis in evangelicalism, and especially in fundamentalism, on "witnessing" to outsiders and on saving souls.

Though the term itself goes back only to 1920, fundamentalism took form around the turn of the century as a reaction to the modernism that was then sweeping American Protestantism. It exists today within many independent congregations and fellowships, such as the Baptist Bible Fellowship, as well as in factions within established denominations, such as the fundamentalist faction currently struggling with "moderates" for control of the Southern Baptist Convention, the nation's largest Protestant denomination (Barnhart 1986). There are probably 4 to 5 million members of fundamentalist congregations in the United States today, while several million other evangelicals show fundamentalist leanings (Marsden 1987).

Historically, fundamentalists have emphasized their separateness from and conflict with the larger society around them. (It is corrupt, in their view.) They have often set themselves apart by avoiding "sinful" behavior like gambling, dancing, and drinking, and have had rather low political participation. Since the 1970s, however, many have exhibited increasing willingness to cooperate with nonfundamentalists in pursuit of common social and political goals. This trend is exemplified by Jerry Falwell, the televangelist and independent Baptist pastor who formed the Moral Majority to work with other Protestants and even with Catholics and Jews. For this, he was denounced by traditionalist fundamentalist leaders like the Reverend Bob Jones III of Bob Jones University.

One aspect of fundamentalist theology that we should briefly discuss is *dispensationalism*, a mode of biblical interpretation originating in the

last century that is accepted by most fundamentalists today (Marsden 1980; McIver 1988a; Hadden and Shupe 1988, 91–108). At first glance, making fine theological distinctions might seem to be straying far afield from an analysis of a social movement, but dispensationalism is an example of the old truism that ideas have consequences.

Dispensationalists divide all of time since creation into several ages (or dispensations), each marked by a different covenant between God and man. They interpret many biblical passages as prophecies of specific events; some of these have come to pass, while others are still to happen. They agree that before the end of the world and the last judgment, there will occur the millennium, a thousand-year period of godly peace and happiness on earth. After this point, however, there is a split among dispensationalists. *Premillennial dispensationalists* believe that Christ's second coming will precede the millennium, over which Christ himself will reign. *Postmillennial dispensationalists,* on the other hand, believe that Christ's second coming will be after the millennium, not before.

This difference, arcane to outsiders, has important implications for believers. For premillennialists, this sinful world will continue to deteriorate until Christ comes to set things right. No human effort can salvage the world; the devout should keep the faith, awaiting the battle of Armageddon and the second coming, which may not be far off. For postmillennialists, the world is just as wicked, but it is within the power of God's people to change. Humans will bring about the millennium, so they should start now to set the world to rights. As we shall see later in this chapter, these theological differences have interesting consequences for modern creationism.

Another category within evangelicalism (in most formulations) comprises *Pentecostalism* and *charismatic Christianity* (Poloma 1982, 1986; Anderson 1987; Marsden 1987). These varieties place strong emphasis on the emotional experience of being possessed by or "filled with" the Holy Spirit, and on other emotion-laden phenomena such as prophecy, glossolalia (speaking in tongues), and faith healing. Pentecostalism began early in this century as a reaction, primarily among the poor, against the formal, doctrine-oriented forms of conventional Protestantism. There are many Pentecostal denominations, including the Church of God in Christ and the Assemblies of God (whose best-known figure, before his defrocking in 1988, was televangelist Jimmy Swaggart [McIver 1986a]), as well as numerous independent congregations.

Charismatics (also known as Neo-Pentecostalists) share many beliefs with Pentecostalists but typically form groups within established non-Pentecostal denominations, ranging from Baptists to Episcopalians (and

even Roman Catholics). Since its beginning in the 1960s, their movement has grown to some prominence. Televangelists Pat Robertson and James Robison are both Southern Baptist ministers who have become charismatics.

All together, there are nearly 7 million Pentecostals and charismatics in the United States. Doctrinally, they tend to be very similar to other evangelicals, and they supply considerable support for the creationist cause.

Other Groups While evangelicals constitute the most important bloc of creationists, distinct but related groupings of conservative Protestants also supply the movement with adherents. Several million, for instance, belong to conservative "reformed" and "confessional" groups (often of German origin). They do not accept the born-again doctrine but proclaim a confession (statement) of faith derived from Martin Luther's. Such denominations include the Missouri Synod Lutherans (numerous in the Midwest). Although not, strictly speaking, evangelicals, conservative confessional Protestants are in most respects doctrinally close to them, and many are creationists.

Creationist positions are also taken by various less conventional groups, sometimes described as sects or even cults because of their adversarial relations with other groups and/or the society around them, such as the Seventh Day Adventists and the Jehovah's Witnesses. Interestingly, the Church of Jesus Christ of the Latter Day Saints (the Mormons) takes no official stand on this issue, though many individual Mormons are creationists (Christensen and Cannon 1978).

Now that we have isolated evangelicals and related groups as those from which creationists generally come, let us turn to the demographic and sociopolitical characteristics of American evangelicals. Not all evangelicals are creationists (or vice versa), but the best approximations we can find to broad social studies of creationists are studies of evangelicals.

Social Characteristics of Evangelicals Are evangelicals different in nonreligious respects from other Americans? In brief, the answer is a qualified yes, but most evangelicals are far from the classic stereotype of southern rural primitives (a caricature at best) that dates back to the days of the Scopes trial.

Hunter's (1983) study characterized evangelicals, compared with the general population, as disproportionately white, female, older, and married. He found them numerically best represented in the rural and small-town South and Midwest, and in the mid-Atlantic states. Conversely,

Table 3.3. Selected Demographic and Opinion Data on
Evangelicals and "Biblical Literalists," 1983

	U.S. Adults (%)	Evangelicals (%)	Biblical Literalists (%)
Females	52	60	63
College grads/Grad school	27	22	12
Family income $30,000+	32	33	27
White-collar occupations	n.a.	35	28
Age 55 or older	24	32	40
Favor voluntary prayer in public schools	81	91	n.a.
Think abortions should be illegal in all circumstances	16	27	33
Favor ERA	59	56	55
Usually vote Democratic	43	47	50

Source: Rothenberg and Newport 1984

they were underrepresented in most big cities. They are more often members of the lower and middle classes—farmers, laborers, skilled and clerical workers, and small businessmen. They tend to have less formal education than most other groups; according to Hunter, 24 percent of them had had at least some college education, compared with 32 percent of liberal Protestants and 46 percent of secularists. These contrasts are differences in degree, however, rather than kind.

Rothenberg and Newport (1984) used somewhat different criteria to identify evangelicals than Hunter, such as dropping the biblical inerrancy criterion. They found evangelicals to be closer to the average American in social and economic characteristics, although the differences noted by Hunter are still apparent (see Table 3.3). Interestingly, they found that when they asked questions about biblical literalism (agreement that the

creation account in Genesis is true), the differences between the sub-sample of evangelicals so chosen and the general population increased greatly. The biblical literalist evangelicals were distinctly less well-off financially, less educated, and more rural than the general population—to an even greater extent than Hunter's evangelicals were. The "biblical literalist" subsample is of particular interest to us here, for this is the best approximation to a national demographic study of creationists. Because of the wording of their item, however, Rothenberg and Newport's category of biblical literalists includes some but not all creationists.[2] Generally, whereas evangelicals differ from the general population, biblical literalists differ even more.

As in Table 3.3 shows, evangelicals (and biblical literalists, especially) tend to be more conservative than the general public on several sensitive public issues that have religious overtones. They oppose abortion and favor prayer in public schools to a greater extent than most Americans. Evangelicals' conservative tenor on social issues has also been noted by Wald (1987), who found that evangelicals (whom he defined on the basis of denominational membership) are less tolerant of marijuana use, homosexuality, extramarital sex, pornography, and abortion than mainline Protestants, Catholics, and others.

However, evangelicals are not necessarily more conservative on *all* social issues, as their support for the Equal Rights Amendment in Table 3.3 shows. Furthermore, even on issues on which many are conservative, others in their ranks take opposing stands. For instance, while 27 percent of evangelicals oppose legalization of any abortions, 29 percent *favor* legalization of *all* abortions (Rothenberg and Newport 1984, 73). Despite the impression that media coverage of the Moral Majority and other such groups has produced, evangelicals are seldom monolithic in their stances on these issues. Indeed, in a 1981 study, most evangelicals did not express support for the Moral Majority (Shupe and Stacey 1982, 1983). Furthermore, Handberg (1984) found in a Florida study that those who supported creationism in the schools gave mixed responses on social issues, although they did tend strongly to agree that the moral fabric of the nation was decaying and that government should have a role in correcting the situation.[3] Moore and Whitt (1986) found similarly mixed responses in a 1982 Nebraska study.

Also surprising to some is that a plurality of evangelicals (47 percent) identified themselves as Democrats (32 percent are Republicans, and 21 percent are ticket splitters) in Table 3.3. This pattern, also found by Wald (1987, 67), shows that Republican efforts to attract evangelicals have

been so far only partly successful, and that social-issue conservatism does not necessarily translate into identification with the more conservative of the two political parties.

Although the demographic and political differences between evangelicals and other Americans are important, these differences have shrinking for some time (Hadden and Shupe 1988, 83–88). Especially since the early 1960s, evangelicals have been increasingly entering the American social, economic, and political mainstream. Recent decades have seen notable increases in their income and educational levels, their representation in managerial and other upper-middle-class occupations, and Republican party identification. For instance, the proportion of evangelical adults with at least some college education, measured at 24 percent by Hunter (1983), was only 7 percent in the early 1960s (Roof 1986). Indeed, given that Republican identification in the general population is associated with higher income and more education, Republican inroads among evangelicals may be due more to appeals to their pocketbooks ("No new taxes!") than to their religious convictions.

While in some respects evangelicals (especially fundamentalists) have resisted changing their religious beliefs, they have also been remarkably flexible in adapting to changing American customs and values (Roof 1986; Hadden and Shupe 1988). What would evangelicals of the 1920s have made of the Christian marriage manuals, success seminars, talk shows, and rock bands of the 1980s and 90s?[4] Today's scientific creationism can be partly understood as another such adaptation by evangelicals to a dominant aspect of in mainstream American life: science.

One sector among evangelicals deserves special comment, namely black evangelicals (who constitute the majority of black Protestants). As blacks are in many aspects of American life, black evangelicals are a group apart. Their denominations and congregations are generally all black. Doctrinally, these groups are typically evangelical, but they are distinguished by the social activism that has been such a powerful force in the civil rights movement. These factors are reflected in Wald's (1987) study, which finds that black Protestants are as conservative as white evangelicals on social issues, including abortion, but that they are overwhelmingly politically liberal and Democratic in voting orientation. The only survey information on creationism specifically among blacks comes from our own college student survey (Harrold and Eve 1987). We found black Protestant students to be even more strongly creationist than white Protestant students. Yet black Americans are strikingly absent from the creationist movement; as far as we know, no prominent crea-

tionist activitists are black. We suspect that this is because civil rights and economic issues are far more salient for black evangelicals.

Varieties of Modern Creationism

Modern creationism takes various forms. But to understand this variety, we must first have some notion of what it is that they all oppose. Hence, this very brief sketch of the main points of the modern scientific consensus on evolution and related issues. (For a concise review, see National Academy of Sciences 1984; more detailed expositions can be found in Strahler 1988; Futuyma 1983; McGowan 1984.)

The Scientific Consensus Although scientists disagree on various points, they have a high degree of consensus in the natural sciences about the main features in the history of the earth and life. Long after the "Big Bang," which began the universe as we know it over 15 billion years ago, the earth formed some 4.5 billion years ago. Sometime before 3.5 billion years ago, primitive forms of life appeared; several theories have been advanced about the origins of life under physical and chemical conditions that were very different from those on today's earth. These theories do not posit supernatural action by God; indeed, scientists widely agree that science is the study of the natural world knowable to us empirically (through the senses), and that therefore supernatural causes are outside its realm. All the panoply of subsequent life, both in the fossil record and around us today, is seen as descended from these ancient beginnings. Through the process of evolution (descent with modification), the "family tree of life" has produced divergent forms in populations of organisms. Genetic variation caused by random mutations is "edited" by natural selection, the main force driving evolution. (In this process, the organisms most successful in surviving and reproducing pass their traits disproportionately to subsequent generations.) We humans are no exception to the evolutionary process; our branch of the primate family tree is estimated to have separated from the ancestors of African apes some 5 to 6 million years ago. Stone tools and evidence of primitive culture appeared over 2 million years in the past; and humans skeletally similar to modern people are dated to at least a hundred thousand years ago.

Scientists stress that this modern consensus is supported by a large and mutually reinforcing body of evidence, not only from geology, paleontology (the study of the fossil record), ecology, and archaeology, but

also from modern biology (comparative anatomy and molecular genetics), physics and chemistry (dating methods based on radioactive decay processes), and even astronomy, with its measurements of objects billions of light-years away.

Creationism rejects this consensus. Some creationists throw it all out in favor of the account of creation in Genesis. Others accept some of it, but deny specifically that humanity arose by the process of organic evolution, or that any evolution could occur without direct supernatural intervention.

Some Caveats   As we mentioned in Chapter 1, many millions of Christians, Jews, and others believe that the universe is indeed God's creation, but they accept the scientific consensus outlined above. Logically, such people should be considered "creationists" because they believe in divine creation of the cosmos. But the usage of the term in the media and by creationists has become narrowed to include only antievolutionists. "Creationists" who accept evolution are now saddled with the awkward name *theistic evolutionists.*

A second caveat is that some antievolutionists are not religiously inspired (at least, not in the conventional sense). Such antievolutionists are not participants in the creationist movement, although some write antievolutionary books. A handful are scientists, like Michael Denton, author of *Evolution: A Theory in Crisis* (1986); others are professional writers, like Francis Hitching (*The Neck of the Giraffe,* 1982) and Paul Fix (*The Bone Peddlers,* 1984). Their books argue against various aspects of the modern scientific consensus, and they especially deny the adequacy of natural selection and other processes to account for evolutionary change. The scientific community has not found these attacks convincing (e.g., Thwaites 1989).[5] Several prominent intellectuals of recent decades, including Arthur Koestler (1971), Jeremy Rifkin (1983), philosopher Mortimer Adler (1967), and historian of science Stanley Jaki (1979), have also attacked one aspect or another of evolutionary theory. Most of these are nonscientists disturbed by what they see as evolution's dismal implications for human morality and dignity or who are unconvinced by the scientific case for evolution.[6] While such authors are readily cited by creationists as secular (and especially, scientific) authors who join them in opposing evolution, they are not intentionally a part of the movement. They do not substitute Genesis for the modern consensus. Indeed, some are nonreligious and highly critical of creationists. They thus do not figure prominently in our discussion.

Finally, we will deal only peripherally with non-Christian antievolutionists. Such people are numerous among Islamic "fundamentalists," and among ultra-Orthodox Jews in Israel, for instance. But they are a negligible force in the United States and they have no impact on the creationist movement.

Young-Earth Creationism   The first of the two main sorts of creationism in the United States today is called *strict,* or *young-earth, creationism.* Strict creationists follow a highly literal and straightforward reading of the first eleven chapters of Genesis. They believe that the entire universe was created in six twenty-four-hour days. Some believe that this happened as recently as Archbishop Ussher's traditional date of 4004 B.C. Other strict creationists, though, allow an age of ten thousand or even twenty thousand years for the universe; since Genesis itself does not fix the date of Creation, there is room for dispute.

But all kinds of life, mankind included, were created *ex nihilo* (from nothing) by God during creation week in essentially their present form. Some strict creationists are willing to accept very limited evolutionary change within "kinds"[7] since creation (such as the domestication of dogs from wolves), but they firmly deny that any large-scale evolution occurred, such as the rise of completely new "kinds" from ancestral ones.

Nearly all strict creationists also accept flood geology, which explains the geological record of sedimentary rocks and the fossil record of past life as products of Noah's flood (Gen. 6–8).

Strict creationism is today the dominant form of creationist belief and is propounded by most of the movement's activists. Indeed, many people who do not follow the controversy closely are unaware that any other sorts of creationism exist. Strict creationism has the advantage of being an apparently completely straightforward interpretation of Genesis, whether it takes the often-simple form of the unexamined faith of a fundamentalist believer or the sophisticated form set forth by the Institute for Creation Research. Its advocates charge other creationists with forced interpretations of the Bible or with adding to it what is not there (Niessen 1980).

Old-Earth Creationism   The other main sort of creationism is *old-earth creationism.* This sort allows that creation may have happened much longer ago than strict creationism asserts. Generally, old-earth creationists accept at least some of the scientific evidence for an ancient earth, such as radiometric dating methods. They reconcile the earth's great age with Genesis in various ways.

Gap theory posits that an undefined amount of time passed between verse 1 of Genesis 1 ("In the beginning God created the heaven and the earth") and verse 2 ("And the earth was without form, and void . . .").[8] Gap theorists claim that while verse 1 describes God creating an ordered universe, verse 2 starts with an already existing but chaotic universe, to which God then proceeds to give form and order (McIver 1988c). This implies to them that one or more earlier cycles of creation and destruction (perhaps representing even millions or billions of years) are encompassed between verses 1 and 2. This leaves plenty of time for geological ages to pass and a fossil record of extinct creatures to be formed. Ultimately, this "pre-Adamic" world perished. All of this left out of Genesis, they say, because the Bible concerns God's relationship with mankind; there was no need for us to know about earlier creations that did not involve us.

Gap theory was popularized by the influential *Scofield Reference Bible* (published in 1909, revised in 1917), which endorsed it (along with premillennial dispensationalism) in its marginal notes. It was the predominant form of creationism before the rise of modern strict creationism in the 1960s, and it is still popular. Gap theory's recent prominent advocates include televangelists Jimmy Swaggart and Jim Bakker, and the late Herbert W. Armstrong of the Worldwide Church of God. Old-earth creationists such as gap theorists carry on vigorous disputes with young-earthers. In McIver's (1988c, 4) words, "Young-earthers think that the gap theory leads to apostasy, heresy, and eventual surrender to evolution; gap theorists think that to insist upon a recent *ex nihilo* creation is so unscientific that it threatens to make the whole idea of creation seem ridiculous and unworthy of consideration." Old-earther Davis Young (1982), a professor of geology at Calvin College in Michigan, strongly criticizes young-earthers for their interpretation of the geological record, though he rejects human evolution. He joined two colleagues at Calvin College in writing a book, *Science Held Hostage* (Van Till et al. 1988), which finds both scientism (as embodied by Carl Sagan) and scientific creationism equally wanting.

A different approach is taken by *day-age theorists*. They point to linguistic evidence that the Hebrew word *yom* that is translated as "day" in English did not always refer to a twenty-four-hour solar day but sometimes referred to periods of indefinite length (Frye 1983; Waltke 1988). They argue that the "days" of creation could have been as long as geological ages. In short, day-age theorists tend to move farther toward a metaphorical interpretation of Genesis than gap theorists. Like the gap theorists, however, they reject evolution, especially in human origins.

A somewhat less well-defined approach, termed *progressive creationism* (Pun 1982; Durbin 1988; Hyers 1984, 80–85), moves farther still toward accepting the scientific consensus. Progressive creationists see the "days" of creation as overlapping and of varying length. They concede that the order in which God created things as related in Genesis differs from the order apparent in the fossil and geological records. Flowering plants, for instance, are created before land animals in Genesis, but they are relative latecomers in the fossil record. Progressive creationists also concede that there are inconsistencies within Genesis itself (for example, plants are created the day before the sun). Some interpret Noah's flood as a regional rather than a worldwide deluge. Nevertheless, for them, accepted scientific theory cannot explain major events in the history of life, such as the appearance of mammals or other groups. Instead, these events required direct divine intervention. In other words, creation did not happen all at once, but throughout time, as God created new forms of life, culminating in the creation of humans.

Some individuals and groups espouse varying combinations of or variations on the three old-earth approaches. Jehovah's Witnesses, for instance, accept both the day-age and the gap theories (Watchtower Society 1985).

Other Forms of Creationism   Some unconventional approaches to interpreting Genesis are more ingenious than they are influential (McIver 1988d, xii). One is called the *revelatory* or *poetic theory* because it proposes that Genesis 1–11 is not a straight narrative account, but the report by Moses (traditionally believed to be Genesis' human author) of a revelatory vision given to him by God. The *literary theory* claims that the creation account is a deliberately poetic account by Moses (or whoever was the human author), not a literal account. These approaches, like old-earth creationism, are usually attempts to justify a move away from a literal interpretation. What separates them from mainstream Christian accommodation to the scientific consensus is their rejection of all or part of the theory of evolution. They see humanity as God's special and direct creation.

Some readers from noncreationist backgrounds may marvel at such beliefs and wonder how creationists can reject such an important part of modern science. But they have a powerful incentive for doing so. Science in the twentieth century has become enormously prestigious, partially (and for some people, completely) displacing religion as an authoritative source of truth. Yet, creationists are sufficiently committed to their par-

ticular religious worldviews that they take the potentially costly step of denying worldview-threatening aspects of science.

How Creationists Deal with Science

What all creationists share is antievolutionism based on commitment to religious faith. But there are two different ways they oppose the theory of evolution, depending on the attitude they take toward science.

Rejectionism The first way of opposing evolutionism we call *rejectionism*. Rejectionists flatly reject out of hand any scientific conclusions that contradict their beliefs. As one popular bumper sticker declares, "God said it, I believe it, and that's that." If science conflicts with God's word, then the rejectionist dismisses science. A rejectionist feels no need to take scientific claims seriously or to study them analytically to see what is wrong with them, for he already knows that if they conflict with Scripture, they are nonsense.

Rejectionism was a dominant attitude of the antievolution movement of the 1920s, and it remains the attitude of many evangelicals, especially those who are less educated and not much given to worrying about intellectual or scientific issues. One person wrote to us after reading a newspaper account of our research on creationism among college students that "I would much rather believe what He [God] says on the subject than what mere men speculate about a bunch of rocks and bones." Americans in general know little about science, and many rejectionists are untroubled by the intellectual difficulties created by dismissing an important part of modern science.

Rejectionism is particularly characteristic of those evangelicals and others whom Toumey (1986) calls *apocalyptic separatists*. Many conservative Protestants are highly particularistic. They regard other forms of religion as not just different but perniciously wrong. Particularism sometimes leads to separatism and a dualistic worldview. Anthropologist Sheila Womack (1982), for instance, studied a Pentecostal group in Texas for whom all people and spheres of activity were either "of God" (associated with their sect), or "of the devil" and to be avoided. Telling such separatists that their beliefs are scientifically indefensible is unlikely to impress them.

Not all rejectionists are simply anti-intellectual. Advocates of an evangelical intellectual movement called *reconstructionism* or *dominion theology* also dismiss scientific objections to creationism (McIver 1988a). Led

by theologians such as Rousas Rushdoony (1980), they want to "reconstruct" American society according to Christian principles. As postmillennial dispensationalists, they believe it is the duty of Christians to bring about the millennium by making God's law the law of the nation. Opponents accuse them of religious totalitarianism, and it does appear that they have little sympathy for religious liberty or for our legal system's toleration of practices condemned by traditional Christianity, such as homosexual behavior.

Reconstructionists are also impatient with evolutionary science. According to their notion of "presuppositional apologetics" (apologetics is the use of argument to explain and defend one's faith), everything in the creation–evolution debate depends on the presuppositions that one brings to the issue. Evolutionists, they say, bring atheistic, materialist presuppositions about reality to the debate, and so of course end up concluding that creationism is wrong. Creationists likewise bring prior assumptions about the existence of God the creator, and these lead them to their conclusions. The difference, for reconstructionists, is that through faith they know that creationists are right. In their view, it is wrongheaded, even blasphemous, to try to justify the ways of God to science; according to one of them (quoted in Bennetta 1988, 18), "it is both impious and just plain stupid to try to prove from science that the Word of God is true."

Scientific Creationism　But for many creationists, it is not enough to ignore the conflict between their religious beliefs and the scientific consensus. They accept the value and authority of science; some are technicians and scientists themselves. Simply rejecting science would contradict a vital aspect of their values and worldview. They resolve this conflict by means of *scientific creationism* (also called *creation science*), which claims that the conflict between science and creationism is only an illusion. For scientific creationists, the correct interpretation of scientific evidence is actually consistent with Genesis; the problem has been with mainstream scientists and their theories, not with science in principle.

Scientific creationists accept the double-revelation theory popular in the last century. If science appears to show that the book of nature contradicts the book of scripture, then there must be a mistake somewhere. And since scripture is God's infallible word, it necessarily follows that the mistake is being made by scientists. The task of creation scientists, then, is to find and explain just where the mistakes are. "What I'm asserting," says biologist Kenneth Cumming of the Institute for Creation Research,

"is that you will never find science proving scripture wrong" (Boxer 1987, 85).

In books and public forums, Cumming and his colleagues argue that their creationism is at least as scientific as evolutionary theory, that it provides evidence to support the accuracy of Genesis, and that it deserves at least equal stature with "evolution-science" in public esteem and public education.

In an age when evangelicals are moving increasingly into the social and economic mainstream, scientific creationism can have great appeal. A creationist who adopts it does not have to directly oppose the power and prestige of science in our society, as adopting a rejectionist stance would require. Instead, he can assert that science actually supports his religious beliefs—in a sense, he can have his cake and eat it too. We believe that this factor explains much of the broad popularity that scientific creationism has achieved among American evangelicals since the 1960s.

It is important for creationists to be able to harmonize their theology with science because many are members of knowledge-intensive occupations in which science is highly regarded (Nelkin 1982, 84–90). Cavanaugh (1983, 57–77) stresses the importance of the growth in the postwar era of what has been variously called the New Class or the knowledge class. These are people valued for their knowledge and technical expertise, such as engineers, technicians, scientists—and astronauts, of whom several, most notably James Irwin, have outspokenly supported creationism. This class is distinguished from the "old" middle class of merchants, middle-management employees, and the like who are losing some of their power and influence in society to the New Class.

As Cavanaugh points out, scientific creationism is produced primarily by religiously conservative members of the New Class for themselves and for like-minded members of the old middle class and, to a lesser extent, the blue-collar working class.

Historical Development Scientific creationism has achieved prominence fairly recently, but its roots go back to the turn of the century (see Numbers 1982, 1986; Marsden 1980, 1983; Cavanaugh 1983; Larson 1985; and for a creationist perspective, Morris 1984a). The forerunner of modern scientific creationism was George McCready Price (1870–1963), a Seventh Day Adventist and self-taught geologist. In his books (for example, Price 1926) he scorned evolution as contrary to true science and common sense and developed the notion of "flood geology," whereby Noah's flood explained the geological and fossil records. He was

the only individual cited by William Jennings Bryan in the Scopes trial as an antievolutionist scientist—a claim that both Clarence Darrow and the scientific community derided.

Price was joined in the 1920s and 1930s by Harry Rimmer (1890–1952), a flamboyant Presbyterian minister who held the first debates with evolutionists. Rimmer, like most creationists of the time, embraced gap theory. He made a standing offer of $1,000 to anyone who could prove the correctness of evolution to his satisfaction; he never paid it out.

Price and Rimmer succeeded in giving encouragement to fellow believers, but they were not very effective in spreading the creationist message to the larger society. They lacked scientific credentials, reached a rather narrow public, and when noticed by outsiders at all, they were usually regarded as cranks. Attempts in the 1930s by evangelicals, Seventh Day Adventists, and others to form organizations to advance creationism on scientific grounds failed due to lack of finances and the old-earth–young-earth dispute.

In 1941, a number of evangelicals with graduate degrees in science formed the American Scientific Affiliation (ASA) in response to the challenges to evangelical faith posed by advances in science and technology. The ASA was not exclusively concerned with creationism, and it included not only creationists (young-earth and old-earth) but theistic evolutionists as well. Some of its strict-creationist members became increasingly dissatisfied with what they regarded as the ASA's failure to take a principled biblical stand on the vital issue of evolution.

A group of them met in 1963 to form the Creation Research Society, (CRS) the seminal association dedicated to scientific creationism, and named horticultural geneticist Walter Lammerts their first president. Among them was the most important figure in the development of scientific creationism, Henry Morris.

Henry Morris and Modern Scientific Creationism   Morris (b. 1918), a Baptist, was a theistic evolutionist when he became an engineering instructor at Rice University in 1942. He soon entered a period of spiritual introspection, however, from which he emerged a dedicated biblical literalist and strict creationist. He read the work of George McCready Price and became convinced that a truly scientific creationism could and should be developed. In his spare time from his career as a hydraulic engineer (culminating as a department chairman at Virginia Polytechnic Institute), Morris worked out his ideas. They were finally definitively published in *The Genesis Flood,* by Morris and theologian John Whitcomb of Grace Theological Seminary (Whitcomb and Morris 1961).

For the first time, flood geology had been set out in detail by a Ph.D., a hydraulic engineer who asserted that not only was strict creationism scientifically defensible, but that mainstream geology and evolution were badly flawed. The book was little noticed in the secular scientific world, but it had a galvanizing effect among evangelicals, especially those with scientific and technical backgrounds.

Morris, Lammerts, Duane Gish, and seven others formed the CRS to promote and publish research supporting scientific creationism. To ensure the quality of their work, they required that full CRS members have advanced degrees; to avoid doctrinal drift toward evolution, members had to sign a statement of belief affirming biblical inerrancy, flood geology, and strict creationism.

Also in 1963, the Reverend Walter Lang, a Missouri Synod Lutheran pastor in Minneapolis, founded the Bible Science Association (BSA). Despite its name, the BSA has always been primarily an organization of nonscientists. While it does publish a journal with creation science articles, its main goals are to encourage scientific creationism among conservative Christians and to form and mobilize local BSA chapters around the country.

The CRS and the BSA soon became influential among evangelicals, persuading many that they did not have to accept evolution in order to be modern and scientific in their thinking. They also made strict, young-earth creationism the dominant force among religious antievolutionists. Their appeal increased in the late 1960s as the last of the antievolutionism laws of the 1920s were repealed or overturned.

In 1970, Henry Morris took an important step in a new direction. He retired from engineering and moved to California at the invitation of Tim La Haye, an independent Baptist pastor in the San Diego area. La Haye was then organizing a new fundamentalist college (Christian Heritage College), and he gave Morris the opportunity to realize a concept that he and others had envisioned as the next logical step beyond the Creation Research Society: a creationist institute with a full-time scientific staff, research facilities, and a graduate degree–granting program. What began as a division of the college emerged in 1972 as the Institute for Creation Research (ICR), the most influential and prestigious creationist organization. ICR staff members have provided the main intellectual structure of creationism; their publications and lectures played a crucial role in the growth of the movement in the 1970s and 1980s. Many newer organizations in the movement have began under the inspiration of the ICR.

Chapter Four

How Creationists View the World

> If humanistic educators in the State's schools and colleges can gain
> control of the minds of young people and train them to reject God as
> Creator, a totally pagan culture will result. All Christians need to know
> the tactics being employed to accomplish this, so they can fight the
> battle.
>
> —Ken Ham, Institute for Creation Research (1989)

There is more diversity among the millions of creationists in the United
States than is commonly realized. But compared with other Americans,
they do tend to exhibit certain tendencies in perception and belief, and it
is these typical patterns we will first describe, especially as they are
articulated by creationist authors.

Creationists characteristically perceive the world and society through
the lens of their particular religious beliefs. Central to their worldview
are the doctrines of conservative Protestantism, especially (from our
point of view) the tenet that the Bible is the inerrant revelation of God's
word to man. Certain perceptions flow from the acceptance of spiritual
revelation as the final authority in all matters. One is that the supernatural order not only exists but is what really counts; the everyday natural
world around us is important only as a prelude to eternity. In this view
the scientific study of the natural world is properly subordinate to theology, the study of its creator (Wilkins 1987).[1] God's word has priority over
that of people: says Henry Morris, "If the Bible teaches it, that settles
it, whatever scientists might say, because it's the word of God" (quoted
in Donaldson 1988, 110).

For most creationists, God has given humanity his plan for us in clear

and direct terms in the Bible; this article of faith colors their attitudes and perceptions in various ways (Frye 1983). For instance, it explains the particularism (Maguire 1987) of their beliefs. If God has spelled out his word in the Bible in terms that any reasonable person can comprehend, then there is really no excuse for being an agnostic or a Muslim or a Catholic, except perhaps ignorance.[2] Creationism's dualistic quality, whereby it sees most matters as either good or evil without shades of gray, is another consequence of this view. For many evangelicals, there are two ways of believing and behaving: God's way, and the wrong way. Many evangelicals see those Christians who accommodate traditional beliefs to contemporary modes of thought (such as evolution) as compromisers, setting foot on the slippery slope to unbelief. Says Morris: "First, Christian leaders compromised on the literal Genesis record of creation and the flood, interpreting Genesis in terms of the geological ages and a local flood. Very quickly, this led them into theistic evolution. Next came an errant Bible, religious liberalism, and the social gospel. Finally, there was nothing left but humanism" (Morris 1984a, 328).

The creationist perception of reality is strong and unitary, and the Bible is its Rock of Gibraltar. At the same time, it is also potentially fragile, as Barker (1985) has noted. As Morris implies, for a literalist the acknowledgment of any error in the Bible has potentially enormous implications. If the Bible is incorrect when it says that creation lasted six days, then how can one be sure that it is correct when it says that Christ rose from the dead? If any factual error in the Bible can discredit it as a reliable spiritual guide, then it becomes understandable why so many creationists defend Genesis as scientifically accurate (Williams 1983). Removing one brick could eventually cause the whole edifice to come crashing down. Morris (1984b, 19) cites John 3:12 thus: "If I have told you of earthly things and ye believe not, how shall ye believe, if I tell you of heavenly things?"

In their insistence that all truth is unitary, to be judged by a single—biblical—standard, creationists are following in the long tradition of Christian Scholasticism (Cavanaugh 1983, 78–114). In this respect they contrast with most mainstream Protestant, Catholic, and Jewish thinkers, whose approach, also venerable, has been characterized by Cavanaugh (1983, 115–37; 1985) as "averroist," after the medieval Islamic scholar Averroës. Averroism is the position that there are different kinds of truth, that they are knowable in different ways, and that each has its own proper sphere and limitations. Thus, to averroists the Bible and science are sources of different kinds of truth. The Bible is a source

of religious truth concerning matters of ultimate meaning and values, not a science textbook; in the phrase of Pope John Paul II, the Bible tells us how to get to heaven, not how the heavens were made. Science, in turn, is a source of truth about the empirical world—that which is accessible directly or indirectly to the senses—but is unable to tell us why we are here or whether there is an afterlife.

Thus most theologians and religious leaders outside the evangelical camp (and some within it) oppose creationism as based on a misperception of the proper roles of revelation and science (e.g., Frye 1983; Skehan 1983, 1986; Hyers 1984; Olson 1982; Prince 1985; Sarna 1983; Murray and Buffaloe 1983).

Cultural Fundamentalism versus Cultural Modernism

Creationists tend to see American society as a complex mixture of positive and negative elements; evangelicals have historically been equivocal about whether America is the new Jerusalem or the new Babylon. On one hand, many creationists, like evangelicals, see America as a Christian nation, perhaps even one with a mission to redeem the world (such as Robertson 1986; see Hadden and Shupe 1988). They typically honor American patriotic values and institutions, and thus are suspicious of foreign religions and ideologies (especially communism).[3]

On the other hand, evangelicals themselves have a long tradition of denouncing the society around them as sinful. They share a widespread sense of alarm at many changes in belief and behavior under way in American society, including everything from the spread of irreligion and unconventional religious beliefs (such as New Age creeds), to proliferating crime and drug use, to the increasing acceptance of abortion and homosexuality. Linking all of these concerns, they perceive that America is losing its way as it turns away from traditional, religion-based mores (see Falwell 1981). Although their perceptions of traditional values and behavior in American history are not always accurate and even idealized (Cavanaugh 1986), evangelicals, including creationists, are certainly correct that conservative Protestant values have lost influence in the United States over the past century.

The process whereby those values have lost ground is referred to as *modernization* or *secularization*. As American society has become more affluent, pluralistic, and organizationally complex, traditional religious symbols and values have become less conspicuous. More and more areas of life have come to be treated as outside the realm of religion. Thus,

many Americans—including some with strong religious convictions—view alcoholism, for example, as a disease or a behavioral disorder rather than a moral problem. They take their problems to a psychologist, not to a minister, and they are untroubled by the Supreme Court's prohibition of prayer in public schools.

Modernization, of course, has been under way for some time. In a perceptive study, Page and Clelland (1978) have noted that it has culminated in a conflict between two generalized worldviews: "cultural modernism" and "cultural fundamentalism."

Cultural modernists may be variously atheistic, agnostic, or religious, but they all agree that people need to find fulfillment in this life, relying mainly on their own moral and intellectual resources. They tend to judge good and evil in relative, situational terms. For modernists, values and social policies are not absolute and given, but are to be arrived at through rational inquiry and analysis. Propositions about human nature and right conduct should, from this perspective, be subjected to "reality testing" to see whether they fulfill or thwart human well-being. Before deciding whether a proposed law against drug use is good or bad, for instance, cultural modernists want to know the actual changes in behavior that the law would be likely to produce, as well as the social costs and benefits it would entail. They are relatively comfortable with social change and see hope for improving the human condition.

By contrast, cultural fundamentalists (or traditionalists, as we shall also call them—and the creationist worldview is certainly traditionalist) usually see changes in values as departures from divinely established rules. As far as they are concerned, modernists are worried too much about this world and not enough about the next. For them, modernism is hubris—a puny creature makes himself, rather than God, the measure of all things. Thus, in a letter to the editor of a Dallas–Fort Worth area newspaper, a reader once castigated a columnist for supporting abortion rights, charging that the columnist in this matter had "graduated from God's opinion to her own."

Not surprisingly, cultural modernists and cultural fundamentalists tend to view each other with suspicion, as misguided at best and dangerous at worst. Cultural modernists tend to entertain negative stereotypes of traditionalists as uneducated, bigoted, and unthinking (stereotypes that, as we have seen, are often misleading). One opponent of creationists denounces them as "a small group of hard-core zealots . . . riding a crest of supernaturalistic fervor to battle against a basic liberating tenet of civilized peoples—the separation of church and state" (Cloud 1977).

Traditionalists, for their part, often fail to perceive the great religious, political, and intellectual diversity among modernists, lumping them together in the despised category of secular humanists.

Secular Humanism

This term warrants some elaboration, for it has no universally accepted definition and means different things to different people. Traditionalists regard secular humanism (sometimes called simply "humanism") as a comprehensive philosophy—or even, since it deals with ultimate values, as a religion.[4] It undergirds all the disagreeable trends accompanying modernization (see Falwell 1987; Morris 1974a, 252). According to evangelical leader Tim La Haye (1980, 9), "Much of thc evils [sic] in the world today can be traced to humanism, which has taken over our government, the UN, education, TV, and most of the other influential things in life."

Citing the Humanist Manifesto, a document whose title is reminiscent of Marx's *The Communist Manifesto,* traditionalists describe secular humanism as the atheistic, morally relativistic philosophy of the powerful forces that are warring against traditional values. From their bastions in the academic and intellectual worlds (Moore 1977a, 1977b), the governmental and educational bureaucracies, and the media, secular humanists advance their philosophy and work to make traditional values of religion, family, and country obsolete. To many traditionalists, the most dangerous aspect of secular humanism is the insidiousness of its attack. Humanists, they say, press their agenda under the guise of promoting fairness, open-mindedness, and alternative views. Yet they teach atheistic evolutionism in public schools and forbid creationism, under the pretext of separating religion and science (for example, Morris 1974c, 171; see Hadden and Shupe 1988, 59–73).

In the traditionalist view the theory of evolution is the God-denying foundation upon which the edifice of secular humanism has been constructed (for example, Ham 1987, especially 83–95; Morris 1989c, 115–17, 153; see Kitcher 1982, 186–202). These traditionalists see secular humanists as "needing" evolution in order to justify their rejection of God and their claim that as evolving creatures in a godless universe, humans can decide their own moral systems. For creationists, moral decay is the inevitable effect of this hubris. According to Ken Ham of the Institute for Creation Research, "As the creation foundation is removed, we see the Godly institutions also start to collapse. On the other hand, as the evolution foundation remains firm, the structures built on that foundation—

lawlessness, homosexuality, abortion, etc., logically increase. We must understand this connection." (Ham 1987, 84)

For many traditionalists, secular humanism is in effect an anti-God conspiracy. Whether its agents know it or not, they are serving Satan by drawing people from God (Jansma 1985, 78; Morris 1984b, 109–11, 1985).

Most modernists are amazed to hear such descriptions of their beliefs (Herbert 1987). As Hadden and Shupe (1988, 65) wryly put it: "Until recently, many liberals had no idea they were Secular Humanists, and there are still many who have yet to find out." Certainly, traditionalists greatly underestimate the diversity of modernists; politically, they range from archconservative libertarians to communists, and religiously, from devout Christians and Jews to militant atheists.

If secular humanism is a religion, it lacks both an accepted doctrine and an institutional base. There is an organization called the American Humanist Association (AHA) that sponsored the second Humanist Manifesto of 1973 (Pfeffer 1988; Herbert 1987) and that publishes a magazine called *The Humanist*. It indeed advocates an atheistic version of humanism (Edwords 1984). But the AHA is a poor candidate for the Vatican of secular humanism. It is a relatively small group, with a 1989 membership of just over five thousand (*The Humanist*'s circulation is seventeen thousand). Most people who could be described as cultural modernists have probably never heard of the AHA or of the Humanist Manifestos. Furthermore, although the manifestos explicitly disavow the supernatural, there is a strong tradition of Christian humanism that stretches back to the Renaissance (Bullock 1985; Spitz 1987). Christian humanists, from Erasmus and Thomas More in the sixteenth century to the present, have extolled human achievement and potential within the context of traditional theistic belief.

Thus, the term *secular humanism* as understood by many traditionalists, attributes a misleading sense of unity and cohesiveness to their opposition, rather like the term *international communism* as utilized by members of the John Birch Society or the term *Moral Majority* as employed by some modernists. However inaccurate it is, the idea of a secular humanist conspiracy provides an identifiable cause for traditionalists' concerns and a named enemy to oppose, as Hadden and Shupe have noted (1988, 71).

But conspiracy theories aside, there is an element of truth to traditionalists' perceptions of modernists. It is beyond dispute that modernist outlooks predominate in society's centers of power and influence (Page

and Clelland 1978; Cavanaugh 1983). It is also true that the scientific and educational establishments tend to favor teaching evolution in public school science classes. This is due not to a grand conspiracy but to shared modernist understandings of the proper spheres of science and religion. Nonetheless, it is easy to see how, given their particularistic and dualistic worldview, many creationists would find it difficult to accept this distinction at face value.

There is another element of truth in the traditionalists' castigation of modernism. Modernists have sometimes presented their philosophical beliefs as if they were scientific findings—with the all the authority that science imparts. But scientists widely agree that science deals only with the natural world and that the supernatural is beyond its scope. A scientist who states categorically that the supernatural does not exist has gone beyond the realm of science. His statement may be true or false, but it is a philosophical one, not a scientific one. Carl Sagan, for one, declared in his book and television series *Cosmos* (1980) that "the cosmos is all there is, or was, or will ever be." Sagan was in fact careful to distinguish between scientific findings and his philosophical positions, which are based in part on those findings. But some readers and viewers probably failed to note his distinction.

Sagan's case exemplifies the philosophical position known as scientism (Midgley 1985, 1987; Barker 1980; Marsden 1983), a position that is undoubtedly popular among modernists. Given the great success that *science* has had in providing an understanding of the empirical world, *scientism* goes on to assert that only the material world and those topics that can be studied by science are real or worth knowing about. To a proponent of scientism, science will provide humanity with all the important answers it needs. Whether true or false, this assertion represents a philosophical position influenced by science rather than a scientific finding.[5]

In the creation–evolution dispute, two worldviews confront each other across a perceptual chasm—not only over the issue of creationism but over other issues on which social movements and countermovements are based: abortion, homosexuality (Adam 1987), women's rights (Ferree and Hess 1985), and so on. Creationism is part of a larger coalition of related movements, termed the Religious Right or New Christian Right (NCR) (Liebman and Wuthnow 1983; Harper and Leicht 1984; Gottfried and Fleming 1988, 82–89). Though they may specialize in different issues, the participants in these various movements tend to be animated by a traditionalist worldview and to regard each other as allies in the struggle to save Christian civilization.

This struggle is carried on both at the political level (court and legislative battles over abortion and creationism) and at the symbolic level (Heinz 1983), where opponents contest whose symbolic interpretations of reality will prevail. On abortion, for instance, "pro-lifers" claim that what is at stake is the high value of human life, while "pro-choicers" say that the real issue is human freedom—the right of a woman to control her reproductive destiny. As in the creation–evolution controversy, each side perceives and presents itself as defending essential civilized values from the other's assault.

Modernists have often assumed that the complete secularization of society and the attendant "withering away" of religion is merely a matter of time, but traditionalism has not only proved very stubborn, it has even made significant gains in recent decades (Hadden and Shupe 1988; Stark and Bainbridge 1985, 429–35), such as the resurgence of the New Christian Right in the 1970s and 1980s.

The cultural and political resurgence of evangelicals and their allies may in large part have been due to their perception (and that of many converts) that cultural modernism has been tried and failed (Wuthnow 1983, 1988; Sweet 1984; Simpson 1983; among others). Many developments of recent decades have deeply troubled American society: Vietnam, Watergate, and other instances of government ineptitude or corruption; the hazards of nuclear weapons and nuclear power; the proliferation of crime and drugs; and changes in sexual mores and family structure. Taken together, these upheavals seem to have persuaded many that the modernist reliance on science, technology, and human rationality alone is inadequate. Perhaps, they think, a return to traditional values and belief is required.

Creationist Epistemology and Science

As we have already seen, modern creationists base their epistemology on the commonsense philosophy that was dominant in the last century and is still popular in the United States. In this view, God has equipped humans with the sensory and mental abilities they need to clearly perceive and cope with the world. Moreover, he has given his revelation to humanity in a straightforward form which (with some work and study) they can comprehend.

God also reveals himself through nature. Like the careful Bible-reader, the scientist patiently documents and arranges the facts of nature until their pattern and significance become self-evident. In this Baconian per-

spective, science consists of sure knowledge—of facts directly observed, repeated, and integrated (Webb 1983, 1986; Cavanaugh 1983, 1985; Marsden 1983, 1984). Speculative theories, full of "what ifs," may have a place in initiating research, but they attain the status of science only when they are empirically proved to be factual. Henry Morris laments the eclipse of Baconian science: "Science was once recognized as the organized body of known truths, or at least a *search* for truth. It dealt with *facts*, demonstrated facts" (Morris 1984a, 24; emphasis in original).

By this standard, evolutionary biology does not qualify as science at all (Gish 1985, 11–25; Morris 1974, 5–8). No one, as Gish points out, directly empirically observed the origin of the earth or of humanity; no one has ever created these processes under controlled conditions in a laboratory. Therefore, like Darwin's contemporary critics, scientific creationists dismiss evolution as mere speculation. As Gish has said, "Now you and I are both aware of many scientific theories and opinions of scientific people that contradict the Scriptures. When we separate that which is merely opinion or theory or ideas from that which is established scientific fact, there are no contradictions" (quoted in Schadewald 1983a, 294).

This reasoning carries considerable weight with many people who hear it. This is because it reflects the ideas about knowledge and science not only of creationists, but of most Americans. Commonsense philosophy and Baconian perceptions of science form the basis of what Cavanaugh (1985) calls the "empiricist folk epistemology" of American culture. By this he means that the everyday epistemology of ordinary people is anchored in reliance upon sensory impressions. For most Americans, (1) reality is perceived simply and directly through our senses, and (2) science is the collection of proved facts.

But the canons of mainstream science as it is practiced today do not coincide with the "empiricist folk epistemology" of creationists and other Americans on either of these counts. A moment's reflection shows that point (1), that reality is perceived simply and directly through our senses, is incomplete. Our senses (and our common sense), for example, tell us that the earth is stationary and more or less flat, while the sun moves across the sky each day. They also tell us that an object like a table is solid matter. Yet according to mainstream science—part of our culture's common knowledge—the earth is neither flat nor motionless, and a table is mostly empty space, owing to the voids between and within the atoms that constitute it. Sensory data, however necessary, are not sufficient. We also need to propose and evaluate ideas to explain our experiences.

Point (2) of folk epistemology, that science consists of collecting facts, warrants more discussion because it is an essential element of the conflict between scientific creationism and mainstream science. Scientific creationism (and much of its popular appeal) is built on a conception of science that is no longer widely accepted in the scientific community or among philosophers of science (Cavanaugh 1983, 1985, 1987; Kitcher 1982; McCain and Segal 1982; Ruse 1984, 1988; Root-Bernstein 1984; Marsden 1983, 1984; Kehoe 1983, 1985, 1987; Wilkins 1987, 52–59). In Cavanaugh's term, Baconianism is "one-eyed" science[6]—better than no science at all, but superseded in practice by more fruitful methodology.

What Is Science? Mainstream versus Creationist Views   A thorough discussion of scientific method is far beyond the scope of this book. But it will be helpful to discuss some basic concepts in order to clarify the differences between mainstream science and science as it is conceived by creationists and many others. When a spokesman for the Institute for Creation Research asserts that creationism is at least as scientifically valid as evolution theory, it is crucial to understand how his conception of science differs from that of most scientists.

Scientists and philosophers of science widely agree that science investigates the empirical universe. It therefore does not and cannot deal with the supernatural. This is not because science presupposes that there is no supernatural reality. In their professional role, scientists can neither affirm nor deny that God or the supernatural exist. (As human beings, they can and do have all sorts of different views on these topics.) But because we cannot systematically make empirical observations about supernatural claims, it is impermissible, in this mainstream perspective, to invoke the supernatural in a scientific explanation. One cannot, in a *scientific* account, say that humanity originated as part of God's plan or that oxygen and hydrogen combine to make water because God wills it. These statements may or may not be true, but do not explain phenomena in terms of causes and effects in the natural world. In contrast, Henry Morris considers theology the "queen of the sciences" (returning to the etymological derivation of *science* from the Latin *scientia,* "knowledge") (Morris 1984b, 25–33). He also thinks that it is atheistic arrogance that has led to the exclusion of the supernatural from the accepted purview of science.

Of course, scientists do more than simply record observations (or data) about the natural world. They try to explain these data by proposing and testing hypotheses and theories. The observation, for instance,

that horses and donkeys have numerous similarities in anatomy and behavior is merely a starting point. From a scientific point of view, what we want to do is explain why those similarities exist. When Darwin proposed that the two species are descended from a common ancestor, he was suggesting a hypothesis to account for such similarities.

Hypotheses, Theories, and Facts   Both hypotheses and theories are propositions framed in order to explain observations. The distinction between them is not always sharply defined or observed, but it may be thought of as a distinction of scale and generality. Theories are complex sets of ideas that are proposed to explain a whole range of data, while hypotheses are more limited, usually involving relations between two or three variables at a time, and may be incorporated within theories. The *hypothesis* that humans share a common ancestry with the great apes, for example, was couched by Darwin in the context of his general *theory* of the origin of species by evolution.

Standard scientific methodology requires that hypotheses and theories be *testable*. Testability is a complicated concept, but it essentially involves the principle that if our proposed theories and hypotheses are correct, we should be able to predict what our investigations will find under certain conditions. If, for example, astronomers are correct about the orbital physics of the solar system, they should be able to predict where to look in the sky for Mars next Tuesday night. And if biologists are correct in proposing that humans share common ancestry with other primates, then we should expect to find certain features of the fossil record and certain biochemical similarities among primates. If the astronomers and biologists find what they have predicted in tests (as they do in these cases), then their hypotheses are supported, or "confirmed."[7] Repeated confirmation increases scientists' confidence in a theory to the extent that they will accept it as correct unless a better explanation is proposed. If its predictions are not borne out, however, a theory will need to be revised or discarded.

A testable hypothesis is *falsifiable,* meaning that we should be able to specify test results that would disconfirm it. If Mars is never found where we predict it will be, then something is wrong with our theory. But if we claim that our theory is right no matter where Mars is (that is, if our theory is so framed that no conceivable test result could show it to be incorrect), then we are not really advancing a scientific theory, because it is not testable.

Note that we have not talked about *proving* a hypothesis or theory. Strictly speaking, it is impossible to do this in science. We can prove propositions in the abstract systems of logic and mathematics, but in the complex empirical world, it is always conceivable that some of the factors influencing a process have not been taken into account. For example, Newton's theory of gravitation was well confirmed by astronomical discoveries until the early nineteenth century, when observations of the planet Uranus showed that its orbit differed significantly from what the theory had predicted (Kitcher 1982, 45–46). Had the many successful previous confirmations of Newton's theory *proved* it? No—there was always the possibility that the next test would be "flunked." Then did the anomalous case of Uranus *disprove* Newton's theory? Not necessarily— it was also possible that a hitherto unsuspected factor was responsible for the anomalous results, such as an undiscovered planet gravitationally affecting Uranus's orbit. In fact, astronomers used Newton's equations to calculate where to seek the hypothetical planet, and they thus discovered Neptune (which had indeed been the cause of Uranus' "misbehavior").

When a theory is repeatedly confirmed by various tests, the level of scientists' confidence in it becomes very high. But their adoption of it is always in principle *tentative;* further, more sophisticated tests may result in disconfirmations indicating that the theory is incomplete (as when, for example, Newton's theories were eventually subsumed by Einstein's, which explained even more phenomena). Repeated disconfirmations of a theory may cause scientists to abandon it entirely. Lamarck's theory of the inheritance of acquired characteristics was so disconfirmed: it eventually became clear that offspring could not inherit characteristics that parents had acquired over their lifetimes. (For example, the children of movie star Arnold Schwarzenegger will not be born musclebound; like their father, they have to acquire extreme muscularity by hard work).

It is rare for even a successful theory to remain totally unchanged for long. Indeed, scientists *expect* theories to undergo change, if only because as a science advances, new phenomena and new levels of complexity are discovered, and theories must be modified to accommodate them. For instance, the atomic theory of matter (that all matter is made up of atoms of a limited number of elements) won acceptance in physics long before anyone conceived of subatomic particles like quarks and mesons. The theory has been repeatedly altered and enlarged to accommodate such ideas. Similarly, the incorporation in this century of the find-

ings of genetics modified and enriched Darwin's evolutionary theory. New methods and findings may prompt debate on whether and how theories are to be modified, and the debate may persist for a long time before it is eventually settled by the weight of observation and experiment.

With this sketch of mainstream science in mind, we can understand why some creationist objections to evolutionary theory do not convince the scientific community. Operating from a perspective of Common Sense philosophy and Baconian science, creationists charge that evolution is not a fact, but only a theory, and that it has never been either proved or directly observed. Furthermore, they say, evolutionists sometimes disagree among themselves, and the theory has been modified over time. These charges are persuasive to many people who share the American "folk epistemology," but to mainstream scientists, they misuse words that have particular meanings in scientific contexts.

For most people, a *theory* is a surmise or a speculation. In the principal American vernacular sense of the word, a theory may be better grounded than a sheer guess but is less so than a fact, which is something known with certainty (Gould 1984). For instance, in everyday language, we know "for a fact" that John F. Kennedy was assassinated, but it is only a speculation, a "theory," that the Mafia was responsible. If someone could actually prove beyond a doubt that his death was a Mafia killing, then the "Mafia theory" would become a "fact." Since Americans usually think of science as dealing with facts, they may construe it as a serious shortcoming if a scientific idea is described as a theory. Ronald Reagan construed it this way during the 1980 presidential campaign, when he said of evolution, "Well, it is a theory, a scientific theory only, and it has in recent years been challenged in the world of science, and is not yet believed in the scientific community to be as infallible as it once was believed" (quoted in Eldredge 1982, 28).

But as we have seen, the scientific community does not consider a theory to be merely a poor substitute for a fact; rather, a theory is a set of ideas that *explains* facts, or data, as scientists usually say.[8] "Only a theory" is a charge that can be leveled against Einstein's theories of relativity as well as against the theory of evolution—which is to say, it is not so much a charge as a misconception.

Mainstream scientists are thus not perturbed that the theory of evolution is not "proved"—no scientific theory is—nor that the process of long-term evolution has not been directly observed by human eyes—neither have electrons. Finally, the modifications of, and controversies

within, evolutionary theory over the years[9] are regarded among evolutionary scientists not as a weakness but as an indication of a fruitful scientific theory that generates research, new findings, and progressively deeper understanding of nature (Kitcher 1982).

Conclusion

Creationists and their opponents tend to differ not over competing theories within the same intellectual framework, but in their most profound understandings of reality, religion, American society, and the nature of the scientific enterprise. Given these differences, it is extremely unlikely that the creation–evolution controversy will end with creationists being persuaded that mainstream scientists are correct (or vice versa).

The dispute continues, and it will continue for some time to come. It is being fought on various fronts, such as the legal-political one, which we will discuss in Chapter 8. It is being contested on a rhetorical front, although not primarily one in which the opponents directly confront each other. Instead—and predictably, given their incommensurable worldviews—each side aims its rhetorical efforts at the general public, which in social and political (if not scientific) terms serves as an arbiter of the dispute. In the next chapter we will examine the nature and style of the creationist attack on evolution. We will look at how successful they have been, and at the counterattack being conducted by mainstream scientists.

Chapter Five

How Creationists Attack Evolution

> The scientific case for special creation, as we will show in the following pages, is much stronger than the case for evolution. The more I study and the more I learn, the more I become convinced that evolution is a false theory and that special creation offers a much more satisfactory interpretive framework for correlating and explaining the scientific evidence related to origins.
>
> —Duane Gish (1985)

> But on the whole, creationists are amateur, anachronistic philosophers of science, acting (unlike either working scientists or professional philosophers of science) to alter the content of scientific knowledge piecemeal through plebiscite and lawsuit rather than systematically through influencing professional debates and research activities.
>
> —Michael Cavanaugh (1985)

Ideology and Its Presentation in a Social Movement

A certain ideology is broadly shared and advanced by most creationists. This ideology can be seen to exemplify certain principles relevant to the study of social movements' ideologies generally. Movement ideologies, in order to be successful, must generally meet several criteria, as Turner and Killian (1987) have pointed out. For example, a proffered ideology must translate individual self-interest into a group ideal and identify group interest with the general welfare of society. That is, it must have moral aims, not self-interested aims. If an ideology is successful in translating self-interest into idealism, its movement will have the force of a moral crusade against injustice, even a revitalization of the culture. Turner and

Killian also note that puritanism, which appears in many widely different movements, may be another way in which a movement establishes itself as a moral crusade rather than as an exercise in self-interest. The temperance movement, for instance, was advanced as something that would benefit not just its advocates but all society, by removing the evil social and health effects of drinking.

Social movements' ideologies also always attempt to reevaluate the worth of certain population segments. The ideology formulates a rationale for viewing the movement's constituency in a more positive and elevated light than it had been before. The ideology also identifies "villains" outside the movement, who are typically regarded as acting against the movement's constituency in the service of their own sinister interests. Thus, for example, the civil rights movement in the 1960s identified as villains individuals (such as George Wallace), groups (the "white power structure"), and opposing ideologies (racism).

The ideology of a movement must also incorporate goals for the movement that have several characteristics, as Turner and Killian (1987) have furthermore suggested. Movement goals must be credible in the eyes of current and potential constituents, and they must unite subelements of the movement rather than divide them. Goals should furthermore be hierarchically ordered; some goals should be almost immediately attainable, and others should be nearly impossible to reach. Movement goals must integrate motives of both tangible and symbolic gain on the one hand with general social betterment on the other. For example, the 1964 Civil Rights Act was an immediate and tangible goal of the civil rights movement in the early 1960s, while "a just society" was a more vague and distant one.

Creationism and Generalized Beliefs   Any well-developed social movement has a set of beliefs that are shared generally among the participants, according to Smelser (1962). Such generalized beliefs have at least two functions: to identify the source of the perceived threat to adherents, and to give prescriptions that are perceived as effective in removing or abating the threat.

The word *perceived* appears twice in the preceding sentence because, as Smelser has pointed out, the identification of the threat and the suggestions for its elimination are often, unfortunately, wrong. This is so because generalized beliefs often arise from highly emotional group interactions, in situations, in which channels for information and lines of

authority are often subject to great fluidity. As a result, many generalized beliefs have an apparently illogical, overly simplistic character, such as the belief among the Nazis that Germany's problems could be solved "if only" the Jews were dealt with, or the widespread perception that the crime problem in the United States could be solved "if only" judges would hand out longer prison sentences.

While such beliefs do identify villains or offer programs of action, they are often based not on a careful and detailed analysis of the situation, but on reactions tinged with emotion, haste, and prejudice. As a result, many generalized beliefs serve more to satisfy the emotional needs of constituents than to accurately depict reality. Smelser calls this type of generalized belief "short-circuited." While Smelser has been criticized for implying that movement adherents' outlook and opinion are more uniform than case studies can fully support, we nonetheless agree that the ideology of a movement, taken as a whole, is largely composed of a set of generalized beliefs that are indeed widely shared by movement adherents, and that many of these are short-circuited. As we will see, a great deal of short-circuiting can be found in generalized beliefs among creationists.

Norms, Values, and Creationism   In general, there are two types of social movements, the norm-oriented and the value-oriented, a distinction also made by Smelser. Sociologically speaking, *norms* are rules for behavior and are therefore more specific than values are. A *norm-oriented movement* is thus one that raises no challenge to the values that organize a society. Instead, the movement's goals are to modify the status, content, or observance of the specific norms that are manifestations of agreed-upon values. A norm-oriented movement, that is, does not challenge a society's values. For example, during the Great Depression, most American workers were concerned to reform the norms of minimum wage levels or unemployment insurance and therefore tended toward norm-oriented movements.

In contrast, a *value-oriented movement* is not content merely to modify rules of behavior but wishes to challenge one or more of the basic values that organize social behavior. Again, during the Great Depression, a smaller percentage of people formed a value-oriented movement, maintaining that the problem was not with the rules of how capitalism operated, but with capitalism itself. Membership in the Communist party attained an all-time high.

Creationists' ideology is usually presented as norm-oriented. One of

their most visible goals is to have their version of origins receive equal time in the schools, not to change the schools. And they argue that evolution does not reflect good scientific procedure, but do not wish to change scientific procedure.

But creationism is at base a value-oriented movement. Its proponents would ultimately be satisfied only with a drastic reorientation of science and education and their subordination to theology (and a somewhat unconventional form of Christian theology at that).

That a value-oriented social movement nonetheless makes norm-oriented presentations of its positions in its everyday activities should not be surprising. Most creationists are well aware that attainment of their ultimate goal of a transformed relation between science and religion is highly unlikely in the foreseeable future. While keeping their eyes on their far-off goal, most creationists are concerned with more immediately realizable ends, pursued in the context of norm-oriented arguments. Thus, they usually argue that the norms of science invalidate evolution, or that the norms of justice merit a place for creationism in the schools— rather than that theology requires the revision of all these norms. Just as many feminists, civil rights advocates, and others with goals of far-reaching change work day-to-day for more modest reforms, creationists realize that "half a loaf" is the best they can expect in the short and medium term, and they adjust the presentation of their movement accordingly. (Indeed, many are more concerned about staving off the triumph of their secular humanist opponents than about their own victory plans.)

The Creationist Case:
What Is Wrong with the Theory of Evolution

Although creationists are not a monolithic bloc, either socially, theologically, or scientifically, they do share two generalized beliefs. One is that the scientific consensus on evolution is incorrect. Evolution didn't happen—or at the very least, *human* evolution didn't happen. Humanity originated in a special divine creation and is not descended from any nonhuman species. The second generalized belief they share is that acceptance of evolutionary theory by individuals and societies is socially as well as spiritually harmful. To creationists, the maleficent effects of evolution are obvious in recent world history. As doctrinal moralists, they see these consequences themselves as further evidence that evolution is false.

Creationists would like to see these two generalized beliefs become more widely accepted in society.

1) Evolution Is Pernicious   As we have seen, most creationists are evangelical or otherwise religiously conservative. That is, they typically believe that salvation depends on accepting several doctrines, including Christ's atonement through his death for humanity's sins. They believe that a person who fails to take these beliefs to heart is doomed to eternal damnation, regardless of how sincerely he may hold his mistaken convictions, or how good a person he may be. Belief in the inerrancy of the Bible is essential to salvation.

But to accept evolution is seen as necessarily to reject the essential doctrine of biblical inerrancy, and leads inevitably to a host of other evil beliefs and practices that are predicated on the idea of a godless universe in which man is a moral free agent: "And today, this God-rejecting, man-exalting philosophy of evolution spills its evil progeny—materialism, modernism, humanism, socialism, Fascism, communism, and, ultimately, Satanism—in terrifying profusion all over the world" (Morris 1963, 83). Creationists point to the many social and political horrors of the twentieth century as the predictable fruits of evolutionary theory. In this ideology, we can see the puritan stance, the identification of a villain that is to be valiantly opposed, and the equation of the agenda of one's own group with the welfare of society.

Especially anathema to creationists is the notion of human descent from "lower" animals, which are believed to lack immortal souls and intellectual or moral capacities, and thus to be separated by a yawning gulf from humanity. To claim kinship with subhuman creatures is seen as a denial of human dignity and encouragement of moral anarchy. Says a creationist high school biology teacher in South Dakota, "I maintain that if you teach a kid he's an animal, and that his behavior is based on his environment, then he's going to act like an animal" (quoted in Parker 1980, 25). So profoundly threatening to their values is evolutionary theory that some creationists have concluded that its true author is Satan himself (such as Morris 1974c, 72–76; 1989c, 258–60).

Few creationists need to be convinced of the evil social consequences of evolution. Many, though, would like to reject evolution without necessarily rejecting an institution as prestigious as science. Furthermore, creationists who wish to attract allies in the struggle against evolution must appeal outside their own circles to people who do not subscribe to their religious doctrines. One goal of movements in general is to develop

a unifying, not divisive, ideology; adherents, to be unified, and outsiders, to be enlisted, must be persuaded that the case against evolution and for creationism is nonsectarian and scientific. Thus the principal task of creationist writers in recent decades has been to make a case that evolutionary theory is incorrect, irrespective of its moral effects.

2) Evolutionists Are Wrong and Creationists Are Right   In attacking evolution, creationists have engendered a huge literature. McIver's (1988d) encyclopedic *Anti-Evolution: an Annotated Bibliography* lists no fewer than 1,852 books and pamphlets (articles in periodicals are not included)—most of them twentieth-century creationist works. The number of particular criticisms that creationists raise against the scientific consensus on evolution is similarly great; one creationist tract (Kofahl 1977) recounts 148 of them. These criticisms tend to boil down to variations on a number of basic themes; a reader familiar with creationist literature finds certain lines of argument appearing again and again. Nonetheless, the sheer number of points of attack is impressive.

It is not our task here to compile or refute this huge corpus of work. The scientific community has already produced a sizable body of refutational literature (such as Strahler 1988; Kitcher 1982; Godfrey, ed., 1983; Montagu 1984; Ruse 1982; Futuyma 1983; McGowan 1984). Rather, we will proffer a few examples of creationist attacks on evolutionism, generally from creationism's most prominent spokesman at the ICR, in order to convey a sense of their style, logic, and variety. We will also offer a sample of the responses from mainstream scientists. We will also look in some detail at the creationist critique of the case for human evolution.

The Creationist Case against Evolution   The creationist charges against the evolutionary consensus (such as Morris 1974a; Moore 1983) include the charge, familiar from our earlier discussion of conventional and Baconian science, that evolution is not a directly observed scientific fact but merely an unproved speculation. Creationists also claim that evolution is precluded by the second law of thermodynamics, under which the universe's constantly increasing entropy (disorganization and loss of energy available for work) makes the evolutionary growth of systems of increasingly complex organization impossible. Scientists note, in response, that despite the common misconception that evolution equals "progress," evolution does not always involve increasing complexity, and furthermore that a thermodynamically open system like the earth,

receiving outside energy from the sun, can locally reverse increasing entropy (Patterson 1983).

Creationists also assert that the fossil record lacks "transitional forms" between claimed ancestral and descendant species (Gish 1985). But many transitional forms do exist at various levels, and there are sound reasons—especially the statistical rarity of fossilization—to expect them to be no more numerous than they are (Eldredge 1985; Godfrey 1983; Strahler 1988, 395–401).

Creationists also attack radiometric dating methods, such as radiocarbon and potassium-argon dating, which indicate the great age of the earth and life. These methods are based on the process of radioactive decay and are used to estimate the age of geological formations, fossils, and ancient artifacts. Creationists claim that decay rates of radioactive isotopes could have been different in the past; if rates were ever much faster than they are now, misleadingly ancient dates could result (see Slusher 1981). They aver that these dating methods produce inconsistent dates all the time and that evolutionists simply accept the ones that fit their preconceived notions and discard the rest. But there is simply no reason to suspect that radioactive decay rates have varied significantly over time—and there is good reason in our understanding of particle physics to expect them *not* to. Furthermore, different dating methods reveal a high degree of agreement when they are cross-checked. The record does not support the charges that dates are arbitrarily accepted or rejected (see Abell 1983; Brush 1983; Strahler 1988, 129–58).

The Creationist Case against Human Evolution   Creationists oppose with particular vehemence the evolutionary consensus on human origins. Even old-earth creationists, who do not necessarily dispute any and all evolution, adamantly deny human evolution (such as Young 1982, 66). We will discuss this issue here in some detail to illustrate the structure of a creationist critique.

The most complete published creationist critique of human evolution is by Duane Gish (1985, 130–228; see also Moore 1983, 185–265; Morris 1974a, 171–96). A biochemist, Gish has done no paleoanthropological research himself; rather, he searches the scientific literature for mistakes, contradictions, and disagreements between specialists in order to refute claims that humans are descended from apelike primate ancestors.

One of Gish's tactics is to impugn the credibility of the anthropologists who study human evolution by citing examples of their mistakes, espe-

cially misidentified fossils. These supposedly show that the "experts" don't know what they're talking about. He cites the cases of "Piltdown Man," a recognized hoax that consisted of doctored fragments of a human skull and of an ape's jaw; "Nebraska Man," a single tooth that actually came from an extinct pig; a bone from Libya that one anthropologist claims is a collarbone of a 5 million-year-old hominid (member of the human biological family) but that another calls a dolphin rib; and "Orce Man" from Spain, which turned out to be a fragment of a member of the horse family, perhaps a donkey. Gish's conclusion: "An ape's jaw in 1912, a pig's tooth in 1922, a dolphin's rib and a donkey's skull in the 1980's—the script is the same, only the actors and props have changed" (Gish 1985, 190). Anthropologists clearly don't know an ass from an ape—why listen to them?

But even a cursory investigation shows that what Gish left out about these cases is at least as important as what he told. The two most important cases are from the early days of paleoanthropology. Piltdown Man, "discovered" in 1912, did indeed dupe the scientific establishment. One reason it did so was that no one even thought to suspect a hoax (Blinderman 1986), but the main reason was that the bones were not examined thoroughly until the work that exposed the fraud in 1953.[1] They finally were studied closely because Piltdown man had a big modern brain but apelike teeth, quite unlike the many other hominid fossils unearthed before and since 1912. The consistent pattern revealed by these fossils showed that (contrary to ideas popular in 1912) upright walking and changes in tooth form preceded brain enlargement in the course of human evolution. Only Piltdown Man seemed to indicate otherwise, and by the early 1950s he had become an anomaly. Some anthropologists had always doubted that the skull and the jaw fragments were from the same creature, though accepting them as genuine fossils. The Piltdown bones were examined to solve the mystery, and the fraud was quickly apparent.

Nebraska man, a tooth found in 1922, was misidentified by a paleontologist, H. F. Osborn, who was not a specialist in primate evolution (Wolf and Mellett 1985; McIver 1987a; Gould 1989). His identification was published in the scientific literature and disputed by other scientists. After reexamination, Osborn publicly retracted the identification: he had mistaken the worn premolar of an extinct pig for a human tooth. Why had the misidentification occurred? Unlike their other teeth, the premolars and molars of pigs do resemble those of humans and can easily be mistaken for them by the unwary or inexperienced. Once again, standard

scientific procedure—detailed publication and discussion of results—rectified the error.

As for the more recent controversies mentioned by Gish: the clavicle-dolphin rib dispute was occasioned by the fact that collarbones are relatively "amorphous"; that is, they vary little in form between different species, and fragments of collarbones can even be mistaken for other bones, such as ribs (Herbert 1983; Johanson and Shreeve 1989, 195–96). The dispute illustrates the need for caution in attributing an isolated, amorphous bone fragment to a particular species. As for Orce Man, this identification was made by paleontologists who were not experienced in primate fossils; it was corrected the first time a physical anthropologist examined the small skull fragment.

Gish fails to report such clarifying details, but he also fails to appreciate the fact that these mistakes were all put right *not by creationists* but by evolutionist scientists. "The creationists who belittle mistakes by scientists cannot admit that science advances, in part, by correcting error" (Wolf and Mellett 1985, 31). Scientists, as human beings, are perfectly capable of mistakes; scientific procedures are designed to open their work to public scrutiny so that errors can be recognized and corrected. To suppose that the "facts" scientists unearth are unalterable and that scientists should never have to change their minds may be characteristic of idealized Baconianism but not of science in the real world. The self-correcting mechanisms of science that are necessary for its progress, Gish perceives as weaknesses.

Regarding the large numbers of fossils that are widely accepted as informing us about human evolution, Gish follows a consistent approach. First, he reiterates the creationist demand for transitional fossils that illustrate the evolution of one species into another. He then proceeds to argue that all relevant fossils are those of *either* apes *or* modern humans; ergo, no transitional fossils; ergo, no evidence for human evolution.

But consider the case of *Homo erectus,* who is inferred to be an ancestor of our own species. *Homo erectus* fossils range in age from roughly 1.7 million to 400,000 years old (see Brace 1983; Klein 1989). They include those popularly known as "Java Man" and "Peking Man." *Homo erectus*'s skeleton, from the neck down, was not greatly different from our own, though more heavily built. The skull, however, was long and low, with large teeth and heavy brows. The brain was roughly two-thirds the size of the modern human brain but about twice the size of an ape's brain. Archaeological sites associated with *Homo erectus* contain numerous stone tools, remains of butchered animals, and sometimes evidence

of fire. *Homo erectus* is characterized by traits more primitive (i.e., reflecting the ancestral condition) than those of modern people, just as he is less primitive than earlier hominids.

Gish dismisses the Java fossils as ancient apes of some sort. To do this, he relies primarily on quotations stressing the skulls' apelike characteristics from *Fossil Men* by French paleontologists Marcellin Boule and Henri Vallois (1957). In this outdated work (a revised edition of a 1921 book), the authors argued that Java Man had apelike traits, the part of their presentation on which Gish draws. But they did this to argue that Java man was not in the line of *direct* human ancestry—that he was a cousin, so to speak, of our ancestors, not an ancestor himself. But Boule and Vallois did not dispute that we and Java Man share common descent from earlier primate ancestors. The weight of current evidence does favor *Homo erectus* as our ancestor, and Boule and Vallois, who argued to the contrary, are seldom cited today. Gish fails to tell his readers that since the original Java finds of 1891 and the 1930s discussed by him and by Boule and Vallois, Indonesian scientists have found more *Homo erectus* fossils using modern excavation methods; like the originals, they show traits that are transitional between earlier, more primitive ancestors and modern humans.

Gish then moves on to Peking Man. Fragmentary remains of dozens of these *Homo erectus* individuals were found in excavations in the 1920s and 1930s in a large cave not far from Beijing (Peking, in the old orthography). They exhibited both humanlike and apelike traits. The originals were lost in World War II, but casts had been made. Gish finds the loss of the fossils suspicious (and hints that their disappearance before their allegedly apelike characteristics became widely known was "convenient"). He furthermore implies that the evolutionist bias of Franz Weidenreich, who made the casts, caused him to alter their appearance in a humanlike direction, although he produces no evidence for such an accusation. Indeed, available photographs of the original fossils indicate that the Weidenreich's casts are faithful reproductions.

Once again, Gish cites Boule and Vallois on the apelike traits of the fossils, but he omits their notations of humanlike traits. He attributes the numerous stone tools and traces of fire found in the cave deposits containing the fossils to anatomically modern people (assuming without discussion that "apes" could not be responsible for tools). There were indeed some remains of modern-appearing humans, *Homo sapiens*, at the Peking site. But these were in the Upper Cave, which was stratigraphically *above*—and much later than—the Peking Man deposits. The site's

excavators categorically stated that the tools and ashes in question came from the same levels as the *Homo erectus* fossils, not from the later *Homo sapiens* ones. Without presenting stratigraphic or geological evidence in support of his argument, Gish claims that the excavators, blinded by their evolutionist presuppositions, were wrong on this point. [2] The Peking site, he concludes, contained remains of apes (Peking "Man") and remains of true men, and it was the latter who made the tools and fire. He does not mention the work done at the Peking site since the 1950s by Chinese scientists, who have discovered more *Homo erectus* fossils with the same characteristics as the lost ones, plus more stone tools, butchered animal bones, and ashes in association with the fossils. Nor does he mention that *Homo erectus* fossils have been found at several other sites in China since the 1960s.

Gish then briefly deals with *Homo erectus* in Africa. He dismisses several fossils from East Africa as being very similar to the Peking and Java fossils and therefore apes. But he treats one remarkable recent find, by associates of Richard Leakey in Kenya in 1984, very differently. The find consists of about 60 percent of the skeleton of a twelve-year-old boy who lived some 1.6 million years ago. Its discoverers remarked that the skeleton was surprisingly modern in appearance, meaning that, although it is one of the oldest *Homo erectus* specimens known, it is not unusually small-brained or primitive in appearance, by *Homo erectus* standards. Gish, however, seizes on their remarks and interprets them as indicating that the specimen is essentially a modern human. The descriptions and photographs of the remains show that this is simply not the case; the individual's characteristics place him firmly in *Homo erectus* (see Day 1986, 234–39).

Gish ignores the various other *Homo erectus* fossil remains in Africa, as well as the consistent association of these hominid fossils with evidences of human culture, such as stone tools. He merely generalizes the unjustified inference he made from the Peking site that modern humans made the tools while the "apes" made none.

Gish deals with the rest of the human fossil record in a similar Procrustean manner: he demands transitional fossils between apelike ancestors and modern humans, then defines all extant fossils as either apes or modern humans (see also Nickels 1986; Zindler 1985; Conrad 1982). He allows none to be transitional, although in fact *Homo erectus* in many respects represents exactly the sort of transitional form Gish demands. Nowhere does he thoroughly consider the anatomical features of the fossils in question, nor other data, such as paleoenvironmental or dating evidence.

Anthropologists familiar with the human fossil record readily see the weaknesses of Gish's attack, but few of his readers know anything about the human fossil record. Creationists, finding that Gish has demolished some or all of the scientific consensus on evolution to their satisfaction, go on to assert that the same evidence, when properly understood, actually supports their beliefs. Gish says that the fossil record actually reveals no intermediate forms but either true humans or various ancient apes—just as the creation "model" would predict.

But he gives no detailed exposition of this creation model or of what and how it predicts. Nor does he explain what happened to all the species of "apes" to which Gish assigns hominid fossils like Peking Man. He does not tell us what various roles they might have played in ancient ecosystems, and why they became extinct. Did they perish in the biblical flood? But their fossils are found in deposits of varying ages, and some forms disappeared before others arrived on the scene. Did they simply come and go as God pleased to create and destroy them? Gish, a strict creationist, rejects radiometric dating and the geological timescale; perhaps he would claim that the various apes were not of different ages at all and did perish together in the flood. But he does not say; indeed, he does not seem interested in understanding very much about the fossils, but only in establishing what they are *not:* evidence of human evolution.

General Characteristics of Creationist Discourse Underlying the multifarious attacks on evolution are some characteristic traits of creationist discourse. Certainly the most rhetorically effective characteristic of modern creationist discourse is what Richard Alexander has termed a "false dichotomy" (Alexander 1983). Strict-creationist writers generally either assume or state that one must be *either* an atheistic evolutionist *or* a biblical-literalist Christian. Theistic versions of evolution, when discussed at all, are usually dismissed as compromise and appeasement, tantamount to secular humanism.

The rhetorical advantages of this tactic, if it is accepted by one's audience, are enormous. If there are two and only two possible positions on an issue, then casting doubt on one necessarily raises the credibility of the other: "Since there are only two possible models, and they are diametrically opposed, it is clear that evidence against evolution constitutes evidence for creation, and evidence against creation is evidence for evolution" (Morris 1977).

By declaration rather than by argument, a spectrum of opinion on many separable issues is polarized into dichotomy between the two endpoints (pure materialism and young-earth biblical literalism). As we have seen,

creationists lump together many distinct scientific and philosophical questions under the term *evolution*—including the origin of the universe, the origins of the earth and of life, the evolution of life-forms, and the evolutionary origins of humanity.

Despite its logical shortcomings, the rhetorical effectiveness of this device is beyond dispute. ICR-style strict creationism has become dominant over old-earth varieties, and public awareness of the issue through the media is generally couched in the dichotomous terms of "evolution versus creation" (Bennetta 1987a; La Follette 1983), as if anyone who accepts evolution must necessarily reject the idea that the universe as a whole was created. The unwary reader easily gets the impression that in this dispute he or she must choose between fundamentalism and atheism. One of us, while teaching physical anthropology courses, has encountered several students who came to the class convinced that it is impossible to accept evolutionary theory without renouncing religion. These students were surprised to learn that many Christians see things otherwise. Indeed, the creation–evolution dichotomy is also often accepted by evolutionists.

Theologian Langdon Gilkey of the University of Chicago Divinity School tells an illuminating incident (Gilkey 1985). Gilkey testified at the Arkansas creationism trial that scientific creationism is a religious doctrine that has no place in science classes. He was invited by his young son's science teachers to participate in an "evolution-versus-creation" discussion at their school. He explained to the students that evolutionary theory is compatible with his religious beliefs. Only afterward did the embarrassed teachers tell him that he had been invited as the "antievolution" speaker. They had simply assumed that anyone who teaches theology necessarily opposes evolution! It came as a shock to them that he had testified *against* the creationist side in the famous trial.

Some 95 percent of Americans believe in God (Associated Press 1985). If creationists succeed in persuading people that evolution is anti-God, they will have a powerful effect on public opinion. The evolution–creation dichotomy gives the advantage to the creationists and allows them to stay on the offensive because they need not develop and defend a detailed scientific theory of their own; they can simply oppose evolution rather than defend their own assertions. At the same time, this strategy leaves anticreationists with much to defend and little to attack.

The second general characteristic of creationist discourse follows logically from the first: it is that creationist discourse consists overwhelmingly of making attacks on various aspects of evolutionary theory rather

than on actively building creationist theory. Creationists at the ICR and their allies spend little effort developing alternative scientific theories to make sense of the huge masses of data that scientists explain via evolution; at least, they do not publish articles attempting to do so in either the scientific literature (Scott and Cole 1985) or in their own outlets. In their view creationism is established merely by discrediting evolution. Creationists feel little need to find out what happened in the past; as far as they are concerned, the Bible has already told us.

Instead, they search the scientific literature for flaws in evolutionary science and claim to find invalid premises, incorrect conclusions from evidence, dogmatism, wild speculation presented as fact, contradictions, disputes among experts, and admissions by evolutionists that something is wrong with their theory. Then they list this catalog of alleged failings in order to discredit evolutionary theory. And of course, if evolution is false, then strict creationism, as the only alternative, must be correct.

Trying to show the shortcomings of previous work in a field is an accepted part of scientific procedure. But accepted procedure also requires one to collect data (in field, laboratory, or library) and analyze it to establish one's own alternative explanations about how the natural world works. Creationists must account in detail for all the data (from fossils to molecular biology to quasar astronomy) that they would, in Isaac Asimov's term, "unexplain" by discarding the mainstream consensus. For instance, if the earth is only a few thousand years old, creationists must explain in detail the immense thickness of the earth's sedimentary rocks and the sequence of changing life-forms in its fossil record. Noah's flood does not account for these data. Strict creationists must account for all the evidence that some distant astronomical bodies are billions of years old. As their adversaries have pointed out, creationists' positive attempts to explain the record of the past have involved little more than the inadequate claims of flood geology (Whitcomb and Morris 1961)[4] and the simple assertion that the "creation model" is just as scientific as mainstream theories and fits the evidence better.[5] They do not attempt (or apparently even recognize the need) to make the wholesale reordering of the natural sciences that their attacks imply.

Not only does scientific creationism lack a detailed scientific program of its own, its attacks on the status quo are strongly rejected as ill-founded by the scientific community. In debates, articles, and books (which can become quite rancorous), mainstream scientists assert that creationist claims are based on misunderstandings and distortions of scientific publications and sometimes on plain dishonesty. Their basic charge

is that creationist authors erect an evolutionary straw man, often selectively using quotations from scientists, and then knock down this distorted image by a combination of "common sense," unsupported assertions, and bombast. We think there is much validity in this charge. Creationists fail to follow the procedures and criteria of mainstream science in their own writings, as Cavanaugh (1985) points out. Mainstream scientists do not, of course, themselves always live up to these standards (Ben-Yehuda 1985). Faulty arguments, flawed procedures, and even frauds have certainly been known in the past and present of mainstream science. But such behavior is well-recognized among scientists as substandard or deviant, and it is usually punished when exposed. The practices of peer review, detailed publication, and open debate among scientists help minimize such failings. Among scientific creationists, by contrast, deviation from scientific practice can be fairly described as typical.

From the mainstream perspective, scientific creationism is not science because it relies on untestable hypotheses (such as that God created the earth, using processes without modern analogues and therefore unknowable). In addition, it abandons natural law in favor of supernatural miracles as an explanatory device, and its conclusions are foreordained. Scientists deny that a field of inquiry in which all the important findings are known in advance can be called a science: "Creationism is not a scientific approach to the origin of species: it is a call to give up scientific research into that particular question" (Bowler 1989, 359).

The charge of deliberate dishonesty is a sensitive issue (Cole 1981). Many evolutionists, including victims of misleading quotation such as Gould (1981) and Eldredge (1982, 130–31),[6] unhesitatingly accuse some creationist authors of being, so to speak, not only fools, but knaves (Cole 1981). One article on the topic is titled, "Telling a You-Know-What for You-Know-Whom" (Bennetta 1988a).

At least one charge of dishonesty has been made against the ICR's premier debater, Duane Gish (Patterson and Schadewald 1984). At issue is molecular biologists' finding that species inferred on traditional anatomical grounds to be closely related by descent from a common ancestor turn out to also be closely similar in their biochemistry. For instance, the genetically determined sequence of amino acids that constitutes a protein like albumin is nearly identical in humans and chimpanzees. But the sequences of amino acids are not so similar between humans and more distantly related forms (say, horses)—and more different still between

humans and even more distant relatives like frogs. Scientists see this as another line of evidence supporting the conclusion that all these forms are related by common descent: in the case of humans and chimps, from a relatively recent ancestor, and in the case of humans and frogs, from a very ancient one (Jukes 1983).

In an interview on the PBS science program *Nova* in 1982, Gish charged that such claims are based on the selective use of evidence. Look at data for some proteins, said Gish, and humans are indeed closest to chimps. But look at the data for other proteins, and humans are closer to frogs; look at still others, and we are most similar to chickens. Protein amino-acid sequences are thus unrelated to supposed evolutionary family trees.

Evolutionists combed the scientific literature to find Gish's proteins, but they could not find them. During debates, they challenged him to document his claims. Who had made the findings about proteins that he mentioned, and where were their results published in the scientific literature? Gish repeatedly promised to produce the documentation but did not, yet he continued to make his claim. After two years, he simply refused to reply to further requests for evidence. He once said that it was the evolutionists' job to ferret out the information, not his (Patterson and Schadewald 1984). Despite Gish's disclaimer, it is widely recognized in science that a person who makes a claim (particularly an extraordinary one) bears the burden of documenting his or her case. Nonetheless, Gish's unsubstantiated assertion has been picked up by other creationist writers and speakers and has been widely disseminated (for example, see Arduini 1984; Kenney 1984). But still no scientific studies that in fact show the protein patterning claimed by Gish are known to evolutionists or specifically cited by creationists.

Such a failure to observe the protocols of scientific debate and procedure lead many evolutionists to dismiss creationists as mountebanks (like Bennetta 1986). If some of these charges of deliberate deception are correct, creationists would hardly be the first zealous proponents of a cause to justify making distortions or even telling lies in the service of what they see as a greater good—nor perhaps the first to see in the scientific literature only what they want to see. But they certainly lack a self-critical, self-policing ethos like that of mainstream scientists (Cavanaugh 1983, 318–21). In any case, it is clear that their criticisms of the scientific consensus are not based on a clear and correct representation of it.

Creationist Pseudoscience? If scientific creationism is not science in the conventional sense, then what is it? The label most frequently used by its opponents is *pseudoscience* (such as Schadewald 1983b; Hines 1988, 1–20, 280–84; Radner and Radner 1982, 27–51). Definitions of this term vary, but their common theme is that pseudoscience involves procedures and assertions that claim to have the status of science but that do not warrant it because of failure to follow accepted scientific methods. Characteristics that have been ascribed to pseudoscience include reliance on untestable hypotheses; uncritical appeal to myths and legends as reliable evidence of past events; "research by exegesis"—that is, by interpreting and criticizing scientific research rather than conducting it oneself (Radner and Radner 1982:47); and an unwillingness to consider modifying one's ideas in the light of criticism or of scientific advances. Commonly cited examples of pseudoscience include "UFOlogy"; von Däniken's "ancient astronauts" books; Immanual Velikovsky's books on cosmic collisions; parapsychology; and even Freudian psychoanalysis (see Hines 1988; Radner and Radner 1982; Stiebing 1984; Cazeau and Scott 1979; Szasz 1974). Elsewhere, we have characterized scientific creationism as pseudoscientific (Harrold and Eve, eds., 1987) because of its parallels in approach and procedure with these other examples, even though its conservative religious roots in some ways set it apart.

Some authors, however, have difficulty applying the term *pseudoscience* to scientific creationism. One reason is the demarcation problem: Can definitions be constructed that always distinguish cleanly between science and pseudoscience? (Dolby 1987). All the above sins attributed to pseudoscience, after all, are found at one time or another in mainstream science, while some "pseudoscientists" (notably in parapsychology) do make efforts to follow scientific procedures. Some philosophers of science find that the demarcation problem puts them in a position like that of the Supreme Court in trying to define *obscenity*. Justice Potter Stewart finally said that while he might be unable to define obscenity precisely, he knew it when he saw it. For some philosophers of science, gray areas like the search for extraterrestrial intelligence (is it farsighted or a waste of time?) and some of the more careful work in parapsychology cause doubt that the boundary can ever be drawn unambiguously.

Thus, physicist and science writer James Trefil (1978) prefers to speak in terms of a concentric series of circles, with established science in the center. Beyond it is a "frontier" of theories, concepts, and procedures that are not now accepted but that show some promise of winning admission to the center in the future. One frontier theory that eventually

won acceptance in the scientific center is plate tectonics (continental drift) theory in geology. Finally, there is a fringe of more outlandish claims (such as geocentrism, biorhythms, and scientific creationism) that will probably never gain acceptance.

Some writers have argued that *pseudoscience* is a vague and unnecessarily pejorative term, a label sometimes used to defend closed minds, that should be replaced by a more neutral term like *unconventional science* (Truzzi 1979). Our own view is that this argument carries relativism too far. Not all knowledge claims warrant equal treatment. Science is not infallible, but it has proven to be a successful means for learning about the empirical world. Despite the ambiguities, distinguishing between science and its imitators is worthwhile.

Another problem regarding scientific creationism's status stems from the fact that the Baconianism that inspires it was itself once conventional science. If the Baconianism of a great figure like Linnaeus was science two centuries ago, is it not still science today? Or is the very definition of *science* changeable? It is for these reasons that Cavanaugh refers to scientific creationism as "one-eyed science" and as a "parascientific movement: one whose members operate outside professional channels of research while still concerned with the criticism, use, and dissemination of scientific findings" (Cavanaugh 1985, 187). Similarly, Dolby (1987), a philosopher of science, calls creationism "archaic science."

Dolby also, however, says that describing scientific creationism simply as archaic science is imprecise. "In addition to being archaic science, it is an especially corrupting form of science. My suspicion is that present publications are to some extent fraudulent, a kind of pious fraud" (Dolby 1987, 209). The fraud to which Dolby refers is not only the misrepresentation of mainstream science in the creationist literature but what he considers the passing-off as science of a political device to install religious doctrine in public schools.

Fraud or no, Dolby and Cavanaugh have hit upon an important point. Scientific creationists not only fail to do conventional science, they also fail to do Baconian science. Although they conceive of science, and criticize mainstream science, in terms of Baconian principles, they themselves do no research to any significant extent, nor gather "facts" in the field and laboratory, nor work to discern the patterns of these facts. Rather, they simply spray the edifice of evolutionary science with numerous volleys in an effort to hit a vital supporting element and bring it down. The structure they would raise in its place is biblical, not scientific.

Because of its shared traits with classic pseudosciences and because

it is not only Baconianism, but incomplete Baconianism, we still maintain that scientific creationism can be fairly described as pseudoscience. But what is more important in this context than the labels applied is the point that scientific creationists do not use the methods, concepts, and communication channels of mainstream science.

Reasons for the Effectiveness of the Creationist Attack

If creationists' goal is to persuade the scientific establishment of the errors of its ways and to present it with a superior alternative, they have failed utterly. The consensus of mainstream scientists is that by scientific standards, scientific creationists present a very poor case. Many scientists are puzzled by the fact that it could persuade anyone.

Why, then, is creationism not simply a footnote in intellectual history, like the once-popular notions of animal magnetism or geocentrism? Why is it still such a controversial issue?

The answer is that creationists are not addressing themselves to the scientific community at all. They do not conduct conventional scientific research. Nor do they publish articles on creation theory in scientific journals. This is not simply because the dogmatic evolutionist editors of scientific journals reject all their articles. As studies of the scientific literature have found, none are submitted (Scott and Cole 1985; Cole and Scott 1982).[7]

Target Audiences   Creationism is still alive because creationist rhetoric is directed not at mainstream scientists but at the lay public. In social movement theory, a movement requires an ideology and goals that will unify real and potential adherents rather than divide them. Creationist literature bypasses scientists and speaks in a consistent ideological language to a reachable public in a language it understands. The principal work of scientific creationists is the production of a steady stream of popularly oriented books, pamphlets, articles, lectures, and debates to substantiate this ideology.

They are interested in reaching two kinds of people. One kind is evangelicals and other conservative Christians who desire solace in the face of perceived threats to their faith: "The very existence of creation science provides considerable reassurance to Biblical literalists. It provides them with the conviction that the most powerful of modern epistemologies, modern science, is on their side" (Barker 1985, 199).

The other kind of people targeted by creationists are those outside the conservative Christian camp and who have no particular stake in the creation–evolution issue but who can be persuaded that there is a scientific case against evolution and for creationism. To use Turner and Killian's (1987) term, they constitute a "bystander public" that perceives itself as uninvolved in the struggle but whose reaction to it could be crucial to its outcome. Most of these outsiders are not expected to become religious converts, but if they can be convinced to support "equal time" for creationism in public education, it will help creationists achieve the legitimization and dissemination of their beliefs in public schools.

Interestingly, these activists make relatively little use of mainstream mass-appeal magazines and television, as Godfrey and Cole (1987) have pointed out. Rather, they rely mainly on in-house and religious channels. Some creationist books, however, are issued in two editions: one for committed Christians, with biblical citations and theological arguments against evolution, and the other for a more general public, without such features and purporting to make its case on purely nonreligious grounds (such as Morris 1974a, 1974b). Furthermore, several creationist books have been published in recent years by commercial presses (Thaxton et al. 1984; Bird 1989) and have received some favorable reviews. They have modulated the highly polemical tone of classic creationist literature and tried to avoid overt misrepresentation of scientists' views. They also eschew evangelical apologetics.

For the most part, though, the creationist case is brought to the public by believers, armed with arguments from creationist literature and citing its authors as scientific authorities in their legal and political struggles.

The Success of Creationist Rhetoric   One might expect that, despite their dedication, creationists would have little success in making their case to the American public. After all, the United States is a world leader in many fields of science, including evolutionary biology. Furthermore, science has high standing and credibility in our society (Walsh 1982; Etzioni and Nunn 1974). Wouldn't the American public heed the scientists who denounce scientific creationism as claptrap?

The answer is that often they do not. As we have seen, some 40 to 50 percent of the American public and around one-quarter of college students agree with strict creationist statements in polls. Moreover, in our study of college students, 42 percent of Texas subjects, along with 25 percent in California and 30 percent of Connecticut, agreed that "There is a good deal of scientific evidence against evolution and in favor of the

Bible's account of creation" (Harrold and Eve 1987). Both directly and indirectly, scientific creationists have managed to persuade many people that there is "something to" their claims.

An even larger segment of the public is willing to support the teaching of creationism in public schools alongside evolution: in a 1981 Associated Press/NBC poll, an overwhelming 76 percent favored just such a policy (Fuerst 1984). Another 10 percent wanted *only* creationism in public schools! Among the college students queried in our study, a majority of the Texas students (57 percent) and nearly half the other two groups—46 percent in Connecticut and 47 percent in California—favored the inclusion of creationism alongside evolution in public school curricula (Harrold and Eve 1987).

Significantly, acceptance of "equal time for creationism" in these studies is higher than acceptance of creationism itself. Many people (apparently in the order of 30 percent of the public) do not themselves embrace creationism but nonetheless support teaching it in public schools.

Why the Success?   We believe that several factors underlie this state of affairs. The first, of course, is that many millions of Americans are conservative Christians who accept creationism as a matter of faith. But many others embrace or tolerate creationism whose religious faith does not require it (such as Catholics or Episcopalians) or who are indifferent to religion.

The second factor is the powerful appeal of creationist rhetoric. To many people, an article or lecture by a creationist like Duane Gish is a very impressive experience. A writer or speaker who is obviously not a fanatic or backwoods primitive constantly stresses the use of common sense and logic as he lists one defect after another in evolutionary theory. He argues, with many citations from the scientific literature, that the creation model explains the fossil and geological records better than the merely speculative theory of evolution. As a Ph.D. in science, he concludes that accepting evolution requires more faith than accepting creationism—and so can the audience, now that they have had a look at the evidence for themselves. Then why can't those scientists in the universities see it too? The audience wonders. Some can, but most *will* not, comes the answer, because of their blind dogmatism and pride, and because the establishment punishes anyone who questions scientific orthodoxy. With a humorous anecdote or two, the speaker reminds the audience that for all their intelligence, academics can be short on common sense—and tolerance. Creationists, he says, do not want to impose an-

other orthodoxy to replace evolution; they simply want their theory to be freely available so that everyone—including public school students—can look at the evidence and decide for themselves.

Especially convincing to many people is the equal-time argument. Named after the Federal Communications Commission policy mandating equal broadcast time for opposing political views, this argument is based on the false evolution–creation dichotomy discussed earlier, and is accepted by many noncreationists. If there are only two possible views of "origins," and if scientific evidence can be advanced to support both evolution and creationism, then what could be fairer than to let both models be presented so that students can make up their own minds? Americans are socialized from early childhood to place a high value on due process and letting everyone have his say. To many people, attempts to keep creationism out of school curricula smack of dogmatism and censorship.

Creationist activists know how to appeal to their audiences. A content analysis of several creationist–evolutionist debates found that the creationist debaters (including Duane Gish) used several forensic devices effective in influencing audiences to a considerably greater extent than the evolutionists did (Stempien and Coleman 1985). They include tactics like Card Stacking (the highly selective use of logic and data to achieve an effect); Testimonial (the use, as evidence, of a respected person's endorsement or criticism of an idea); and Glittering Generality (associating an idea with an esteemed concept such as family values or fairness). While anticreationist debaters often bored and baffled their audiences with scientific discourse, their creationist opponents showed a keen awareness of techniques useful for winning, not scientists, but a lay audience. The creationists "use appeals that ordinary folks can relate to easily. They often appeal to folk beliefs about science. They ask the public to 'come to their own conclusions.' . . . They are not afraid to employ devices that appeal more to sentiment than to intellect" (Stempien and Coleman 1985, 173).[8]

Creationist rhetoric also succeeds in part because it appeals to the populism, antielitism, and anti-intellectualism that are part of American culture (Hofstadter 1963), as Nelkin (1982, 165–79) has noted. Who should control our school curricula, creationists ask—an arrogant elite out of touch with the rest of us, or the taxpayers who foot the bill? Isn't this country supposed to be a democracy? The scientific authorities who oppose creationism inhabit an intellectual and academic world that many Americans associate with some powerful negative stereotypes—from the absentminded professor who spins abstruse theories but lacks the

horse sense to be able to fix his own plumbing, to the Ivy League snob, to the bearded campus liberal who opposes prayer in schools but thinks flag-burning is fine. Such negative associations have been used by creationists to help build an effective ideology that defines population segments outside the movement as villains.

Along with distrust of intellectuals, creationism appeals to a growing sense of disillusionment with science that many people feel (Nelkin 1982; Walsh 1982). As we are increasingly beset by technological and environmental problems, many people seem to conclude that science (which they do not distinguish from its technological applications) is doing more harm than good.

Perhaps most crucial to the success of creationist attacks on evolution is the low level of knowledge and understanding of science among Americans. In the words of science writer William Bennetta (1986, 10): "Like it or not, the general population of the United States is composed of people who know precious little about the history and content of modern science, and precisely nothing about its precepts and methods."

Bennetta's unsparing judgment is supported by a good deal of evidence. Sociologist Jon Miller (1983, 1987a, 1987b), for instance, has conducted national surveys of American adults' scientific literacy. Using a fairly modest definition of *scientific literacy* as involving a basic understanding of scientific methods (the meaning of scientific study of a subject) and constructs (concepts such as DNA), he found that only about 5 percent of the U.S. public can be considered scientifically literate—able, for instance, to read a newspaper story about genetic engineering, and understand its content and implications for public policy (Miller 1987b). Only 16 percent reported having a "clear understanding" of what DNA is, while 57 percent had "little understanding." Seven percent think that astrology is "very scientific," and another 29 percent think that it is "sort of scientific." And no less than 41 percent agreed that "Rocket launchings and other space activities have caused changes in our weather" (Miller 1987a). In a more recent study (National Science Foundation 1989), only about 45 percent of U.S. respondents were aware that the earth revolves around the sun in a period of one year (not one day or one month).

Unsurprisingly, scientific literacy increased with education, although only 12 percent of college graduates were judged literate (Miller 1987a). Even among people with graduate degrees, the proportion rose to only 18 percent.

The somewhat higher rates of scientific knowledge and understanding among younger people should not be interpreted too optimistically. On

standardized science tests, American students typically score lower than students from many other countries. For instance, in a recent study by the International Association for the Evaluation of Educational Achievement (IEA), science achievement levels of secondary students from thirteen developed nations were assessed between 1983 and 1986 (IEA 1988; Walsh 1988). U.S. students made discouragingly low scores in all areas of science tested, never finishing higher than eighth. In biology they scored last. (We must ask whether this is connected to the chilling effect that creationism has had on high school instruction in evolution, the central organizing principle of biology [see Chapter 8].) The generally poor state of U.S. science education has drawn criticism and expressions of concern from many educators and scientists (National Commission on Excellence in Education 1983; American Association for the Advancement of Science 1986; Lehman 1982; Volpe 1984). D. Allen Bromley, director of President Bush's Office of Science and Technology Policy, has said that at the precollege level, science education "can only be described as scandalous," while at the college level there are "peaks of excellence and valleys of mediocrity that defy description" (quoted in Beardsley 1989).

The significance of this situation for this book is that average Americans are ill-equipped to evaluate the claims of scientific creationism. They can hardly be expected to analyze creationist claims about the second law of thermodynamics, for instance, if they lack any idea of what the first or third laws are about. If they have no notion of the wealth and range of evidence for human evolution, they may find perfectly reasonable the claim that all *Homo erectus* fossils are either apes or modern humans. If they subscribe to the common misconception that evolutionary change is the result of "blind chance," they may perceive creationist arguments of its extreme improbability as compelling. If they have little understanding of the roles of critical thinking and "rules of evidence" in science, they may cling to unsubstantiated beliefs even after seeing them effectively refuted; even if they do change their minds, they may revert after a time to their former beliefs (Singer and Benassi 1981; Gray 1987). Average Americans may be convinced by creationist arguments (especially if they are religiously conservative), or they may simply throw up their hands in puzzlement. There are Ph.D.s on both sides of this issue, they may decide, so let's allow the schoolkids to hear both points of view; that seems fair.

Godfrey (1981a) found striking instances of such reactions when she asked a class of students who had some background in anthropology to

read some creationist material and then write their responses. Some were won over by the standard creationist arguments. Even those who disagreed were often unable to summon arguments or data to show why the creationist claims were wrong. Those who tried to do so often revealed that they had fundamental misunderstandings of modern evolutionary theory, such as the notion that equates evolution with progress. Wrote one: "Look, I can't answer these questions. Sorry I can't help you out, but this is beyond me" (Godfrey 1981, 385).

Conclusion

The efforts of scientific creationists have not affected the scientific consensus on evolution because creation scientists do not function in the research tradition of modern science. They use Baconian standards of evidence and argument. They launch scattershot attacks on the evolutionary consensus based on the notion that evidence that damages evolution is evidence that supports creationism. Their actual criticisms of scientific findings are characterized by misunderstandings, omissions, and distortions. They do not attempt to develop detailed alternative scientific explanations of the data that they claim to have "unexplained" in their criticisms of the consensus. Instead, they appeal to the supernatural.

Yet despite its shortcomings as scientific discourse, the creationist assault on evolution has enjoyed significant success. Creationists have spread their generalized beliefs that evolution is both nonsensical and, as the foundation of secular humanism, destructive of traditional values, with some effect. Many Americans accept creationist claims, and many others have been persuaded that fairness requires us to give scientific creationism a place in public science education. The reasons for this success include religious beliefs (bolstered by assurances that creationism is scientific); the skilled presentation of the creationist case; Americans' sense of fair play; their growing mistrust of the scientific establishment; and their generally poor understanding of science.

It seems safe to conclude that creationist rhetoric has indeed effectively bolstered the ideology's credibility. Despite the mainly norm-oriented tone of their discourse, creationists' ultimate recourse to value-oriented arguments indicates that their primary interest is not so much to develop an alternative science as to defend a traditional worldview or even advocate the establishment of a conservative Christian theocracy. In either of these cases, there would be no role left for sci-

ence to play, except when its findings could be used to support scripture. Modern science generally, which rationally deduces hypotheses from preexisting knowledge, tests them with data, and then lets the philosophical and theological chips fall where they may, would have little place in a society such as creationists envision.

The Genesis of Creationism: Psychological and Sociological Perspectives

This monkey mythology of Darwin is the cause of permissiveness, promiscuity, pills, prophylactics, perversions, pregnancies, abortions, pornotherapy, pollution, poisoning, and proliferation of crimes of all types.

—Braswell Deen, chief justice of the
Georgia Circuit Court of Appeals (1981)

To those trained in science, creationism seems like a bad dream, a sudden reliving of a nightmare, a renewed march of an army of the night risen to challenge free thought and enlightenment.

—Isaac Asimov (1982)

Storm in the Mountains: The Kanawha County Textbook Confrontation

In 1974, in Kanawha County, West Virginia, Alice Moore, a public school board member who was also the wife of a fundamentalist minister, ushered in a new era in the creation–evolution debate when she objected at a school board meeting to some of the 175 books the board had chosen as supplementary reading selections for the language arts program.

To fully understand her objections, we should note that West Virginia law requires that local school districts choose their books from a state-approved list if they expect the state to pay for the books. As a result, a good deal of weight had been given to the mandate of the West Virginia

State Board of Education that districts should select reading materials that place emphasis on "minority and ethnic group contributions to American growth and culture and which depict and illustrate the intercultural character of our pluralistic society" (Moffett 1988, 11).

We should also note that although Kanawha County contains the state capital, Charleston, it is otherwise composed of many small, rural communities. "The population is distinctly non-ethnic and Protestant. Less than 1 percent of the population is non-white and only 2.9 percent are first or second generation foreign born" (Page and Clelland 1978). These numbers alone should suggest that Kanawha County was a potential site for conflict because several previous studies have found that rural and small-town dwellers are somewhat more likely to support creationist doctrine.[1]

Alice Moore had been elected to the school board in 1970 as a result of her instigation of a 1969 campaign to remove sex education from the county schools' health education program. This conflict, too, may be seen as largely a conflict between rural Appalachian values and those of the county's burgeoning cosmopolitan sector. Moore had asserted that sex education was anti-Christian and anti-American and violated God's law.

When Alice Moore began to read the newly adopted language arts books (itself unusual because previously the board had left book selection to the professional educators), she was shocked. In her first public denunciation of the books at a school board meeting on 23 May, she denounced the books as "filthy, trashy, disgusting, one-sidedly in favor of blacks, and unpatriotic" (Moffett 1988, 14). Moore appeared on TV and before local church congregations to attempt to rally support for her protest against the language books. In June the PTA voted against several of the books, citing them as "full of anti-Americanism . . . [and] woefully lacking in morally uplifting ideas. Many of the statements flout law-and-order and respect for authority. Several passages are extremely sexually explicit" (Moffett 1988, 15). On the other hand, the local NAACP and YWCA supported the books, and so did the West Virginia Human Rights Committee and the Episcopal Church (and most of the other mainline denominations). On 27 June at the next school board meeting, more than a thousand antitextbook protestors attended. Not to be intimidated, the board voted to adopt the disputed books. This decision became a precipitating event.

According to Ann Page and Donald Clelland (1978), "On September 3, the new school term was started for some 45,000 students. Protesting parents withheld their children from the schools (10,000 by school board estimates), picketed businesses and mines throughout the county, and

prevented school and city buses from operating." Unwilling to cross lines of picketing parents, thirty-five hundred miners declined to go to work, in spite of orders to do so from United Mine Workers officials. After about a week, the schools closed for a three-day period and the controversial books were removed from the classroom—at least temporarily.

But "During this so-called cooling off period, violence escalated," according to Page and Clelland (1978, 269). Random sniping by both sides was reported; vandalism of school property was commonplace; schools were firebombed and dynamited; school buses were fired upon; and so were two highway patrol cars escorting a school bus. In addition, the county board of education building was dynamited. Still refusing to be intimidated, the school board voted to reinstate the books; but they arranged only for the most controversial ones to be placed in the schools' libraries and further decreed that they should be read only with parental consent. The mayor of one town sympathetic to the protesters managed to have the superintendent and at least two board members arrested for supposedly contributing to the delinquency of minors (Page and Clelland 1978, 269; Moffett 1988, 23).

What, one might well ask, kind of books had created such a volatile situation? The books contained a highly diverse selection of poetry, nonfiction, drama, short stories, and other fiction, mostly by recent American authors. The protesting parents had pointed to passages in the books that they believed promoted a climate of sexual immorality, a lack of patriotism, communism, drug and alcohol use, violence, and (most notable for our purposes) belief in evolution. Many of their opponents felt that this very eclecticism was proof that the protesters were suffering from collective schizophrenia or other fragmentation of the intellect. But once we understand the dynamics involved, we will see the coherence of these topics, even if we disagree with the meaning assigned to them.

One result of these events was almost unbelievable. In November, several mayors of towns in one region of the county presented a plan for the secession of their portion of the county! In addition, a number of private Christian schools were created, which, interestingly, separated the most militant parents from the public schools. The violence and confrontation subsided.

Beyond Kanawha County

The events in Kanawha County, while fascinating in their details, would be only a minor footnote to history if it were not for the fact that they

contributed to a general movement that appeared to gain momentum exponentially. A fascinating account of the Kanawha County conflict has been recorded in detail by the individual in charge of developing the language arts program that set off the confrontation. In his 1988 book *Storm in the Mountains,* James Moffett (general editor of the book series that was at issue) suggests that the events in Kanawha County had widespread impact. "Leaders of the textbook controversy boasted that their example set rolling a conservative buildup that swept the country by the eighties. . . . The momentum gathering there set off alarms throughout the publishing and educational worlds that sound more insistently even at this writing" (Moffett 1988, 187). Since the 1974 battle of the books in Kanawha County, there has been a sharp increase in the number of incidents of censorship or attempts at censorship (Jenkinson 1979, 29). During the 1977–78 school year, more incidents of removing or censoring books were reported nationally than at any other time in the last twenty-five years.

Many other authors have documented the rise in attempts at textbook censorship (Arons 1981; Katz 1985; Skoog 1979, 1984). In 1988, People for the American Way produced a booklet entitled *Attacks on the Freedom to Learn* that summarized a number of attempts at school censorship during the 1987–88 school year. According to that publication, "Censorship attempts occurred in 42 states and in every region of the country. The most frequently attacked book was *Of Mice and Men.*" In more than one-third of the incidents, books or programs were removed or restricted. Interestingly, the 157 incidents reported in the booklet (which includes incidents other than direct attempts at censorship) is almost evenly divided among the West, the South, and the Midwest (with forty-two to fifty incidents each). Only the Northeast had a noticeably different number (nineteen).

We have so far described what happened in Kanawha County and elsewhere; it remains to explain *how* it happened and *why.* It should become obvious that much of the explanation appropriate to the West Virginia case can help explain many other incidents of cultural militancy by conservative Christians—including, of course, their fervor against evolution.

The Creationists and the New Christian Right

Creationism is to some extent related to a larger ideological totality that is often referred to as the New Christian Right (NCR). Several authors have suggested that the New Christian Right is itself but one facet of an

even broader conservative social movement of recent years, the New Right. One author has suggested that "the New Right consists of the network of activists, organizations, and constituencies that have been the most militant opponents of the Equal Rights Amendment, the Panama Canal Treaty, SALT II, affirmative action, federal social programs, and government regulation of business; the most vocal critics of liberalism and 'secular humanism;' and the most ardent proponents of the Human Life Amendment, the Family Protection Act, increased defense spending, prayer in public schools, and *the teaching of "scientific creationism"* (Himmelstein 1983, 13; our italics).

Not surprisingly, the New Right had its first stirrings in the Old Right—a reaction on the part of conservative portions of the Republican party to the New Deal of Roosevelt. The Old Right flowered into adulthood with the Joseph McCarthy hearings of the 1950s, then was quiescent for several years. But the right enjoyed a rebirth of energy and visible membership during the Nixon-Agnew and, most especially, the Reagan-Bush administrations. The specific concerns of this more recent New Right, so clearly reflected in the topics the Kanawha County protestors found objectionable, are built upon the three doctrinal cornerstones of the New Right: laissez-faire capitalism, social traditionalism, and militant anticommunism (Lieberman and Wuthnow 1983). Part of what is new about the New Christian Right is its mobilization of conservative Christians, many of whom had historically been politically inactive due to a conviction that church and state should be separate spheres and, in some cases, due to the belief that the world outside their groups was irredeemably corrupt. The New Christian Right has also been the beneficiary of the demise of the old Roosevelt Democratic coalition. Many religious conservatives changed their voting patterns and came eventually to oppose the Democrats, whom they often now see as too liberal. Certainly during the Reagan years, many who would have voted Democratic on strictly economic issues in the past nonetheless began to support the agenda of conservative values put forth by the Republicans.

We partially agree with the assertion that the New Christian Right is generally harmoniously embedded in the larger New Right movement. But we take the position here that the relationship between the New Christian Right and the hard-liners in the Old Right is in many ways a limited alliance of convenience because the New Christian Right often does not share the same depth of commitment to laissez-faire economics or social Darwinism as the Old Right; nor do they necessarily reflect other elements historically characteristic of the hard-line rightists. The

most accurate summary of the relationship would seem to be that the New Christian Right and the rest of the political right seem to find in each other convenient—if not particularly like-minded—allies. For example, Ronald Reagan and many others in his administration were not deeply committed to the specific goals of the New Christian Right, but there is little doubt that some of their success stemmed from their willingness to ally themselves with the New Christian Right politically. Therefore, we will try to explain the dynamics of creationists without regarding them as being precisely interchangeable with the older and more mainstream elements of the right wing.

Explaining Creationism:
Pathology versus Rationality

Most attempts to understand creationists invoke some form of personal psychopathology or irrationality to explain their beliefs. Creationist belief, by the same token, has often been seen as a bizarre adjustment to life, the result of personality aberrations among its adherents or as a throwback to a prescientific era.

But in recent years the field of collective behavior analysis has increasingly moved away from a view of collective behavior (including social movements) as inevitably reflecting irrational impulses and a high level of emotionality among participants. To gain a full explanation of the sources of the creationist movement, we must focus more on the rationality of the adherents and on their demonstrated organizational expertise. But because psychopathological interpretations of the New Right and creationism have a long history, it is necessary to understand them before a critique of such explanations will be meaningful.

Personality Factors and Attraction to Creationism Many authors have argued that right-wing politics tends to be particularly appealing to individuals with certain personality types. Such people, for example, are said to have an "authoritarian personality." It would seem in order to briefly discuss what the authoritarian personality *is*, before assessing the validity of the claim.

Before World War II, a number of talented Jewish psychiatrists and psychologists worked together at the Institut für Sozialforschung in Frankfurt, among them the now famous figures of Erich Fromm and Theodor W. Adorno. These fugitive social scientists fled for their lives

from the terrors of Hitler's Germany and reorganized themselves after arriving in New York as The Institute for Social Research. There they became, not surprisingly, deeply concerned with the question of how Hitler and Nazism could have come to dominate an entire nation. They became convinced that "the political, economic and social convictions of an individual often form a broad and coherent pattern, as if bound together by a 'mentality' or 'spirit,' and that this pattern is an expression of deep-lying trends in his personality" (Madge 1962, 379). In part, this thesis asserted that in the typical German family the father was an extremely dominating figure. It was widely argued that this would establish a pattern that would lead young men to need to replace the dominant father of the family with another authoritarian figure after leaving the family. Presumably, the new authority figure could fill the void of existential anxiety left by the absence of having a domineering father to tell one what was correct and how to behave. In addition, such sons were said to be socialized to find strict, black-and-white moral codes attractive. Thus, having grown accustomed to an authoritarian father, it was an easy step to adopting the authoritarian figure of the Führer to tell one what to do.

This view of German family dynamics was to lead Erich Fromm to write his famous book *Escape from Freedom* (1941). Fromm argued that during the Hitler era, the rank-and-file members of German society voiced platitudes about how much they desired freedom, but when actually presented with it, they usually felt great anxiety about the self-responsibility and the moral decision-making that freedom entails. As a result, they rushed to abdicate their freedom to an authority figure. Such an authority figure, we should note, need not be a head of state but could as readily be a teacher, a minister, a local politician, a seer, or even a licensed psychiatrist.

This reasoning remained only a hypothesis until the late 1940s, when Adorno began a research project involving in-depth interviews, not with Germans but with Americans, to see whether psychometric scales could be developed to identify individuals whose personalities incorporated a constellation of interrelated authoritarian beliefs. Adorno reasoned that anyone might have an authoritarian belief or two, but he hypothesized that in people with an authoritarian personality, such beliefs tended to be inexorably intertwined into a major personality dimension. Although there have been many criticisms of the methodology Adorno et al. used in producing *The Authoritarian Personality* (1950), today a large majority of social scientists accept that something very like the authoritarian personality does exist. In empirical studies since Adorno's, many other

researchers have found that certain people are likely to combine some, if not all, of the traits that were hypothesized to characterize authoritarians.

Such traits include prejudice, ethnocentrism, excessive concern with conventional middle-class morality, an obsession with dominance and submission in all relationships, repressed hostility and aggression toward anyone different from themselves, opposition to sensitivity or "tender-mindedness," inclination toward superstition and stereotyping, a belief in a hostile world, a belief in grand conspiracies, intolerance of ambiguity, a tendency to holding contradictory beliefs, a preoccupation with masculine toughness, cynicism, an obsession with sex as dirty or out of control, and a tendency to "project" many of one's undesirable subconscious impulses onto others while remaining unaware of their inner source. Not every authoritarian individual manifests all of these traits, but some combination of them seems unusually likely to occur together in those who qualify as authoritarians. (For further information on the authoritarian personality and related research, see Madge 1962; Moffett 1988, 193–197; Rokeach 1960).

Goldstein and Blackman (1978, 35) contend that high levels of authoritarianism are most often found among the less educated, the older, the rural, the disadvantaged, members of dogmatic religious organizations, members of lower socioeconomic groups, and those emotionally isolated from other persons. It is, of course, among just these groups that creationism has found its greatest support. But there seems to be little or no empirical research that specifically ties individual creationists to high scores on psychometric tests for authoritarianism.

A number of authors have also made cogent arguments that those with authoritarian personalities are likely to be attracted to—and overrepresented in—right-wing politics (see, for example, Lipset 1960). The bases for these arguments are relatively easy to see. Right-wing religions and right-wing politics often place great emphasis on unquestioning acceptance of authority (whether secular or godly), the acceptance of rules at face value, a view of such rules as hard-and-fast in nature, and the need for coercive control of antisocial impulses in individuals. Since these are the same themes that held center stage in the authoritarian's childhood, it is not hard to understand why such a person would be attracted to this type of political or religious organization.

It should be noted, however, that creationists often espouse certain beliefs that are not consistent with this image of them. Those who originally developed the concept of the authoritarian personality wished to identify a personality type that was susceptible to antidemocratic dog-

mas. But many creationists would, at least by their own reports, be among democracy's strongest supporters. Their rhetoric is highly populist, as we saw in Chapter 5, and they often support parental or local governmental authority when it conflicts with federal or state-level authority (such as the mandates of national politicians and educational elites to cover evolutionism in the public schools). These hardly seem like the same personality traits that one would have found among those who supported the dictatorship of Hitler. If the word *authoritarian* merely indicates people who are rigidly committed to a belief system and to its coercive implementation, then there obviously exist left-wing authoritarians as well.

To definitively establish whether creationists are any more authoritarian than others from the same sociodemographic backgrounds, we will need to go beyond a "debate of competing intuitions." Often those on opposing sides of a social movement issue employ "atrocity tales" about the behavior of their enemies. (Atrocity tales are lurid, often exaggerated tales employed by those on both sides of controversial issues such as charges of brainwashing in recent American religious cults. Such tales are told in an attempt to influence undecided members of the public to support one's position by portraying those on the opposite side as completely evil and inhuman). Such tales act as an important mechanism for justifying the use of whatever punishment or control one believes is necessary to keep the opposition in line. Social scientists will need to perform more carefully designed and controlled studies before we can conclude beyond doubt that creationists are unusually likely to be authoritarians. The alternative is that such a characterization will be seen as only a half-truth or even an example of an atrocity tale masquerading as a valid scientific finding.

Explaining Creationism: Status Politics

The everyday use of the word *politics* is more or less synonymous with phenomena for which sociologists and political scientists reserve the more specific terms *class politics* or *positional politics*. These terms are used to identify people's relationship to the economic or material resources of their society. Such politics form the very backbone, for example, of Marxist theory, which sees history as being determined by the political conflict between classes that have material advantage and those without it. But in recent decades, a new category of politics, called *status politics*, has been introduced into the social sciences. The unique aspect

of status politics is that they are based on one's *worldview* and *life-style* (defined in terms of traditional ways of doing things), rather than on one's class position. In status politics, it is one's worldview, not one's wealth, or other material advantage that is threatened by an outside collectivity.

The concept of "status politics" was first put forward by Richard Hofstadter (1955) in an attempt to explain the origins of right-wing extremism in the United States. Hofstadter's thesis was that the theoretical conceptualizations that were commonly used for examining social movement conflicts were often overly concerned with economic factors, and that many modern American social movement conflicts could be better explained by recognizing that in many such cases the prime mover was actually a sense of threatened worldview that cut across traditional social class boundaries. Such an assertion can be seen to reflect a critique of Marx by early sociologist Max Weber. Weber suggested that while class was undoubtedly important in many social conflicts, status groups (or what he referred to in German as *Stände*) had received insufficient attention from Marx as a source of both within-group cohesion and between-group conflict. Weber intended by his use of the term *status group* to mean a collectivity defined by its adherence to a common life-style and its associated claims to "social honor and prestige" (Wald, Owen, and Hill 1989, 13). Weber further suggested that such groups often find themselves to be locked in "constant struggles [with other status groups] for control of the means of symbolic production through which their reality is constructed" (Page and Clelland 1978). In making this assertion, Weber set the stage for a major schism in modern explanations of social movements.

The analysis of social movements, at least since Marx, has been sensitive to the role of material and economic factors as a source of conflict between segments of a society (and between societies). But a fundamental modification of strict Marxian class-centered social analysis presented itself within the study of social movements beginning with the work of Ralf Dahrendorf (1959). Darhendorf placed greater emphasis on the individual's craving not for material comfort but for control over his life. Those of us accustomed to life in modern capitalist society are unduly inclined to think that having personal wealth means having control over one's own life. But such an exact overlap is not inevitable. University professors, for example, as well as most ministers, generally have relatively low incomes compared with others with equivalent educational credentials, but they nonetheless enjoy unusually enhanced control over their own lives. They set their own hours to a large extent, and after

they receive tenure, they seldom have to justify their research interests to anyone else. Indeed, many professors say that they would rather enjoy the freedom of academic life than the greater income that they might earn from many other occupations. Thus, while income and control are frequently found together, their connection is not a fundamental requirement. Unlike Marx, Dahrendorf proposed that the bases for social conflicts, and associated social movements, may not rest solely on material advantages or class position. This line of thinking has led several recent observers of social movements to recognize that movements such as the temperance movement (Gusfield 1963), the antipornography movement (Zurcher 1971), and the gay-rights movement (Adam 1987) are best explained in terms of issues that cut across traditional class lines.

Individuals who feel that their way of life is in danger of being absorbed or supplanted by that of an outside group are likely to suffer anxieties because of their declining status (or at least their belief that such a decline is imminent), according to authors like Trow (1958) and Gusfield (1963). They will be attracted to social movements that they believe will delay or prevent this outcome. Wald, Owen, and Hill (1989) have applied this conception of status politics with considerable success to an analysis of support for the New Christian Right among churchgoers in a southern community. Unlike class politics, status politics are more concerned with self-expression than with a struggle for economic dominance, more concerned with symbolic goals than with tangible or instrumental goals, and are more likely to occur during prosperous times than in times of economic hardship.

Why this last point should be so may need clarification. In psychologist Abraham Maslow's (1973) concept of a "hierarchy of human needs," human needs are arranged hierarchically so that "lower" or more "primitive" needs must be met before individuals will have the time or the inclination for "higher" thoughts or activities. Thus, a hungry and destitute individual, because he is mainly concerned with having enough to eat, is unlikely to be concerned with whether his job is meaningful or with world peace or global crises. Maslow's line of thinking suggests that in prosperous times, such as those now generally characterizing industrial and postindustrial societies such as the United States, most people have their basic needs met and therefore have enough health, time, and energy to concern themselves with symbolic issues as well as with purely material or economic ones. Indeed, during the late twentieth century in the United States and in other modern nations, there has been an explo-

sion of social movements concerned with advancing the values or norms of certain subgroups of these populations.[2] At the same time, these movements threaten others within the same societies, and thus contain within themselves the seeds of countermovements by adherents of traditional life-styles. With people's essential needs generally met, we find ourselves living in societies that are increasingly segmented, not only on the basis of class or economic conflicts but on the basis of conflicts over whose values and worldview shall predominate in the media, the courts, the schools, and so on.

In several Western countries, including the United States, the soil is thus fertile for status politics to arise because conservative Protestants have increasingly found themselves locked into a competition with groups with other worldviews and norms. In the U.S., they have fallen from a position of near total national dominance in the mid-nineteenth century to a less powerful position after the ethnic immigrations at the turn of this century, and then to an even less powerful position as the United States has been transformed from a primarily rural society to an industrial (or perhaps even postindustrial) one, a transformation accompanied by notable secularization.

It is little wonder then, that members of the older prestige group should feel that their life-styles and values are jeopardized by various newcomers. As a consequence, the traditionalists find themselves needing at every turn to defend their general way of life. In the resulting conflict, each group defends powerful emotional symbols of its own life-style with a fervency every bit as intense as in any confrontation over material factors. Among the traditionalists, such life-style symbols include religious piety and an *assertion of the sanctity of a traditional account of creation.*

Thus, seen from the status politics perspective, those who join social movements are motivated by anxiety resulting from a sense of status insecurity. They join movements that they believe may remove this status anxiety by anchoring their beliefs securely at the top of the social prestige hierarchy.

Several authors have suggested that status inconsistents[3] are particularly likely to be drawn to extremist movements, and usually to ones on the political right. For example, Trow (1958) found among the members of the John Birch Society a disproportionate number of status inconsistents. Trow also described how the Nazi party in Germany was disproportionately composed of small businessmen who were politically marginal because, while they had no use for labor unions, neither were

they in favor of large-scale corporate capitalism. The reason for the latter is, of course, that large corporations can exercise power and benefit from economies of scale in ways that threaten the very livelihood of small merchants and artisans. Small businessmen thus seem to crop up often in far-right conservative movements, rejecting not only left-wing organizations such as trade unions but supporting laissez-faire and free-market economics.

Other instances in which status inconsistents are overrepresented in traditionalist movements can be seen in Gusfield's (1963) analysis of the temperance movement, and in Zurcher's (1971) examination of the anti-pornography movements. The findings have been fairly consistent that individuals who belong to groups that are either declining in prestige or that are at least at risk of such a decline (such as small farmers, craftsmen and artisans, small businessmen, unskilled and semi-skilled laborers) are unusually likely to suffer from status anxiety, which in turn propels them into right-wing social movements. They often see such movements as attempts to stave off threatening social change and to defend what they perceive as the "natural" status quo.

Nelkin (1982) advanced this type of explanation for the creationist movement itself; consistent with this explanation, Michael Cavanaugh has observed that "if we glance at the career patterns of the leading figures of one of the major organizations [of scientific creationism], the Institute for Creation Research, we find considerable downward mobility" (Cavanaugh 1983, 193). But were these scientific creationists downwardly mobile before joining the creationist ranks, or after? Most of the evidence seems to suggest that creation scientists were already previously committed to a literal interpretation of the Bible and that this forced them into marginal scientific institutes funded by conservative Christians as the only places they could actually practice scientific creationism.

But it is the *older* versions of status politics theory that try to explain membership in right-wing movements primarily on the basis of the status anxieties of individual adherents. New refinements of status politics theory have brought it more into line with recent developments in the study of social movements, and the newer versions appear to explain creationism better than has previously been possible. It is to these recently refined versions of status politics theory that we now turn.

Explaining Creationism: Worldviews in Conflict

Those who have advanced status politics theories to explain how individuals are attracted to right-wing social movements have been recently

criticized for too quickly resorting to explanations in terms of the individuals' mental processes and motivations. It is tempting for many evolutionists, too, to explain creationists as having pathologies of character such as authoritarianism, or as ignorant, or as poor, or status-declining, or as responding to structurally induced anxiety.

But such conceptions of status politics are inadequate to account for most adherents to the creationist movement. It seems likely that status decliners (and those threatened with such decline) are indeed unusually likely to be attracted to creationism, but it does not logically follow that the majority of creationists can be characterized this way. Indeed, most analyses do not find creationists to be generally poor or downwardly mobile. They are often quite well off. As we saw earlier, most indications are that, on the average, creationists are not much worse off than other Americans, and they have been closing the gap in recent years. In some locations, such as the Dallas–Forth Worth area (a stronghold of creationism), many or even most of the population, of all economic strata, are conservative Protestants. It is absurd to suppose that all, or even most, creationists in such areas are poor, ignorant, or downwardly mobile.

A calm assessment of the situation suggests that other modes of explanation are necessary. A full account must explain, for example, why large numbers of educated and well-to-do persons are creationists.

The argument we will present below follows in the footsteps of recent developments in the study of social movements. In the early days of the field, as we have seen, it was fashionable to see social movements as driven by irrational, subconscious, and primitive impulses. Ever since LeBon (1897) formulated his law of "the mental unity of crowds" it has been popular to see individuals engaged in collective action as having a unitary psyche or a "group mind"—and not a very good mind at that. The group mind was said to be of low intelligence, given to wild and illogical emotional behavior, and extremely suggestible.

But recent analyses have tended to discover that the behavior of movement adherents is actually reasonably logical and rational *when seen from the perspective of the participant*. Page and Clelland (1978) suggest that previous conceptions of status politics (such as Gusfield's or Zurcher's) were in error because the central dynamic behind the revival of creationism is not the actual or threatened decline of an individual's prestige or income. Page and Clelland claim that these views underestimated the extent to which groups within a larger society can develop systems of values and norms that represent much more than merely the internal mental life of individual members. Through socialization, whole groups learn to promote and defend the values and symbols of the way

of life (the subculture, as anthropologists would call it) that they share with other members. Thus, status groups (in Weber's sense of a vertical cleavage in society, not a horizontal economic one) "are consequently involved in constant struggles for control of the means of symbolic production. . . . status politics is not, in essence, the attempt to defend against declining prestige but the attempt to defend a way of life" (Page and Clelland 1978, 266). We will try to explain just what we mean by the creationists' "symbolic construction of reality," why it is logical and plausible from their point of view, and why their view of reality is completely incompatible with that of the evolutionists and twentieth-century science. But first, we need to look at a few fundamental ideas drawn from the general study of symbolic interactionism—that is, the study of how humans attempt to give meaning to their world.

Symbolic Interactionism and the Struggle over the Means of Cultural Reproduction   Around the turn of the century, social psychologist George Herbert Mead was interested in accounting for how humans come to think in abstractions and how they use abstract, culturally shared symbols (including language and gestures, as well as the more obvious types) to try to make sense of their world. Mead called his theory "symbolic interactionism," and he developed its concepts in a series of extemporaneous lectures at the University of Chicago in the early 1930s. Mead might have explained a conflict in two groups' perceptions of reality in the following way.

Most modern Americans have an immediate and visceral reaction to a black symbol that they generally recognize as a swastika. Most Americans associate this symbol with deeply internalized revulsion against the Nazi excesses of Hitler's Germany. But the exact same design can be found against a red background (among others) on Navaho blankets and pottery that were created hundreds of years before the rise of Hitler and where, of course, it is absolutely unconnected to the Nazi Party. The vexing question is what *is* the swastika—one of the most hated symbols in modern Western democracies, or an interesting artistic motif among prehistoric southwest Indians?

The symbolic interactionist's answer would be that it is both, because human beings act toward a thing on the basis of the symbolic meaning of the thing that is communicated to one by the way one's fellows act toward one in relation to the thing. One's own group "agrees upon" meanings for the nature of the objects in their world. A swastika has no innate meaning, only that which is attached to it by people. To an infant at birth, no

symbols are yet defined because the infant has had no interaction with others that would communicate the shared symbolic meanings. After many years, we usually enter into a subconscious agreement that our culture's symbolic definitions are the only "natural" or "right" ones. The rub comes when we make contact with other groups who don't share our "natural" symbol systems. The Navaho, for example, traditionally believe every part of the natural world contains an inner spirit—every rock, every tree, every brook. But if you try to communicate with the spirit of a wolf or a tree in your local Protestant chapel, you may well be considered insane, possibly dangerous, and perhaps a good candidate for a mental institution. After all, your aberrant behavior in what people consider a sacred setting calls into question the validity of the symbol system that people usually believe is immutably correct. And if your apparently bizarre interpretation of the symbols turns out to be right, wouldn't that imply that there's at least a chance that many of the other symbols in our system could be wrong too? One possible result, especially if the individual calling the symbol system into question is perceived as intelligent, trustworthy, or of high status or power, would be an existential fear that the "natural" symbol system is breaking down. If it did, people might no longer know why they are here, what they are supposed to do while they are here, or even how to do it.

While this example may seem a bit far-fetched, the conflict between the creationists and the evolutionists is just such a symbolic conflict over the nature of reality, and the nature of human existence. As such, many people on both sides believe that the conflict threatens to tear apart the very fabric of the symbol system that created and sustains their entire worldview.

Cultural Fundamentalists and Cultural Modernists   As we have noted, Ann Page and Donald Clelland (1978) have called the two general worldviews involved in the evolution–creationism controversy "cultural fundamentalism" and "cultural modernism." Each has its own symbol system.

Cultural fundamentalists, of whom creationists are a subcategory use a symbol system that places great emphasis on authority, tradition, and revelation of God's truth through the Bible. They are strongly opposed to "situational ethics" or to "placing man before God."

The influence of cultural fundamentalism has steadily declined in the face of urban heterogeneity, consumerism, and increased rationalization and secularization of society. As we have seen, their recent self-asser-

tion is not necessarily based on economics. "Cultural fundamentalism . . . cuts across economic classes and is not a prestige class. There is little, if any, evidence . . . that their real concerns are a sublimated response to status frustration. . . . The central concern of status group members is the viability of their way of life. It is, therefore, no accident that the politics of life style concern should so often center on the school system." (Page and Clelland 1978, 275–76)

By contrast, cultural modernists (among whom are to be counted most twentieth-century scientists and most cosmopolites) are far less likely to believe the Bible is the incarnate and inerrant word of God. Some cultural modernists may still accept the Bible as divinely inspired, but they think that it is nonetheless to be interpreted by humans rationally and with an understanding of the ancient cultural context in which it was produced; others think that the Bible may not be completely adaptable to the currently rapid social change. For cultural modernists, truth is the hard-won result of human enterprise, not revelation given directly by a deity. For cultural modernists, truth about the physical universe (and often about moral issues too) is discovered through rational hypothesis-testing against observations gleaned from the physical world, and the subsequent interpretation of such data according to unvarying physical laws. Cultural modernism is largely an adaptation to affluence, rationalized large-scale organizations, and a service economy and it emphasizes "cultural relativity (thus teaching the tolerance of a variety of life styles), the segmentation of religion from other spheres of life . . . , rationality, creativity, [and] moderate consummatory hedonism (including alcohol use and sexual practices)" (Page and Clelland 1978, 276–77).

For cultural fundamentals, the highest purpose of man is the glorification of God and doing his work, guided by scripture and revelation. If this requires the denial of hedonism (or even the endurance of suffering), so be it. Cultural modernists, by contrast, believe that the purpose of human existence is to maximize human potential and to minimize human suffering—enterprises that may require frequent and quick man-made judgments about morality and behavior in the context of rapidly changing modern society.

Since the beginning of this century, the conflict between these two worldviews has often been most intense in areas experiencing a rapid transition from a rural past to an urban or suburban "high-tech" future (as in Kanawha County). Moral crusades are most likely to take place in rapidly growing urban areas where cosmopolitanism represents a new and intense form of rationality, as several studies of status politics (such

as those by Gusfield, Zurcher, and Page and Clelland) have found. The new symbol system, cosmopolitanism, like its parent worldview, cultural modernism, advocates a relativistic, flexible moral code and hence inevitably threatens adherents of traditional mores, who see such moral rules as God-given and not open to question. Cavanaugh found this pattern in 1983, when he identified creationism as particularly strong within North America in rapidly expanding metropolitan areas such as "Seattle, Atlanta/Marietta, Vancouver, B. C., Portland, San Francisco, Los Angeles/San Diego, Phoenix, Denver, Minneapolis/St. Paul, Milwaukee, Cleveland, Detroit, and Tampa" (1983, 182). Unfortunately, these two symbolic systems and their worldviews are profoundly incompatible.

This does not mean, however, that one of them is necessarily irrational; contrary to the opinions of many evolutionists, creationist belief systems may be rational. In saying this, we hasten to add that rational may not always mean "correct," and that rationality is a complex, multidimensional concept. Loosely following Cavanaugh (1983), we suggest that a belief system should be conceptualized in terms of its position on three dimensions. Specifically, we need to ask whether a belief is *logical,* whether it is *plausible,* and whether it is *creditable.*

If we mean *logical* in the formal sense (as, if A = B and B = C, then A = C), some forms of creationism—especially scientific creationism—are logical; they do not represent bizarre or magical thinking. For instance flood geology adherents recognize that a scientific account of earth history logically requires a physical mechanism to explain the accumulation of the earth's sedimentary rocks. Similarly, scientific creationism is *plausible* in the sense that there is no obvious reason that it could not be true; flood geology has surface plausibility to a person not versed in the methods, philosophy, and research results of science.

But if *creditable* assertions are those that can be shown to match the actual operation of the physical laws that govern the universe and the results of sustained scientific investigation, creationism is not creditable. It cannot be made to correspond with the totality of modern observed data about the natural world.

Rejectionists　　Some self-identified creationists make statements like, "God said it, I believe it, and that's the end of it!" and "Look at all the problems of the world that man has failed to solve. We must turn back to an omnipotent source for answers because we can see what a mess vain humans have made of things." These statements reflect what we have called rejectionism, for whose adherents the politics of life-style

dictate that things are true by reason of tradition or authority. Such creationists do not require scientific confirmation for beliefs. After all, they see their beliefs as based on relevation from an inerrant source and therefore are not in need of testing. While the belief systems of the rejectionists may be internally logical (in that their actions follow logically from their acceptance of a certain view of the Bible), they are neither plausible nor creditable.

Scientific Creationists

Compared with the rejectionists, the scientific creationists not only have beliefs with logical coherence, they have managed to make a scientific defense of creationism at least sound plausible. But, scientific creationism has not been able to do an adequate job of explaining observed data and is therefore, in the final analysis, not creditable.

Explaining Creationism: Beyond the Dichotomy

As we have seen, early explanations of creationism relied upon assertions of individual pathology (such as authoritarian character structure). More recent theories emphasized the status anxieties of individuals. Still others suggested that the evolution–creationism conflict can be understood as a conflict between two worldviews.

While we believe that the third approach is correct in general, it remains unclear why many who have testified in creationist trials *in favor of evolution* are Christians. While Page and Clelland's worldview explanation advances our understanding a great deal, many mainstream theologians and Christians do not fit the picture they draw of cultural traditionalists. While the basis of an adequate explanation must rest on the notion of conflicting worldviews, it may be an oversimplification to see only *two* groups involved. We suggest here that an analysis that stresses the interplay of several groups is a much more satisfying one.

. Since the end of World War II, the West has seen the arrival of a New Class (Mills 1951) or "the new middle class" (Gouldner 1979; Medawar 1973). This New Class[4] is neither the traditional bourgeoisie nor the proletariat. "The new class is defined by the twin features that it possesses its own stock of knowledge-capital in the form of trained technical skills but is employed by large organizations in salaried positions" (Gouldner 1979, 18–27). Members of this class would be those who work for aerospace companies as scientists and engineers, geologists and chemists

who work for major oil corporations, university scientists, information and computer systems analysts who work for IBM, and so on. (Both Nelkin [1982] and Patterson [1983], himself an engineer, have noted the strong representation of engineers in the ranks of prominent creationists.)

The prestige of the New Class lies in its scientific talent and its technical expertise. As such, this class is in conflict with the traditional elite, whose prestige was based on business expertise, personal character, creditworthiness, and skillful entrepreneurship.

It is precisely in this category of businessmen located in the older modes of production that we find a disproportionate number of creationists.[5] Gusfield (1963) has described those who engage in status politics on the conservative side as "tradition enforcers" who attempt to maintain intact the norms and values that legitimize and perpetuate their high status. Traditionally, this required he who would be successful to respect tradition, authority, Protestant religion, and "fitting in." But those in the new class of scientists, computer systems designers, laser optics technicians, and yet others are more likely than members of the older modes of production to prefer evolution. This is partly because they are quite likely to have received more formal education, including advanced scientific training that casts doubt on creationist beliefs.

However, because the power of the New Class resides in its stock of scientific knowledge or technical expertise—an expertise that is increasingly required by the industrialist in order to be competitive in an increasingly rationalized and streamlined market—its members enjoy a relatively greater intellectual freedom to base their beliefs on empirical data rather than on traditional authority.

But we cannot classify the entire old elite as cultural traditionalist and the entire New class as cultural modernist. It leaves unexplained why those in the vanguard of the creationist movement are often engineers and Ph.D.s in the physical and natural sciences (Nelkin 1982).[6] Cavanaugh (1983, 63–66) has suggested that this is so because in modern high-tech societies, people are bound together in a vast interdependency brought about by extreme specialization (or what sociologists call "organic solidarity"), rather than by each person sharing the same knowledge and values (or "mechanical solidarity"—a condition much more common in preliterate, more functionally homogeneous societies). Cavanaugh cites Peter Medawar in support of his point: "To be a first-rate scientist it is not necessary . . . to be extremely clever, anyhow in a pyrotechnic sense. One of the great revolutions brought about by sci-

entific research has been the democratization of learning. Anyone who combines strong common sense with an ordinary degree of imaginativeness can become a creative scientist" (Medawar 1973, 103). The result, says Cavanaugh, is: "the creation of a class, though a rather large one, of scientific and technical workers whose competence does *not* [my italics] depend on the high degree of theoretic and philosophic awareness we would expect to find in scientific and technical elites" (Cavanaugh 1983, 65). Because of this, it is entirely possible that many of the new class of scientific and technical workers operate with little knowledge of the intellectual foundations and history of science or of the areas of science outside their own.

This last point is especially important because it seems to be widely believed (even among many in the New Class) that if one has memorized enough discrete "scientific" facts, one must be a good scientist. In reality, doing good science requires much more than merely accumulating discrete bits of information. In the end, the primary goal must be to understand the *pattern* into which these atomistic bits must be fitted. For example, at various sites from Oklahoma to Minnesota, and especially in New England, there are claims that rock surfaces display markings left in the New World by numerous Viking (and other Old World) settlers long before Columbus. If we look only at the scratches on some of the rocks, we might (just barely) consider such a claim reasonable. The claim is scientifically dubious because in the same areas there are none of the physical remains that such settlers would have produced (i.e., bones of Old World domestic animals, architecture and artifacts of European manufacture; Stiebing 1984, 133–66; Cazeau and Scott 1979). In other words, "runestone" claims that seem reasonable as isolated facts do not meet the pattern test of good science; that is, what patterning of our data would we expect to find if a given claim were true? It should be noted that this mistake repeatedly characterizes the claims of "creation science."

The importance of the pattern test and other concepts central to science cannot be understood without some knowledge of the history and philosophy of science. By this standard, many people working in "science and technology" today are not actually scientists.[7] They are, unfortunately, unlikely to know this. It is on this point that creation science can be faulted.

Another characteristic of good science is that it must be openly debated. (Unfortunately, open debate often gives the lay public the impression of confusion.) Usually the forum for debate is research articles

published in scientific journals. But the scientific creationists content themselves with trying to pick holes in the findings of mainstream science. They themselves almost never conduct original research, nor publish findings in mainstream peer-reviewed professional journals.

Conflict within the New Class   Social conflicts occur not only between social classes but within them. Just as in recent years many writers have come to believe that revolutions are better explained by conflicts between factions of the bourgeoisie (rather than between the bourgeoisie and the workers; for example, Goldstone 1986), we suggest that there are also conflicts within the New Class of science and technology workers. Peripheral members of the New Class may contest with those at the center of class's prestige hierarchy. Indeed, "creating the appearance of alternative intellectual positions is an instrument in the jockeying for shares of credit that goes on within Class I [the New Class]" (Cavanaugh 1983, 74).

Thus, it can be argued that scientific creationists maintain a love-hate orientation to mainstream science. A sizable proportion seem to envy the status and credibility that being at the center of the scientific establishment confers, but they are simultaneously unable to compete successfully with the philosophically and historically better-informed scientists at the center. As a result, some seem to attempt to advance scientific creationism as an alternative science deserving of equal time. In this endeavor, they are very likely to be supported by the old elite because, as we have seen, creation science is founded upon a view of science that favors commonsense explanations and upon a rejection of the legitimacy of the power at those at the center—including big science, big corporations, and big government. These big institutions are, of course, the historical enemies of the entrepreneurial businessmen who constitute the old elite. Thus, creation science, produced by a marginal group in the New Class, is ideologically wedded to the politics of another marginal group, specifically "a disestablished local bourgeoisie of insurance salesmen, clerks, small businessmen, retired Air Force officers and others" (Cavanaugh 1983, 66). Both the creation scientists and the old elite feel besieged by the New Class, which controls access to major schools and which is often aligned with centralized, usually national power (educational, governmental, and media) against local power.

Thus, Page and Clelland's dichotomous classification of cultural modernists versus cultural traditionalists is in need of certain qualifications. Not all self-identified scientists are cultural modernists, because creation

scientists appeal to biblical scripture as their criterion of the validity of ideas. Nor are all religious persons necessarily cultural fundamentalists and opposed to evolution; many of the witnesses at the Arkansas creationism trial who spoke in favor of evolution were mainstream theologians and Christians (Gilkey 1985). For such theologians, as for many other Christians, the confrontation between science and religion has been neutralized by averroism, the philosophical stance that there is more than one kind of truth and more than one way of knowing. In other words, liberal Christians perceive that science will not give humankind an explanation of the meaning of their existence; nor will it answer other difficult existential and ethical questions. At the same time, religion will not be very useful for NASA space flight computations or estimating the age of the earth. For such liberal Christians, the prestige of science does not threaten to erode the legitimacy of religion because each attempts to explain very different things.

Creation scientists, on the other hand, reject averroism. They themselves are part of the New Class, but they have committed themselves to a species of biblical inerrancy that contradicts mainstream science. Their resolution of this conflict puts them at odds then with mainstream scientists, big business, political liberals, and perhaps even with the vast majority of their fellow Christians. This leaves them with a powerful reason to ally themselves with other elements of the religious right.

For some people, specifically rejectionists, creationism is true simply because the Bible *says* it is true; they probably do fit the description of cultural traditionalists because for them, things are "true" by reason of tradition or authority. (Many people in this category believe in a literal hell of fire and brimstone, and for them, to entertain evolution as valid is to risk eternal damnation.) Such people often look to the creation scientists as a source of legitimization for their beliefs. Others who are seeking upward mobility out of the blue-collar stratum, and people from the older elite whose worldview and even livelihood are threatened by the new elite, join them. Thus, creation scientists provide the leadership for a movement whose rank and file comes from several different sectors of society who find in creationism a symbol for several different varieties of worldview conflicts (local control versus national control, situational ethics versus God-given values, and the like).

Creation scientists are thus neither crazy nor simply ignorant, as some detractors claim, but represent an older, less sophisticated version of science, one congenial to their religious beliefs. Creationism is at least partially based upon a logical and plausible belief system, but not a creditable one. The result is what Cavanaugh (1983) has called a "one-eyed"

social movement that embodies some elements of rationality and whose organizational characteristics are rational. It is this element of rationality, coupled with widespread ignorance of science among the general public, that gives creationism its potency and its widespread appeal.

In the end, the creation–evolution struggle results from the pervasive and overwhelming force of modern science and technology. Many people in these groups feel relatively powerless and isolated from control of the science that so buffets them at every turn. (Who has not had his credit checked by a computer, had to take an auto mechanic's word for the malfunction of a mysterious "black box" under the hood, or on a grander scale, worried that he has no control over nuclear policy or environmental decisions?) When people feel powerless, they are likely to initiate social movements to attempt to empower themselves.

The social movement of twentieth-century science contains within itself the seeds of its own countermovements. One of these countermovements—Christian conservatism—is composed of people who invoke divine authority to reclaim control over their life-style and over the socialization of their own children. From their point of view, culturally alien entities (big government and the national scientific-educational elite) are trying to "indoctrinate" their children with values that would destroy their life-style. Of course, those who support evolution react with the same intense ire when their children come home from school telling them about the "creation science" that teaches that men and dinosaurs coexisted and that the geological record is a result of Noah's flood.

On a related but quite different note, it is of interest that the much-maligned New Age movement is also composed of persons who feel alienated from big science and big industry, but for a variety of reasons they find conservative Christianity unpalatable. They, too, attempt to reempower themselves, but with concepts and devices such as channeling, astral soul transport, communication with aliens, and healing crystals.[8] It may well be that because both movements are locked in a contest not only with the New Class, but also with each other over which alternative is a worthy one, they are generally extremely hostile toward each other.

Cultural Modernists and the Anticreationist Movement

The creationists' opponents are greatly disturbed by the efforts of creationists for various reasons. But many of these reasons mirror the concerns that move the creationists themselves.

Anticreationists, too, are often moved by the politics of life-style concern and a struggle for dominance over the means of the cultural reproduction. A struggle to advance a certain symbolic social construction of reality is also the prime mover of proevolution organizations just as it was for the creationists. Those who favor evolution often worry that if the creationists were ever to gain the upper hand in society, their own organizational bases and worldview might well not survive.

Just as the creationists' fears that teaching evolution will lead to abortion, sexual hedonism, homosexuality and so on seem out of proportion to the actual situation, the politics of life-style concern also seem to stimulate terrifying nightmares among proevolutionists. For instance, they fear that their children will be taught that the purpose of science is to validate a literal reading of the Bible. They worry that schools would require equal time for creationism and evolution, or perhaps teach neither. Many parents who are science professionals and workers fear that they may suffer an occupational death blow. Many such parents regarded the 1988 presidential campaign of Pat Robertson with great trepidation. Since Robertson is a dedicated creationist, might not his election have had dire consequences for the research agenda of organizations like the National Institutes of Mental Health, the Department of Education, and the National Science Foundation? Anticreationists thus fear a creationist-controlled government uninterested in funding research on topics that might threaten scripture in any way (such as research into recombinant DNA, which could be seen as "man playing God") or attempts to find intelligent life elsewhere in the universe. Abortion might be outlawed, resulting in massive changes in the medical establishment. Those interested in providing sex education to young people at a time when they are facing the AIDS crisis fear that they would be disempowered to do so.

Thus, despite their diametrically opposed substantive positions, creationists and their opponents uncannily resemble each other in their sense of threat to their respective worldviews—and in the appeals for money and other help that they make to like-minded people. Both are in effect saying, "Our opponents are bent on destroying the values that underlie our society's greatness, and they are indoctrinating our children in their ideology. You must help us stop them before it's too late!"

Conclusion

Creationists react so powerfully against evolutionary theory not simply because they disagree on specific scientific matters but because they

a small Museum of Creation and Earth History (visited by nearly six thousand people in 1988) is maintained at the ICR itself.

The content of the ICR's public message, the venues of most of its lectures, and the channels it employs for the distribution of its literature indicate that evangelicals and other conservative Christians constitute its primary direct audience. Most of its presentations are couched in religious terms, attempting to convince readers and listeners that evolution is spiritually dangerous nonsense, while strict creationism is truly scientific, and that Christians should work to promote creationism in society (particularly in the schools) as part of their evangelical duty. But it also makes efforts, most noticeable in the college lectures and debates, to reach a more general public. In these settings, ICR speakers tone down or eliminate the religious language and argue that young-earth creationism can be established on purely scientific grounds but that it is being suppressed by the scientific establishment.

Significantly, the report of ICR activities for 1988 (Morris 1989a) gave no details on the two other aspects of the institute's program, its research and teaching. The ICR has very little in the way of laboratory or other research facilities, and almost no creation-science papers have been submitted by its staff (or other creation scientists) to scientific journals (Scott and Cole 1985). The research done by ICR staff is primarily a search in the scientific literature for flaws in evolutionary biology and other components of the scientific consensus. The occasional exceptions include the study of supposed human footprints in the same rocks as dinosaur prints in the Paluxy River valley of Texas (J. Morris 1980) and expeditions in search of Noah's ark on Mount Ararat in Turkey (J. Morris and La Haye 1976).

As for teaching, in 1981 the ICR began to offer a graduate program, with master of science degrees in geology, biology, "astro/geophysics," and science education (Bennetta 1989a). Students in the ICR Graduate School (ICRGS) have never been numerous (twelve at last count), but several graduates have gone on to engage in further work in creation science, such as Dave and Mary Jo Nutting, who founded the Alpha Omega Institute (patterned on the ICR) in Colorado.

The ICRGS has never sought accreditation; Henry Morris thinks it would be futile to try, since higher education is controlled by evolutionists. But in 1981 the ICRGS applied for and received official approval from the state superintendent of public instruction. For any unaccredited postsecondary school in California to legally award degrees, this approval

is necessary. In late 1988 their application to renew the approval encountered difficulties (see Bennetta 1989a, 1989b). According to Superintendent of Public Instruction Bill Honig, this was due to substandard academic resources, facilities, and programs. According to *Acts & Facts* (February 1989), however, the reason was evolutionist intolerance.

The ICR called on its political and religious allies in the state for help in a letter-writing campaign. The apparent denial of approval by the state's Department of Education began to soften as the department entered into negotiations with the ICR.

In early 1989 they reached a temporary compromise. The institute was allowed to continue its programs, pending a five-member committee's evaluation in the summer of 1989. In February 1990 the committee finally recommended the "death sentence" for the ICRGS. As of this writing (winter of 1990), Superintendent Honig has not yet officially denied approval, but he is expected to do so by all observers, including the ICR. The institute has vowed to exercise its right of administrative appeal if the decision is negative, and it does not rule out a court battle, should that avenue fail.[1] Clearly, the ICR is going to try to save its graduate program (Morris 1989b); but whatever its fate, the institute's main work—disseminating scientific creationism—will continue unabated.

Although ICR personnel draw modest salaries, their enterprise is expensive (the 1989 budget was $1,690,000). The funds are raised through a combination of book and tape sales, speakers' honoraria, tuition, and donations from congregations and individuals on the ICR's mailing list of more than eighty thousand names. Each issue of *Acts & Facts* also contains an appeal for donations.

More than any other organization, the Institute for Creation Research has set the terms for the creation–evolution dispute and has supplied the movement with its intellectual armamentarium of strict scientific creationism and equal-time claims. Such success as the movement has enjoyed is due in considerable part to Henry Morris and this group.

Other Centrist Organizations   A new organization whose purposes and goals are similar to the ICR's is the Center for Creation Studies at Liberty University in Lynchburg, Virginia. Liberty University is the fundamentalist institution run by televangelist Jerry Falwell. With over 4,200 on-campus students, Liberty is now the central project of Falwell's ministry (Hadden and Shupe 1988, 136–38). Its creationist-oriented Biology Education Program has been accredited by the Virginia Board of Edu-

cation to train teachers. That is, there will one day be accredited biology teachers in the public schools of Virginia (and no doubt other states as well) who were trained in a creationist biology curriculum. All Liberty University students must take a semester-long creationism course, History of Life (Scott 1986; Schadewald 1987). In 1989, Chancellor Falwell awarded Henry Morris an honorary doctorate at Liberty University's commencement ceremonies. The Center for Creation Studies, which claims to have the world's largest creationist museum, is directed by former ICR staff member Lane Lester.

Still important in the movement is the Creation Research Society (Nelkin 1982, 78–79; Morris 1984a, 170–203; Cavanaugh 1983, 217–22). It has about six hundred voting members—members have graduate science degrees and sign a required statement of belief—and a thousand or so associate members, whose dues help to support the society's main enterprise, the *Creation Research Society Quarterly.* The journal is the most prestigious in its field, featuring articles with titles such as "An Analysis of the Post-Flood Population Growth." CRS also sponsored a 1974 creationist high school biology text, *Biology: A Search for Order in Complexity,* by John N. Moore and Harold Slusher. A "two-model" treatment that left no doubt as to which model was superior, it was widely used in Christian schools and was approved for public school adoption in several states. But the Indiana Supreme Court struck it from that state's approved book list in 1977 on the grounds that it unconstitutionally advanced religious beliefs. Thereafter other states also disavowed it, and it subsequently went out of print.

The CRS is composed primarily of young-earth creation scientists. Some of its important members and officers have been ICR staffers, as well as people from other creationist groups.

An organization wholeheartedly devoted to the promotion of creationism through legal action is the Academic Freedom Legal Defense Fund, formerly the Creation Science Legal Defense Fund (Bennetta 1987a; Morris 1984a, 289–93). It was formed in 1981 to help defend the Arkansas creationism law by Bill Keith, who was then a Louisiana state senator and author of that state's 1981 creationism law. The fund later aided the Louisiana law's progress through the court system. By the end of 1986, according to Keith, the fund had collected over $200,000 (including a $25,000 donation from televangelist Pat Robertson). The fund's name change illustrates a recent trend in the movement toward eliminating overt public references to religion. But ideology seems not in the least affected. Keith wrote in a 1987 "Dear Friends and Patrons" letter, "We

are still going to blow evolution out of the public schools!" (Bennetta 1987c, 7).

Also involved on creationism's legal front is Citizens for Fairness in Education (CFE), headed by Paul Ellwanger of Plano, Texas. Ellwanger, a respiratory therapist and—unusual among creationists—a Roman Catholic, has long worked for state laws and school policies to mandate equal time for creationism in public schools. He also helped to found a group called Citizens against Federal Establishment of Evolutionary Dogma, with the goal of equal-time treatment for creationism in the federal government's support of education, museums, and scientific research. Ellwanger supplied the suggested bills that formed the bases of both the Arkansas and Louisiana creation science acts of 1981 (see chapter 8). In the wake of unfavorable court decisions on those bills, Ellwanger is circulating a new suggested "Policy for Academic Freedom in Origins Teaching," designed to avoid those aspects of the laws that ran afoul of the courts.

The Right Wing   A bit to the right of the ICR on the creationist spectrum is the Bible Science Association (BSA) of Minneapolis, Minnesota (Nelkin 1982, 83–84; Morris 1984a, 212–19; Schadewald 1989a, 1989b; Cole 1988; Cavanaugh 1983, 213–15). It was founded in 1963 by Walter Lang, a Missouri Synod Lutheran pastor, and its current leaders are predominantly of that denomination. Lang, a tireless speaker and writer, is now director emeritus. After a major shakeup in 1989 owing to some BSA board members' belief that the organization was being inefficiently run, a new executive director was hired. The director, a former pastor named Gregory Hull, oversees a staff of seven and a $250,000 annual budget.

In its monthly *Bible-Science Newsletter* (circulation twenty-seven thousand), the association publishes a broad range of creationist opinion, including statements that the ICR would find embarrassing, such as those promoting geocentrism. The range of scientific sophistication in the newsletter articles varies greatly, but overall it is lower than that of ICR publications; the BSA requires no scientific credentials for its membership. The BSA's new leadership began in 1989 to try to improve the newsletter's quality. It is too soon to tell whether they will succeed.

The Bible Science Association has an active program of publication and outreach. From 1973 to 1987, it produced a series of creation science-oriented reading books for kindergarten through high school students. It

sponsors geological tours, seminars, films, and radio programs, and it holds annual meetings at which papers are presented in the manner of scientific societies. It also sponsors biennial National Creation Conferences.

In 1988, one of us (FBH) attended a lecture and videotape presentation by Walter Lang on flood geology and the search for Noah's ark at a Missouri Synod Lutheran church in Arlington, Texas. By ICR standards, his performance was unsophisticated, as were the questions and comments from the audience of some two dozen congregation members. But Lang was warmly received by his listeners (who bought a goodly number of BSA publications), and his talk seemed to provide real reassurance to them that their religious beliefs were consistent with scientific evidence.

The grass-roots nature of the BSA, with its twenty thousand members, is reflected in its thirty or so regional and twenty local chapters around the nation. Several organizations have spun off from the BSA after originators as chapters, such as the Creation Science Research Center. Some of these still retain close connections with it, such as the Genesis Institute, the focus of Walter Lang's ministry since he stepped down as head of the BSA; it publishes *The Ark Today,* "a family creationist magazine."

Another group to the right of the ICR is the Creation Social Science and Humanities Society, organized in 1977 by Paul Ackerman, a psychologist at the University of Wichita (Morris 1984a; Cavanaugh 1983; 222–23). Counting some six hundred members, it offers seminars and speakers, bestows scholarships, and publishes a quarterly journal on the destructive effects of Darwinian dogma on the social sciences and humanities.

A somewhat different approach to promoting creationism has been adopted by the Creation Science Research Center (CSRC) (Nelkin 1982; 79–80; Morris 1984a, 231–34; Cavanaugh 1983, 215–17). The origins of this group lie in the California textbook disputes of the late 1960s. These disputes led fundamentalist housewives Jean Sumrall and Nell Segraves and the latter's son, Kelly, to form a local chapter of the Bible Science Association. In 1970, this group merged with what was then the creation research division of Christian Heritage College, led by Henry Morris. The Segraveses wanted a series of creation–oriented textbooks to be developed for the public schools, and Morris's group was interested in producing such texts. But after less than two years, the groups split over policy disputes. Morris's organization became the ICR, and the Se-

graveses' group retained the CSRC identity. Today, their director is Kelly Segraves, and their science coordinator is chemist Robert Kofahl, president of Highland [Christian] College in Pasadena. The CSRC works in two main areas. The first is publication. They produce a newsletter, *Creation Science Report*, as well as a science and creation textbook series for Christian schools (with reported sales of over seventy thousand for one of their books), plus filmstrips and cassettes. Their best-known book is probably *Handy Dandy Evolution Refuter* (Kofahl 1977, 1980), a breezy paperback full of brief antievolution arguments. In its literature, the CSRC very explicitly identifies evolution as a cause of modern social and moral decay and relies on biblical citations as evidence for its assertions.

In its second area of work, and in a departure from ICR-style creationism, the CSRC promotes legal challenges to the current system of science instruction in the California public schools. In 1981, for instance, a suit was filed against the state on behalf of Kelly Segraves's children, alleging state interference with the free exercise of their religion because of the exclusive teaching of evolution. "If it is unconstitutional to teach of God," said Nell Segraves "then it is equally unconstitutional to teach the absence of God" (quoted in B. Parker 1980, 31).

A relatively new organization in the creationist movement is Maranatha Bible Fellowship. Under the name of Maranatha Campus Ministries, Maranatha is particularly active on college campuses. A dominion-oriented (reconstructionist) group, Maranatha is not exclusively concerned with creationism, but through its Society for Creation Science it offers noncredit, off-campus creationism courses at over thirty colleges and universities (Cole 1988). Its goal is to install chapters at most of the colleges in the nation. It plans to particularly target students who are majoring in education, in order to enhance treatment of creationism in the schools. The Maranatha organization cosponsored with the BSA the 1987 National Creation Conference (Schadewald 1987); its director of evangelism, Rice Broocks, gave a fiery keynote speech. Aggressive, expanding, and hostile to evolution, Maranatha is a growing force in the antievolution movement.

Another organization with reconstructionist leanings is the Baltimore Creation Fellowship, which sponsors a yearly Creation Convention. At the 1988 meeting, reconstructionist theologian James Robbins delivered a talk entitled "The Hoax of Scientific Creationism," excoriating scientific creationists for trying to justify the ways of God to scientists (McIver 1988a).

One creationist group is concerned with the implications of a particular paleontological locality. Near Glen Rose in north-central Texas, the Paluxy River cuts through limestones of the Cretaceous Period (130 to 65 million years ago) and in some areas exposes dinosaur tracks, many of which have been incorporated into Dinosaur Valley State Park. Creationists have long claimed that human footprints appear in the same rocks. This is said to prove that dinosaurs and humans are contemporaries (before Noah's flood) and make nonsense of the sequence of geological ages and fossil forms worked out by scientists (for example, J. Morris 1980). But recent scientific studies have concluded that the purported "man-tracks" are variously erosional features, misinterpreted partial dinosaur tracks, and in a few cases, deliberate forgeries (Cole and Godfrey, eds., 1985; Hastings 1988). "Mainstream" scientific creationists have since withdrawn or downplayed their earlier claims regarding the "man-tracks"—but not the Reverend Carl Baugh and the volunteer staff of the small Creation Evidences Museum (located a few miles from the sites of the disputed fossil tracks).

Baugh claims a Ph.D. in anthropology from the College of Advanced Education in Irving, Texas. This Bible college is located on the grounds of the Sherwood Park Baptist Church in an old house. It has no library or research facilities (Hastings et al. 1989; Kuban 1989). Other creationists, such as those at the ICR, are distressed by Baugh's lack of scientific credentials and by his conspicuous failure to use standard scientific terminology; he is regarded in the movement as something of an embarrassment (McIver 1987b). Nonetheless, he is supported in his work by a Dallas–Fort Worth-area group called the Metroplex Institute of Origin Science, and he manages to garner publicity in the local media. Most recently, Baugh and his associates appeared on an area television station's evening news claiming that a Cretaceous fossil tooth found at Dinosaur Valley State Park was human and thus invalidated the standard geological column. They later recanted when microscopic examination demonstrated that the item in question was a fossil fish tooth (Hastings 1989), but their recantation was not covered by the media.

On the extreme creationist right wing are the geocentrists, who maintain that, Copernicus and Galileo notwithstanding, the sun revolves around the earth (Schadewald 1981–82; Coburn 1988). Geocentrists argue that the Bible plainly presupposes that the earth is stationary and at the center of the universe and that all heavenly bodies revolve around it. They further claim that the data of astronomy, properly interpreted, support this view completely. They generally do accept that the earth is

spherical, not flat—although the human author of Genesis obviously conceived of the earth as flat and the sky as a sort of inverted bowl (Sarna 1983), and thus a fully literalist reading would seem to require such a belief.

Geocentrists are represented by the Tychonian Society, which publishes a bulletin. Its leader, Gerardus Bouw of Baldwin-Wallace College, has written a book on the topic (Bouw 1984; for an unflattering review by a fellow creationist, see Talty 1988). Other creationists regard Bouw and his allies as scientifically backward literalists who do more harm than good by holding the cause up to ridicule.

The Left Wing   Those at the center of the spectrum regard more "liberal" creationists, on the other hand, as compromisers. This left wing includes the Geoscience Research Institute (GRI) of Loma Linda University, a Seventh Day Adventist institution in Riverside, California (Morris 1984a, 221–22; McIver 1988d, 234). The GRI has a staff of five research professionals and publishes a semiannual journal, *Origins*. But witnessing to a large public is not its main goal; rather, it serves mainly as a source of expert advice for Seventh Day Adventist teachers. Like most of the left wing, the GRI accepts an old earth but not evolution. Its staff regard the ICR as naive both in scientific method and in biblical interpretation.

An old-earth creationist group that is very interested in getting its message across to the public is the Foundation for Thought and Ethics (FTE) of Richardson, Texas (a suburb of Dallas). Its former director of curriculum, a chemist and fellow of the American Scientific Affiliation named Charles Thaxton, is coauthor of a book, *The Mystery of Life's Origins* (Thaxton et al. 1984), that was printed by a commercial publishing house and received some fairly favorable reviews in scientific publications—probably the only creationist book in modern times to accomplish this. It consists primarily of a negatively disposed but competent review of current theories of the origin of life, concluding in the last chapter with a plea for supernatural creation as the best available explanation.

The FTE has also sponsored a textbook supplement for high school biology classes (Davis and Kenyon 1989; see Scott 1989). Titled *Of Pandas and People*,[2] it too after some effort found a commercial publisher (Haughton, a small Dallas firm, not to be confused with the giant Houghton-Mifflin). The book, which mentions Charles Thaxton prominently as "academic editor" and author of an afterword for teachers, is apparently

intended for use in both public and private schools, since it carefully avoids any references to God or religion. Explicitly distancing itself from scientific creationism, it borrows heavily from the work of Geisler and Anderson (1987) and Denton (1986) to argue that the fossil record, the chemistry of DNA, and other evidence are best explained by appealing to "intelligent design" rather than to evolutionary processes. It contains nothing new intellectually, but it is novel as a sophisticated, well-crafted attempt to insert creationism into science curricula in a "soft" form acceptable to the courts (Scott 1990).

In late 1989, Haughton and the FTE lost the first round of their attempt to gain public school acceptance for *Of Pandas and People*. The Alabama Board of Education declined to accept it as an approved supplemental biology text despite a petition with 11,800 signatures promoted by a Tuscaloosa Christian radio station (Brande 1990). The foundation also holds "in-service seminars" for high school teachers who want to teach creationism in a way that will not run afoul of course decrees on church-state separation.

The FTE's public pronouncements avoid explicit religious references and imply that it is a scientific and philosophical (rather than a religious) organization. But when filing for tax-exempt status, it stated its purpose as "proclaiming, publishing, and preaching, . . . and otherwise making known the Christian gospel and understanding of the Bible and the light it sheds on the academic and social issues of our day." The FTE appears to be more sophisticated, and less confrontational and abrasive, than most other creationist groups, and it will probably play an increasingly important role in the movement in coming years.

Still another organization, Students for Origin Research (SOR), has been characterized by an adversary as "the most responsible creationist organization" (Schadewald 1987; see also Morris 1984a, 283; McIver 1988d, 262). Founded in 1976 at the University of California at Santa Barbara, SOR publishes *The SOR Bulletin* as well as a semiannual journal, *Origins Research*. It also offers a computerized bibliography database on the creation–evolution controversy that contains thousands of entries. Old-earth creationist in orientation, SOR does not require members to accept a statement of belief (as the ICR and the CRS do). Indeed, its publications sometimes criticize creationists and print anticreationist views.

Other creationist organizations, none as influential as those we have discussed, could also be arrayed along the ideological spectrum we have described. Many are small local organizations and are thus local in

their impact. Some are primarily discussion groups rather than action oriented (such as the group described in Cavanaugh 1983, 230–43). Some "groups" actually consist of one or two people. Others are found in unexpected corners; for example, although the Roman Catholic Church has long accepted evolution (Ewing 1956), there are nonetheless small Catholic creationist groups with names like Keep the Faith and Children of Mary (McIver 1988b). There is even a Jewish group called the Association of Orthodox Jewish Scientists. Perhaps most intriguing of all is the Creation Health Foundation, which holds that one's view of the world's origins directly affects one's nutritional patterns and health, and that evolutionary dogma is gradually destroying the nation's physical well-being. It advocates natural foods, preventive medicine, and biblical creationism.

Creationism as a Sideline   Of some importance in the creationist movement are a number of organizations whose main purpose is not antievolutionism but who contribute to that cause in various ways. Most of these organizations (like creationist groups) are part of the loose coalition of the New Christian Right.

Few religious denominations take an official stand explicitly opposing evolution. But the Jehovah's Witnesses do, and their publishing arm, the Watchtower Bible & Tract Society, has produced several books condemning evolution and promoting old-earth creationism with standard creation science arguments. The most recent (*Life—How Did It Get Here? By Evolution or Creation?* 1985) has already passed the 2 million-copy mark. (Most are distributed free.) Its predecessor had 18 million copies and was printed in thirteen languages—making it surely the most widely distributed creationist book ever.

The American Scientific Affiliation (ASA) is not exclusively concerned with the creation–evolution issue, and the statement of faith it requires of its three thousand full members is evangelical but takes no position on creationism. Doubtless, many ASA members are theistic evolutionists. But in 1986 the ASA issued a booklet, *Teaching Science in a Climate of Controversy* (Price et al. 1986), that in essence takes an old-earth creationist position. It was written in response to a 1984 booklet from the National Academy of Sciences (NAS) that was strongly critical of creationism. Like the NAS publication, it is scheduled to be distributed widely to U.S. high schools (McIver 1988c, 4; Bennetta 1987b). In a calm and nonpolemical tone, it characterizes both the evolutionary consensus and young-earth creationism as extreme views, and it leaves the reader with

the message that old-earth creationism is a sensible and moderate alternative, both scientifically and politically.

Several evangelical educational organizations promote antievolutionism as part of their mission of defending traditional values in education. The Christian Educators' Association International offers curriculum materials, instructs parents' action groups, and gives legal counseling to those of its twenty-five hundred members who may run afoul of public school administrators for teaching creationism in class. The National Association for Christian Educators (NACE) is a similar organization; it and an associated group, Citizens for Excellence in Education (CEE) have been active in state and local educational controversies. In 1989, for example, the CEE's Texas director, David Muralt, testified before that state's board of education against a proposal to mandate coverage of evolution in biology textbooks. Robert Simonds, president and founder of both NACE and CEE, argues that there are many opportunities for teachers to teach creationism in public schools under existing laws and regulations in all states, and he supplies advice and encouragement for those who wish to do so (see Simonds 1989).

Educational Research Analysts, of Longview, Texas, is a small but potent organization run by Mel and Norma Gabler. The Gablers have been appearing at state textbook hearings since the 1960s and distributing literature in opposition to the spreading of secular humanism in the public schools (see, for example, Gabler and Gabler, eds., 1988). With some success, especially in the 1970s, they have fought against textbooks with material reflecting political liberalism, nontraditional sex roles and morality, and evolution. The resulting toned-down textbooks have been used not only in Texas but around the nation. The Gablers once objected to the appearance of the story of Robin Hood in a reader, on the grounds that it could be used to promote socialism (Bennetta 1986, 23).

Unsurprisingly, evangelical educational institutions at all levels tend to be hostile—or at least cool—toward mainstream scientific concepts of evolution. Many conservative Christian colleges (including Liberty University, Christian Heritage College, and Bob Jones University) teach creationism. And at the elementary and secondary levels, increasing numbers of students are learning creationism in private Christian academies (Peshkin 1986; Rose 1988). These schools constitute a large and rapidly growing segment of American private education, currently enrolling about a million students (Rose 1988, 34–39). They are overwhelmingly evangelical and conservative, and they are generally opposed

to evolution and other aspects of "secular humanism." Perhaps two-thirds of all Christian schools use a standardized curriculum called Accelerated Christian Education (ACE) that is staunchly strict creationist. Several Christian media organizations have lent a hand to the creationist movement. Most televangelists, notably Pat Robertson and Jerry Falwell, occasionally feature and support creationist speakers on their programs (and preach creationism themselves). Films for Christ, of Mesa, Arizona, has produced a six-film series called *Origins,* featuring ICR creationism. Rising televangelist star D. James Kennedy has produced a highly polished and widely distributed film, *The Case for Creation.* The Moody Institute of Science (a division of the fundamentalist Moody Bible Institute of Chicago) produces a wide range of high-quality nature films that emphasize the idea of design and purpose in nature; several are antievolutionist, though not strict creationist. A number of religious publishing houses, such as Apologetics Press (Montgomery, Alabama) and Baker Book House and Zondervan (both of Grand Rapids, Michigan) issue creationist books. An evangelical mission group called Teen Mission USA sends a creationist book to high school and other libraries free of charge—if and only if it is placed in the library's *science* reference section (as opposed to, say, sections for religious books) (Bennetta 1987d).

Many other conservative, religiously oriented organizations with at least partly political agendas lend support to creationist goals, including Tim La Haye's American Coalition for Traditional Values, Beverly La Haye's Concerned Women for America (which claims a larger membership than the National Organization for Women), and Phyllis Schlafly's Eagle Forum. In the more secular political arena, creationists are sometimes supported by various foes of modernism and secular humanism, such as conservative columnists like Joseph Sobran and M. Stanton Evans, and politicians like Representative William Dannemeyer of California and Senator Jesse Helms of North Carolina. The Heritage Foundation, a conservative think tank, supports the struggle against secular humanism, as does the Rutherford Institute (McIver 1988d, 162). Rutherford lends legal support to conservative Christians opposing what they see as state interference with religious freedom on such issues as school prayer and creationism.

Finally, literally thousands of conservative Protestant church congregations and their ministers play an essential role in the movement. It is typically these congregations (sometimes individually, sometimes in local coalitions) that sponsor creationist speakers, debates, and films and

promote the sale of creationist literature. They also apply most of the grass-roots pressure to teachers, administrators, and state boards of education. These part-time local groups would be less effective without the guidance and inspiration supplied by the creationist SMOs we have discussed, but the SMOs would likewise be ineffective without the foot-soldiers the congregations supply.

It is important to note that not all evangelical Christian groups support creationism. For instance, Morris (1984a, 305) disapprovingly cites such organizations as Youth for Christ, the Inter-Varsity Christian Fellowship, and many evangelical colleges and publishing houses for tolerating theistic evolution.

Summary The many creationist organizations vary in size, influence, ideology, and sophistication. They sometimes seem to contend almost as much with each other as with evolutionists, although (following the old social-psychological maxim that external threat creates internal cohesion) they generally unite in the face of the common foe. They develop arguments against mainstream evolutionary theory on grounds both religious and (in their view) scientific, and they communicate their case to both believers and nonbelievers. They are supported by thousands of individuals and congregations who give them money and time, buy their books and media offerings, incorporate their ideas into their evangelistic activities—and press the creationist case on political fronts.

SMOs in the Countermovement

Although anticreationists are not the main subject of our study, it is essential to have some grasp of the social movement organizations that they use to confront creationists in the pages of journals and books, in debates before college audiences, in court trials, and in testimony and argument before public officials. We will deal with only the most important groups.

The NCSE In many ways the most important group is the National Center for Science Education (NCSE). It is the only national organization that devotes itself primarily to opposing creationism. It was organized in 1981 as a national network of the local and state organizations (known as the Committees of Correspondence), which had begun to form in the late 1970s in reaction to the advance of creationism (Moyer 1989).

The anticreationist committees, begun among scientists and other ac-

ademics, teachers, and intellectuals, felt the need for a national clearing-house that would provide information, warnings of new creationist tactics, and ideas for coping with local creationist activities. What began as an occasional newsletter edited by Iowa science teacher Stanley Weinberg was eventually formalized in 1984 as the *Creation/Evolution Newsletter*, then and now the most important channel of communication in the countermovement.

Incorporated in 1983, the organization itself gradually became more formalized. In 1986 it received a $150,000 grant from the Carnegie Foundation (other grants have helped underwrite the NCSE since then), allowing it to open an office and hire an executive director, anthropologist Eugenie Scott. It broadened its focus from directly fighting creationism to including education in evolution and the nature of science. Textbook reform is a major priority. The NCSE now has a task force to put publishers in contact with scientists for prepublication reviews of textbooks for scientific accuracy. It also publishes a textbook review newsletter, *Bookwatch Reviews*. Its other task forces are working in the following areas: the Resource Center, which furnishes information to the public and the media; teacher education, for high school science teachers; audiovisual programs and videos on science and evolution; and a speakers' program. In 1989 the newsletter was revamped and retitled *NCSE Reports*.

Despite these changes, the principal object of concern to the NCSE and its twelve hundred-plus members is still creationism. The NCSE still acts as the intellectual nucleus of the anticreationist movement and as the meeting place for the Committees of Correspondence (such as the Texas Council for Science Education and the Ohio Committee of Correspondence) in forty-six states and three Canadian provinces.

Other Organizations   Also important, although not exclusively concerned with creationism, is the Committee for the Scientific Investigation of Claims of the Paranormal, better known by its initials as CSICOP. Formed in 1976 by a number of scientists and intellectuals (including such well-known figures as Carl Sagan, Isaac Asimov, science author Martin Gardner, and professional magician James Randi), CSICOP skeptically investigates and criticizes a whole range of unconventional claims. Its quarterly journal *The Skeptical Inquirer* (circulation about thirty-five thousand) carries articles intended to debunk and otherwise examine "paranormal" claims, ranging from ESP and ancient astronauts to New Age crystals and channeling—and, of course, creationism. It pro-

motes critical thinking, the scientific method, and skepticism toward extraordinary and supernatural claims.

CSICOP members number some two hundred Fellows who are invited to membership on the basis of their professional qualifications and their skeptical interest in paranormal claims. It is informally affiliated with forty local and state groups with similar aims, such as the Bay Area Skeptics and the Wisconsin Committee for Rational Inquiry, plus kindred groups in nineteen foreign countries. CSICOP's chairman is Paul Kurtz, a professor of philosophy at the State University of New York at Buffalo. He also heads a nonmembership group called the Council for Democratic and Secular Humanism, which publishes the magazine *Free Inquiry*. Unabashedly secular humanist in orientation, it often turns a critical eye on creationism.

Another organization in the forefront of the countermovement is the American Humanist Association (AHA). Despite the alarm among creationists and their allies about the specter of secular humanism, there seem to be relatively few officially self-declared humanists in the United States. The AHA's membership of about five thousand is proportionately (and even absolutely) smaller than the rosters of similar organizations in Europe. Its counterpart in Norway, for instance, counts thirty thousand members among a total population of 4.2 million. But the AHA is growing, perhaps because many modernists perceive that cultural fundamentalism is on the upswing. Membership increased by 19 percent in 1988–89. Many AHA members are highly influential in the sciences, arts, and humanities, such as science fiction writer (and current president of the AHA) Isaac Asimov, writer-publisher Gloria Steinem, psychologist B. F. Skinner, and paleontologist Stephen Jay Gould.

Needless to say, this membership roster is tantamount to a rogues' gallery to most creationists, just as the AHA's positions on social and political issues are anathema to them. The AHA is concerned with many issues from a viewpoint of nontheistic secularism; it favors free access to abortion and divorce, decreased defense spending, euthanasia, gay rights, and sexual equality. In the "Humanist Manifesto II," the AHA unequivocally denies the existence of the supernatural, characterizes belief in an afterlife as illusory, and claims that the moral life is the result of human reason and effort, not of faith and obedience to divine law. In short, the AHA's position statement is antithetical to the deeply held beliefs of creationists.

The AHA devotes a good deal of attention to creationism. It publishes the journal *Creation/Evolution* (not to be confused with the NCSE's *Cre-*

ation/Evolution Newsletter), which occasionally carries articles by creationists but consists mostly of refutational articles. Its official magazine,
The Humanist, sometimes carries anticreationist articles as well.

Also active in the anticreationist ranks is People for the American Way
(PFAW), a civil liberties advocacy group founded in 1980 by television
producer Norman Lear and several associates who were alarmed at the
growth of the Moral Majority. It opposes the New Christian Right on
many of the issues on its agenda, particularly those regarding education,
censorship, and governmental relations with religion. The PFAW's executive director is John Buchanan, a liberal Baptist minister and former
congressman. It produces an annual report entitled *Attacks on the Freedom to Learn,* a compilation of attempts by parents, minsters, and groups
to remove materials from school curricula or libraries, usually on the
charge that they advocate secular humanism or atheistic evolutionism.
They also sponsored *A Consumer's Guide to Biology Textbooks* (Moyer
and Mayer 1985) to draw attention to the gingerly treatment of evolution
in many of these books.

PFAW actively lobbies before state legislative and governmental bodies. For example, Mike Hudson, Texas state director of the PFAW, testified before the state board of education in favor of the proposed
regulation to include coverage of evolution in biology texts (Stutz 1989).

Concerned with similar issues is the American Civil Liberties Union
(ACLU), which has been involved in the creationism controversy since it
defended John Scopes in 1925. The ACLU takes on a great variety of
cases in which it believes essential civil liberties are being threatened by
governmental action. It helped assemble on a pro bono basis the teams
of trial lawyers who successfully opposed the Arkansas and Louisiana
1981 creation science laws in court (see Chapter 8).

Last, a host of scientific and scholarly professional societies became
sufficiently alarmed by the creationist movement (usually in the early
1980s) to issue official resolutions, pamphlets, and special journal issues
decrying scientific creationism as highly unscientific and unworthy of inclusion in public school science curricula. One partial compilation (Mc-
Collister and Saladin 1986) lists fifty-six statements against creation
science from national, state, and local scientific and educational organizations, including the American Anthropological Association, the Geological Society of America, the American Association for the Advancement
of Science, the American Society of Biological Chemists, the National
Education Association, and the National Science Teachers Association.
A number of groups with a cultural modernist religious orientation, in-

cluding the American Jewish Congress and Americans United for the Separation of Church and State, have also taken positions against creationism. Several, including the American Society of Zoologists, filed briefs with the Supreme Court in the Louisiana creationism case (Bennetta 1988b).

Support for the anticreationist countermovement is broad among a host of intellectual and educational organizations, as well as the press and publishing establishments. But it also tends to be shallow. These groups have other tasks and priorities, and they tend to pay attention to creationism only when it becomes "news" and is perceived as a threat. After being roused to action, they forget the matter until the next crisis (Cole and Godfrey 1987). For this reason, the fact that they are opposed by nearly the entire intellectual/scientific establishment does not overwhelm the creationists as one might expect.

In the next chapter we will examine how the creationist SMOs have carried their cause to the courts, legislatures, schools, and other venues. We will look at their strategies and tactics, and at the response by anticreationist SMOs.

Mobilizing the Movement: The Politics of Equal Time

> Forget, if need be, the high-brow both in the political and college world, and carry this cause to the people. They are the final and efficiently corrective power.
>
> —William Jennings Bryan

> If we're going to teach evolution in the public schools, why not teach scientific creationism? They're both theories.
>
> —Arkansas Governor Frank White (1981)

Introduction

Neither creationists nor their opponents suffer from a dearth of strong feelings on the topic of evolution, but emotion alone is not enough to cause social movements to rise and fall, or to determine their success or failure, as students of social movements have increasingly realized in recent years.

Klandermans (1984), for example, has pointed out that although traditional social movement theories were almost exclusively social-psychological and explained social movements in terms of personality traits, marginality and alienation, grievances, and/or ideology, the research literature does not contain much actual evidence that most of these factors were prime movers in the social movements. Some studies, which he cites, have indicated that marginality and alienation were *not* typical of the backgrounds of participants in such divergent social movements as German fascism, the 1960s U.S. student movement, the civil rights

movement, labor unionism, and the environmental, antiabortion, and antinuclear movements. Klandermans concludes that "The importance of grievances and ideology as determinants in a social movement has been ambiguous" (Klandermans 1984, 583).

A related point is made by Freeman: "It is a common assumption among students of social movements that a movement's strategy is largely determined by its ideology. That is, a movement first analyzes its situation and decides on its goals, then fashions an appropriate strategy for obtaining them. Yet new movements often arise in response to a crisis situation or a long history of more subtle grievances, and find themselves embroiled in action long before they develop elaborate concepts of where they want to go, let alone how to get there. Once an ideology begins to form, it may redirect the group's strategy, or it may merely confirm it. . . . whatever strategy a group desires, it must be developed within certain confines. The group can do no more than its resources and its environment permit." In other words, while it is quite true that few social movements could succeed without considerable emotional involvement on the part of their adherents, such involvement is only a necessary but by no means a sufficient condition for success (Freeman 1979, 167). History is replete with examples of whole masses of people who were engulfed in a shared sense of righteous indignation but who nonetheless were unable to take meaningful action to correct the situation. In many cases, what was lacking was an ability to obtain and mobilize sufficient resources to sustain the movement.

Out of this observation in the past twenty years a whole body of theory has grown, entitled *resource mobilization theory*. Rather than focus exclusively on outbursts of emotion, as early theorists had, and rather than see such outbursts as the results of formerly repressed, sometimes primitive and irrational impulses, "resource mobilization theory emphasizes the importance of [social] structural factors, such as the availability of resources to a collectivity and the position of individuals in social networks, and stresses the rationality of participation in social movements" (Klandermans 1984, 583).

Since, as we have seen, the motivations of creationists are rational from their own point of view, their willingness to become dedicated adherents could result in part from their subjective perceptions of the costs and benefits of such involvement, according to this type of resource mobilization theory. But Klandermans (1984) has criticized these resource mobilization theorists precisely for promoting the idea that an adherent joins a movement on the basis of a rational calculation of the ratio of costs

to rewards. As Klandermans points out, such a decision is necessarily based on the individual's perception of the costs and rewards of participation—which may, of course, differ from reality on occasion. He propose to bridge traditional collective behavior approaches (with their emphasis on emotional motivation) and newer resource mobilization perspectives (which examine more logical, organizational, and institutional factors).

Even though creationists have had plenty of emotion to motivate them for decades, it is only in recent years that their visibility has increased and their fortunes seemed on the ascendency. The importance of Klandermans's work is to help explain why this is so. A complete understanding of their increased success will require us to consider not only their emotional arousal but also how the past and future of the creation–evolution controversy have been shaped by differential access to resources such as funding, media coverage, legal sanctioning, and so on. In the same vein, we will also need to examine how the choice of different tactics and organizational principles has produced (and will continue to produce) differential prospects for success on both sides of the conflict.

Creationist Tactics   A movement's choice of tactics tends to be determined by whether the main orientation of the movement is "strategic" or "expressive" (Turner and Killian 1987, 300–301). If the orientation is strategic, tactics are chosen based on the perceived probability of their effectiveness in reaching movement objectives. In contrast, if a movement has an expressive orientation, its tactics will tend toward symbolic displays and the exercise of power in the name of the movement's cause.

Presumably, the expressive orientation is characteristic of movements in which participants are involved primarily for the emotional satisfactions of seeing themselves as righteously correct and confronting the rascals perceived as the source of the problem. But expressive movement adherents have sometimes found that after making a satisfying frontal confrontation, their power was insufficient to prevail. Under such conditions, the movement may conclude that it must forgo some emotionally satisfying tactics in favor of more subtle tactics that are less likely to provoke an overwhelmingly hostile response from a dangerous enemy. Thus, "The major difference between expressive and strategic considerations is found in the tendency to use and display maximum or minimum power. Expressive tendencies mean a preference for coercion rather than for bargaining, facilitation, or persuasion [the tactics more typical of a strategic movement]" according to Turner and Killian (1987, 301).

We hope to show that the creationist camp has undergone such a transformation, from expressive to strategic. Its initial strategy emphasized using the power of law to *force* evolution out of the schools and, later, to force creationism in. Even when antievolutionist legislation failed, applying pressure on school boards and textbook publishers was often effective in banishing or restricting instruction in evolution. But such efforts have generally failed to win support from the courts in the second half of this century; this failure apparently led the creationist forces to adopt new tactics. Faced with the disappointing outcome of an expressive approach, the movement seems to have decided to increase its effectiveness by adopting more carefully calculated, tactics. We will see that bargaining, facilitation, and persuasion have increasingly characterized creationist tactics over the past ten years or so. (Fortunately, the rifle shots and bombings of the Kanawha County controversy now seem banished to the past.)

Although recent years have seen this tendency toward a strategic approach, this was not always the case. The Sputnik crisis of the 1960s with its new emphasis on science in education revitalized the creationist movement, first with an intensely expressive orientation (as, for example, in Kanawha County). In keeping with Turner and Killian's proposal that expressive orientations usually result in a choice of coercive tactics, the creationists' tactics focused on attempting to have the courts' authority imposed on those advocating evolution.

We begin with the courts as we survey the development of the strategy, tactics, and resource mobilization of the creationist movement over the several decades of its modern (post-Sputnik) phase. We examine the four main arenas of creationist activity and how successes and failures in each have modified subsequent struggles. This treatment is topical rather than strictly chronological, since at any one time efforts were under way in each arena. It is true, however, that different arenas have predominated at different times as creationist tactics shifted over time.

The Four Arenas of Creationist Effort

1) The Courts In this section we will discuss creationist attempts to use the federal courts as an "offensive weapon." Occasions when creationists have found themselves in court in a defensive role will be discussed later.

As described in Chapter 2, the impetus of the modern creationist revival of the 1960s and early 1970s came from two main events. One

was the Sputnik-inspired rejuvenation of U.S. science education, including especially the Biological Sciences Curriculum Study (BSCS) textbooks. The other was the demise of the 1920s antievolution laws in the wake of the Supreme Court's 1968 *Epperson v. Arkansas* decision, which ruled that state prohibition of evolution instruction violated the First Amendment.

Stripped of their legal protection from evolution just when, thanks to the BSCS textbooks, they felt they needed it most, creationists began to seek redress for their perceived grievances. One path open to them— one used successfully by a number of other social movements—was the courts. The Supreme Court had clearly proclaimed that banning evolution was out of the question; but perhaps constitutional arguments could still be used to diminish and qualify (if not actually outlaw) evolutionary instruction in the schools and to allow the presentation of creationism as well.

'The First Amendment has proved crucial to all recent court cases involving creationism. Part of the Bill of Rights added to the Constitution in 1791, the amendment reads: "Congress shall make no law respecting an establishment of religion, or prohibiting the free exercise thereof; or abridging the freedom of speech, or of the press; or the right of the people peaceably to assemble, and to petition the government for redress of grievances." The part of the amendment that concerns religion is contained in the first two clauses, which are referred to respectively as the "establishment" clause and the "free exercise" clause. The exact interpretation of these clauses, and their implications for numerous laws and practices, have been the subject of a long and contentious legal history (see Wald 1987, 100 ff.; Larson 1985, 93–96). For much of American history, standard construals of these clauses were different from today's. For instance, the establishment clause was long interpreted to mean merely that Congress could establish no national church on the model of the Church of England. Many early American jurists did not interpret it as meaning *states* were forbidden to establish churches or to prescribe religious instruction in public schools.

But Supreme Court decisions gradually extended the application of the First Amendment to the states, and furthermore took on a general interpretive pattern. Regarding the establishment clause, government at all levels was required to adopt an attitude of neutrality toward both religion in general and any creed in particular (hence the famous 1963 decision forbidding the states to prescribe prayer sessions for public school children). As for the free exercise clause, it was usually construed so as

to allow people very wide latitude to practice their religion, even an unconventional one and even if they had to be specially exempted from laws that were conceded to be generally beneficial. For instance, the Court has allowed Amish children to be exempted from laws requiring attendance at public schools.

Given creationists' attitudes toward evolution and secular humanism, it is no surprise that many of them have long felt that their beliefs are being denied constitutional protection. An attempt was made to gain such protection in 1970, when Rita Wright filed suit against the Houston public schools (*Wright v. Houston Independent School District*) (Larson 1985, 124, 132–33). Wright argued that the school system was violating her daughter's constitutional rights when it taught evolution but not creationism. It did so in two ways: by telling her that her beliefs about creation were wrong, and thus inhibiting the free exercise of her religion (free exercise clause); and by lending official support to the "religion of secular humanism" (establishment clause). But her suit was dismissed before reaching a trial. The judge ruled that the free exercise clause did not imply a right to be insulated from scientific findings incompatible with one's beliefs. In Larson's (1985, 133) words, the judge decided that "scientific opinion could determine science teaching even if that teaching offended religious beliefs."

Two other suits were filed on similar grounds in the 1970s (Nelkin 1982, 100–2; Larson 1985, 133). In 1972, William Willoughby, religion editor of the *Washington Evening Star,*[1] sued the National Science Foundation to force it to spend as much money to promote creationism as it had on the BSCS project (*Willoughby* v. *Stever*). In 1978, Dale Crowley and the National Foundation for Fairness in Education sued the Smithsonian Institution (*Crowley* v. *Smithsonian Institution*) to block an exhibit, "The Emergence of Man," that dealt with the human fossil record. Both suits alleged that one-sided federal support had been given to the religion of secular humanism. Both were dismissed on the grounds that the federal institutions had been disseminating scientific findings, not promoting secular humanism.

Thus, creationists failed completely to get the federal courts to secure equal time for creationism or to have evolution defined as religion and deemphasized accordingly in curricula. Evolutionary science, said the courts, is not a religion, and it cannot be excluded from education or museums because it offends some people's religious beliefs. Creationist activists still generally believe that their First Amendment rights are being violated, but they have been unable to devise a new legal strategy

that would succeed in the federal courts, and they have not tried using them to attack the status quo since these cases.

A less ambitious strategy involves a 1988 lawsuit filed in federal district court by Ray Webster, a junior high school science teacher in New Lenox, Illinois. Forbidden by his school district to teach creationism, he sued on grounds that his rights of free speech and academic freedom were violated. He lost but is appealing.

Two highly publicized 1987 lawsuits did not directly concern creationism but did involve New Christian Right opposition to secular humanism. In both cases, groups of parents sued local boards of education over books that students were required to read that, the parents said, advocated secular humanism in place of traditional values (Norgren and Nanda 1988, 135–37). The specific issues involved included gender roles, the place of religion in American history, and stories in readers which contained material allegedly unsuitable for children. In short, the suits raised the same sorts of issues that had fueled the Kanawha County dispute. In one of the cases (*Smith* v. *Board of School Commissioners*), an Alabama federal district judge ruled that the offending books were indeed advancing the religion of secular humanism, but he was overruled by the court of appeals. In the other case (*Mozert* v. *Hawkins City Board of Education*), an initially favorable ruling that excused Tennessee children from classes that employed the offending books was also later overturned. But NCR activists, including creationists, were encouraged by the parents' initial successes and by the national publicity, which generated much support. There is some reason for creationists and other opponents of secular humanism to hope for future lawsuits similar to the two just discussed.

2) Legislation   It was in state legislatures that creationists achieved their most prominent successes in the 1920s, and unsurprisingly, they turned to them in the 1970s to try to recover the ground they had lost to the BSCS textbooks and the Epperson decision. During that decade, they introduced dozens of bills in state legislatures that would have mandated that instruction in evolution be balanced by instruction in creationism, generally identified explicitly as a religious doctrine.

Equal Time for Religion   In 1973, Tennessee's legislature passed an act providing that biology textbooks identify evolution as a theory rather than as "scientific fact" and that "the Genesis account in the Bible" be given equal space in the texts (note the colloquial uses of the terms *theory*

and *fact*) (Larson 1985, 134–39; Webb 1986).[3] The law was quickly challenged in court (*Daniel v. Waters*) by a coalition of organizations, including the National Association of Biology Teachers and Americans United for Separation of Church and State. In 1975, a federal appeals court struck down the law, ruling that it violated the establishment clause by mandating instruction of a religious doctrine in public schools. In the wake of this decision, the many "equal time for religion" bills in state legislatures died quiet deaths.

The sole exception was a 1976 Kentucky law that took a different tack (Larson 1985, 147–50). It neither mandated nor forbade anything, but it allowed teachers the option of presenting the Genesis account (straight from the Bible, and without particular denominational interpretations) alongside evolutionary theory. Students "who receive such instruction, and who accept the Bible theory of creation" could receive academic credit for learning the Genesis story. Interestingly, this statute has never been challenged in court, perhaps because of its lack of coercion.

Equal Time for Creation Science   The Kentucky law found no imitators, however. In the wake of *Daniel v. Waters,* creationists converged instead on a new approach that would avoid the Tennessee law's apparent fatal flaw: its explicit provision for instruction in religious doctrine. The new approach was to present creationism not as a religious dogma (which would always make it subject to establishment clause sanction) but as a *scientific theory* that on grounds of academic freedom, equal time, and complete education deserved to be presented alongside evolutionary theory. The fact that its tenets paralleled the Genesis creation story should be considered, from a legal standpoint, merely coincidental.

The introduction of creation science into legislation owed its impetus to several developments. One was the development of scientific creationism, the earnest Baconian endeavor of men of scientific and technical backgrounds who were trying to square their faith with their professional training. Henry Morris and his allies laid the necessary groundwork by producing a body of literature that could be adduced as *scientific* evidence for creationism and against evolution.

A second development was that the rhetoric of scientific creationism was translated into a form acceptable in the specialized legal world of legislatures and courts. The man most responsible for doing this is attorney Wendell Bird, now of Atlanta, Georgia. Bird graduated with honors from both Vanderbilt University and Yale Law School, where he studied under later Supreme Court nominee Robert Bork. At Yale he

began to formulate the legal rationale underlying the equal-time-for-creation-science approach, which was published in detail in two law journal articles (Bird 1978; 1979a; see also Larson 1985, 147–50). Bird argues that scientific creationism is science, not religion, and therefore is not subject to challenge on establishment clause grounds. But the policy of *not* teaching it in public schools, he claims, violates both religion clauses of the First Amendment. It is inconsistent with the establishment clause because teaching only evolution "causes preference to religious Liberalism, Humanism, and other religious faiths" (Bird 1979b). It does this, he argues, by putting the prestige of science and of state approval behind the religious beliefs of some students. Furthermore, an evolution-only policy violates the free exercise clause, according to Bird, because it states or implies official disapproval of some religious beliefs, which forces children to learn material that both they and their parents believe to be inimical to God's truth. Bird argues that it is irrelevant whether such a policy is *intended* to favor some "religions" over others; the important matter is that it unconstitutionally has the effect of doing so. The solution Bird recommends is a policy of state neutrality, providing instruction in both scientific theories. This would ensure academic freedom, well-rounded science education, and the protection of everyone's First Amendment rights.

While he was on the staff of the Institute for Creation Research, Bird wrote a model resolution (Bird 1979b) for local school boards that wanted to institute a policy of equal time for creation science. The resolution, which briefly recapitulated these legal and scientific arguments, was mailed to thousands of people as part of the ICR's *Impact* series. Bird agreed with Henry Morris that in view of the fate of the Tennessee law, the legislative route was unproductive for creationists; education and local school board policies encouraging creation science were seen as more effective in the long term (Bird 1979c).[4]

But one recipient of Bird's resolution was very interested indeed in the legislative route, and he provided the third development in the process leading to creation science laws. Paul Ellwanger of Citizens for Fairness in Education long favored state laws as a direct path to big results; why labor to urge thousands of individual local school boards toward an equal-time policy, when a mere fifty state legislatures could quickly produce the same effect? In Bird's resolution he saw an approach that might work. He modified it into a suggested legislative bill and circulated it widely among his network of contacts, mostly in the churches.

By 1981, over twenty bills based on the Bird-Ellwanger model had

been introduced in state legislatures. Most died in committee, but two were enacted in 1981. They represent the high-water mark of creationist legislative efforts and of national publicity for the movement. Both, however, were ultimately overturned in the federal courts. We will discuss them in order of their enactment.

The Arkansas Law One copy of Ellwanger's proposed bill was sent to the Reverend W. A. Blount of the Sylvan Hills Community Church in North Little Rock, Arkansas (La Follette, ed., 1983; Larson 1985:151–63; Nelkin 1982:137–47; Lewin 1982; Lyons 1982; Ruse 1984; Geisler 1982). In 1981, Blount gave the proposal to State Senator James Holsted, who was sympathetic to conservative religious causes. Holsted drafted and sponsored a bill that closely followed Ellwanger's. The Greater Little Rock Evangelical Fellowship Committee (of which Reverend Blount was president) joined with a group called FLAG (Family Life, America and God) to mount a vigorous lobbying campaign. Most legislators seem to have needed little convincing. To many of them the bill seemed fair, nondogmatic, and clearly popular with religious conservatives, who are numerous in Arkansas. Said one of the few members who expressed dislike for it, "This is a terrible bill, but it's worded so cleverly that none of us can vote against it if we want to come back up here" (quoted in Larson 1985, 152). The bill quickly and overwhelmingly passed both houses of the legislature and was signed into law by Governor Frank White on 19 March 1981.

Officially known as Act 590, the Balanced Treatment of Creation Science and Evolution Science Act, the law required that a "two-model" approach be adopted in textbooks and curricula. It defined "creation-science" as "the scientific evidences for creation and inferences from those scientific evidences," including "sudden creation of the universe, energy and life from nothing." Creation had to be taught alongside "evolution-science," in order, among other ends, "to protect academic freedom by providing student choice; to ensure freedom of religious exercise, to guarantee freedom of belief and speech; to prevent establishment of religion; to prohibit religious instruction concerning origins"; and "to bar discrimination on the basis of creationist's or evolutionist's belief." Creationists had gotten exactly what they wanted in a state law.

The act was immediately challenged in federal court by the ACLU and a coalition of local Protestant, Catholic, and Jewish clergy and national educational and religious organizations. The suit alleged that the law violated the establishment clause of the First Amendment, as well as

teachers' academic freedom, and was furthermore unconstitutionally vague in its requirements.

The ensuing trial in December 1981 (*McLean v. Arkansas Board of Education*) was heavily covered by the national news media. Inevitably dubbed "Scopes II,"[5] it focused more national attention on the creation–evolution dispute than at any time since 1925. The ACLU legal team concentrated most of its effort on its allegation that Act 590 violated the establishment clause. To this end, they assembled a distinguished and well-prepared group of expert witnesses. Some, including theologian Langdon Gilkey, historian of religion George Marsden, and sociologist Dorothy Nelkin, were called to establish that "creation-science" was religious in nature and inspiration. The others, such as Stephen Jay Gould and geophysicist G. Brent Dalrymple, testified that scientific creationism failed to meet the methodological criteria necessary to qualify as science.

In contrast, the defense operated in some disarray. It was led by Arkansas attorney general Steve Clark, who incurred the anger of many creationists by deciding not to accept the proferred help of Wendell Bird, the author of the resolution that had been modified into Act 590. Some, including Pat Robertson and Jerry Falwell, even accused Clark of not wanting to win the case—a charge he strongly denied.

The defense called a number of witnesses—both scientific and theological specialists—to testify that creation science was indeed real science, that it was no more essentially religious than "evolution-science," and that the conformity between the findings of creation science and conservative Christian belief was therefore legally irrelevant. Clark decided not to ask the best-known potential witnesses—Henry Morris, Duane Gish, and others from the Institute for Creation Research—to testify. Their writings make the religious inspiration and purpose of creation science obvious, and the plaintiffs could have used this fact to great advantage during cross-examination. The witnesses the defense did call included Harold Coffin of the Geoscience Research Institute, biologist Wayne Frair of the Creation Research Society, and surprisingly, mathematician Chandra Wickramasinghe. Wickramasinghe seems to have been called not because he is a creationist or even a Christian, but because he disagrees with the scientific consensus on several matters, such as the origin of life (that is, he believes it was "seeded" on earth rather than originating here).

The defense witnesses were less effective than those of the plaintiffs. Norman Geisler of Dallas Theological Seminary—whose book (Geisler 1982) provides a creationist perspective on the trial—created embar-

rassment when he affirmed under cross-examination that he believes that UFOs are satanic manifestations. The defense's scientific witnesses turned out to be unable to point to concrete scientific achievements for creation science. And Wickramasinghe agreed on the stand that one would have to be "crazy" to believe that the earth is only a few thousand years old.

On 5 January 1982, federal Judge William Overton handed down his verdict: Act 590 violated the establishment clause of the First Amendment and was accordingly overturned. In essence, he accepted the plaintiffs' arguments, relying heavily on the above-mentioned testimony as well as that of philosopher of science Michael Ruse (1984), who had laid out a widely accepted definition of modern science that excluded scientific creationism. "Since creation-science is not science," Overton concluded, "the conclusion is inescapable that the only *real* effect of Act 590 is the advancement of religion."

Overton's trenchant and sweeping verdict did not leave much room to maneuver, and Attorney General Clark decided not to appeal. The decision's effects were significant. No further equal-time bills were passed, and there was a widespread impression that the creationists had been decisively defeated. Indeed, many in the anticreationist countermovement in effect declared that the war was won and began to demobilize (Cole and Godfrey 1987).

Creationist activists were all deeply disappointed by what they saw as an unfair verdict, but they were divided in their interpretation of the trial's outcome. Some saw it as proving once again that the legislative route was unproductive. For others, however, it meant that the next attempts had to be more carefully fashioned and better defended. Their strategy was soon put to the test, for the legal battle over the other equal-time law was soon to begin.

The Louisiana Law   In 1980, Louisiana state senator Bill Keith (founder of the Creation-Science Legal Defense Fund, now the Academic Freedom Legal Defense Fund) introduced an equal-time creationism bill into the state legislature. After numerous modifications in committees and in the differing House and Senate versions, it was passed. Governor David Treen reluctantly signed the popular bill in July 1981 (see Bennetta 1988b; Larson 1985, 153–67; Boone 1989; Bird 1987; Scott 1987; Zimmerman 1987b; Gould 1987b).

Like the Arkansas law, the Louisiana bill mandated the teaching of creation science alongside evolution. There were some differences, how-

ever, that its supporters hoped would make it less vulnerable to court challenge. In particular, the law defined creation science simply as "the scientific evidences for creation and inferences from those scientific evidences."[6] It did not list any of those inferences, as Act 590 had (such as the sudden creation of all life), nor did it say just what *creation* meant. Neither did it mention God. In other words, explicit Christian religious doctrine was excised from the law's language, apparently so that a courtroom defense of the law could deny a religious element or intent more plausibly than in Arkansas. But this left a nearly content-free vacuum: what *was* creation science, then, and why was it important?

Predictably, the law's passage was quickly followed by a federal suit (*Aguillard* v. *Treen*) by the ACLU and a coalition very similar to the one in the Arkansas case. The legal struggle that ensued was fought over issues like those in *McLean* v. *Board,* but it differed in important respects. One was that it dragged on for over five years before a decision was reached. Another difference was that the defense in Louisiana was better organized and prepared. It had had the benefit of the Arkansas case to study, and it had the services of Wendell Bird, who was named a special assistant attorney general for Louisiana. Curiously, the Louisiana case never actually came to trial.

We will not follow in detail the complex legal history of this bill but note that after a side excursion to the Louisiana Supreme Court (whence it was referred back to federal district court), the struggle began with a request from the plaintiffs for a summary judgment (that is, one without a trial) against the state to overturn the law. To simplify somewhat, the plaintiffs' reasoning was that this was just another law mandating the teaching of creation science, such as had already been found unconstitutional in Arkansas, and that therefore no trial was merited. The defense, using their vague definition of creation science, contended that unlike Act 590, their law was not specifically religious in content and therefore should not be summarily dismissed; it deserved a full trial.

In January 1985, Judge Adrian Duplantier, relying on the Arkansas precedent, granted a summary judgment to the plaintiffs and declared the Louisiana law unconstitutional. The state promptly appealed, asking again for the right to a trial. The case, now known as *Edwards* v. *Aguillard* (since the state and its governor, Edwin Edwards, were now the plaintiffs in an appeal), went before a three-judge panel of the U.S. Court of Appeals for the Fifth Circuit. The panel upheld Judge Duplantier's decision. The state then requested that their appeal be held *en banc*—

reheard before all fifteen judges of the Court of Appeals. The judges voted narrowly (8–7) to deny the request. So far, the state had lost at every turn. But their last reversal had been narrow, and they were encouraged by the fact that several judges thought their appeal worth hearing again. Thus, Bird and his associates decided to follow their appeal to the final resort, and in December 1985 they took it to the Supreme Court.

Oral arguments before the Court took place on 10 December 1986. The case generated nearly as much publicity as the Arkansas trial had five years before, even though a victory for Louisiana would have resulted not in implementation of the law, but merely in the right to a full trial of the sort that Act 590 had received. Its chances of victory in such a trial would probably have been slim. Nonetheless, creationists realized the tremendous value in publicity, prestige ("We won in the Supreme Court!"), boosted morale, and financial contributions that would ensue if the Supreme Court upheld Louisiana's appeal. Their opponents realized this as well, and both sides made strong efforts. Amicus curiae briefs were entered for both sides (especially the anticreationists) by many individuals and organizations. The most impressive was a brief signed by seventy-two Nobel laureates in the natural sciences, joined by twenty-four scientific organizations, contending that creation science was a scientific fraud that would debase science education (Bennetta 1986b).

The oral arguments pitted Wendell Bird against the ACLU attorney, Jay Topkis. Their disputation centered mainly on the issue of whether creation science, as defined in the law, was necessarily a religious concept.

On 19 June 1987, the Court issued its opinion, written by Justice William Brennan. It voted 7–2 to uphold the summary judgment against the law and thus to support overturning it. The Court found the statute unconstitutional because it served no clear secular purpose but instead favored creation science—and, despite the law's vague definition, it had clearly been intended by the legislature as a way to mandate the teaching of the Genesis story in the public schools. Chief Justice William Rehnquist and recently appointed Justice Antonin Scalia disagreed. The latter wrote a strong dissent, arguing that the Court should believe the wording of the law itself regarding its intent rather than what legislators had said to the media and to their constituents while the bill was under debate. In this dissent, Scalia showed a misunderstanding of some of the basic differences between mainstream science and scientific creationism (Gould

1987b), perhaps comprehensible given the creationist strategy of telling what creation science is *not,* rather than what it is.[7] Nonetheless, the majority ruled, and creationists had suffered a major defeat.

In the aftermath of this setback, many creationists are more convinced than ever that the legislative arena is unproductive. Even those who support the legislative approach have retired for the time being to produce new strategies.

The Federal Legislative Front   Congress has never come close to passing a federal creationism law comparable to the state laws we have discussed, largely because of the limited federal role in education. Many members denounce secular humanism and evolution, though, and one issue merits some discussion.

The first incident is the controversy over Man: A Course of Study, or MACOS (Nelkin 1982, 47–51, 121–36). MACOS was a curriculum developed in the late 1960s and promoted for adoption in fifth and sixth grades, with funding from the National Science Foundation. It examined humans from a comparative, evolutionary perspective (comparing human behavior with that of animal species) and looked at American culture in cross-cultural terms (comparing American and Netsilik Eskimo cultures and values).

In the early 1970s, MACOS began to generate a good deal of grass-roots controversy ("'We're all animals,' kids are taught"). Members of Congress led by conservative Representative John Conlan of Arizona and Senator Jesse Helms of North Carolina put considerable pressure on the NSF. Eventually, the NSF found itself being investigated by congressional committees on allegations that it was underwriting an attempt to inject secular humanism and evolutionism into the schools. No drastic consequences ensued, but the MACOS program foundered in the controversy, and the NSF has been left "gun shy" of congressional critics.

So when the *Chronicle of Higher Education* ran a story on the reaction of social and natural scientists to creationism (McDonald 1986), the head of the NSF's science education directorate declined to be interviewed on the topic. And when biologist Michael Zimmerman (1989) was invited to give a talk at the NSF's headquarters on his research on students' and teachers' belief in creationism, he found that unlike other people's appearances there, his speech had not been publicized. He charges that the NSF's research grants to scientists are routinely given new and uncontroversial-sounding titles (and never feature the word *evolution*) before

lists of the research grant awards are made available to members of Congress and their aides. Clearly, the NSF feels a need to be careful in its treatment of evolutionary topics, lest one or more of its grants trigger further investigations and perhaps loss of funding or political influence over grant awards.

Summing up the Legislative Arena   Apart from temporary successes, no creationist-inspired legislation has taken effect since the repeal of the 1920s antievolution laws. Nonetheless, some activists are still trying, like Paul Ellwanger, who is now circulating a revamped Uniform Origins Policy. The creationists' problem lies less in mobilizing antievolutionist sentiment and legislative votes than in fashioning a bill that would survive the inevitable trip to the courts.

3) State Educational Bodies   State governments play an important role in financing and regulating education. When their boards of education and other regulatory bodies select textbooks and set curriculum guidelines, creationist activists try to influence the process to defend and promote their interests.

Members of some state boards of education are elected; others are appointed by elected officials. In any case, they are seldom immune from political pressure and indeed can be particularly susceptible to it. Since relatively few people are politically aware of and active over educational issues, the support or opposition of a small group can be very significant. Although in this arena another lobbying effort must be mounted every time guidelines or textbooks are up for reconsideration, this is the strategy Wendell Bird recommends for creationists.

One way creationists try to curtail evolution or promote creationism in public schools is to influence general curriculum guidelines. Getting a board of education to require the inclusion of scientific creationism in biology courses may be nearly as effective as a getting a law passed by the legislature, and it is less likely to be overturned in a court.

Second, creationists try to influence textbook selection. In twenty-two states, the state board of education adopts a list of approved textbooks and subsidizes their purchase by school districts. Particularly important in the struggle are the two largest of these "adoption states," California and Texas. Texas and California both represent huge markets, so textbook publishers are very keen on winning their adoption, and they tailor their books to their adoption criteria. It would not pay publishers to pro-

duce different editions of their textbooks for various states, so schools in smaller or "nonadoption" states tend to be offered books whose content is largely determined by its acceptability in California and Texas.

Textbook Travails Textbook content is vulnerable to political pressure. Both creationists and their opponents have many complaints about textbooks and their treatment of evolution. Their vexation is part of a widespread national dissatisfaction on the part of educators and the public alike with elementary and secondary textbooks in all subjects. As Tyson-Bernstein (1988) points out, textbook publishers are in a highly competitive business, and they try to suit their product to the market. That market can be highly politicized, characterized by the demands of many interest groups (cultural fundamentalists, feminists, and minority group advocates) for the favorable treatment, inclusion, or omission of various topics. Add the strong editorial control of publishers (rather than authors) over textbook content, "readability formulas" (which supposedly ensure that books will not be too difficult to read), and the standardized achievement tests for which books are to prepare students—and bland, confusing, even incoherent textbooks often result. Publishers also generally choose profitability over intellectual integrity. Says one industry executive: "If the customer wants a pink stretch Cadillac, I may think it's tacky and wasteful, but I would be a fool to produce a fuel-efficient black compact if nobody is going to buy it" (quoted in Tyson-Bernstein 1988, 2). Given these circumstances, anticreationists in academia who expected commercial textbooks to faithfully reflect the scientific consensus on an explosive topic like evolution were in for a rude shock (Bennetta 1985b, 1986, 19–26).

Textbooks and "Dogmatism" in California The struggle over evolution in the California State Board of Education was one of the first manifestations of the modern creationist movement (Nelkin 1982, 107–19; Moore 1974; Larson 1985, 140–43; Bennetta 1985b, 1986; Padian 1989a, 1989b). In 1963, Nell Segraves and Jean Sumrall (later to found the Creation-Science Research Center) petitioned the state Board of Education to require that evolution be taught as theory rather than fact, and conservative Superintendent of Education Max Rafferty ordered that all texts be so labeled.

In the late 1960s, Governor Ronald Reagan appointed increasing numbers of conservatives to state boards, and creationist dissatisfaction with evolution instruction became more vocal and influential. In 1969, crea-

tionists achieved major changes in the state's Science Framework, the curriculum guidelines for science teaching. Their leader was Vernon Grose, an aerospace engineer, political conservative, and Assemblies of God member. Grose successfully proposed that the Framework call for the inclusion of scientific creationism as an alternative "theory of origins" in all public school biology courses. The advisory committee that had prepared the Framework for the board fought back, enlisting academic scientists, and a complicated political struggle ensued.

By the time the dust settled in 1974, creationists had managed to secure an "antidogmatism policy" from the board, which required evolutionary statements to be qualified. The findings of evolutionary biology were now described in textbooks as what "some scientists believe," or using similar "fudge words" that were not used for other theories (like gravitation). Compare these sentences from textbooks before and after the new policy:

Before: "As reptiles evolved from fishlike ancestors, they developed a thicker scaly surface."

After: "If reptiles evolved from fishlike ancestors, as proposed in the theory of evolution, they must have developed a thick scaly surface." (Nelkin 1982, 115).

But Grose and his allies were still far from happy. The textbook changes were less thoroughgoing than they had wanted, and their other goal, a policy mandating equal time for creation science, had slipped from their grasp in a narrow board vote. The Creation-Science Research Center decided to go to court.

In 1979, the CSRC's Kelly Segraves petitioned a California court to overturn the Framework for being insufficiently undogmatic. The petition was denied. Then the CSRC took another tack: in 1981, Segraves sued in state court alleging that the state was violating his children's religious rights because, despite the nondogmatism rule, evolution was actually being taught in a dogmatic way.

Segraves v. *California's* complex legal maneuvers centered on the question of whether evolution was being taught dogmatically. Its verdict was a partial victory for creationists; certainly it is the sole recent court result that was not clearly damaging to the creationist cause. The judge did not overturn the Framework or order drastic changes, but he did praise the nondogmatism policy as necessary in a pluralistic society, and he required that copies of it be sent to all school districts in the state.

More recent developments in California have not been favorable for creationists. Their influence on the board of education has faded. In 1985

and 1986, anticreationists, led by academics, managed to get treatment of evolution in textbooks strengthened somewhat (though not to their own satisfaction; see Bennetta 1985b, 1986a). The old Anti-Dogmatism Policy was replaced in late 1988 by a statement on science teaching that removed the features objectionable to evolutionists (Padian 1989a). In November 1989 the board of education adopted a revised Science Framework requiring presentation of the scientific consensus on evolution. Creationists managed to get several sentences deleted or reworded, but overall the revising committee, dominated by anticreationists, prevailed (Padian 1989b). Nonetheless, creationists remain a force to be reckoned with. And their past activities have left a distinctive educational legacy: in our study of creationism among college students (Harrold and Eve 1987), far more California students reported having been taught creationism in high school than students from Connecticut or even Texas (see Table 8.4).

Texas: the Gablers versus Secular Humanism   In 1963, Mel Gabler, an oil company clerk in Longview, Texas, and his wife, Norma, became so fed up with the secular humanism permeating public education that they began to monitor textbooks and testify at state board of education hearings. Ten years later, Gabler retired to form Educational Research Analysts and work full-time for the cause. The Gablers became well known and effective foes of evolution in the schools, aided considerably by a strange rule in the Texas book-adoption system that provided that no one except textbook publishers could testify in *favor* of a book under consideration; citizens could express only disapproval. Express it the Gablers did, inspiring like-minded textbook-watchers all over the state and nation, and communicating with them through a mailing list of several thousand names (Nelkin 1982, 63–65; Gabler and Gabler 1988; Larson 1985, 139–40). They also arranged for creation scientists to testify against books and encouraged campaigns of letters and phone calls to influence members of the elected board.

Their first major success came in 1969, when the board struck the NSF-developed Biological Sciences Curriculum Study textbooks from the approved list. These were the only existing high school biology texts to give evolution thorough coverage. In 1974, the Texas Education Policy Act adopted the Gablers' suggested provision that all biology texts prominently carry a statement that evolution is a theory rather than a fact and is only one of several explanations of origins.

As in California, however, the 1980s saw some discouraging developments for the Gablers and their allies. In 1984, educational reforms by the state legislature made the state board of education an appointed body, and thus one step removed from direct political pressure. The board's textbook review procedures were reformed to allow citizens to testify for as well as against books. Furthermore, anticreationist individuals and groups, notably People for the American Way and the Texas Committee for Science Education, or TCSE (a Committee of Correspondence), began to testify in opposition to the Gablers at textbook hearings. Finally, the state attorney general issued an opinion that the "evolution-as-a-theory" disclaimer required in textbooks violated the state constitution and it was subsequently removed.

In 1988, the guidelines for geology textbooks were up for review, and the board, despite strong opposition, required in its Proclamation No. 65 that evolutionary theory be mentioned and explained in approved textbooks. Anticreationists were encouraged, but they knew that the big contest was coming the next year, when the Textbook Proclamation (guidelines) for biology books would be considered. Far more students study biology than geology in high school. Furthermore, in 1989 a new, elected board would be in place (due to passage of a recent referendum replacing the appointed board).

In January 1989, the Texas Education Agency staff sent to the board a proposed text of Proclamation No. 66 explicitly requiring biology books to include the "scientific theory of evolution" and "scientific evidence of evolution." There was no mention of scientific creationism or alternative theories (Faust 1989–90; Scott 1989).

The board's public hearings in February featured impassioned testimony from both sides (Stutz 1989). Creationists wanted discussion of evolution toned down or at least balanced by "creation theory." The Gablers were absent due to Mel Gabler's illness, but a number of their allies, including David Muralt of Citizens for Excellence in Education, pressed their case. Said one witness to the board, "God is watching you. Please do not provoke his wrath." Between the board's February and March meetings, creationist groups initiated a barrage of letters and telephone calls to the board; the TCSE and university scientists did likewise.

In March 1989, the board met to consider a slightly modified Proclamation. Changes seemed to have been made in response to both sides' pressures. Darwin's theory, for instance, had been added to a list of important biological discoveries that were required to be discussed. But

the section calling for inclusion of "scientific evidence of evolution" now also required mention of "other reliable scientific theories to the contrary," clearly a gesture to the creationists. At the last minute (perhaps in response to some final lobbying by anticreationists), that last phrase was changed to read "other reliable scientific theories, *if any,*" and the Board voted 12–3 to accept the new Proclamation.

Evolutionists were jubilant, but creationists too found something to cheer about in the changes allowing creationism to be presented if interpreted as a "reliable theory." Wording had also been retained that required treatments of evolution (but *not* other scientific theories) to examine "alternative evidence" against the theory. From the creationist point of view, a disaster had been headed off. In early 1990, both sides began to gear up their lobbying efforts for the six-month-long process of choosing the textbooks to be approved for use. Only then would the real result of Proclamation No. 66 be clear. Nonetheless, a significant shift in state policy toward evolution in textbooks had occurred. In both Texas and California, resurgent anticreationists, effectively lobbying board and staff members and using the support of the scientific establishment, had convinced education boards that the scientific consensus on evolution should weigh heavily in state educational policy.

How Complete a Defeat?   Creationists have clearly lost ground recently at the state agency level in two important adoption states, but their actual influence is probably greater than this fact would lead one to think.

For one thing, some other states' agencies held firm for creationists. In 1986, for example, New Mexico's state board of education voted to retain its "evolution-is-a-theory" disclaimer and to encourage local boards to consider presenting "multiple theories of origin." (*Creation/Evolution Newsletter* 8(5), 9, 1988).

Second, even the "improved" biology texts assembled by publishers in the mid-1980s to meet new guidelines still tend to treat evolution sketchily and to use "weasel words" (like "some scientists think . . .") (Skoog 1984; Bennetta 1985b, 1986). Furthermore, one analysis of several biology texts (Woodward and Elliott 1987) has concluded that publishers are implementing "market segmentation": offering a range of texts, from those that almost completely ignore evolution to those that treat it in detail. Thus there are still texts for states, districts, and teachers who want to avoid evolution.

Finally, at the local level—in classrooms, principals' offices, and local school board meetings—creationists still have influence. Just as there are still public schools where the Supreme Court's 1963 ban on school prayer is violated daily, there are many teachers and local administrators who choose to heed their own beliefs and/or local preferences, whatever state boards or even textbooks may say about evolution.

4) The Grass-roots Level The most effective creationist campaigns against evolution and for their beliefs are being waged at the level of local boards of education and individual schools. But reliable information is hardest to obtain for this level. Unlike many other nations, in which education is controlled by a central national ministry, the United States has an extremely decentralized system (Wald 1987). Most decision-making power in education rests at the local level, in the thousands of school districts across the country. In these contexts, creationist appeals to elected local officials and to principals and teachers who are their neighbors can be very effective. Like other social movement advocates who have been rejected repeatedly by major institutions of change (courts and legislatures), creationists have taken to exerting grassroots pressure. In this context, Wendell Bird has recommended a procedure for creationist activists: First, "learn the Biblical teaching about creation." Then, become familiar with scientific creationism and with Bird's legal arguments for equal time. Next, learn what bodies and individuals in your state and district determine curriculum and textbook guidelines. Finally, petition these bodies to adopt equal-time resolutions and two-model textbooks (Bird 1979c). Clearly, many creationists have followed Bird's advice.

Tales Told Out of Class Most of our information on creationist activities at the local level consists of anecdotal reports that have made their way to the national press, *NCSE Reports,* or People for the American Way's annual report, *Attacks on the Freedom to Learn.* Several illustrative examples come from the 1987–88 report of that publication:

• In Fisher, Illinois, a group of parents petitioned the school board to grant equal time to creationism in biology classes. After consulting legal counsel, the board decided it could not do so, but it did buy creationist books for school libraries.

• In New Lenox, Illinois, a social studies teacher sued his school district for violating his First Amendment rights by prohibiting him from teaching creation science.

• In Dubuque, Iowa, members of Citizens for Excellence in Education met with school officials urging an equal-time policy in the name of nondiscrimination.

• In Burleson, Texas, parents associated with a local church requested alternative creation science lessons for their children in place of the coverage of evolution in the regular biology curriculum. The school board at first decided to comply with their request, but it changed its policy when threatened with an ACLU lawsuit.

A number of school districts have adopted some form of two-model policy, including Dallas, Texas; Columbus, Ohio; Tampa–St. Petersburg, Florida; and Racine, Wisconsin (Fowler 1982).

Probably more important than the publicized cases, however, are the informal or unpublicized policies made by many boards and principals, and individual teachers' decisions to downplay evolution and/or to include discussion of creationism.

For example, a brief scrutiny of teachers' and school administrators' reactions in the Dallas–Fort Worth area to the 1989 Texas biology Textbook Proclamation is instructive:

A science teacher said: "It won't change the way I teach evolution in my classroom. I teach it in the way of change. Everything has change. I do not spend a lot of time saying who came from whom."

A district director of curriculum: "Care is taken in these courses by teachers to explain [that] many of the ideas presented are conjecture."

Another director of curriculum: "Evolution is taught along with several other theories. We do not say that there is one interpretation, nor do we tell students with strong religious convictions, for example, that the creation theory is wrong. We feel that we should inform our students of all the major theories that are widely accepted—theories that have a strong group of specialists that believe them. Then, they can make their own judgements" (Mulé 1989; Matulich 1989).

Their consensus seems to be that, whatever may be decreed in Austin, treatment of evolution in the district will change little if at all. Note the terms they use—*change, creation theory, conjecture, make their own judgments*. These are just the catchphrases favored by creationists who advocate equal-time policies.

These quotations are consistent with the (admittedly anecdotal) evi-

dence from our conversation with area students and educational officials: evolution is considered a potentially explosive topic in Dallas–Fort Worth area schools. From what we have been told, some science teachers simply avoid the subject, or it is conveniently relegated to the last chapter of the book, the one the class never reaches before the end of term. Others give equal (often brief) time to evolution and creation. And all are uneasily aware of the possibility of complaints from irate parents and clergy. A local minister who was keeping in touch with other pastors in the area on the 1989 Texas Proclamation said: "I will read and monitor" (quoted in Matulich 1989).

Survey Evidence   Information on the effectiveness of grass-roots creationist pressure can also be found in surveys, mostly of high school science teachers. These surveys must be regarded cautiously, for none is a fully representative national sample, and no two asked precisely the same questions.[8] Nonetheless, taken together, they give a rough indication of the scale of creationist success.

These surveys indicate that the schools are fertile territory for creationists—that is, a significant number of teachers agree that scientific creationism has a place in the curriculum (see Table 8.1).

As we noted in Chapter 3, schoolteachers do not seem to vary much from college students in their acceptance of creationism. A significant proportion of them accept the idea of equal time—though far fewer than

Table 8.1. Agreement That Creationism Should Be Taught in Public School Science Classes

Population	Those Agreeing (%)
Ohio teachers (Zimmerman 1987a)	38
Kentucky teachers (Ellis 1986)	69
Georgia teachers (Eglin 1983)	30
Georgia teachers (Buckner 1983)	32
Illinois teachers (Nickels and Drummond 1985)	30
National sample of science teachers (Affannato 1986)	45
Ohio school board presidents (Zimmerman 1987–88)	53

among the public as a whole. Equal time seems to be even more popular among board presidents than teachers—though again, less than among the public. The board presidents' figure supported by an informal poll of readers of *The American School Board Journal* (167, 3, March 1980, 52): 48 percent of respondents favored teaching both evolution and creationism in public schools. Twenty-five percent wanted evolution only, while no less than 19 percent favored creationism *only*, and 8 percent preferred to avoid both topics. Clearly, one reason that creationism is found in the classroom is that many teachers and administrators think it belongs there. Some NCR organizations (such as the National Association of Christian Educators) enthusiastically support the right of teachers to promulgate scientific creationism. Following the reasoning of Wendell Bird (1987), they argue that state or district policies forbidding creation science unconstitutionally violate academic freedom.

Interestingly, a poll of readers reported in the American Bar Association's *ABA Journal* supports them (Reidinger 1987). When asked in a mail questionnaire whether the First Amendment prohibits the teaching of creationism in public schools, only 28 percent of the 578 lawyers responding answered yes. Sixty-three percent answered no. While policies that *mandate* creationism in science curricula so far have been ruled unconstitutional, the right of a teacher to *voluntarily* include creation science is a different issue, and its First Amendment implications have not been definitively settled. Along with Bird (1987), we suspect that legal defenses of a teacher's right to teach creationism will become more common in the future.

If some teachers need little persuading, there is also some evidence that creationists are pressuring them, although the data are sketchier than we would like (Table 8.2).

Table 8.2. Teachers Reporting Pressure to Teach Creationism and/or Downplay Evolution

Population	Those Reporting Pressure (%)
Ohio teachers (Zimmerman 1987a)	12
Kentucky teachers (Ellis 1986)	21
Georgia teachers (Buckner 1983)	29

In one study, nearly one-third of teachers reported receiving pressure from parents, ministers, or administrators. Furthermore, Eve and Dunn's (1989, 1990) pilot national study indicated that 16 percent of teachers had been pressured by parents, 8 percent by ministers, and 8 percent by administrators. These figures are not negligible, especially when one considers that a teacher need not be the direct object of creationist urgings to feel coerced. He or she need merely talk to colleagues who have received pressure, or even simply hear through the grapevine about a past incident or two, to draw the conclusion that saying anything that offends creationists is asking for trouble.

Given the many stresses to which high school teachers are subjected daily, it is quite understandable that science instructors would want to avoid bringing more complications into their lives.

To what extent does grass-roots creationist effort actually pay off? How often is creationism taught and evolution deemphasized? Again, our statistics are insufficient. We know that some school districts have some form of official equal-time policy and that many others practice an unofficial, de facto policy of making concessions to creationists (like the Dallas–Fort Worth area administrators quoted above). But we lack comprehensive statistics on how often this is done, and on just what form the two-model teaching takes.

Again, teacher surveys provide our best indications (see Table 8.3).

Table 8.3. Science Teachers Who Report Teaching Creationism in Their Classes

Population	Those Who Teach Creationism (%)
Ohio teachers (Zimmerman 1987a)	22
Kentucky teachers (Ellis 1986)*	30
Georgia teachers (Eglin 1983)	27
Oregon teachers (Study by Boring, cited in Affannato 1986)	26

*Those who reported giving "strong emphasis" to creationism.

Table 8.4. College Students Who Received
High School Instruction in Creationism and Evolution

Population	Responses to the Question, "Were you taught evolution in high school?"		
	Yes, *without* creationism (%)	Yes, *with* creationism (%)	No (%)
Texas students	43	33	24
California students	8	83	9
Connecticut students	46	31	22

Source: Harrold and Eve 1987

The available surveys indicate consistently that about one-fifth to one-third of science teachers actually teach creationism in their classes, although there is no indication of the amount or enthusiasm of such instruction.

Further confirmation that creationism is being taught in public high schools to a significant extent comes from one study of college students in three states (Harrold and Eve 1987). We asked them whether they had received such instruction while in high school. Their responses (Table 8.4), while not directly comparable with those in Table 8.3, are congruent with them.

We do not know how many of the surveyed students were taught creationism only, but it is obvious that a significant portion of them received instruction in creationism along with evolution in high school, and (just as important) many others seem never to have been taught about evolution. This latter finding is important, since total avoidance of evolution in school curricula would probably satisfy most creationists as much as inclusion of their own beliefs. The results of the aforementioned California antidogmatism policy also show up clearly. Because ours was not a random national sample, we cannot generalize with certainty to the nation as a whole, but over half of our polled students received the sort of instruction concerning "origins" that creationist activists want: either no coverage of evolution or the inclusion of creationism.

On the basis of our combined teacher and student survey results and keeping in mind the nature of the samples queried, it is fair to suggest

(though we need confirmation by more complete studies) that over a quarter—and perhaps as many as half—of the nation's high school students get science educations shaped by creationist influence—in spite of the overwhelming opposition of the nation's scientific, educational, intellectual, and media establishments.

How effective is the teaching of creationism. How thoroughly and how well is it taught? How much of it do students learn? Does such instruction actually make any difference in student beliefs?

Of course, the answers to these rarely raised questions vary greatly from teacher to teacher and school to school. But in general, it is clear that exposure to creationism (or lack of exposure to evolution) is not the only factor that influences actual acceptance of evolution. If it were, then creationist belief in California would be higher than in Texas, considering Table 8.4. As we saw in Table 3.2, though, this is not the case. Indeed, our 1987 study indicated that the most important determinant of acceptance of creationism among college students is (unsurprisingly) strong prior conservative religious belief.

Yet learning experience does have some influence on belief; for instance, in our study and in Fuerst's (1984), the more one was exposed to evolution in college coursework, the more likely one was to accept evolution. Furthermore, acceptance of evolution is related to understanding it (Fuerst 1984) and science (Johnson and Peeples 1987). Thus, it is likely that teaching creationism and/or downplaying evolution in the schools not only comforts creationists, but has some effect on students' views.

One unhappy effect of the two-model approach was found by Jones (1987). Among students in her study, instruction in creationism was associated statistically with poorer thinking skills. Specifically, students with secondary school instruction in creationism were found to be more likely to accept mutually contradictory aspects of evolutionary theory and creationism as *both* true, despite the logical impossibility. In this case, two-model instruction, far from increasing the effectiveness of science education as creationists often claim, led some students to end up with Orwellian doublethink, simultaneously holding two contradictory views.

The Countermovement's Response

The countermovement that arose among scientists, educators, intellectuals, civil liberties groups, and others in response to the creationist advance has had some success in rebuffing its opponents. There was a

considerable lag between the 1960s rejuvenation of creationism and the mobilization of the countermovement, in part no doubt because of the compartmentalization of American education. Scientists in the universities—those best equipped to oppose creationist knowledge claims— were seldom directly affected in their own work by sociopolitical tempests in the high schools. Like their predecessors of the 1920s, today's creationists have made no serious attempts to control science curricula in public colleges and universities.

Moreover, the prevailing attitudes of academics toward creationism have also discouraged scientists from becoming involved in anticreationist activities. Scientists who urged others to confront creationism received cool responses. "You can't change the minds of religious fanatics," they were told. "Besides, responding to them only lends them spurious credibility. Ignore them and get back to doing science."

Only in the late 1970s, when it became clear that the creationists, intellectually armed with scientific creationism, might really change the direction of biology education—and perhaps eventually the status and funding of mainstream science—did the countermovement form and gather momentum. Scientific and educational societies began to issue statements and pamphlets. For example, in the early 1980s the American Anthropological Association issued several pamphlets for students and the public on the fossil record of human evolution and on the nature of origin myths. And in 1984 the prestigious National Academy of Science produced a widely distributed booklet criticizing creation science.

Scientists and others also responded with a blizzard of books and articles in the scholarly and popular presses. A survey of several databases for the period 1977–85 by Godfrey and Cole (1987) found that the number of articles on the creation–evolution controversy in scholarly journals and popular magazines began to increase from low levels in 1980, shot up the next year, peaked at a high level in 1982, then fell off precipitously in 1983 and continued to decline thereafter. Natural scientists were well represented among the authors. They generally wrote articles refuting creationist claims, pointing to dangerous educational or sociopolitical implications of creationism, or both. Interestingly, articles in which social scientists analyzed (as opposed to castigated) creationism were relatively rare, as Godfrey and Cole point out.

At the same time, anticreationist social movement organizations confronted creationists in legal, political, and public relations struggles. From the turn of the decade on, creationists increasingly encountered organized opposition in court, at textbook hearings, and in debates. The

National Center for Science Education and the Committees of Correspondence, People for the American Way, and the ACLU have been especially active in this regard.

After the anticreationist victory in the 1981 Arkansas trial, many activists, having made their point in the courts and in print, in effect declared victory and marched home. Niles Eldredge, author of a well-regarded anticreationist book (Eldredge 1982), said at a 1985 scientific meeting that evolutionists had won the war and should now get back to their scientific work. Many did just that.

But the countermovement never ceased entirely, and most of the anticreationist SMOs have continued their work. The scientific establishment and its allies in the countermovement have not returned to their old levels of apathy and noninvolvement, and they probably will not for some time to come.

The countermovement's success was highly publicized in the national and state court battles and legislation where the creationists were effectively checked. The countermovement's enormous resources of scientific and legal expertise, and the prestige and authority of the scientific establishment, have helped them gain the upper hand over the creationists by winning the support of crucial bystander publics, especially the judiciary, the legislatures, the educational bureaucracies, and the media. At the level of state educational bodies, success has been more mixed for the countermovement, but they have offset earlier creationist gains in the two biggest textbook adoption states. It is at the local level that anticreationists have encountered the greatest difficulties, mainly because of the sheer number of local educational bodies with their own (often populist) standards of curriculum policy, and the lack of publicity most cases receive. When an alert Committee of Correspondence or other group becomes aware of creationist activity, it often is effective in checking it at the local level—and when a threatened ACLU lawsuit convinced a Texas local school board not to accommodate creationist parents (discussed above), or when Reverend Carl Baugh's Paluxy "human tooth" claim was refuted by high school science teacher Dr. Ron Hastings (1989) and others. But as we have noted, many creationists' successes at the local level go unchallenged.

Partly because it is impossible to put out a thousand brush fires, some anticreationist SMOs—in particular, the National Council for Science Education—are modifying their strategies. Reasoning that a major cause of the success of creationism is scientific illiteracy, they are increasingly emphasizing education in scientific method and concepts and in critical

thinking. In effect, they are shifting to a strategy of "prevention" as well as "cure" for creationism. One form these efforts are taking is an increasing number of college courses on the creation–evolution controversy, or more generally on scientific and critical thinking (Nelson 1986; Saladin 1986; Feder 1985–86; Gray 1984, 1987; Thwaites 1986). These courses seem to have had some success in reducing creationist and other unconventional beliefs among students who take them, although the effect sometimes is temporary. Other planned measures include lecture series (CSICOP) and television productions (NCSE).

Conclusion

As the creation–evolution conflict evolved, creationists advanced their case in different arenas, gradually concentrating their efforts on those arenas that have shown the greatest successes. In the process, their orientation evolved from a more expressive phase to a more strategic one as they found the tactics that work best—pressing for equal time in local and state arenas, and advocating "fairness" and compromise rather than coercion. They are adapting to the reality that, at least for the present, they can appeal with far more success to some bystander publics (school administrators, teachers, and the general public) than to others (judges, legislatures, the media). This change is also becoming apparent in their literature, as the zealous and sometimes strident rhetoric of the ICR is joined by the quieter, less polemical approach of the Foundation for Thought and Ethics. The persuasion, facilitation, and compromise characteristic of the strategic orientation are increasingly apparent in creationist literature, in the ICR's growing emphasis on workshops and field trips over debates, and in the "soft" creationist line for school curricula, which eschews terms like *God* and *creation* in favor of *intelligent design* and *abrupt appearance*. The Creation-Science Legal Defense Fund was renamed the Academic Freedom Legal Defense Fund, and the second edition of Gish's *Evolution? The Fossils Say No!* was given the vaguer and less polemical title *Evolution: The Challenge of the Fossil Record.*

There is still plenty of emotion in the conflict, but many creationists seem to be coming to the conclusion that it is counterproductive for them to be perceived as extremists angrily demanding accommodation for their beliefs. This trend among creationists is being paralleled elsewhere in the New Christian Right; activists who oppose sex education and secular humanism in the schools and government-sponsored day care and who

support home schooling are also adopting less flamboyant tactics, building coalitions with non-NCR forces, and becoming established in the structure of the Republican party (Shribman 1989).

By the same token, many anticreationists have come to realize that denouncing creationists as benighted fanatics is insufficient, as is scientifically refuting creationist claims, and are adding improved science education to their agendas. Both creationists and their opponents are aware that they are in for a long struggle that is unlikely to end in total victory for either side. In the final chapter we will venture some predictions about the course this conflict will follow in the 1990s and beyond.

Chapter Nine

Looking Backward and Forward: Some Conclusions and Predictions

Eventually the modern creationist revival had to be taken seriously. For a long time, it was all but ignored; more recently it began to be ridiculed. Now it is being intensively and viciously opposed. At least we finally have their attention!

—Henry Morris (1984)

Scientific creationism may be poor science, but it is powerful politics. And politically, it may succeed.

—Laurie Godfrey (1981)

Introduction

In this final chapter we summarize the most important points made in earlier chapters and try to venture some predictions about the intensity and form of future conflicts between creationists and evolutionists. Toward this end, we have chosen to use an analytical scheme that draws upon Smelser's (1962) theoretical framework for analyzing collective behavior.[1] Smelser has suggested that most forms of collective behavior (including social movements) can best be understood by examining the interplay of six "determinants" of collective behavior: (1) structural conduciveness, (2) structural strain, (3) a precipitating event, (4) the growth and spread of generalized beliefs, (5) the mobilization of participants for action, and (6) the operation on the movement of social control.

We use Smelser's scheme here in support of the contention that the creation–evolution conflict will continue for years to come—in fact, we expect the conflict to escalate rather than abate. Smelser's scheme should enable us to organize a large mass of data and a multitude of ideas presented in previous chapters to demonstrate that such predictions are the logical outcomes when we use solid social-science theory. Let us turn our attention to the first of Smelser's determinants.

Structural Conduciveness

Structural conduciveness refers to factors that do not themselves *cause* collective behavior but that do make it more *likely* that a situation is ripe for collective behavior. Among the elements of structural conduciveness that may act much as a catalyst in a chemical reaction does are (1) the existence of overlapping social structural cleavages, (2) channels of grievances that are closed to potential movement adherents, (3) a lack of a clear line of responsibility for resolving the problematic situation, and (4) rapid and ready communication among potential movement members.

A good example of the importance of overlapping structural cleavages in promoting the longevity of a social movement is the case of the Irish Republican Army (IRA). In examining the activities of the IRA, it can be readily seen that the issue is not just one of nationality (English versus Irish) but also one of religion (Protestant versus Catholic) and, indeed, even one of social class conflict (Irish Catholics are generally less well off). Hence, the degree of overlap among structural cleavages (in other words, the issues of nationality, religion, and economics) is great. Such situations are notoriously difficult to resolve because solving the strain deriving from one structural cleavage generally does little or nothing to eliminate conflict related to the other structural divisions that overlap the first. The result is that the unresolved issues tend to lead to a return to conflict even after some issues are apparently individually resolved. In such situations, social movement conflicts tend to be long-lived.

Structural Cleavages and the Creationism–Evolution Debate
The creationist movement is not simply a squabble over what constitutes good scientific evidence or procedure for explaining human origins. At a deeper level, it is a conflict between two fundamentally different world-views for control of the "means of cultural reproduction." There is some

evidence that other cleavages in the social structure overlap with and affect the creationism–evolutionism debate. Differences in educational backgrounds, denominational preferences, ages, and urban-versus rural residence of the combatants are all overlapping structural cleavages that make the prognosis for a resolution of the conflict poor, and to make matters worse channels for the expression of grievances are not readily available. Also, there are few clear lines of responsibility for the resolution of the conflict. While each side has certain outlets to express its grievances (e.g., its own visual media outlets and its own publishing outlets), these outlets tend to represent only one side without bringing together the contenders in a single forum. Even if this were done, there appears to be no readily agreed upon lines of responsibility, or even procedures, that would allow a final authority to arrive at a decision by a set of rules acceptable to both sides.

Turning our attention to the availability of channels for communication among potential participants, we observe that it is well known that if actual or potential movement adherents are out of touch with one another, it is unlikely that a social movement can be originated or sustained. But in recent years, both sides seem to have improved their intermember communication. The creationists historically published only through small publishing houses that sold primarily to Christian bookstores, but in recent years they have been able to find more mainstream publishers, have developed long lists of direct-mail recipients, have begun to target biology teachers, and have made other strides in enhancing communication among their members and potential recruits. Their opponents, after producing a spate of rebuttal articles during 1981–84 (Cole and Godfrey 1987, 107), appear to have generally been overly optimistic about the results of these publications and assumed victory prematurely. It would appear that the evolutionist forces assumed that when the truth was announced, the fight would be over. Social movements do not normally cease simply because the truth is announced, however; instead they tend to come to a close only when the situation is no longer considered problematic by movement adherents. Since the creationist movement involves a conflict of worldviews, not simply conflicting interpretations of scientific data, the conflict continues.

Currently, the evolution forces have quite a few nationwide organizations, composed largely of professionals in the natural and social sciences, such as the National Center for Science Education, the Committee for the Scientific Investigation of Claims of the Paranormal, the American Humanist Association, the National Association of Biology

Teachers, the American Association for the Advancement of Science, and so on. They are continuing, and sometimes increasing, their anticreationism efforts. But the proevolutionism contingent has generally failed to develop a widespread communication network at the local level that equals that of the creationists. The creationists currently have in place a much better communication system for reaching the rank-and-file members. On the other hand, the proevolutionist movement has probably been more successful in reaching elites in key academic, legal, and political positions.

Taken together, the factors related to structural conduciveness seem to indicate that the situation is structurally conducive to continuing the conflict for some time and that it will not be resolved soon. Instead, it can be expected to continue throughout the 1990s and beyond.

Structural Strains

Structural strains are the actual motive or driving forces that propel social movements. Precipitating events may at first appear to be the source of a social movement, but in reality they represent only the triggers that release the stored potential energy (the gunpowder) created by deep-seated strains within the social structure. Such underlying strains can be massive in their effects, but they tend to be perceived "but through a glass darkly" by both movement adherents and bystander publics. Like tectonic plates in the drift of the continents, the forces involved are awesome, but they tend to be noticed only when they give rise to a volcano or an earthquake. Similarly, the activation of various social movements may appear unrelated on the surface, but they are in fact often driven by the same deep social forces. (The other "volcanos" and "earthquakes" are, for example, such social movements as those concerning the issues of abortion, homosexual rights, women's rights, and pornography.) Several structural strains are at work in the creation–evolution conflict.

Local Control and Structural Strain   One source of structural strain occurs not in the area of religion specifically but in the political foundations of American government; specifically, the tradition of local control in American democracy. By contrast to the U.S., as Cavanaugh (1983) has pointed out, in the United Kingdom (and much of the rest of the developed world), the clergy tend to be educated in mainstream, nationally prominent institutions of higher education. Historically, theological dissent in Great Britain has largely been institutionalized in the

has largely been institutionalized in the activities of the evangelical church (or in the Presbyterian Church, in Scotland). But in the United States, because of the existence of the frontier, there developed a strong tradition of the lay preacher whose primary qualifications for the job often seem to have been that God called him and that he had enough charisma to draw some followers.

Both education curriculum decisions and religious activities are unusually decentralized in the United States, compared with most European countries. This results in plenty of room, both literally and metaphorically, for dissenters to establish their own churches, colleges, and other institutions. Therefore the governmental center and the national educational and intellectual elites are less powerful in the United States than in Britain. In Great Britain, the clergy have, by comparison, usually been much better educated in the arts and sciences. Consequently, doctrinal differences tend to be worked out within the major centers of religious life. In the United States, however, when those at the center of big science attempt to send forth science books developed in major urban, cosmopolitan universities and think tanks, some local congregations—and even entire local communities—are likely to regard such books as largely alien to their belief systems (witness the sometimes violent rejection of the Biological Sciences Curriculum Study funded by the National Science Foundation).

The Politics of Life-style Concern Probably the most powerful strain in the evolution–creationism controversy—yet the least clearly perceived by both sides—is the headlong collision of the worldviews that, following Page and Clelland (1978), we have called "cultural fundamentalism" and "cultural modernism."

Modernism can be understood to be the system of thought that arose out of the Enlightenment. As Giddens (1978, 267) has pointed out, "The progenitors of the Enlightenment set out to effect the disenchantment of the world, to replace myth by solidly founded knowledge, applying that knowledge practically in technology. In so doing they prepared the way for the domination of modern culture by technical rationality. . . . In the name of freedom from the domination of myth, the Enlightenment created a new form of domination, hidden from view by its own philosophy: domination by instrumental rationality."

Frederick Turner (forthcoming) helps connect Giddins's remark with the fundamentalists' rejection of modernism in general and non-Baconian science in particular. Modernism, he says, "took a deterministic and ma-

terialistic view of nature, a hostile view of traditional society and its economic base. . . . It existed within and fed upon the western liberal capitalist democracies and the established body of scientific knowledge and technological power." Turner argues that the social paroxysms of the 1960s in the United States and in other Western societies heralded a breakdown in the popular acceptance of modernism. Faced with the problems of environmental exploitation and degradation, a runaway military-industrial complex, and the collapse of shared moral values reflected in the rise of free love, drug use, and abortion upon demand, increasing numbers of individuals began to reject modernism. Tradition-minded conservative Christians, of course, occupy a primary position among those rejecting modernism in general and what they see as its excessive reliance on technological rationality and materialism.

Those who subscribe to a cultural fundamentalist construction of reality tend to believe that humans cannot solve the social problems of the Western world in the late twentieth century without divine assistance. They believe instead that solutions can be found only through faith in an all-powerful and inerrant deity. Indeed, many of them believe that the problems themselves originated from a widespread lack of piety. To conservative Christians, things tend to be true by reason of revelation, faith, tradition, or authority. Such truths are not open to question—"God said it, I believe it, end of argument!" For these people, the ultimate purpose of human existence is the glorification of God.

On the other side of this volatile mix, the cultural modernists believe that their opponents' dogmatic inflexibility and adherence to "outdated" ethical codes bode disaster for the human race. In contrast to the cultural fundamentalists, cultural modernists have tended to see the development of flexible moral codes and situational ethics as essential for successful adaptation to rapid social change. For modernists, the end purpose of existence on this earth is less to glorify God than to maximize human, and even personal, development; to minimize human suffering; and generally to improve the human condition through rational—and often scientific—means.

The Advent of Postmodernism In the past few years, many scholars have offered the opinion that we are now entering a "postmodern" age. Even many people who are not conservative Christians—including sizable factions within the scholarly fields of art, literature, philosophy, and rhetoric—have begun to feel that modernism has failed to give to most of us a fulfilling worldview or to improve the human condition

or potential. For example, within the philosophy of science a number of critics have emerged recently who argue that modern science has no claim as a superior way of finding out about the natural world. Instead, they continue, it serves primarily to legitimate power and privilege for scientists and for those for whom they work (Kuhn 1970; Habermas 1972; Feyerabend 1975).

The postmodernists argue that modernism has done little more than rob man of his spirituality, reduce him to little more than a consumer, produce war on a heretofore unknown scale, precipitate a global environmental crisis, and either promote or cause the breakdown of the traditional family. To date, the postmodernist critics have done a thorough job of decrying the effects of modernism, and they have arguably robbed it of much of its legitimacy. Unfortunately, however, they have also failed to propose a meaningful alternative to modernism. Instead, their collective effect appears to have been largely to aggravate the alienation that began with the rise of modernism by casting further doubt on the utility of its values and worldview. As F. Turner (forthcoming) has summarized the current situation, "Postmodern relativism and nihilism are producing their own conservative reaction . . . so now in many quarters a convulsive and hysterical fundamentalism is attempting to vomit up the postmodern disease. Most obvious, of course, is the wave of Islamic fundamentalism that is sweeping Asia and Africa; but we can see the same tendency among Christian and Jewish fundamentalists."

In our view, the rise of postmodernism has introduced a new sense of urgency and concern into the social movements of conservative Christians. This is because they find postmodernism's nihilistic and relativistic quality even more frightening than they did the secularization and rationalization attendant on "old" modernism. Conservative Christianity had almost found a way to make its peace with the values of modernism that promoted industrial development and consumerism. Postmodernist ethics and values, however, are profoundly antithetical to cultural fundamentalism. (Oddly, the rise of postmodernism has made potential allies of conservative Christians, "deconstructionist" intellectual critics of postnodernism—who often work within mainstream institutions—and New Age seekers.) It seems clear that conservative Christians are reacting, just as are many other segments of the world's population, against a very real threat that their entire way of life may be destroyed and replaced with what they perceive as a vacuous and morally ambiguous alternative. In one sense, then, the antievolution movement that we have been con-

trasting with the countermovement to protect evolution is itself actually a broad and deeply based countermovement against modernist trends in society.

Modernism, Postmodernism, and Emotional Isolation   There are around 4 to 5 million fundamentalists in the United States (drawn from 40 to 50 million evangelicals—many of whom are potential converts to creationism). Their numbers appear to be growing fairly rapidly as members leave the mainstream churches for more fundamentalist and charismatic ones. Much of this denominational migration seems to be due to another structural strain: the greater social and psychological isolation of the individual. This isolation has grown as a result of the disappearing sense of family and community in the United States during recent decades. Currently, fewer than 25 percent of all Americans live in families if we define a family as having two or more related generations under one roof. Mainstream church activity is apparently often perceived as too abstract, too divorced from emotional support, and too busy with South Africa, nuclear disarmament, and Social Gospel in general to meet its members' psychological needs. To find emotional support, or a cathartic emotional resolution for bereavement or for sin, the current choice would appear to be not the family but a mental health professional, a New Age "healer,"[2] or to involve oneself in the activities of conservative Christian churches, such as group prayer meetings or speaking in tongues—activities that offer many of the benefits of secular group therapy.

Scientific Creationists and Modernism   Still another structural strain in the creation–evolution debate are the varying conceptions of science itself, which affects how one properly "constructs" one's view of reality. When creationists accept science at all, their science of choice is Baconian inductivism. Their choice of this older version of science is consistent (just as it was in the nineteenth century) with a belief that the Bible is the inerrant and literal word of God. For those who embrace inductivism, the only job left to science is to collect and categorize discrete "facts" (which are assumed to be self-evident and not subject to phenomenological interpretation) and interpret them to show how the book of nature fits into the overall picture provided by the book of scripture. Twentieth-century science, in contrast, uses formal logic to deduce hypotheses from what is already known about the physical world and then tests such hypotheses, allowing the chips to fall where they may philo-

sophically and theologically. In addition, in twentieth-century science, even "facts" are not seen as self-evident but as inevitably colored by the inner experiences of the observer and by the instruments chosen to use to look for facts (after all, it is unlikely one would find something that he did not design an instrument a priori to look for). Creationists in general, and creation scientists in particular, see this twentieth-century science as leading to moral and ethical bankruptcy, since it often suggests that some aspects of nature are at odds with a literal reading of scripture and may even imply the absence of a divine plan (Hawking 1989).

Some observers (like Norelli and Proulx 1982) have suggested that the creationist movement is driven by the triple forces of populism, antielitism, and anti-intellectualism. While there is certainly some truth in this thesis, by itself it does not take into account the diversity within the creationist movement. It is certainly true that a good portion of the creationist movement can be characterized as consisting largely of the reaction of common people to a sense of alienation and exclusion from "the center," that is, big business, big government, and big science. These forces often do in fact buffet the man or woman in the street with blithe disregard for his or her opinions, sacred beliefs, or even well-being. It is also not surprising that many ordinary citizens come to feel that their government is unresponsive and dominated by special interests and that big business sees them primarily as a market to be exploited (while often simultaneously neglecting to protect them from fraud, toxic dumping, etc.). They also often feel that big science is awesome in its power to affect their lives, as well as remote, incomprehensible, and inaccessible, and it is often perceived also as the handmaiden of big politics and big business. Worse yet, modern science is seen as dangerous in its readiness to build surveillance devices and space weapons and to pollute the natural environment. It was, after all, only a few decades ago that science was touted as the answer to everyone's problems, a force that would lead to the good life for each person on the planet. But public opinion polls over succeeding decades have shown a steady increase in the number of people who have come to feel that, far from being a salvation, science itself (one of the "tools of choice" of modernism) is the source of many of the social problems that afflict twentieth-century man. Even small businesspeople become alienated from science when they see it as the henchman of giant corporations—entities that threaten to ruin them just as completely as they ever feared any labor union might.

When we turn our attention to the practitioners of *scientific* creationism, however, we note immediately that many of these individuals don't

fit such a mold. They are actually part of the New Class, whose members represent an alternative source of power to the old elite (Medawar 1973). The New Class "most generally consists of those college and professionally trained people who are occupationally associated with the knowledge industry" (Hunter 1983, 107). Put differently, the New Class is largely comprised of those who derive their livelihoods from the creation and manipulation of symbols. The conditions under which this new class arose make it very likely that its members will be devoted to "rationalistic modes of thought and discourse," as well as to liberal cosmopolitanism and humanistic morality (Hunter 1983, 107–9). Therefore, members of the New Class, *including* scientific creationists, can hardly be considered ignorant or backwoodsy.

Most members of the New Class are typically committed to modernism and even humanism, but a handful are clearly not. The leaders of the scientific creation movement, for example, tend to be drawn from the New Class. Many of them hold Ph.D.s in the sciences from respectable universities. They are not greatly anti-intellectual in orientation. On the contrary, many of them are by choice deeply engaged in lecturing, debating, and writing about their concerns. Their only distinguishing characteristic in comparison to their brethren in the New Class is their immutable belief that the Bible is completely literal and inerrant.

The view of scientific creationists as antielitist and anti-intellectual seems less valid than some recent thinking in the neo-Marxist school. Although Marx himself believed that modern societies are shaped by conflicts between the working class and the elite class, recent neo-Marxist analyses (such as Goldstone 1986) have suggested that it is much more common for a rift to develop *within* the elite class. Then those on each side of the rift attempt to recruit members of bystander publics to their particular interpretation of reality.

Unlike most Christians, scientific creationists have no use for averroism. Their belief in biblical inerrancy means that this particular portion of the New Class will find itself largely excluded from power and prestige within the mainstream scientific establishment (especially if they are vocal about their beliefs). This, of course, is a powerful structural strain for scientific creationists—a strain that is more than sufficient to galvanize them into action as leaders of the creationist movement.

We can, of course, see the mirror image of this situation when mainstream scientists are faced with scientific creationism's attempt to control the means of cultural reproduction through the schools. They call for

the reform of science education, arguing that if students become more staunchly committed to a twentieth-century scientific way of thinking, the threat to the legitimacy of mainstream science will be greatly lessened.

It would appear then that while the creationism–evolution conflict is in part traceable to a split between the common man and the big institutions at the center, in the end this alone would not be sufficient to mobilize the current creationist movement. Instead, the scientific creationists (themselves often members of the New Class) provide much of the ideology, rhetoric, and even specific resources (books, speakers, pamphlets, texts, and the like) that make the movement viable. To a large degree, they have decided in the past which tactics were used by the overall movement, and in what specific manner these tactics were used.

Many Overlapping Sources of Strain   There are thus many overlapping structural strains in the creationism–evolution conflict, and little reason to believe that any of these cleavages will diminish soon. Certainly, the local control issue in a democratic society is not likely to vanish in the near term. Nor is the conflict between the old political and business elite and the New Class, or even the conflict between scientific creationists and other members of the New Class. In addition, the dissolution of family and community support and the erosion of traditional values that results from modernism and postmodernism—forces that have probably led to increased growth of the evangelical churches—are not likely to abate anytime soon. Consequently, there is every reason to believe that the number of those who are exposed to and embrace creationist doctrine will continue to rise. Many potential converts will undoubtedly have no difficulty believing in sudden creation because, as we have seen, the vast majority can be expected to know very little about science.

Precipitating Events

A precipitating event in an episode of collective behavior is one that "releases" pent-up energies. It is not so much the *cause* of collective behavior (that role is reserved for structural strains) as the trigger that transforms the potential energy of participants into kinetic activity. It is usually easier to identify a specific precipitating event in an episode of one of the elementary forms of collective behavior (such as a riot or a panic) than it is in the case of a social movement. But nonetheless at least two precipitating events may be identified in the creation–evolution debate.

One precipitating event was the Russian success in orbiting Sputnik. That a hostile nation's hardware was orbiting over the United States and the United States was unable either to shoot it down or to launch a satellite of its own sent Americans into paroxysms of agony. It was widely argued that at least one reason for this situation was inadequate American science education. The federal government tried to remedy this situation by pouring more resources into the nation's science classrooms. In one example of this new trend, we have seen that The National Science Foundation developed the BSCS textbooks for the nation's high school biology classrooms. The BSCS books featured evolution as central to the study of biology. This, of course, earned the ire of conservative Christian parents and educators because the BSCS books were widely perceived as potentially disrupting the means of their own cultural reproduction. The militant protest in Kanawha County, West Virginia, was widely repeated in many other locations.

The other precipitating event was the Supreme Court's 1968 *Epperson* v. *Arkansas* decision, which ruled that state prohibitions of evolution instruction violated the establishment clause of the First Amendment. The long-term effect, as we have seen, was to overturn most of the existing antievolution laws. *Epperson* v. *Arkansas* outraged conservative Christians and galvanized them into action.

The Growth and Spread of Generalized Beliefs

As Neil Smelser has suggested, movement participants have a tendency to develop a set of generalized beliefs—that is, a set of beliefs that are shared by movement adherents and that increasingly lead toward a common worldview. Indeed, without outside information to contradict generalized beliefs, a whole collectivity may easily drift, without conscious awareness, into extreme or even bizarre worldviews. This is true because there are in such circumstances few reality-testing mechanisms available within the collectivity itself. Instances of this problem are described by Fromm in his 1941 analysis of the rise of Nazism and by Chidester in his 1988 analysis of Jim Jones's People's Temple cult.

There are generally two types of generalized beliefs. One type is the generalized beliefs that identify and define the source of the strain that gave rise to the movement. It should be noted, however, that such shared beliefs are often erroneous because they are often based more on their emotional appeal than upon strict logic and because participants lack the feedback mechanisms mentioned above. The second type of generalized belief consists of prescriptions for how to resolve the strain

that is perceived as impinging upon the collectivity. This type of belief is subject to the same potential for inaccuracy as the first type.

In the case of the creationist movement, over much of the twentieth-century fundamentalists increasingly perceived that their goals and values were threatened and could possibly be replaced by those of outsiders. In trying to explain this to themselves, they reasoned that if evolution had taken place in ways that contradicted the biblical account of origins, then it would cast doubt on the existence of God's plan (with man as the ultimate and lasting pinnacle of the process). If people accepted evolution it would lead to a rejection of godliness and turn society toward secular humanism and its doctrine of flexible situational ethics. Moreover, they reasoned to themselves, the acceptance of such humanist ethics would lead to homosexuality, abortion, pornography, drug use, and many other problems.

The result of this chain of reasoning was that creationists established within their own minds, and to some extent have successfully propagated the idea into society, that a strict dichotomy exists between creationism and evolution. Specifically, they advocate the position that the Bible is the literal and inerrant word of God and they consequently regard even their less conservative Christian brethren as hopeless compromisers. Thus, the large majority of Christians who are prepared to believe that God directed the creation of mankind but did so over many millions of years, are denied the right to call themselves creationists. From the point of view of creationists, even their fellow Christians who do not accept the inerrancy position are drifting into secular humanism and will become yet another source of the social problems of the late twentieth century. For biblical literalists, *no* error in any area of the Bible can be accepted lest the Bible become suspect in all other areas. As a consequence, it is not surprising that they see a great necessity to demonstrate how the Bible can be shown to be scientifically accurate. This line of thought, of course, led them to the belief that in order to drive the evolutionists and secular humanists from the gates it is necessary, among other things, to develop a convincing scientific version of the creationist position on human origin.

Their prescription for eliminating their source of strain was to begin developing scientific creationism. Next, other beliefs about how best to accomplish the dissemination of scientific creationism had to be agreed on. Having met with little success in the academic community and the courts after the Scopes trial, they seem to have agreed that the field of action would have to be the local community in general and its school-

rooms in particular. Thus, creationists began to argue in public the essential "fairness" of presenting both models of origins in the science classroom and then letting the students "decide for themselves." What could be more American than to argue that each side should be given equal time to present its case?

Generalized Beliefs and "Short-Circuiting" When collectivities develop erroneous generalized beliefs, they are "short-circuited," argues Neil Smelser (1962). Many generalized beliefs are developed primarily on the bases of emotional needs and symbolic appeal in order to fill the need of movement adherents for an easily understood and satisfying worldview. Such beliefs are often therefore cast into conflict with a strictly rational and realistic analysis of the situation. Creationism, like many other movements, appears to have succumbed to this tendency to develop short-circuited beliefs about the situation and the appropriate means for removal of associated strains. For example, their rejection of the validity of evolution-based science reflects confusion over the directions of causation involved. Acceptance of evolution has not *caused* modernism and humanism, nor will its elimination automatically solve the problems arising out of the Enlightenment.

Creationists' claims that evolution has not occurred or is bad science will not magically do away with modernism, humanism, situational ethics, and so on. Such a belief is short-circuited. Indeed, the most likely result of imposing such a claim would be similar to that which occurred when the medieval church tied itself to Ptolemy's geocentric view of the universe. The ultimate effect of connecting theological doctrine to an erroneous view of scientific knowledge was disastrous. When it turned out the earth was *not* the center of the universe, (as Ptolemy had claimed and the church had seconded), the legitimacy of the church suffered a blow from which it has never completely recovered. To make a similar mistake now cannot advance the cause of conservative Christians.

Mobilization of Participants for Action

We have mentioned before that early theorists in the study of social movements have sometimes been accused of implying that social movements arise only when structural strain becomes psychologically meaningful to potential participants to such a degree that their emotional arousal provides both a necessary and sufficient condition for activism. Such emotional arousal, however, is in and of itself insufficient to wholly

account for the pattern of activation of actual social movements. In many situations individuals have been hugely frustrated and angry, but were nonetheless unable to initiate a viable social movement. What was often missing from a full explanation in these cases was an adequate consideration of the resources necessary to form a movement and the readiness and effectiveness with which adherents can put such resources to work.

This type of problem faces both sides in the creation–evolution conflict. Militant creationists probably far outnumber the corresponding category of militant mainstream scientists (partly because scientists tend to eschew involvement in activity outside of their labs). On the other hand, mainstream scientists are probably better connected to policy-setters and decision-makers within society's powerful large-scale institutions. Apparently because of this, until recently most creationist campaigns could expect to meet with the same fate as the Scopes trial; that is, even if they won on paper, the overall results would be either minimal or perhaps even negative.

But a few recent developments have enhanced the creationists' prospects very substantially. The appearance of scientific creationism and its associated institutes (such as the Institute for Creation Research) greatly increased the mobilization potential of the creationist movement. The ICR and its kindred organizations were the architects of two new thrusts that breathed new life into the creationist movement during the 1960s. Specifically, they introduced the idea that plenty of *scientific* evidence could be found that would support a sudden-creation model. And in keeping with a deeply ingrained American value, they began to advocate equal time for the creationist model in the science classroom and generally met with very good receptivity to this argument.

A truism in the study of social movements is that when a movement finds that it is powerless, it must make its ideology and goals creditable to bystander publics in hopes of recruiting new members and new resources. Both the scientific claim for creationism and the call for equal time (or "balanced treatment") have successfully broadened the credibility of the creationist movement. This attempt to widen its credibility continues today.

Creationists of the 1960s were catapulted into action by a sense of moral outrage at what they believed to be a loss of their control of the means of cultural reproduction in the classrooms of their children. In such a climate, their movement initially had a strongly expressive character. One way this character was manifested was in their immediate resort to

the court system to try to settle their grievance: They would *force* the evolutionists right out of the classroom by means of a good, sound legal bludgeoning. This, however, was not to be. Such confrontational tactics are often chosen initially because of their potential for great emotional satisfaction, but when they fail because a movement lacks the power needed to make them effective, the movement will generally find itself forced to adopt less strident and confrontive tactics. Tactics such as persuasion and bargaining, while less satisfying at the gut level, may be selected as more likely to succeed.

Clearly, the new emphasis on the scientific nature of creationism and the call for equal time can be seen as initial steps in a shift from expressive to instrumental tactics. A still more recently developed instrumental tactic has also involved persuasion: robust grass-roots campaigns waged at the local level and intended to influence parents, school board members, and even individual teachers.

Creationists' Attempts to Mobilize Schoolteachers   Expressive tactics by the creationists (such as attempts to ban the teaching of evolution), have been generally unsuccessful to date. Not yet to be denied, however, the creationists developed still another tactic that is less expressive and more persuasive in character than scientific creationism. Specifically, they have begun to speak in terms of the theory of abrupt appearance. According to Bennetta (1988b, 20) this idea could be found as early as the summer of 1983, when one well-known creationist advised his fellows to focus on how the fossil record demonstrates the abrupt appearance of various life-forms. Advocates of the doctrine of abrupt appearance studiously avoid explicit references to supernaturalism and will not speak of any god, but instead will sometimes refer to a nebulous "intelligence" or "intelligent cause" or "intelligent design." The inaccurate use of the word *kinds* is being dropped, as are references to a worldwide flood and all other topics that are clearly biblical in origin (Bennetta 1988, 22). Even the term *creation science* itself will be increasingly avoided in the future. The new creationism has a generally calmer, less angry tone and is more willing to accept an old age for the earth. In other words, creationism is being sanitized, until it is no longer overtly recognizable as religious in origin. (Good examples of the new approach are a 1984 book by Charles Thaxton et al. entitled *The Mystery of Life's Origins: Reassessing Current Theories* and Davis and Kenyon's 1989 *Of Pandas and People.*)

All of the above factors indicate a move toward a new, less strident

creationism that, it appears, may eventually largely replace the tactics heretofore typical of the Institute for Creation Research and the Bible Science Association.

There is much reason to believe that the new instrumental tactics of bargaining, facilitation, and persuasion will give creation science a broad and ready acceptance among a sizable percentage of American high school biology and life-science teachers. As we have seen, several studies appear to indicate that on the order of 25 to 30 percent of these teachers already privately believe in special creation. We have also seen that probably 20 percent or more of these same teachers actually do present creationism in a favorable light within their classrooms. These instrumental tactics are potentially very effective for mobilizing support among schoolteachers.

Have Creationists Forgotten about the Courts and Legislatures?   The success that the creationists have enjoyed at the grass-roots level makes it likely that they will continue to press their campaign vigorously at this level, although one should not assume that they have abandoned the courts altogether. As we have seen, they seem to have come for now, however, to a substantial impasse in the courts and legislatures, having apparently exhausted their most likely legal claims. For the immediate future, little more is likely to occur than occasional suits by individuals teachers claiming First Amendment protections that they feel should allow them to present creationism in the science classroom. But the Reagan appointees to the Supreme Court have shifted the balance of the Court very considerably in a conservative direction. In particular, the current chief justice, William Rehnquist, has been quoted (in a recent national direct-mail campaign by Americans United for Separation of Church and State) as having said that "The 'wall of separation between church and state' is a metaphor based on bad history, a metaphor which has proved useless as a guide to judging. It should be frankly and explicitly abandoned." The presence of Rehnquist and his conservative Christian allies on the Supreme Court bench must surely give the creationists new hope for their long-term future in the legal arena.

Nor do the creationists have reason to totally despair of influencing state legislatures. Many of the new Supreme Court justices are themselves conservative Protestants, and others like Justice Scalia seem disposed to let state legislatures make laws to govern areas of life that more liberal judges have considered subject to constitutional restrictions. We may expect conservative judges, for instance, to regard more sympa-

thetically the populist argument that final authority over public school curricula belong to the taxpayers, not to educational experts.

In conclusion, during the very near term, little of the creationist campaign is likely to be waged in the courts or legislatures. The ground seems much more fertile for influencing local schoolteachers, local school boards, and local and statewide textbook adoption committees.

The Operation of Social Control

Smelser's final determinant of collective behavior is *the operation of social control*. The shape and ultimate success of a social movement is based in part on this determinant. For example, in a riot situation, much depends on the presence and effectiveness of social control agents like the police or the military. Their effectiveness influences the extent, duration, and intensity of a riot.

It is a bit difficult to apply this analytical determinant to forms of collective behavior beyond the elementary forms, but certain analogous effects do have an impact on social movements such as the creationist movement. Probably the most obvious of these control agents are the teachers, scientists, and mainstream institutions who try to discredit creationism.

To date, the operation of social control in this form has failed to win a clear victory, and this situation is not likely to change in the near future. Indeed, there is much reason to believe that the proportion of evangelicals and fundamentalists in the general population will continue to increase in a reaction against modernism, and this in turn will bring many new adherents to creationism. On the other hand, creationists' campaign to control school curricula and the textbook selection process seems to have been slowly and widely deteriorating. In both Texas and California, recent textbook adoption hearings have resulted in minor compromises intended to defuse creationist ire, but in both states (the two states with the biggest influence on textbook publishers) the main body of the emerging guidelines gave evolution a more secure place in the curriculum. While these de jure outcomes are reassuring to evolutionists, the de facto practices of individual teachers in their own classrooms may well be expected to depart from official guidelines.

In past years the creationists have been able to influence textbook publishers to "water down" or omit coverage of evolution in their textbooks. In the light of recent history, especially the Texas and California

cases, this ability seems to be on the wane. Juxtaposed against this, however, must be the knowledge that publishers are increasingly adopting a policy directed toward marketing segmentation—that is, give Arkansas the books it wants, and give New York what it wants. It is, however, reassuring to note that the best-selling biology text—Holt, Rinehart and Winston's *Holt's Modern Biology*—has recently expanded its coverage of evolution, in a largely accurate manner. But, it still falls short of the centrality that many of its professional reviewers desire.

Summary

In summary, while evolutionists often suggest that creationists are crazy, or at least ignorant, such accusations seem unfounded for the most part.

For most creationists, the debate over the adequacy or interpretation of the scientific data is ultimately subordinated to the conflict between the worldview they have been socialized to believe in and the worldview created and sustained outside their communities by the forces of modernism and postmodernism. The debate is much less a fistfight in the kitchen between scientists than a struggle for the means of cultural reproduction by people who often know little of science. In modern society, this struggle for control of the means of cultural reproduction is almost inevitably focused upon the schools and their curricula.

We have also seen that scientific creationists do not share all the characteristics of the rank-and-file members of the creationist movement. In particular, their educational experiences would ordinarily make them members of the New Class (that is neither traditional business elites nor traditional laborers). But scientific creationists' commitment to the Bible as both literal and inerrant forces them, unlike most other members of the New Class, to reject evolution and to attempt to replace it with scientific creationism. To this end, they have adopted Baconian inductivism. Baconian inductivism (popular among mainstream scientists in the nineteenth century) sees the Book of Scripture as inerrant. As a result, the only work left to the scientist is to collect and categorize data and show how it "fits" scripture. But such science cannot reflect current scientific practice because by its very nature its assertions are not falsifiable (one of the prime requirements of modern science). Nor do the followers of scientific creationism do much original research, instead contenting themselves with trying to pick holes in the theory of evolution. When they do publish "research," it is almost never submitted to review by the

scientific community at large, nor is it subjected to peer review by fellow scientists. The conclusion is inescapable: creation science is not science; its true purpose is to provide the overall creationist movement with a way to combat evolution, which creationists think is the first step down a slippery slope into crime, homosexuality, drug use, pornography, the decline of the traditional family, and a host of other evils. While creationism is not good science, it was nonetheless the scientific creationists who provided much of the leadership, materials, and tactics that have been employed by the overall creationist movement.

The creationists' first challenges to evolutionism since the late 1950s came in the courts. They originally attempted to simply have evolution banned from the school curriculum. When this failed, they moved on to argue that evolution was "just a theory" and, therefore, just as much a religion as creationism. This, too, met with no long-term success in court. The next tactic was to argue that there was much scientific evidence that creationism was correct and that therefore the two-model approach should be adopted. This would allow each side equal time in the school science classroom, and the students would be left to decide for themselves which to believe. The courts, however, have consistently ruled in the final analysis that creationism is religious in nature and intent and is therefore in violation of the establishment clause of the First Amendment. The courtroom seems to have become a dead-end for the creationists.

Partly in reaction to their lack of progress in the courts, the creationists are currently working hardest at the local level, where they are trying to influence state and local textbook selection committees, and even local school boards and individual teachers. They are now emphasizing a new version of creationism: the theory of abrupt appearance, which is actually nothing more than low-profile recycled creationism. It is nonetheless more likely to infiltrate the science classroom in the future than the older versions because it has been shorn of all references to a supernatural being, as well as any other recognizable religious terminology. Instead, it argues that a nontheistic origin of the universe is statistically wildly improbable and that therefore it must be the result of intelligent design. This newest form of creationism is also more willing to accept an ancient age for the earth (although not, of course, for humankind). The strength of the new creationism is that it is more difficult to recognize as based on an assumption of biblical inerrancy. Since one must be a very sophisticated natural scientist to subject the abrupt appearance doctrine to adequate tests, its more reasonable tone will almost

certainly lead to its adoption by many teachers who would have been quick to reject older versions of creationism.

The Institute for Creation Research's influence, and its relatively strident language, is likely to be less at the forefront of the new creationism. Henry Morris and Duane Gish are nearing retirement age, and although the succession of leadership is assured (Morris's son John will succeed him), the continuation of current strategy is not. The newer, more tactically effective, creationism will be carried forth by less visible groups who are currently based more at the local level. It is also these organizations that are likely to be the architects of the future tactical decisions of the creationist movement.

Finally, the United States (as well as several other modern Western societies) is likely to become increasingly polarized as a result of the conflict between cultural fundamentalism and cultural modernism and postmodernism. This broader conflict, taking place at the deepest sociocultural level, will be reflected in an intensification of debates about many issues, and the creation–evolution debate will almost certainly remain one of these.

Far from being a mere debate over scientific evidence or good scientific method, the creation–evolution debate reflects a major dialectic within Western culture. Because one part of this dialectic is a backlash against modernism and postmodernism, it seems likely that the numbers of conservative Christians will continue to swell. This in turn will provide a ready, and perhaps widening, market for creationism. Simultaneously, those being educated outside of the conservative Christian environment will be increasingly less likely to find creationism palatable, and they can be expected to grow increasingly hostile toward the symbolic issues they associate with the cultural fundamentalists. Their rejection of creationism is especially likely if the looming struggle to improve educational achievement in the area of science is successful.

But those within the creationist-dominated schools are unlikely to have to change their ways drastically. Science textbook publishers increasingly tend to adopt a policy of segmental marketing. This publishing trend and the fact that individual science teachers are likely to continue to present creationism in their classes in a favorable light, regardless of official guidelines, shows us that no resolution of the conflict is in sight.

There is much reason to believe that Nelkin's (1982) "Space Age Fundamentalism" is not going to go away anytime soon but instead will prosper and increasingly conflict with those it sees as its enemies. This will intensify the creation–evolution debate for many years to come. The fact

that evolution represents the most scientifically valid conception of physical reality does not necessarily mean it will be widely accepted. As many social scientists, literary figures, news commentators, and even good salesmen of wares material or religious are acutely aware, most individuals construct their reality far more on the basis of what they *need* or *wish* for it to be than on the basis of the laws of science. The creation–evolution controversy is likely to be no different.

Notes

Chapter Two

1. Nineteenth-century scholars were not the first to recognize inconsistent, vague, and problematical passages in the Bible. For instance, Augustine (A.D. 354–430) took the creation account in Genesis figuratively, not literally. For him, what counted was not exactly when or how the universe began but that it had been created by God (rather than, for example, always existing) (Frye 1983).

2. Note, by the way, that the book is titled *The Origin of Species*, not *Origin of the Species*. It was concerned with the problem of how species in general originate, and in fact it had almost nothing to say about human evolution specifically. Darwin dealt with that topic in his 1871 *The Descent of Man*.

3. Although Darwin's claim that evolution had occurred was indeed quickly and widely adopted, there was less unanimity about his argument that natural selection was the mechanism that drove the process. Some scientists thought natural selection only a partial explanation, while others, called Neo-Lamarckians in the United States, espoused a kind of progressionism based on a supposed ability of individual creatures to pass on to their offspring adaptations they acquire during their separate lives. Only after the development of the science of genetics in the twentieth century did the workings of natural selection become clearer and more widely accepted.

Chapter Three

1. Deciding when scriptural language is figurative is not always easy. In Mark (10:21), for example, Jesus tells a man that he should sell all he has and give it to the poor (cited in Barr 1982). Christians—fundamentalists included— seldom interpret this as a direct command to Christ's followers to sell all they have, yet the plain reading of the passage is very straightforward.

2. Respondents were given three possible responses about the Genesis story of creation: (1) that it is literally true that God made the world in six twenty-four-hour days; (2) that "The story of creation is a true account of how God

created the world"; and (3) that "The story of Creation reflects *man's* feelings about how the world may have been created" (Rothenberg and Newport 1984, 165). Only respondents who selected the first response were considered biblical literalists. Clearly, many creationists (in our terms, old-earth creationists) might select the second answer.

3. Handberg's three-question "creationism scale" asked respondents about their support for *teaching* creationism in the schools, which is a logically distinct proposition. As we shall see in chapter 6, not only creationists but some non-creationists support such a policy for public schools.

4. When used by evangelicals, the term *Christian* usually does not have its broad meaning (which would, for instance, include Catholics) but refers only to conservative Protestants.

5. These authors generally replace or supplement evolutionary theory with purposeful divine guidance of the evolutionary process and/or a version of Lamarckianism, which involves notions (discarded by mainstream science) that acquired traits can be inherited and that evolution progresses inevitably toward complexity and perfection.

6. As Dawkins (1987) has acerbically pointed out, such rejections of evolution by nonscientists are often based on a very imperfect knowledge and understanding of relevant data, concepts, and arguments.

7. As we noted in chapter 1, creationists cannot agree among themselves on what a "kind" corresponds to in the formal taxonomic system for classifying life-forms—species, genus, order, and so on. To mainstream scientists, this indicates that *kind* is not a scientific term.

8. In adopting creationist terminology in this passage, we are using (or misusing) the term *theory* in the very broad sense of an interpretation, rather than in the more precise scientific sense discussed in chapter 5.

Chapter Four

1. Indeed, Henry Morris claims in *The Biblical Basis for Modern Science* that all the sciences, from astronomy to geophysics to anthropology, can profit from using the Bible as scientific evidence: "Whenever a Biblical passage deals either with a broad scientific principle or with some particular item of scientific data, it will inevitably be found on careful study to be fully accurate in its scientific insights. Often it will be found even to have anticipated scientific discoveries" (Morris 1984b, 20).

2. Weber (1982) and Marsden (1982; 1980, 219–21) have noted the paradox lurking in acceptance of the commonsense principle that the meaning of the Bible is plain for any reasonable person to see. If this is so, critics ask, then why are there so many different interpretations of scripture, even among those who accept the commonsense principle (such as premillennial versus postmillennial dis-

pensationalists)? Perhaps common sense is not in fact very widespread, or perhaps the meaning of the Bible is not self-evident after all.

3. Although some premillennialist and other groups are separatist, based on their belief that the society around them is irredeemably sinful (such as Womack 1982), the primary emphasis among evangelicals, including fundamentalists, in recent decades has been on patriotism and what Bellah (1975) calls civil religion, animated by the view of the United States as a nation favored by God (Wuthnow 1988, 245–51).

4. Traditionalists often assert that the Supreme Court has ruled that secular humanism is a religion. The House of Representatives seems to agree; its 1976 amendment to the National Defense Education Act provided that "no preference be granted to the religion of secular humanism" in government-aided curricula (Nelkin 1982). This claim, however, is based not on a case in which the Court directly made such a ruling but on a 1961 case (*Torcaso* v. *Watkins*) in which Justice Black, in a footnote to the decision, included secular humanism in a list of religions that, like Buddhism, do not feature belief in a personal God (Pfeffer 1988). The footnote does not constitute a definitive ruling by the Court on the question of secular humanism's religious status. This issue quickly becomes bogged down in the definition of a religion. Must a religion necessarily feature belief in the supernatural, or need it simply involve ultimate values? More fundamentally, is there a sharply defined set of widely shared beliefs and values called secular humanism? Traditionalists seem to think so, but many of those whom they label as secular humanists disagree.

5. Furthermore, Wilkins (1987) discusses *Darwinisticism* (more commonly known as evolutionism), the position that we should derive our ethics from the evolutionary process. Kitcher (1982, 198–200) and Ruse (1982, 266–81), among others, have criticized this position as a confusion of *what is* (how animals behave) with *what ought to be* (how humans, as moral agents, should behave).

6. From the old saying, "In the land of the blind, the one-eyed man is king."

7. A test is not necessarily a laboratory experiment. Scientific theories may also be tested by predicting what will be observed in the fossil record, in a sociological survey, or on the surface of the sun, and then conducting appropriate observations to see whether these predictions are fulfilled (Kitcher 1982; Brown 1986; Gould 1982b).

In an interesting variation on the "evolution-isn't-science" theme, Geisler and Anderson (1987) have proposed that the study of "origins" constitutes a different kind of science from normal "operation science." They call it "origin science" and assert that consideration of supernatural causation is permissible in such science. Such reasoning does not convince philosophers of science (such as Kitcher 1982, 75–81) for whom the concept of origin science has two serious flaws. First, it falsely proposes that the scientific study of the past (origin science) is innately different from that of the present. This would come as news to the many geologists, paleontologists, and others who propose and test theories about

the past. Secondly, Geisler and Anderson's notion confuses physical causation in the past ("How did the earth accrete from existing matter?") with questions of ultimate causation ("Is the universe itself caused?"), which are in the domain of metaphysics and theology.

8. Whether mainstream scientists regard evolution as a fact depends on the sense in which the word is used. In the strict sense, evolution is a *theory* that explains the "facts" of science—the data of the fossil record, genetics, and so on. In another sense, scientists do generally regard evolution as a fact, if by *fact* we mean a proposition regarded as "confirmed to such a degree that it would be perverse to withhold provisional assent" (Gould 1984, 119). In this vernacular sense, scientists regard atoms, gravity, and evolution as facts.

9. One such dispute among evolutionary biologists is that between the synthetic version of Darwinian theory (Mayr 1982) and the more recently proposed theory of punctuated equilibrium (Gould and Eldredge 1977; Eldredge 1985). The debate is not over whether evolution happened or the general course of evolutionary history, but over the mode and tempo of evolutionary change. Does the evolution of a descendant species from an ancestral one typically occur gradually, as synthetic theory proposes, or relatively abruptly, as punctuated equilibrium theory argues? Consensus has not been reached among evolutionary biologists. This dispute has been used (misused, according to scientists) by creationists to try to discredit evolutionary theory altogether.

Chapter Five

1. The importance of the bones was announced after only a superficial examination, and for complicated reasons, they were not thoroughly studied until the early 1950s, whereupon their bogus status became immediately apparent (Blinderman 1986). This reflects poor scientific procedure on the part of the principals early in this century, but not dishonesty—except, of course, on the part of the still-unidentified hoaxer.

2. Gish's principal source for this line of argument is O'Connell (1969), a creationist Catholic priest without apparent anthropological or geological qualifications who lived in China during the period of the discoveries. Although he never even visited the site, O'Connell decided that it was not a cave at all, but a limeworks.

3. One of the unexplored implications of strict creationism is the extraordinarily crowded and complex antediluvian ecology that is necessitated by the requirement that all known living and extinct species of organisms coexisted before the deluge. Imagine a world populated not only by all of today's living species, but also by all those found in the fossil record—dinosaurs included.

4. As Strahler (1988, 188–243) and others (such as Kitcher 1982, 128–34;

Gould 1982b) have demonstrated, flood geology suffers from fatal logical and evidentiary flaws; the fossil and geological records simply cannot be accounted for by a worldwide flood. Similarly, the supposedly human origin of the Paluxy River "mantracks" (J. Morris 1980) has been refuted (Cole and Godfrey, eds., 1985; Hastings 1988). And creationist efforts to find Noah's ark on Mount Ararat in Turkey (Zindler 1986a, 1986b) have also been fruitless.

5. In what is now the creationists' standard (Baconian) approach, Morris (1974a, 8–16) argues that evolution and related scientific ideas do not qualify as scientific theory because no one has directly observed the beginnings of the earth or humankind. He admits, however, that despite some creationists' claims to the contrary, strict creationism also fails to qualify as a theory. So he substitutes the more general term *model*. Then he argues that the "creation model" is better supported by scientific evidence than the "evolution model."

6. As originators of the theory of punctuated equilibrium (see chapter 4, note 9), Gould and Eldredge argue that traditional theory depicts evolution as too consistently slow and gradual. Their work has been quoted by creationists in such a way as to seem to agree with contentions that a lack of transitional fossils and other flaws make any evolutionary theory untenable.

7. To anyone familiar with the frequently contentious pages of scientific journals in fields such as evolutionary biology, the creationist charge that evolutionist scientists will not tolerate challenges to orthodox ideas rings hollow. What such journals do demand is that standard scientific procedures be followed, but creationists typically do not do this. Creationists seem to want to have it both ways on the issue of scientific disagreements: scientific unanimity in defending evolutionary theory against their attacks is cited as evidence of blind dogmatism, while any scientific disputes over the mode and tempo of evolutionary change are interpreted as disarray in the scientific camp, heralding the collapse of the mainstream consensus.

8. After faring unevenly in public debates (especially against Gish) in the 1970s, evolutionists began to prepare studiously for them, adopting some of the creationists' own forensic tactics (see Milne 1981). They found, for instance, that a good offense is the best defense and vigorously attacked the "science" in scientific creationism (such as their challenge to Gish concerning protein sequences). Their performances generally improved, and some debaters, such as biologist Kenneth Miller of Brown University, became especially formidable (Morris 1984a, 319). Who "wins" more debates is a largely subjective question; both sides regularly claim victory (see Lubenow 1983 for a creationist account of Gish on the debate trail, and the *Creation/Evolution Newsletter* [since 1989 called *NCSE Reports*] for anticreationist accounts). Creationists usually "pack" the audience with sympathizers from local church congregations. The side winning a majority vote of the audience in a debate, of course, may or may not have won by the sophisticated standards of forensic (debate) competition. In turn, forensic

skill in presenting a case has little relationship to the actual scientific merits of that case. In any event, the ICR has recently deemphasized debates in its overall strategy in favor of more seminars and workshops.

Chapter Six

1. The largest rural-urban difference we have found was in a study of twenty-one hundred college students at forty-one U.S. colleges and universities over the years 1974–83. It found that, when asked if evolution should be taught in public schools, only 10.4 percent of rural residents said yes, but only 9.7 percent of urban students said no (Almquist and Cronin 1988). Sharp differences in rural and urban life-styles and outlook existed very close together in Kanawha County (Moffett 1988), and these made the area ripe for conflict over which group's values should prevail in the schools.

2. Of course, these issues may also have huge economic or material implications (such as comparable worth doctrines in the case of women's liberation or medical costs passed to the taxpayers in the case of legalized abortion). But conceptualizations of status politics have claimed such issues as their own because the conflict is thought of by the participants themselves as a moral one rather than an economic one.

3. Status inconsistents are those whose levels of occupational prestige, educational attainment, and wealth or income are not congruent—for example, the uneducated small farmer who becomes rich when oil is discovered on his land or the Mafia boss with high income but very low social prestige.

4. In keeping with our earlier discussion, this New Class might be better conceptualized as a vertical status group than a horizontal class. But it remains true that in general the members of the New Class can be characterized as "middle" and "upper middle."

5. In a study by the authors of 979 college and university students around the United States, those majoring in business administration were the most likely to support creationism—over 50 percent (Harrold and Eve 1987, 80).

6. At least among the students surveyed by the authors (see note 5), creationist sentiment was likely to be higher among those majoring in the physical sciences than among those in the social sciences or in liberal arts. Interestingly, those physical sciences that tend to confront students with earth history (geological strata, fossils, and the like) had fewer creationism supporters. We suspect that students who believe in creationism have a tendency to select themselves out of majors and courses that would create cognitive dissonance for them. Perhaps this also helps explain why most of scientists who support creationism are found in the physical and applied sciences that do not normally confront the diachronic (long-term) aspects of earth history (chemists, engineers, and so on).

7. The "creation scientists" present no gestalt of science. Could creation science, for instance, get one to the moon? They will turn the table on such

charges and try to discredit evolution by pointing to missing fossil "links." Such criticism, however, overlooks the fact that the *pattern* of evidence for evolution is the crucial test, not the validity of datum considered individually.

8. Ironically, many New Age beliefs actually involve elements from non-Christian religions (such as reincarnation from Hinduism, healing the earth from many North American Indian religions, etc.).

Chapter Seven

1. According to the detailed account by Bennetta (1989a, 1989b), the original five-man evaluation appointed by the Department of Education in August 1988 included two associates of Henry Morris. It voted 3–2 to recommend approval of ICR's graduate program. The two dissenters protested strongly that the commission's report did not reflect the real situation at the institute. After examining further information on the ICR's program, the third member (who was not a Morris ally) in effect changed his vote, and the department indicated that approval was going to be denied.

However, perhaps because of political pressure applied by ICR supporters, Superintendent Honig did not then actually issue a denial of approval. Instead, the department entered into negotiations with the ICR and its representative, lawyer Wendell Bird. In March 1989 a temporary compromise was announced: the ICR could keep its program pending another review in August, but meanwhile it had to begin to upgrade it and to keep creationist "interpretations" out of its courses. This development was greeted with relief by ICR supporters and with consternation by anticreationists; as Bennetta (1989b) wondered, how could science of any sort be taught without interpretations?

In August 1989, the second committee of five examiners evaluated the ICR's program. It comprised one institute nominee and four well-known mainstream scientists from California state institutions. By a 4–1 vote, they found the ICR's program still substandard and recommend denial of approval (*NCSE Reports* 1990). The affair resulted in considerable publicity and bitterness. Both sides criticized Honig and the Department of Education bureaucracy. The creationists claimed an evolutionist conspiracy to silence them, while anticreationists charged that the department had conducted the process clumsily and had for a time bowed to political pressure in reaching the interim compromise with the ICR.

2. Without apologies to paleontologist Stephen Jay Gould, whose *The Panda's Thumb* (1980) is a best-selling collection of essays on natural history and evolutionary biology.

Chapter Eight

1. Willoughby is now editor of *The Crusader: The Voice of Religious Freedom*, the official publication of the Religious Freedom Crusade. Its publisher is a

minister of the Church of Scientology, the cult religion founded by the late science fiction writer L. Ron Hubbard. *The Crusader* covers a host of religious liberty topics, sympathetically portraying groups from Amish to Scientologists to creationists as struggling against the power of the state to practice their religious beliefs freely.

2. One exception to this generalization (*Segraves* v. *California*, in 1981) was pursued in a state court and arose directly out of a state school board struggle. For that reason we will discuss it later.

3. The same legislature, only six years before, had repealed the state's famous antievolution law—in Webb's (1988, 42) analysis, largely in an "attempt to build a more favorable image in the hope of attracting new business and industry to improve the state's poor economy." By contrast, the 1973 law, while not trying to ban evolution, took the popular step of legitimizing creationism while appearing to be "fair."

4. In view of Wendell Bird's strenuous efforts over the past decade on behalf of the creationist cause (including a stint as staff attorney for the ICR and an appearance before the Supreme Court advocating the Louisiana creationism law), we were surprised and intrigued when Bird denied (in a 1989 letter to Raymond Eve) that he is a creationist and asked that we not refer to him as such. He did not say what he *does* consider himself to be; perhaps we are to infer that he is aiding creationism in the service of a principle of his own, as ACLU attorneys defend people whose views they do not share in order to protect what they consider basic civil liberties. Complying with Bird's request, we refrain from calling him a creationist and leave the reader to arrive at his or her own judgment.

5. This is not the first time the sobriquet Scopes II has been applied; *Segraves* v. *California* was also so termed.

6. Note that here and in the Arkansas law, the word *evidences* is in the plural—a usage common in Christian apologetics but not in scientific terminology.

7. For instance, Justice Scalia, like most creationists and many others, confounded the issue of the *origin* of life with the separate question of the *evolution* of life once it had come into existence (Gould 1987b).

8. Zimmerman (1987a) sent questionnaires to all high schools in Ohio and analyzed the responses received from 404 biology teachers; he followed a similar procedure with school board presidents in that state (Zimmerman 1987–88), receiving 336 replies out of 730 questionnaires. Ellis (1986) similarly collected data on 794 Kentucky biology teachers. Eve and Dunn (1988, 1989) drew a random sample of 190 science teachers from the rolls of the National Science Teachers Association. Similarly, Affannato (1986) drew a national sample of 999 science teachers, of whom 467 responded. Nickels and Drummond (1983) surveyed 132 science teachers at a state convention. Buckner (1983) surveyed ninety-seven teachers in one Georgia county, while Boring (in an unpublished study cited in Affannato 1986) surveyed three hundred Oregon teachers.

Chapter Nine

1. We are only loosely adhering to the exact scheme that Smelser has proposed. It has been argued that his scheme is most successfully applied to the analysis of relatively short-lived "events" of collective behavior (e.g., a riot). Nonetheless, much of his scheme and terminology can be of assistance in our current task by way of providing a broad analytical structure for viewing creationism as a movement in a longitudinal perspective.

2. Seen in this context, it is not hard to see where the so-called New Age movement fits into this same schema. Many readers are aware that there has been a widespread increase in recent years in belief in occult and paranormal phenomena. Actress Shirley Maclaine has attracted millions of followers with her claims of out-of-body experiences, communication with those long dead through "channelers," and the healing power of crystals. Interest in voodoo and satanic religion has been on the increase among drug dealers and high school students. While these phenomena seem far removed from the revival of the conservative Christian movement, they are probably other facets of the same stone. What binds these topics together is the sense of threat—and often outright powerlessness—that all these groups experience in the face of modernism, with its emphasis on corporate life, secularism, consumerism, and technical expertise and rationality. Faced with a sense of powerlessness, these marginal groups are attempting to empower themselves from alternative sources.

3. *American Demographer* (September 1988, 36) reports on a study by the *Los Angeles Times* of a sample of housewives in Los Angeles. Among women whose household incomes were over $40,000, more respondents reported having sought the services of a New Age "channeler" than those of a psychotherapist, psychiatrist, or marriage counselor.

Works Cited

Abell, George, O. 1983. "The Age of the Earth and the Universe." In *Scientists Confront Creationism*, ed. L. Godfrey, 33–48. New York: Norton.

Adam, Barry. 1987. *The Rise of a Gay and Lesbian Movement*. Boston: Twayne.

Adler, Mortimer. 1967. *The Difference of Man and the Difference It Makes*. New York: Holt, Rinehart.

Adorno, T. W., et al. 1950. *The Authoritarian Personality*. New York: Harper.

Affannato, Frank E. 1986. *A Survey of Biology Teachers' Opinions about the Teaching of Evolutionary Theory and/or the Creation Model in the United States in Public and Private Schools*. Unpublished Ph.D. dissertation, University of Iowa.

Alexander, Richard. 1983. "Evolution, Creation, and Biology teaching." In *Evolution versus Creationism: The Public Controversy*, ed. J. P. Zellerburg, 90–111. Phoenix: Oryx Press.

Almquist, Alan J., and **John E. Cronin.** 1988. "Fact, Fancy, and Myth on Human Evolution." *Current Anthropology* 29(3):529–22.

American Association for the Advancement of Science. 1986. *The Continuing Crisis in Science Education: The AAAS Responds*. Washington: AAAS Publication 86-12.

Anderson, Robert Mapes. 1987. "Pentecostal and Charismatic Christianity." In *The Encyclopedia of Religion*, ed. Mircea Eliade, vol. 11:229–35. New York: Macmillan.

Arduini, Frank. 1984. Letter to editor. *Creation/Evolution Newsletter* 4(5): 14–15.

Arons, S. 1981. "The Crusade to Ban Books." *Saturday Review*, June, 17–19.

Asimov, Isaac. 1982. "The 'Threat' of Creationism." In *Speak Out*, ed. H. Vetter, 166–74. Boston: Beacon.

Associated Press. 1985. "Faith Remains Stable in U.S." *Dallas Times-Herald*, October 26.

Bainbridge, William S., and **Rodney Stark.** 1980. "Superstitions: Old and new." *The Skeptical Inquirer* 4(4):18–31.

Barker, Eileen. 1980. "Thus Spake the Scientist: A Comparative Account of

the New Priesthood and Its Organizational Bases." *Annual Review of the Social Sciences of Religion* 3:79–103.

———. 1985. "Let There Be Light: Scientific Creationism in the Twentieth Century." In *Darwinism and Divinity*, ed. John Durent, 181–204. London: Basil Blackwell.

Barr, James. 1982. "Religious Fundamentalism." *Current Affairs Bulletin* 59: 24–30.

Beale, Howard K. 1936. *Are American Teachers Free?* New York: Scribner's.

———. 1941. *A History of Freedom of Teaching in American Schools.* New York: Scribner's.

Beardsley, Tim. 1989. "Science Gains a Voice." *American Scientist* 26(1):14.

Becker, Howard. 1963. *The Outsiders.* New York: The Free Press.

Beckwith, Burnham P. 1981–82. "The Effect of Education on Religious Faith." *Free Inquiry* (Winter):26–31.

Bellah, Robert. 1975. *The Broken Covenant: American Civil Religion in Time of Trial.* New York: Seabury Press.

Bennetta, William J. 1985. "Faking It." *Pacific Discovery* 38(4):29–34.

———. 1986. *Crusade of the Credulous: A Collection of Articles about Contemporary Creationism and the Effects of That Movement on Public Education.* San Francisco: California Academy of Sciences Press.

———. 1987a. "News Reports of 'Creation Science' Are Misleading Readers." *Bulletin of the American Society of Newspaper Editors* 694 (March): 18–19.

———. 1987b. "A question of integrity." *California Science Teacher's Journal* (Spring).

———. 1987c. "Presidential Candidate Pat Robertson." *Creation/Evolution Newsletter* 7(5):8.

———. 1987d. "Two Groups Sponsor Clandestine Efforts to Put 'Creation Science' into Schools." *Creation/Evolution Newsletter* 7(6):6–8.

———. 1988a. "Telling a You-Know-What for You-Know-Whom." *California Science Teacher's Journal* 18(3):10–12.

———. 1988b. "The Rise and Fall of the Louisiana Creationism Law." *Terra*, part 1, 26(6):20–27; part 2, 27(1):16–23.

———. 1989a. "Degrees of Folly." *Bay Area Skeptics Information Sheet*, part 1, 8(2):1–4; part 2, 8(3):1–5; part 3, 8(4):3–6; part 4, 8(5):3–6; part 5, 8(7): 6–8; part 6, 8(9):6–8; part 7, 8(10):6–8; part 8, (11):6–7.

———. 1988b. "ICR Still in Business, Still Has State Approval." *The Skeptical Inquirer* 14(1):7, 9.

Ben-Yehuda, Nachman. 1985. *Deviance and Moral Boundaries: Witchcraft, the Occult, Science Fiction, Deviant Sciences, and Scientists.* Chicago: University of Chicago Press.

Bird, Wendell R. 1978. "Freedom of Religion and Science Instruction in Public Schools." *Yale Law Journal* 87:515.

——— 1979a. "Freedom from Establishment and Unneutrality in Public School

Instruction and Religious School Regulation." *Harvard Journal of Law and Public Policy* (Summer):125–205.

———. 1979b. "Resolution for Balanced Presentation of Evolution and Scientific Creationism." *Impact* series, no. 71. San Diego: Institute for Creation Research.

———. 1979c. "Evolution in the Public Schools and Creation in Students' Homes: What Creationists Can Do." *Impact* series, nos. 69–70. San Diego: Institute for Creation Research.

———. 1987. *The Supreme Court Decision and Its Meaning.* ICR *Impact* series, no. 170.

———. 1989. *'The Origin of Species' Revisited.* 2 vol. New York: Philosophical Library.

Blinderman, Charles. 1986. *The Piltdown Inquest.* Buffalo, N.Y.: Prometheus.

Blumberg, Rhoda L. 1984. *Civil Rights: The 1960s Freedom Struggle.* Boston: Twayne.

Blumer, Herbert. 1939. "Collective Behavior." In *Principles of Sociology,* ed. A. M. Lee, 67–121. New York: Barnes & Nobel.

Boone, Keith, 1989. "Reconfigured Court and Creationism." *Newsletter of the Ohio Center for Science Education* (January):1–4.

Boule Marcellin, and Henri Vallois. 1957. *Fossil Men.* New York: Dryden Press.

Bouw, Gerardus D. 1984. *With Every Wind of Doctrine: Biblical, Historical, and Scientific Perspectives of Geocentricity.* Cleveland: The Tychonian Society.

Bowler, Peter. 1989. *Evolution: The History of an Idea.* Rev. ed. Berkeley: University of California Press.

Boxer, Sarah. 1987. "Will Creationism Rise Again?" *Discover* (October):80–85.

Brace, C. Loring. 1983. "Humans in Time and Space." In *Scientists Confront Creationism,* ed. L. Godfrey, 245–82. New York: Norton.

Bronde, Scott. 1990. "Science Text Adoptions in Alabama: Part II." *NCSE Reports* 10(1):8–11.

Brown, Harold I. 1977. *Perception, Theory and Commitment: The New Philosophy of Science.* Chicago: University of Chicago Press.

———. 1986. "Creationism and the Nature of Science." *Creation/Evolution* 6(2):15–25.

Brubacher, John S., and Willis Rudy. 1976. *Higher Education in Transition.* 3rd ed. New York: Harper & Row.

Brush, Stephen G. 1983. "Ghosts from the Nineteenth Century: Creationist Arguments for a Young Earth." In *Scientists Confront Creationism,* ed. L. Godfrey, 49–84. New York: Norton.

Bryan, William Jennings. 1969 [1922]. "Education without Morality." In *Controversy in the Twenties,* ed. W. Gatewood, 226–32. Nashville: Vanderbilt University Press.

Bullock, Alan. 1985. *The Humanist Tradition in the West.* New York: Norton.

Buckner, Edward M. 1983. *Professional and Political Socialization: High School Science Teacher Attitudes on Curriculum Decisions, in the Context of the "Scientific" Creationism Campaign.* Ph.D. dissertation, Georgia State University. Ann Arbor, Mich.: University Microfilms International.

Caplow, Theodore, Howard M. Bahr, and **Bruce A. Chadwick.** 1983. *All Faithful People: Change and Continuity in Middletown's Religion.* Minneapolis: University of Minnesota Press.

Cavanaugh, Michael A. 1983. *A Sociological Account of Scientific Creationism: Science, True Science, Pseudoscience.* Ph.D. dissertation, University of Pittsburgh. Ann Arbor, Mich.: University Microfilms International.

———. 1985. "Scientific Creationism and Rationality." *Nature* 315:185–89.

———. 1986. "Secularization and the Politics of Traditionalism: The Case of the Right-to-Life Movement." *Sociological Forum* 1(2):251–83.

———. 1987. "One-eyed Social Movements: Rethinking Issues in Rationality and Society." *Philosophy of Social Science* 17:147–72.

Cazeau, Charles J., and **Stuart D. Scott, Jr.** 1979. *Exploring the Unknown: Great Mysteries Reexamined.* New York: Plenum.

Chidester, David. 1988. *Salvation and Suicide: An Interpretation of Jim Jones, the People's Temple, and Jonestown.* Bloomington, Ind.: University of Indiana Press.

Christenson, Harold T., and **Kenneth L. Cannon.** 1978. "The Fundamentalist Emphasis at Brigham Young University: 1935–1973." *Journal for the Scientific Study of Religion* 17(1):53–57.

Cloud, Preston. 1977. "'Scientific Creationism'—a New Inquisition Brewing?" In *A Compendium of Information on the Theory of Evolution–Creationism Controversy,* 83–94. National Association of Biology Teachers.

Coburn, Cynthia. 1988. "Trouble in Paradise." *Newsletter of the Ohio Center for Science Education* (July):9–11.

Cole, Henry P., and **Eugenie C. Scott.** 1982. "Creation-Science and Scientific Research." *Phi Beta Kappan* 63:557–58.

Cole, John R. 1981. "Misquoted Scientists Respond." *Creation/Evolution* 6:39–41.

———. 1988. "Some Leading Creationist Organizations." *Creation/Evolution Newsletter* 8(4):18–19.

———, and **Laurie R. Godfrey,** eds. 1985. *The Paluxy River Footprint Mystery Solved.* Special issue of *Creation/Evolution* 5(1).

Conrad, Ernest C. 1982. "Are There Human Fossils in the 'Wrong Place' for Evolution?" *Creation/Evolution* 8:14–22.

Dahrendorf, Ralf. 1959. *Class and Class Conflict in Capitalist Society.* Stanford, Calif.: Stanford University Press.

Davis, Percival, and **Dean H. Kenyon.** 1989. *Of Pandas and People.* Dallas, Tex.: Haughton.

Dawkins, Richard. 1987. *The Blind Watchmaker.* New York: Norton.

Day, Michael H. 1986. *Guide to Fossil Man.* 4th ed. Chicago: University of Chicago Press.

De Camp, L. Sprague. 1968. *The Great Monkey Trial.* Garden City, N.Y.: Doubleday.

Denton, Michael. 1986. *Evolution: A Theory in Crisis.* Bethesda, Md.: Adler and Adler.

Dolby, R. G. A. 1987. "Science and Pseudo-science: The Case of Creationism." *Zygon* 22(2):195–212.

Donaldson, Ken. 1988. "The Creationism Controversy: It's Only the Beginning." *School Library Journal* 34(7):107–113; 34(8):16–17.

Durbin, Bill, Jr. 1988. "How It All Began." *Christianity Today* (12 August): 31–46.

Eckberg, Douglas, and **Alexander Nesterenko.** 1985. "For and Against Evolution: Religion, Social Class, and the Symbolic Universe." *Social Science Journal,* 22(1):1–17.

Edwords, Frederick. 1984. *The Humanist Philosophy in Perspective.* Pamphlet distributed by the American Humanist Association, Amherst, N.Y.

Eglin, P. G. 1983. *Creationism versus Evolution: A Study of the Opinions of Georgia Science Teachers.* Ph.D. dissertation, Georgia State University.

Eiseley, Loren. 1958. *Darwin's Century.* New York: Doubleday.

Eldredge, Niles. 1982. *The Monkey Business: A Scientist Looks at Creationism.* New York: Washington Square Press.

———. 1985. *Time Frames.* New York: Simon and Schuster.

Ellis, William E. 1986. "Creationism in Kentucky: The Response of High School Biology Teachers." In *Science and Creation,* ed. R. W. Hanson, 72–91. New York: Macmillan.

Etzioni, Amitai, and **Clyde Nunn.** 1974. "The Public Appreciation of Science in Contemporary America." *Daedalus* 103:191–205.

Eve, Raymond A., and **Dana Dunn.** 1989. "High School Biology Teachers and Pseudoscientific Belief: Passing It On?" *The Skeptical Inquirer* 13(3): 260–63.

———, and ———. 1990. "Psychic Powers, Astrology, and Creationism in the Classroom." *The American Biology Teacher* 52(1):10–21.

———, and **Francis B. Harrold.** 1986. "Creationism, Cult Archaeology, and Other Pseudoscientific Beliefs: A Study of College Students." *Youth and Society* 17(4):396–421.

Ewing, J. Franklin. 1956. "The Present Catholic Attitude towards Evolution." *Anthropological Quarterly,* 24(4):123–39.

Falwell, Jerry. 1981. *Listen America!* New York: Bantam.

———. 1987. "Listen America!" In *Taking Sides: Clashing Views on Educational Issues.* 4th ed., ed. J. W. Noll, 44–52. Guilford, Conn.: Dushkin.

Faust, Scott. 1989–90. "'Only a Theory': Evolution in Texas Textbooks, New Requirements, and a Bit of History." *The Skeptic* 4(1):1, 4–6; 4(2):3–7.

Feder, Kenneth L. 1985–86. "The Challenges of Pseudoscience." *Journal of College Science Teaching* 15(3):180–86.

Ferree, Myra, and **Beth Hess.** 1985. *Controversy and Coalition: The New Feminist Movement.* Boston: Twayne.

Feyerabend, Paul. 1975. *Against Method: Outline of an Anarchistic Theory of Knowledge.* London: Verso.

Fireman, B., and **W. Gamson.** 1979. "Utilitarian Logic in the Resource Mobilization Perspective." In *The Dynamics of Social Movements,* eds. M. Zald and J. McCarthy. Cambridge, Mass.: Winthrop.

Fix, William R. 1984. *The Bone Peddlers: Selling Evolution.* New York: Macmillan.

Fowler, Dean R. 1982. "The Creationist Movement." *American Biology Teacher* 44(9):528–42.

Frazier, Kendrick. 1988. "Do 'One-fifth of *All* Scientists Reject Evolution'?" *Creation/Evolution Newsletter* 8(4):9–10.

Freeman, J. 1979. "Resource Mobilization and Strategy: A Model for Analyzing Social Movement Organization Actions." In M. Zald and J. McCarthy, eds., *The Dynamics of Social Movements.* Cambridge, Mass.: Winthrop.

———. 1983. *Social Movement of the Sixties and Seventies.* New York: Longman.

Friedman, Richard E. 1987. *Who Wrote the Bible?* New York: Summit.

Fromm, E. 1941. *Escape from Freedom.* New York: Holt, Rinehart and Winston.

Frye, Roland M. 1983. "Creation-Science against the Religious Background." In *Is God a Creationist?,* ed. R. M. Frye, 1–28. New York: Scribner's.

———, ed. 1983. *Is God a Creationist?* New York: Scribner's.

Fuerst, Paul A. 1984. "University Student Understanding of Evolutionary Biology's Place in the Creation/Evolution Controversy." *Ohio Journal of Science* 84:218–28.

Funk, Richard B., and **Fern K. Willits.** 1987. "College Attendance and Attitude Change: A Panel Study, 1970–1981." *Sociology of Education* 60:224–31.

Futuyma, Douglas J. 1983. *Science on Trial: The Case for Evolution.* New York: Pantheon.

Gabler, Mel, and **Norma Gabler,** eds. 1988. *Scientific Creationism.* Handbook no. 10. Longview, Tex.: Educational Research Analysts.

Gatewood, Willard B., Jr. 1969. Introduction. In *Controversy in the Twenties: Fundamentalism, Modernism, and Evolution,* ed. W. Gatewood, 3–46. Nashville: Vanderbilt University Press.

Geisler, Norman L. 1982. *The Creator in the Courtroom: Scopes II.* Milford, Mich.: Mott Media.

———, and **J. Kerby Anderson.** 1987. *Origin Science: A Proposal for the Creation/Evolution Controversy.* Grand Rapids, Mich.: Baker Book House.

Gilkey, Langdon. 1985. *Creationism on Trial: Evolution and God at Little Rock.* Cambridge, Mass.: Harper and Row.

Ginger, Ray. 1958. *Six Days or Forever?* Boston: Beacon.

Gish, Duane T. 1978. *Evolution: The Fossils Say No!* San Diego: Creation-Life Publishers.

————. 1985. *Evolution: The Challenge of the Fossil Record.* El Cajon, Calif.: Creation-Life Publishers.

Godfrey, Laurie R. 1981a. "Science and Evolution in the Public Eye." In *Paranormal Borderlands of Science,* ed. K. Frazier, 379–90. Buffalo, N.Y.: Prometheus.

————. 1981b. "The Flood of Antievolutionism." *Natural History* 90:4–10.

————. 1983. "Creationism and Gaps in the Fossil Record." In *Scientists confront creationism,* ed. L. Godfrey, 193–218. New York: Norton.

————. ed. 1983. *Scientists Confront Creationism.* New York: Norton.

————, and John Cole. 1987. "A Century after Darwin: 'Scientific Creationism' and Academe." In *Cult Archaeology and Creationism,* eds. F. Harrold and R. Eve, 99–123. Iowa City: University of Iowa Press.

Goldstein, K. M., and **S. Blackman.** 1978. *Cognitive Style: Five Approaches and Relevant Research.* New York: John Wiley.

Goldstone, Jack. 1986. *Revolutions: Theoretical, Comparative, and Historical Studies.* San Diego: Harcourt Brace Jovanovich.

Gottfried, Paul, and **Thomas Fleming.** 1988. *The Conservative Movement.* Boston: Twayne.

Gould, Stephen Jay. 1980. *The Panda's Thumb.* New York: Norton.

————. 1982a. "Genesis versus Geology." *Atlantic* 250(3):10–17.

————. 1982b. "On Paleontology and Prediction." *Discover* 3(7):56–57.

————. 1984. "Evolution as Fact and Theory." In *Science and Creationism,* ed. Ashley Montagu, 117–25. New York: Oxford.

————. 1987a. "William Jennings Bryan's Last Campaign." *Natural History* 96(11):16–26.

————. 1987b. "Justice Scalia's Misunderstanding." *Natural History* 96(10): 14–21.

————. 1989. "An Essay on a Pig Roast." *Natural History* (January):14–25.

————, and **Niles Eldredge.** 1977. "Punctuated Equilibria: The Tempo and Mode of Evolution Reconsidered." *Paleobiology* 3:115–151.

Gouldner, A. W. 1976. *The Dialectic of Ideology and Technology.* New York: Seabury.

————. 1979. *The Future of Intellectuals and the Rise of the New Class.* New York: Oxford University Press.

Grabiner, Judith V., and **Peter D. Miller.** 1974. "Effects of the Scopes Trial." *Science* 185:832–37.

Gray, Thomas. 1984. "University Course Reduces Belief in the Paranormal." *The Skeptical Inquirer* 8:247–51.

————. 1987. "Educational Experience and Belief in the Paranormal." In *Cult Archaeology and Creationism,* eds. F. Harrold and R. Eve, 21–33. Iowa City: University of Iowa Press.

Grose, Elaine C., and **Ronald D. Simpson.** 1982. "Attitudes of Introductory College Biology Students toward Evolution." *Journal of Research in Science Teaching* 19:15–24.

Gusfield, Joseph R. 1963. *Symbolic Crusade: Status Politics and the American Temperance Movement.* Urbana: University of Illinois Press.

Habermas, Jürgen. 1972. *Knowledge and Human Interests.* Boston: Beacon.

Hadden, Jeffrey K., and **Anson Shupe.** 1988. *Televangelism: Power and Politics on God's Frontier.* New York: Henry Holt.

Ham, Ken. 1987. *The Lie: Evolution.* San Diego: Master Books.

———. 1989. "Is God Being Outlawed in California?" *Back to Genesis,* April: a–d.

Handberg, Roger. 1984. "Creationism, Conservatism, and Ideology: Fringe Issues in American Politics." *Social Science Journal* 21(3):37–51.

Harper, Charles L., and **Kevin Leicht.** 1984. "Explaining the New Religious Right." In *New Christian Politics,* eds. D. G. Bromley and A. Shupe, 101–10. Macon, Ga.: Mercer.

Harris, Marvin. 1974. *Cows, Pigs, Wars, and Witches: The Riddles of Culture.* New York: Random House.

———. 1980. *Cultural Materialism: The Struggle for a Science of Culture.* New York: Vintage Books.

Harrold, Francis B., and **Raymond A. Eve.** 1986. "Noah's Ark and Ancient Astronauts: Pseudoscientific Beliefs about the Past among a Sample of College Students." *The Skeptical Inquirer* 11(1):61–75.

———, and ———. 1987. "Patterns of Creationist Belief among College Students." In *Cult Archaeology and Creationism: Understanding Pseudoscientific Beliefs about the Past,* eds. F. Harrold and R. Eve, 68–90. Iowa City: University of Iowa Press.

Hastings, Ronnie J. 1988. "The Rise and Fall of the Paluxy Mantracks." *Perspectives on Science and Christian Faith* 40(3):144–55.

———. 1989. "Creationists' 'Glen Rose Man' Proves to Be a Fish Tooth (as Expected)." *NCSE Reports* 9(3):14–15.

———, **Rick Neeley**, and **John Thomas.** 1989. "A Critical Look at Creationist Credentials." *The Skeptic* (North Texas Skeptics) 3(4):1, 5.

Hawking, Stephen W. 1988. *A Brief History of Time.* Toronto: Banting.

Heinz, Donald. 1983. "The Struggle to Define America." In *The New Christian Right,* eds. R. C. Liebman and R. Wuthnow, 133–48. New York: Aldine.

Herbert, Wray. 1983. "Hominids Bear Up, Become Porpoiseful." *Science News* 123:246.

———. 1987. "Fundamentalism vs. Humanism." In *Taking Sides: Clashing Views on Controversial Educational Issues.* 4th ed., ed. J. W. Noll, 53–61. Guilford, Conn.: Dushkin.

Himmelstein, J. L. 1983. "The New Right." In *The New Christian Right,* eds. R. C. Liebman and R. Wuthnow, 13–30. New York: Aldine.

Hines, Terence. 1988. *Pseudoscience and the Paranormal*. Buffalo, N.Y.: Prometheus.

Hitching, Francis. 1982. *The Neck of the Giraffe: Darwin, Evolution, and the New Biology*. New York: Mentor.

Hofstadter, Richard. 1955. "The Pseudo-conservative Revolt." In *The New American Right*, ed. Daniel Bell. New York: Criterion.

————. 1963. *Anti-Intellectualism in American Life*. New York: Knopf.

————, and Walter P. Metzger. 1955. *The Development of Academic Freedom in the United States*. New York: Columbia University Press.

Hovenkamp, Herbert. 1978. *Science and Religion in America, 1800–1860*. Philadelphia: University of Pennsylvania Press.

Hunter, James Davison. 1983. *American Evangelicalism: Conservative Religion and the Quandary of Modernity*. New Brunswick, N.J.: Rutgers University Press.

Hyers, Conrad. 1984. *The Meaning of Creation*. Atlanta: John Knox Press.

Industrial Chemist. 1988. "Readers Question Evolution." 9(2):47.

International Association for the Evaluation of Educational Achievement. 1988. *Science Achievement in Seventeen Countries: A Preliminary Report*. Oxford: Pergamon Press.

Jaki, Stanley L. 1979. *The Origin of Science and the Science of Its Origins*. South Bend, Ind.: Regnery/Gateway.

Jansma, Sidney J., Jr. 1985. *Six Days*. Grand Rapids, Mich.: privately printed.

Jenkinson, E. B. 1979. *Censors in the Classroom: The Mind Benders*. Carbondale, Ill.: Southern Illinois University Press.

Johanson, Donald, and James Shreeve. 1989. *Lucy's Child: The Discovery of a Human Ancestor*. New York: William Morrow.

Johnson, Ronald L., and E. Edward Peoples. 1987. "The Role of Scientific Understanding in College Student Acceptance of Evolution." *The American Biology Teacher* 49(2):93–98

Jones, Rhondda E. 1987. "Evolution and Creation: The Consequences of an Analysis for Education." *Interdisciplinary Science Reviews* 12(4):324–32.

Jukes, Thomas H. 1983. "Molecular Evidence for Evolution." In *Scientists confront creationism*, ed. L. Godfrey, 117–30. New York: Norton.

Katz, G. 1985. "School Censorship Rise Cited." *USA Today*, 15 August.

Kehoe, Alice B. 1983. "The Word of God." In *Scientists confront creationism*, ed. L. Godfrey, 1–12. New York: Norton.

————. 1985. "Modern Antievolutionism: The Scientific Creationists." In *What Darwin began*, ed. L. Godfrey, 165–185. Newton, Mass.: Allyn and Bacon.

————. 1987. "Scientific Creationism: Worldview, Not Science." In *Cult Archaeology and Creationism*, eds. F. Harrold and R. Eve, 11–20. Iowa City: University of Iowa Press.

Kelley, Dean M. 1972. *Why Conservative Churches Are Growing*. New York: Harper and Row.

Kenney, Robert W. 1984. Letter to the editor. *Creation/Evolution Newsletter* 4(5):15–17.

Kitcher, Philip. 1982. *Abusing Science: The Case against Creationism.* Cambridge, Mass.: MIT Press.

Klandermans, B. 1984. "Mobilization and Participation: Social-psychological Expansions of Resource Mobilization Theory." *American Sociological Review* 49:583–600.

Klein, Richard G. 1989. *The Human Career.* Chicago: University of Chicago Press.

Koestler, Arthur. 1971. *The Case of the Midwife Toad.* New York: Random House.

Kofahl, Robert E. 1977. *Handy Dandy Evolution Refuter.* San Diego: Beta Books.

———. 1980. *Handy Dandy Evolution Refuter.* Rev. ed. San Diego: Beta Books.

Kuban, Glen J. 1989. "A follow-up on Carl Baugh's Science Degrees." *The Skeptic* (North Texas Skeptics) 3(5):1–2.

Kuhn, Thomas S. 1970. *The Structure of Scientific Revolutions.* Chicago: University of Chicago Press.

La Follette, Marcel C. 1983. "Creationism in the News: Mass Media Coverage of the Arkansas Trial." In *Creationism, Science, and the Law: The Arkansas Case,* ed. M. La Follette, 189–207. Cambridge, Mass.: MIT Press.

———, ed. 1983. *Creationism, science, and the Law: The Arkansas Case.* Cambridge, Mass.: MIT Press.

La Haye, Tim. 1980. *The Battle for the Mind.* Old Tappan, N.J.: Fleming H. Revell.

Larson, Edward J. 1985. *Trial and Error: The American Controversy over Creation and Evolution.* New York: Oxford University Press.

Lebon, Gustave. 1897. *The Crowd.* London: T. Fisher.

Lehman, James D. 1982. "The Creation-Evolution Debate: Is Science Education Failing?" *Journal of College Science Teaching* 11(5):280–82.

Lewin, Roger. 1982. "A Tale with Many Connections." *Science* 215:484–87.

Liebman, Robert C., and Robert Wuthnow, eds. 1983. *The New Christian Right.* New York: Aldine.

Lipset, Seymour M. 1960. *Political Man.* New York: Doubleday.

Lubenow, Marvin L. 1983. *From Fish to Gish.* San Diego: Creation-Life Publishers.

Lyons, Gene. 1982. "Repealing the Enlightenment." *Harper's* (April):38–40, 73–78.

Madge, J. 1962. *The Origins of Scientific Sociology.* New York: The Free Press.

Maguire, Meredith B. 1987. *Religion: The Social Contract.* 2d ed. Belmont, Calif.: Wadsworth.

Marsden, George M. 1980. *Fundamentalism and American Culture.* New York: Oxford University Press.

———. 1982. "Everyone One's Own Authority? The Bible, Science, and Authority in Mid-nineteenth Century America." In *The Bible in America: essays in cultural history,* eds. N. O. Hatch and M. A. Noll, 101–20. New York: Oxford University Press.

———. 1983. "Creation vs. Evolution: No Middle Way." *Nature* 305:571–74.

———. 1984. "Understanding Fundamentalist Views of Science." In *Science and creationism,* ed. A. Montagu, 95–116. New York: Oxford University Press.

———. 1987. "Evangelical and Fundamental Christianity." In *The Encyclopedia of Religion,* ed. M. Eliade, vol. 5, 190–97. New York: Macmillan.

Maslow, Abraham. 1973. *Dominance, Self-esteem, Self-Actualization: Germinal Papers of A. H. Maslow.* R. J. Lowry, ed. Monterey, Calif.: Brooks, Cole.

Matulich, Keith. 1989. "Tarrant Divides along Familiar Lines." *Ft. Worth Star-Telegram* (11 Feb.):25–26.

Mayr, Ernst. 1982. *The Growth of Biological Thought: Diversity, Evolution, and Inheritance.* Cambridge, Mass.: Harvard University Press.

McCain, Garvin, and Erwin M. Segal. 1982. *The Game of Science,* 4th ed. Monterey, Calif.: Brooks, Cole.

McCollister, Elizabeth M., and **Kenneth S. Saladin.** 1986. "84 position statements against 'creation science.'" *Creation/Evolution Newsletter* 6(5):3.

McDonald, Kim. 1986. "Pervasive belief in 'creation science' dismays and perplexes researchers." *Chronicle of Higher Education* (Dec.)10:5, 6, 10.

McGowan, Chris. 1984. *In the beginning . . .* Buffalo N.Y.: Prometheus.

McIver, Tom. 1986a. "Ancient Tales and Space-Age Myths of Creationist Evangelism." *The Skeptical Inquirer* 10(3):258–76.

———. 1986b. "The Diversity of Creationist Bible-Science and Anti-Evolutionism." Paper delivered at the annual meeting of the American Anthropological Association.

———. 1987a. "Nebraska Man Strikes Again and Again." *Creation/Evolution Newsletter* 7(4):13–14.

———. 1987b. "A Creationist Walk through the Grand Canyon." *Creation/Evolution* 7(1):1–13.

———. 1988a. "Christian Reconstructionism, Post-millennialism, and Creationism." *Creation-Evolution Newsletter* 8(1):10–17.

———. 1988b. "Catholic Anti-Evolutionists and Historical Revisionism." *Creation/Evolution Newsletter* 8(3):15–16.

———. 1988c. "Formless and Void: Gap Theory Creationism." *Creation/Evolution* 8(3):1–24.

———. 1988d. *Anti-Evolution: An Annotated Bibliography.* Jefferson, N.C.: McFarland.

Medawar, Peter B. 1973. *The Hope of Progress.* Garden City, N.J.: Anchor.

Metzger, Walter P. 1987. "The Academic Profession in the United States." In *The Academic Profession: National, Disciplinary, and Institutional Settings,* ed. B. R. Clark, 123–208. Berkeley: University of California Press.

Midgeley, Mary. 1985. *Evolution as a Religion: Strange Hopes and Stranger Fears.* London: Methuen.

———. 1987. "Evolution as a Religion: A Comparison of Prophecies." *Zygon* 22(2):179–94.

Miller, Jon D. 1983. "Scientific Literacy: A Conceptual and Empirical Review." *Daedalus* 112:29–48.

———. 1987a. The Scientifically Illiterate." *American Demographics* 9(6):26–31.

———. 1987b. "Scientific Literacy in the United States." In *Communicating science to the public,* eds. D. Evered and M. O'Connor, 19–40. New York: Wiley.

Milne, David H. 1981. "How to Debate with the Creationists—and Win!" *American Biology Teacher* 43(5):235–45.

Mills, C. W. 1950. *White Collar.* New York: Oxford University Press.

Moffett, J. 1988. *Storm in the Mountains.* Carbondale, Ill.: Southern Illinois University Press.

Montagu, Ashley, ed. 1984. *Science and Creationism.* New York: Oxford University Press.

Moore, Helen A., and **Hugh P. Whitt,** 1986. "Multiple Dimensions of the Moral Majority Platform: Shifting Interest Group Coalitions." *The Sociological Quarterly* 27(3):423–39.

Moore, James R. 1979. *The Post-Darwinian Controversies.* Cambridge: Cambridge University Press.

Moore, John A. 1974. "Creationism in California." *Daedalus* 103:173–89.

Moore, John N. 1977a. *The Impact of Evolution on the Sciences.* ICR *Impact* series, no. 52.

——— 1977b. *The impact of evolution on the humanities and science.* ICR *Impact* series, no. 53.

———. 1983. *How to Teach Origins without ACLU Interference.* Milford, Mich.: Mott Media.

———, and **Harold S. Slusher.** 1971. *Biology: A Search for Order in Complexity.* Grand Rapids: Zondervan.

———, and ———. 1974. *Biology: A Search for Order in Complexity.* 2d ed. Grand Rapids: Zondervan.

Morris, Henry M. 1963. *The Twilight of Evolution.* Grand Rapids, Mich.: Baker.

———. 1974a. *Scientific Creationism,* general edition. San Diego: Creation-Life Publishers.

———. 1974b. *Scientific Creationism,* public school edition. San Diego: Creation-Life Publishers.

———. 1974c. *The Troubled Waters of Evolution.* San Diego: Creation-Life Publishers.

———. 1977. *The Scientific Case for Creation.* San Diego: Creation-Life Publishers.

———. 1984a. *A History of Modern Creationism.* San Diego: Master Books.

————. 1984b. *The Biblical Basis for Modern Science.* Grand Rapids, Mich.: Baker.

————. 1985. Introduction to *Six Days,* by S. Jansma, p. 5. Grand Rapids, Mich.: privately published.

————. 1989a. "1988 A Great Year! Annual Report of ICR activities." *Acts & Facts* 18(1):2, 9.

————. 1989b. "Why Fight for the ICR Graduate School?" *Acts and Facts* 18 (10):3.

————. 1989c. *The Long War against God.* Grand Rapids, Mich.: Baker.

————. 1990. *ICR, Creationism, and the 1990's.* ICR *Impact* series, no. 52.

Morris, John D. 1980. *Tracking Those Incredible Dinosaurs and the People Who Knew Them.* San Diego: Creation-Life Publishers.

————. 1988. *Noah's Ark and The Lost World.* San Diego: Master Books.

————, and Tim La Haye. 1976. *The Ark on Ararat.* Nashville: Thomas Nelson.

Moyer, Wayne. 1989. "Quality Science Education and the National Center for Science Education Goals." *NCSE Reports* 9(1):7–10.

————, and William V. Mayer. 1985. *A Consumer's Guide to Biology Textbooks.* Washington, D.C.: People for the American Way.

Mule, Lisa. 1989. "Schools Foresee No Change." *Arlington Citizen-Journal* (26 Feb.):1A, 9A.

Murray, N. Patrick, and Neal D. Buffaloe. 1983. "Creationism and Evolution: The Real Issues." In *Evolution vs. Creationism: The Education Controversy,* ed. J. P. Zetterberg, 454–76. Phoenix: Oryx Press.

National Academy of Sciences. 1984. *Science and Creationism: A View from the National Academy of Sciences.* Washington: National Academy Press.

National Commission on Excellence in Education. 1983. *A Nation at Risk: The Imperative for Educational Reform.* Washington: U.S. Government Printing Office.

National Science Foundation. 1989. "Scientific Literacy: New Survey Finds Levels Still Low in U.S., U.K." *The Skeptical Inquirer* 13(4):343–45.

NCSE Reports. 1990. "ICR's Graduate Programs Blasted by State Committee." 10(1):1, 13–15.

Nelkin, Dorothy. 1982. *The Creation Controversy: Science or Scripture in the Schools.* New York: Norton.

Nelson, Craig E. 1986. "Creation, Evolution, or Both? A Multiple Model Approach." In *Science and Creation,* ed. R. W. Hanson, 128–59. New York: Macmillan.

Nickels, Martin K. 1986. Creationists and the Australopithecines. *Creation/Evolution* 6(3):2–15.

————, and Boyce A. Drummond. 1985. "Creation/Evolution: Results of a Survey Conducted at the 1983 ISTA Convention." *Creation/Evolution Newsletter* 5(6):7–11.

Niessen, Richard. 1980. *Theistic Evolution and the Day-Age Theory.* ICR *Impact* series, no. 81.

Norelli, Richard J., and **Robert R. Proulx.** 1982. "Anti-science as a Component in the Growing Popularity of Creationism." In *Confronting the Creationists,* eds. S. Pastner and W. Haviland, 4–11. Northeastern Anthropological Association, occasional proceedings no. 1.

Norgren, Jill, and **Serena Nanda.** 1988. *American Cultural Pluralism and Law.* New York: Praeger.

Numbers, Ronald L. 1982. "Creationism in 20th-century America." *Science* 218:538–44.

————. 1986. "The Creationists." In *God and Nature: Historical Essays on the Encounter between Christianity and Science,* eds. D. Lindberg and R. Numbers, 391–423. Berkeley: University of California Press.

O'Connell, P. 1969. *Science of Today and the Problems of Genesis.* Book 1. Hawthorne, Calif.: Christian Book Club of America.

Olson, Edwin A. 1982. "Hidden Agenda behind the Evolutionist/Creationist Debate." *Christianity Today* 26(8):26–30.

Padian, Kevin. 1989a. "California Framework Committee: Victory for Evolution with a New Anti-Dogmatism Statement." *NCSE Reports* 9(1):20–21.

————. 1989b. "The California Science Framework: A Victory for Science Integrity." *NCSE Reports* 9(6):1, 10–11.

Page, Ann L., and **Donald A. Clelland.** 1978. "The Kanawha County Textbook Controversy: A Study of the Politics of Lifestyle Concern." *Social Forces* 57:265–81.

Parker, Barbara. 1980. "Creation vs. Evolution: Teaching Origin of Man." *American School Board Journal* 167(3):25–32.

Patterson, John. 1983. "Thermodynamics and Evolution." In *Scientists Confront Creationism,* ed. L. Godfrey, 99–116. New York: Norton.

————, and Robert J. Schadewald. 1985. "Creationist Science." *Creation/Evolution Newsletter* 4(4):16.

Peshkin, Alan. 1986. *God's Choice: The Total World of a Fundamentalist Christian School.* Chicago: University of Chicago Press.

Pfeffer, Leo. 1988. "How Religious Is Secular Humanism?" *The Humanist* 48(5):13–18, 50.

Pfeifer, Edward J. 1974. "United States." In *The Comparative Reception of Darwinism,* ed. T. Glick, 168–206. Austin: University of Texas Press.

Poloma, Margaret M. 1982. *The Charismatic Movement: Is There a New Pentecost?* Boston: Twayne.

————. 1986. "Pentecostals and Politics in North and Central America." In *Prophetic Religions and Politics,* eds. J. Hadden and A. Shupe, 328–52. New York: Paragon House.

Price, Jerome B. 1989. *The Antinuclear Movement,* rev. ed. Boston: Twayne.

Price, David, John Wiester, and **Walter Hearn.** 1986. *Teaching Science in a Climate of Controversy.* Ipswich, Mass.: American Scientific Affiliation.

Price, George McCready. 1926. *The New Geology,* rev. ed. Mountain View, Calif.: Pacific Press.

218 *Works Cited*

Prince, Robert W. 1985. *An Examination of Henry M. Morris's Interpretation of Biblical Creation.* Ph.D. dissertation, Southwestern Baptist Theological Seminary. Ann Arbor, Mich.: University Microfilms International.

Pun, Pattle P. T. 1982. *Evolution: Nature and Scripture in Conflict?* Grand Rapids, Mich.: Zondervan.

Quebedeaux, Richard. 1978. *The Worldly Evangelicals.* New York: Harper.

Radner, Daisie, and **Michael Radner.** 1982. *Science and Unreason.* Belmont, Calif.: Wadsworth.

Reapsome, James W. 1980. "Religious Values: Reflection of Age and Education." *Christianity Today* 24(9):23–25.

Reidinger, Paul. 1987. "Creationism and the First Amendment." *ABA Journal* (Jan.) 1:35.

Rescher, Nicholas. 1967. *Studies in Arabic Philosophy.*

Robertson, Pat. 1986. *America's Dates with Destiny.* Nashville, Tenn.: Thomas Nelson.

Rokeach, M. 1960. *The Open and Closed Mind.* New York: Basic Books.

Roof, Wade Clark. 1986. "The New Fundamentalism: Rebirth of Political Religion in America." In *Prophetic religions and politics,* eds. J. K. Hadden, and A. Shupe. New York: Paragon House.

Root-Bernstein, Robert. 1984. "On Defining a Scientific Theory: Creationism Considered." In *Science and Creationism,* ed. Ashley Montagu, 64–94. New York: Oxford University Press.

Rose, Susan D. 1988. *Keeping Them Out of the Hands of Satan: Evangelical Schooling in America.* New York: Routledge.

Roszak, Theodore. 1987. "Evolution." In *The Encyclopedia of Religion,* ed. Mircea Eliade, vol. 5, 208–14. New York: Macmillan.

Rothenberg, Stuart, and **Frank Newport.** 1984. *The Evangelical Voter: Religion and Politics in America.* Washington: The Institute for Government and Politics.

Ruse, Michael. 1979. *The Darwinian Revolution: Science Red in Tooth and Claw.* Chicago: University of Chicago Press.

———. 1982. *Darwinism Defended: A Guide to the Evolution Controversies.* Reading, Mass.: Addison-Wesley.

———. 1984. "A Philosopher's Day in Court." In *Science and Creationism,* ed. Ashley Montagu, 311–42. New York: Oxford University Press.

———, ed. 1988. *But Is It Science? The Philosophical Question in the Creation/ Evolution Controversy.* Buffalo, N.Y.: Prometheus.

Rushdoony, Rousas J. 1980. "The Necessity for Creationism." *Creation Social Science and Humanities Quarterly* 3(1):5–14.

Sagan, Carl. 1980. *Cosmos.* New York: Random House.

Saladin, Kenneth S. 1986. "Educational Approaches to Creationist Politics in Georgia." In *Science and creation,* ed. R. W. Hanson, 104–27. New York: Macmillan.

Sarna, Nahum. 1983. "Understanding Creation in Genesis." In *Is God a Creationist?* ed. R. M. Frye, 155–74. New York: Scribner's.

Schadewald, Robert J. 1981–82. "Scientific Creationism, Geocentricity, and the Flat Earth." *The Skeptical Inquirer* 6(2):41–48.

———. 1983a. "The Evolution of Bible-Science.' In *Scientists Confront Creationism,* ed. L. Godfrey. 283–300. New York: Norton.

———. 1983b. "Creationist Pseudoscience." *The Skeptical Inquirer.* 8:22–35.

———. 1987. "The 1987 National Creation Conference." *Creation/Evolution Newsletter* 7(6):17–22.

———. 1988. "The ICR Summer Institute, July 11–15, 1988." *Creation/Evolution Newsletter* 8(5):14–16.

———. 1989a. "Shake-up at the Bible-Science Association." *NCSE Reports* 9(3):18.

———. 1989b. "Creationism in Flux." *NCSE Reports* 9(5):4–5.

Scott, Eugenie C. 1986. "Anti-evolutionism, Scientific Creationism, and Education." *Practicing Anthropologist* 8(3–4):24–25.

———. 1987. "Anti-evolutionism, Scientific Creationism, and Physical Anthropology." *Yearbook of Physical Anthropology* 30:21–39.

———. 1989a. "New Creationist Book on the Way." *NCSE Reports* 9(2):21.

———. 1989b. "Good News, Bad News from Texas." *NCSE Reports* 9(2):4–6.

———. 1990. Review of *Of Pandas and People,* by D. Kenyon and P. Davis. *NCSE Reports* 10(1):16–18.

———, and **Henry P. Cole.** 1985. "The Elusive Basis of Creation 'Science.'" *Quarterly Review of Biology* 60:21–30.

Shrivman, David. 1989. "Religious Right Drops High-Profile Tactics, Works on Local Level." *Wall Street Journal,* 26 September.

Shupe, Anson, and **William A. Stacey.** 1982. *Born-again Politics and the Moral Majority: What Social Surveys Really Show.* New York: Edwin Mellen.

——— and ———. 1983. "The Moral Majority Constituency." In *The New Christian Right: Mobilization and Legitimation,* eds. R. C. Liebman and R. Wuthnow, 103–16. New York: Aldine.

Simonds, Robert L. 1989. *Teachers Can Teach Creation Science in the Classroom.* ICR *Impact* series, no. 196.

Simpson, John H. 1983. "Moral Issues and Status Politics." In *The New Christian Right,* eds. R. C. Liebman and R. Wuthnow, 187–205. New York: Aldine.

Singer, Barry, and Victor A. Benassi. 1981. "Occult Beliefs." *American Scientist* 69:49–55.

Skehan, James W. 1983. "Theological Basis for a Judeo-Christian Position on Creationism." *Journal of Geological Education* 31:307–14.

———. 1986. *Modern Science and the Book of Genesis.* Washington: National Science Teachers Association.

Skoog, Gerald. 1979. "The Topic of Evolution in Secondary School Biology Textbooks: 1900–1977." *Science Education* 63(5):621–40.

———. 1984. "The Coverage of Evolution in High School Biology Textbooks Published in the 1980s." *Science Education* 68:117–28.

———. n.d. "Fact Sheet on Evolution/Creationism Controversy" (Unpublished document).

Slusher, Harold S. 1981. *Critique of Radiometric Dating Methods*, rev. ed. San Diego: Creation-Life Publishers.

Smelser, Neil J. 1962. *Theory of Collective Behavior.* New York: The Free Press.

Spitz, Lewis W. 1987. "Humanism." In *The Encyclopedia of Religion*, ed. Mircea Eliade, vol. 6:511–15. New York: Macmillan.

Stark, Rodney, and **William Sims Bainbridge.** 1985. *The Future of Religion.* Berkeley: University of California Press.

Stempien, Richard, and **Sarah Coleman.** 1985. "Processes of Persuasion: The Case of Creation Science." *Review of Religious Research* 27(2):169–77.

Stiebing, William H., Jr. 1984. *Ancient Astronauts, Cosmic Collisions, and Other Popular Theories about Man's Past.* Buffalo, N.Y.: Prometheus.

Strahler, Arthur N. 1988. *Science and Earth History: The Evolution/Creation Controversy.* Buffalo, N.Y.: Prometheus.

Stutz, Terrence. 1989. "Fundamentalists Assail Proposed Evolution Rule for Textbooks." *Dallas Morning News,* 11 February, 32A.

Sweet, Leonard I. 1984. "The 1960s: The Crisis of Liberal Christianity and the Public Emergence of Evangelicalism." In *Evangelicalism and Modern America*, ed. G. Marsden, 29–45. Grand Rapids, Mich.: Eerdmans.

Szasz, Thomas. 1974. *The Myth of Mental Illness.* New York: Harper and Row.

Talty, William R. 1988. Review of Gerardus Bouw's *With Wind of Doctrine. Bible-Science Newsletter,* April 26:18.

Tanner, Daniel. 1972. *Secondary Education: Perspectives and Prospects.* New York: Macmillan.

Tatina, Robert. 1988. "Creationism in South Dakota Schools." *Newsletter of the Ohio Center for Science Education* (October): 1–2.

Thaxton, Charles B., Walter L. Bradley, and Roger L. Olsen. 1984. *The Mystery of Life's Origins: Reassessing Current Theories.* New York: Philosophical Library.

Thwaites, William M. 1986. "A Two-model Creation versus Evolution Course." In *Science and Creation*, ed. R. W. Hanson, 92–103. New York: Macmillan.

———. 1989. Review of *Evolution: A Theory in Crisis*, by Michael Denton. *NCSE Reports* 9(4):14–17.

Toumey, Christopher P. 1986. "Three Species of Creationism." Paper presented at the annual meeting of the American Anthropological Association.

Trefil, James S. 1978. "A Consumer's Guide to Pseudoscience." *Saturday Review* (April):16–21.

Trow, M. 1958. "Small Businessmen, Political Tolerance and Support for McCarthy. *American Journal of Sociology* 64:270–81.

Truzzi, Marcello. 1979. "On the Reception of Unconventional Scientific Claims." In *The Reception of Unconventional Science,* ed. S. Mauskopf, 125–37. Boulder, Colo.: Westview.

Turner, Frederick. (forthcoming). *Rebirth of Values.* Albany, N.Y.: State University of New York Press.

Turner, Ralph H., and Lewis M. Killian. 1987. *Collective Behavior.* 3rd ed. Englewood Cliffs, N.J.: Prentice-Hall.

Tyson-Bernstein, Harriet. 1988. *A Conspiracy of Good Intentions: America's Textbook Fiasco.* Washington: Council for Basic Education.

Van Till, Howard J., Davis A. Young, and **Clarence Menninga.** 1989. *Science Held Hostage: What's Wrong with Creation Science and Evolutionism.* Downer's Grove, Ill.: Intervarsity Press.

Vaughan, Ted R., Douglas H. Smith, and **Gideon Sjoberg.** 1966. "The Religious Orientations of American Natural Scientists." *Social Forces* 44:519–26.

Volpe, E. Peter. 1984. "The Shame of Science Education." *American Zoologist* 24:433–41.

Wald, Kenneth D. 1987. *Religion and Politics in the United States.* New York: St. Martin's Press.

———, **Dennis E. Owen,** and **Samuel S. Hill, Jr.** 1989. "Evangelical Politics and Status Issues." *Journal for the Scientific Study of Religion* 28(1):1–16.

Walsh, John. 1982. "Public Attitude Toward Science Is Yes, but—." *Science* 215:270–72.

———. 1988. "U.S. Science Students near Foot of Class." *Science* 239:1237.

Waltke, Bruce. 1988. "The First Seven Days." *Christianity Today* (12 August):42–46.

Watchtower Bible and Tract Society. 1985. *Life—How Did It Get Here? By Evolution or Creation?* New York: Watchtower Bible and Tract Society of New York.

Webb, George E. 1983. "The 'Baconian' Origins of Scientific Creationism." *National Forum* 62:33–35.

———. 1986. "'Facts' or 'mere theory?' Continuity among American creationists." Paper delivered at the annual meeting of the American Anthropological Association.

———. 1988. "Demographic Change and Antievolution Sentiment: Tennessee as a Case Study." *Creation/Evolution* 8(3):37–44.

Weber, Timothy P. 1982. "The Two-edged Sword: The Fundamentalist Use of the Bible." In *The Bible in America: Essays in Cultural History,* eds. N. O. Hatch and A. Noll, 101–20. New York: Oxford University Press.

Whitcomb, John C., and **Henry Morris.** 1961. *The Genesis Flood: The Biblical Record and Its Scientific Implications.* Grand Rapids, Mich.: Baker.

Wilkins, Walter J. 1987. *Science and Religious Thought: A Darwinism Case Study.* Ann Arbor, Mich.: UMI Research Press.

Williams, Robert C. 1983. "Scientific Creationism: An Exegesis for a Religious Doctrine." *American Anthropologist* 85(1):92–102.

Wilson, R. J., ed. 1967. *Darwinism and the American Intellectual.* Homewood, Ill.: Dorsey.

Wolf, John, and James S. Mellet. 1985. "The Role of 'Nebraska Man' in the Creation/Evolution Debate." *Creation/Evolution* 5(2):31–44.

Womack, Sheila A. 1982. Creationism vs. Evolutionism: The Problem for Cultural Relativity. In *Confronting the Creationists*, eds. S. Pastner and W. Haviland, 27–34. Northeastern Anthropological Association, Occasional Proceedings, no. 1.

Woodward, Arthur, and David L. Elliott. 1987. "Evolution and Creationism in High School Textbooks." *The American Biology Teacher* 49(3):165–70.

Wuthnow, Robert. 1983. "The Political Rebirth of American Evangelicals." In *The New Christian Right: Mobilization and Legitimation,* eds. R. C. Lieberman and R. Wuthnow, 168–85. New York: Aldine.

———. 1988. *The Restructuring of American Religion.* Princeton: Princeton University Press.

Young, Davis A. 1982. *Christianity and the Age of the Earth.* Grand Rapids, Mich.: Zondervan.

Zald, M., and J. McCarthy. 1979. *The Dynamics of Social Movements: Resource Mobilization, Social Control, and Tactics.* Cambridge, Mass.: Winthrop.

Zimmerman, Michael. 1986. "The Evolution-Creation Controversy: Opinions from Students at a 'Liberal' Liberal Arts College." *Ohio Journal of Science* 86:134–139.

———. 1987a. "The Evolution–Creation Controversy: Opinions of Ohio High School Biology Teachers." *Ohio Journal of Science* 87:115–25.

———. 1987b. "That Court Ruling Won't Stop the Creationists." *Creation/ Evolution Newsletter* 7(5):4–5.

———. 1987–88. "Ohio School Boards Presidents' Views on the Evolution–Creation Controversy." *Newsletter of the Ohio Center for Science Education,* October 1987 and January 1988.

———. 1989. "Hiding at the National Science Foundation." *Newsletter of the Ohio Center for Science Education* (April):1–2.

Zindler, Frank. 1985. "Maculate Deception: The 'Science' of Creationism." *American Atheist* (March):23–26.

———. 1986a. "Of Astro-Nuts and Arko-nauts: Noah's Ark and the Space Age." *American Atheist* (July):36–39.

———. 1986b. "Stalking the Elusive Mountain Boat: The Quest for Noah's Ark." *American Atheist* (August):28–31.

Zurcher, L. A. 1971. "The Anti-pornography Campaign: A Symbolic Crusade." *Social Problems* 19:217–38.

Bibliographic Essay

The literature relevant to the creation–evolution controversy is truly vast, even if one ignores periodicals and concentrates on books alone. Here we can only suggest some of the most important and influential works.

Antievolutionist Books

McIver's encyclopedic *Anti-evolution: An Annotated Bibliography* (1988) is an indispensable guide to the literature. Still the best overall introduction to the dominant form of antievolutionism—classic strict creationism—is Henry Morris's *Scientific Creationism* (1974), while his *The Biblical Basis for Modern Science* (1984) updates and extends the scope of creation science; for Morris, science and all other sources of knowledge are subordinate to the Bible. In *The Long War against God* (1989), Morris details his view of the origins and pernicious effects of evolution. *Evolution: The Challenge of the Fossil Record* by Duane Gish (1985) is the most detailed creationist critique of mainstream understandings of the fossil record and a good exemplar of Gish's combative style. It is a revised and retitled version of his *Evolution? The Fossils Say No!* (1978), which, like Morris's *Scientific Creationism,* was issued in two editions: a "general" edition, complete with scriptural arguments and citations, and a "public school" one, with those elements removed. Wendell Bird's *The Origin of Species Revisited* (1989) is a massive two-volume work based on his legal briefs prepared for the Supreme Court in the 1987 Louisiana case. It presents detailed analyses of the scientific, philosophical, and legal aspects of creationism from the cause's main legal advocate.

Old-earth antievolutionism is not so well represented by published works, but a good starting point is the pamphlet *Teaching Science in a Climate of Controversy* (Price et al., 1986), sponsored by the American Scientific Affiliation. The Foundation for Thought and Ethics's commercially published *The Mystery of Life's Origins* (Thaxton et al., 1984) is complex and demanding, saving its creationist message for the last chapter. Young's (1982) *Christianity and the Age of the Earth* shows in detail why a geologist who is an old-earth creationist cannot accept a recent creation. And *Science Held Hostage* by Van Till, Young, and Menninga

223

(1988) presents strict creationism and evolutionary naturalism as equally incorrect. Michael Denton's *Evolution: A Theory in Crisis* (1986) is probably the best of the noncreationist books criticizing evolutionary theory.

Anticreationist Books

There are a host of books intended primarily to refute creationist claims and defend mainstream science but that inevitably include some analysis of creationism as well. Perhaps the best short treatment is *The Monkey Business* by paleontologist Niles Eldredge (1982). Paleontologist Douglas Futuyma's *Science on Trial: The Case for Evolution* (1983) is a well-written medium-length treatment. Chris McGowan's *In the Beginning. . .* (1984) concentrates on creationist claims about the fossil record. And geologist Arthur Strahler's monumental *Science and Earth History: The Evolution/Creation Controversy* covers nearly all aspects of the dispute in detail. Two edited collections of essays are especially valuable for broad coverage and expert analyses: Laurie Godfrey's *Scientists Confront Creationism* (1983) and Ashley Montagu's *Science and Creationism* (1984).

Of particular interest as clearly written analyses of creationism from the perspective of the history and philosophy of science are Philip Kitcher's unsparing *Abusing Science: The Case Against Creationism* (1982) and Michael Ruse's *Darwinism Defended: A Guide to the Evolution Controversies. Is God a Creationist?*, edited by Roland Frye (1983), examines the theological basis of creationism from a mainstream religious viewpoint and finds it wanting.

Religious, Historical, and Sociological Background

An invaluable source for understanding creationism in its historical religious context is George Marsden's *Fundamentalism in American Culture* (1980). Insightful sociological studies of contemporary conservative Christianity include James Hunter's *American Evangelicalism: Conservative Religion and the Quandary of Modernity* (1983), and *Televangelism: Power and Politics in God's Frontier* (1988), by Jeffrey Hadden and Anson Shupe. Kenneth Wald's *Religion and Politics in the United States* (1987) helps to set creationism in a context of church-state disputes, as does *The New Christian Right*, edited by R. C. Liebman and Robert Wuthnow (1983). Sociologist Dorothy Nelkin's *The Creation Controversy: Science or Scripture in the Schools* (1982) is an informative chronicle and analysis of the creationist movement up to the early 1980s. And *Trial and Error: The American Controversy over Creationism*, by Edward Larson (1985), combines thorough coverage of the legal aspects of the struggle with a broad historical overview. Finally, Henry Morris's *History of Modern Creationism* (1984) is a valuable account by a major participant in the movement.

Evolution

For the historical development of evolutionary thought and its replacement of natural theology, see Peter Bowler's *Evolution: The History of an Idea* (2d ed., 1989) and Michael Ruse's *The Darwinian Revolution: Science Red in Tooth and Claw* (1979). *The Blind Watchmaker* by Richard Dawkins (1987) is a highly readable account of current evolutionary theory. Finally, Richard Klein's *The Human Career* (1989) is an excellent and up-to-date account of human biological and cultural evolution.

Sociological Theory and Analysis

For an excellent account of recent thinking on the sociology of science and pseudoscience, see Nachman Ben-Yehuda's *Deviance and Moral Boundaries: Witchcraft, the Occult, Science Fiction, Deviant Sciences, and Scientists* (1985). For a very good reference on the sociology of science and the phenomenological forces and history involved in the production of scientific creationism, see Michael Cavanaugh's article "Scientific Creationism and Rationality" (1985) as well as his "One-eyed Social Movements: Rethinking Issues in Rationality and Society" (1987). Joseph Gusfield's article entitled "Symbolic Crusade: Status Politics and the American Temperance Movement" (1963) is a classic and early presentation of the analytical conception of status politics and its application to a specific social movement. B. Klandermans's "Mobilization and Participation: Social-psychological Expansions of Resource Mobilization Theory" (1984) and M. Zald and J. McCarthy's *The Dynamics of Social Movements: Resource Mobilization, Social Control, and Tactics* (1979) give an excellent overview and critique of the latest thinking in the use of resource mobilization theory for the analysis of social movements. Ann Page and Donald Clelland's "The Kanawha County Textbook Controversy: A Study of the Politics of Lifestyle Concern" (1978) is a seminal article on the politics of life-style concern and resultant struggles for the control of the means of cultural reproduction. Neil Smelser's *Theory of Collective Behavior* (1962) is probably still the most widely used scheme for analyzing episodes of collective behavior, and he presents his classic determinants of collective behavior in great detail. Finally, L. A. Zurcher's "The Anti-Pornography Campaign: A Moral Crusade" (1971) is another very good example of the application of status politics theory to the analysis of a specific social movement.

Index

ABA Journal, 164
ACLU, 25, 138, 149–50, 152, 169
Aardsma, Gerald, 121
abortion, 42, 61, 118
academic freedom, 16, 25, 150
Academic Freedom Legal Defense Fund,
125
Accelerated Christian Education (ACE),
134
Act 590, 149–50
Acts & Facts, 121, 124
Adam and Eve, 17
Adler, Mortimer, 45
Adorno, Theodor W., 99, 100: The
Authoritarian Personality, 100
Agassiz, Louis, 13
Aguillard v. Treen, 152
AIDS, 118
Alabama Board of Education, 131
Alexander, Richard, 79
alienation, 140–41, 180
Alpha Omega Institute, 123
American Anthropological Association,
138
American Association for the
Advancement of Science, 138, 175
American Civil Liberties Union. See
ACLU
American Coalition for Traditional
Values, 134
American Humanist Association (AHA),
59, 137–38, 174
American Jewish Congress, 139

American School Board Journal, 164
American Scientific Affiliation (ASA), 52,
132–33
American Society of Biological Chemists,
138
American Society of Zoologists, 139
Americans United for the Separation of
Church and State, 139
amino acids, 82–83
antievolution movement of the 1920s,
20–29; see also countermovement
antipornography movement, 104, 106
apocalyptic separatism, 49
Apologetics Press, 134
Ark Today, The, 127
Arkansas Law, 149–51
Armstrong, Herbert W., 47
Asimov, Isaac, 81, 136, 137
Associated Press/NBC poll, 88
Association of Orthodox Jewish
Scientists, 132
atomic theory, 65
"atrocity tales," 102
Augustine, 195n1
Australia, 5
"authoritarian personality," 99–102
Averroës and averroism, 55–56, 116, 181

BSA, 53, 126–27, 188
BSCS, 28–29, 144, 158, 176, 183
Bacon, Francis, and Baconianism, 14–15,
18, 19, 61–62, 73, 76, 85–86, 147,
179, 190; see also facts; theories

226

Baker Book House, 134
Bakker, Jim, 47
Balanced Treatment of Creation Science Act. *See* Act 590
Baltimore Creation Fellowship, 128
Baptist Bible Fellowship, 38
Baugh, Reverend Carl, 129, 169
Bay Area Skeptics, 137
Bible, inerrancy of, 2, 10, 37, 41–42, 54–56, 72, 110, 116, 179, 181, 184, 190, 191, 196n1, 196–97n2; *see also* Genesis; Noah's flood
Bible Science Association. *See* BSA
Bible-Science Newsletter, 126
"Big Bang," theory, 44
biology education, 10, 27–29; *see also* textbook issues
Biology for Beginners (Moon), 27
Biological Sciences Curriculum Study. *See* BSCS
Bird, Wendell, 147–48, 150, 152, 153, 155, 161, 164, 202n4
black evangelicals, 43–44
Blount, Reverend W. A., 149
Blumer, Herbert, 7
Bob Jones University, 133
Bookwatch Reviews, 136
Boule, Marcellin, and Henri Vallois: *Fossil Men,* 77
Bouw, Gerardus, 130
Brennan, Justice William, 153
Bromley, D. Allen Bromley, 91
Broocks, Rice, 128
Bryan, William Jennings, 22–25, 26, 52
Buchanan, John, 36, 138
"bystander public," 87

CRS, 52, 53, 125–26, 150
California State Board of Education, 156–58
capitalism, robber-baron, 23
Card Stacking, 89
catastrophism, 15–16
Cavanaugh, Michael, 5, 51, 55, 62, 85, 106, 111, 113–14
Center for Creation Studies, 124–25
charismatic Christianity, 39–40
Children of Mary, 132

Christian Educators' Association International, 133
Christian Heritage College, 53, 121, 127, 133
Christian Nation concept, 189
Christian Scholasticism, 55
Christians of Rome, 7
Chronicle of Higher Education, 154
Church of Jesus Christ of the Latter Day Saints, 40
Church of Scientology, 202n1
Citizens against Federal Establishment of Evolutionary Dogma, 126
Citizens for Excellence in Education (CEE), 133, 159
Citizens for Fairness in Education (CFE), 126, 148
Civil Rights Act, 69
civil rights movement, 43–44, 69
Clark, Steve, 150
class politics or positional politics, 102
Coffin, Harold, 150
colleges, American, 13; *see also* Ph. D. degree; professionalization
College of Advanced Education, 129
Committee for the Scientific Investigation of Claims of the Paranormal (CSICOP), 136–37, 174
Committees of Correspondence, 136, 169
Concerned Women for America, 134
Conlan, Representative John, 154
Constitution of the United States, 10; *see also* First Amendment
Consumer's Guide to Biology Textbooks, A, 138
cosmpolitanism, 110–11
Council for Democratic and Secular Humanism, 137
countermovement, 6, 135–39, 167–70
courts, 143–46, 188–89
Creatio ex Nihilo, 5
Creation Evidences Museum, 129
creation-evolution controversy, 3, 28, 60–61, 89, 117: implications of, 9–11
Creation/Evolution, 137–38
Creation/Evolution Newsletter, 136, 137–38

DATE DUE			
DEC 04 99			
MAY 0 1 20			

STOP!

This is the back of the book.
You wouldn't want to spoil a great ending!

This book is printed "manga-style," in the authentic Japanese right-to-left format. Since none of the artwork has been flipped or altered, readers get to experience the story just as the creator intended. You've been asking for it, so TOKYOPOP® delivered: authentic, hot-off-the-press, and far more fun!

DIRECTIONS

If this is your first time reading manga-style, here's a quick guide to help you understand how it works.

It's easy… just start in the top right panel and follow the numbers. Have fun, and look for more 100% authentic manga from TOKYOPOP®!

ALSO AVAILABLE FROM 🐢 TOKYOPOP®

MANGA

.HACK//LEGEND OF THE TWILIGHT
@LARGE
A.I. LOVE YOU February 2004
AI YORI AOSHI January 2004
ANGELIC LAYER
BABY BIRTH
BATTLE ROYALE
BATTLE VIXENS April 2004
BIRTH May 2004
BRAIN POWERED
BRIGADOON
B'TX January 2004
CARDCAPTOR SAKURA
CARDCAPTOR SAKURA: MASTER OF THE CLOW
CARDCAPTOR SAKURA: BOXED SET COLLECTION 1
CARDCAPTOR SAKURA: BOXED SET COLLECTION 2
    March 2004
CHOBITS
CHRONICLES OF THE CURSED SWORD
CLAMP SCHOOL DETECTIVES
CLOVER
COMIC PARTY June 2004
CONFIDENTIAL CONFESSIONS
CORRECTOR YUI
COWBOY BEBOP: BOXED SET THE COMPLETE
    COLLECTION
CRESCENT MOON May 2004
CREST OF THE STARS June 2004
CYBORG 009
DEMON DIARY
DIGIMON
DIGIMON SERIES 3 April 2004
DIGIMON ZERO TWO February 2004
DNANGEL April 2004
DOLL May 2004
DRAGON HUNTER
DRAGON KNIGHTS
DUKLYON: CLAMP SCHOOL DEFENDERS
DV June 2004
ERICA SAKURAZAWA
FAERIES' LANDING January 2004
FAKE
FLCL
FORBIDDEN DANCE
FRUITS BASKET February 2004
G GUNDAM
GATEKEEPERS
GETBACKERS February 2004
GHOST! March 2004
GIRL GOT GAME January 2004
GRAVITATION
GTO

GUNDAM WING
GUNDAM WING: BATTLEFIELD OF PACIFISTS
GUNDAM WING: ENDLESS WALTZ
GUNDAM WING: THE LAST OUTPOST
HAPPY MANIA
HARLEM BEAT
I.N.V.U.
INITIAL D
ISLAND
JING: KING OF BANDITS
JULINE
JUROR 13 March 2004
KARE KANO
KILL ME, KISS ME February 2004
KINDAICHI CASE FILES, THE
KING OF HELL
KODOCHA: SANA'S STAGE
LAMENT OF THE LAMB May 2004
LES BIJOUX February 2004
LIZZIE MCGUIRE
LOVE HINA
LUPIN III
LUPIN III SERIES 2
MAGIC KNIGHT RAYEARTH I
MAGIC KNIGHT RAYEARTH II February 2004
MAHOROMATIC: AUTOMATIC MAIDEN May 2004
MAN OF MANY FACES
MARMALADE BOY
MARS
METEOR METHUSELA June 2004
METROID June 2004
MINK April 2004
MIRACLE GIRLS
MIYUKI-CHAN IN WONDERLAND
MODEL May 2004
NELLY MUSIC MANGA April 2004
ONE April 2004
PARADISE KISS
PARASYTE
PEACH GIRL
PEACH GIRL CHANGE OF HEART
PEACH GIRL RELAUNCH BOX SET
PET SHOP OF HORRORS
PITA-TEN January 2004
PLANET LADDER February 2004
PLANETES
PRIEST
PRINCESS AI April 2004
PSYCHIC ACADEMY March 2004
RAGNAROK
RAGNAROK: BOXED SET COLLECTION 1
RAVE MASTER
RAVE MASTER: BOXED SET March 2004

ALSO AVAILABLE FROM ⚬TOKYOPOP®

REALITY CHECK
REBIRTH
REBOUND
REMOTE June 2004
RISING STARS OF MANGA December 2003
SABER MARIONETTE J
SAILOR MOON
SAINT TAIL
SAIYUKI
SAMURAI DEEPER KYO
SAMURAI GIRL REAL BOUT HIGH SCHOOL
SCRYED
SGT. FROG March 2004
SHAOLIN SISTERS
SHIRAHIME-SYO: SNOW GODDESS TALES December 2004
SHUTTERBOX
SNOW DROP January 2004
SOKORA REFUGEES May 2004
SORCEROR HUNTERS
SUIKODEN May 2004
SUKI February 2004
THE CANDIDATE FOR GODDESS April 2004
THE DEMON ORORON April 2004
THE LEGEND OF CHUN HYANG
THE SKULL MAN
THE VISION OF ESCAFLOWNE
TOKYO MEW MEW
TREASURE CHESS March 2004
UNDER THE GLASS MOON
VAMPIRE GAME
WILD ACT
WISH
WORLD OF HARTZ
X-DAY
ZODIAC P.I.

NOVELS

KARMA CLUB APRIL 2004
SAILOR MOON

ART BOOKS

CARDCAPTOR SAKURA
MAGIC KNIGHT RAYEARTH
PEACH GIRL ART BOOK April 2004

ANIME GUIDES

COWBOY BEBOP ANIME GUIDES
GUNDAM TECHNICAL MANUALS
SAILOR MOON SCOUT GUIDES

CINE-MANGA™

CARDCAPTORS
FAIRLY ODD PARENTS MARCH 2004
FINDING NEMO
G.I. JOE SPY TROOPS
JACKIE CHAN ADVENTURES
KIM POSSIBLE
LIZZIE MCGUIRE
POWER RANGERS: NINJA STORM
SPONGEBOB SQUAREPANTS
SPY KIDS
SPY KIDS 3-D March 2004
THE ADVENTURES OF JIMMY NEUTRON: BOY GENIUS
TRANSFORMERS: ARMADA
TRANSFORMERS: ENERGON May 2004

TOKYOPOP KIDS

STRAY SHEEP

For more
information visit
www.TOKYOPOP.com

FLCL

PREVIEW VOLUME 02

Naota goes from high school nothing to mutant warrior in the blink of an eye. But what does it all mean? The town stirs with gossip when the Mayor's adulterous affair makes headlines. But his daughter, Ninamori, the class president and Naota's friend, is having a hard time of it. So hard, in fact, that she turns into a giant balloon to challenge Naota in battle. Plunge deeper into the dream with FLCL Volume 2.

stepped out into the road. One bowed and one curtseyed. Then they cartwheeled neatly into an empty lay-by and began to dance.

'What are they, Daddy? What are they doing?'

They were like humming birds in their brilliant, sequined costumes, wheeling and dipping and somersaulting beneath the blue parking sign. Mr Barker drove slowly towards them, staring. One of them, a clown, was now running backwards, beckoning with his arms, inviting them into the lay-by; while the ballerina danced on alone in her golden mask.

'He wants us to stop, Daddy! Please, Daddy! Can we, Daddy?'

The car drew into the lay-by and the doors opened. Behind the clown's white mask, two shrewd eyes assessed the family as they got out. Two little girls, flushed and excited, a boy of about ten, fancying himself too old for enjoyment. The mother — not so good! Spends all her money on her back and wants value for it. The father — hey, here's a fine, smiling gentleman for you! Good for a pound at the very least. A fiver, if we're lucky.

The clown and the ballerina joined hands, bowed and began their act. Mr Barker watched them in pleased astonishment.

'They must be from the circus,' his wife said, 'There were posters up in the last village, did you notice? I suppose they'll want money.'

Of course, she was right, thought Mr Barker,

5

they must be circus children. They were not, after all, shining visitors from a brighter world. The boy's legs were dirty and the girl's hairslide was made of pink plastic. Still, they were charming, dancing in the sunlight in their flamboyant costumes. They might have stepped out of any century, wayside acrobats amazing travellers with their tinselled skills. When he was a boy, he had once dreamed of running off to join a circus.

'They're good,' he said.

Their act was simple enough. The clown was in love with the ballerina. He pressed his hands to his heart, blew her kisses, walked upside down and somersaulted before her, but all in vain. She did not seem to see him, but danced as if in a dream, serious and self-absorbed.

'Why won't she look at him, Daddy?'

'I don't know, dear.'

Now the clown held his hand in the air, shook it, and 'a red rose blossomed in his fingers. He offered it to the ballerina. Still ignoring him, she did a high kick and the flower shot from his hand. As he bent to pick it up, another dancing kick sent him staggering forward. He straightened up, rubbing his behind, and a third kick narrowly missed knocking off his head. The children laughed.

Cold water and hard knocks for the clowns, Punch beating Judy, . . . there was always cruelty.

The ballerina had danced away, leaving the

clown disconsolate, holding the rejected flower in his hand. He turned his back on the dancer and, coming forward, offered the paper rose to the smallest girl. Perhaps it was the white mask that frightened her. She shrank away from him and hid her face in her mother's skirts.

'She's shy,' Mrs Barker said. 'Don't you want the pretty flower, Jenny? I'll take it for you, shall I?'

The little girl peeped and nodded.

'I want one, too.' It was the second little girl, her face about ready to cry. At any moment she'd wail that it wasn't fair.

Life isn't fair, Charlie could have told her. And these flowers don't grow on bushes, you know. Your daddy'd better pay well.

He brought his hand out from behind his back, flicked his fingers and there was another rose, blue this time. Now the older boy had come up — don't say *he* wanted a flower! No, he only wanted to tell Charlie how the trick worked.

'You've got them in your back pocket,' he said. 'They're folded flat and you sort of shake them out. I saw! It's not much of a trick.'

Clever little snot! Let him try it with sweating fingers, and the thin paper all too ready to stick and tear.

'It was splendid,' Mr Barker said, 'I enjoyed it.' He put his hand in his pocket. Charlie held out his hat hopefully. Now Belle came dancing up beside him, all gold and yellow and shining.

She sank into a deep curtsey.

The smallest girl, fascinated, toddled up to her on fat legs. 'Pretty,' she said, and put out her hand to touch the golden mask. Belle jerked her head away sharply, but the child's fingers had caught in the elastic and it snapped. The mask fell off.

The child stared, her face crumpling. Then she burst into tears and ran back to her mother.

'What's that on her face?' whispered the other girl, too audibly.

'It's a scar, silly,' said the boy. 'What did you think it was? A worm?'

The clown sprang on him, and, knocking him to the ground, began punching his head.

2

Her son was yelling for help, but Mrs Barker could not move. Her two small daughters, crying and clinging to her, kept her anchored to the ground.

'Do something, Bill!' she shouted to her husband, who just stood there like a dolt, while their son was being punched to pieces, 'Do something!'

Mr Barker caught hold of Charlie's arm and pulled him roughly to his feet. There was the sound of ripping cloth. Immediately Mr Barker's back was pummelled by hard, furious fists. The ballerina was attacking him, shouting.

'You're tearing it! You're tearing it! He's got to wear it tonight!'

Looking round, he thought for a startled moment that her head was on back to front. But then, seeing the tip of her nose just visible, he realised that she had hidden her scarred face behind curtains of hair. Oh, poor girl! he thought, with a pang. Then he felt a sharper pain as Charlie bit his hand. He yelped and let go the boy's arm.

'Scarper!' shouted Charlie, and ran.

Let them try and catch us, he thought, knowing he was fast. When he reached the gap in the hedge on the other side of the road and looked back, he saw the flatties had hardly moved. But Belle, — Belle who should have been at his heels, being as fast as he was, was now lying on the ground. Blinded by her own hair, she had tripped and fallen.

'Come on!' he shouted.

In answer, she made a furious gesture, that said as plainly as words, Get out of sight. He hesitated, then obediently pushed through the gap in the hedge, and crouching down opposite the lay-by, looked through the leaves.

Belle seemed in no hurry. She had picked herself up, and was now examining her leg. Charlie saw her wipe away a trickle of blood before it reached her yellow satin pump. Blood, like grass stains, did not wash out easily. Then she turned to look at the man.

'He bit me!' Mr Barker was saying, sounding astonished, 'Look, it's bleeding.'

Belle took his hand in her dusty finger and peered at it through her hair.

'That's nothing. Scarce broke the skin,' she said, unable to keep the scorn from her voice. 'You won't die. He cleaned his teeth this morning.'

'I'm glad to hear it,' Mr Barker said.

The little girls had been bundled into the back of the car, their wailing now muffled with chocolate. Mrs Barker was holding a handkerchief to her son's bloody nose.

'Come and sit down, Donald,' she said. 'Tilt your head back. I'll guide you to the car.'

'Best throw cold water over him,' advised Belle. It was difficult to tell whether she was suggesting a cure or a drowning. Mrs Barker turned on her furiously.

'You're from that circus, aren't you? I've a good mind to complain. I wonder what they'll say when they hear how you've behaved . . .'

'*Me?*' Belle said, 'I done nothing! I'm the injured party. I've been insulted, I have!'

'My dear, I'm sure Donald never meant . . .' Mr Barker began.

'He said I got a worm on my face!'

'I didn't! I said it wasn't a worm!'

'You got no call to mention worms at all!' shouted Belle, her voice thick with tears.

'I didn't mean . . .' the boy began, but his mother pulled him towards the car, telling him not to argue with that girl, he was only making matters worse, getting blood all over his shirt.

Mr Barker looked at Belle. Her lowered head was moving slowly from side to side, her face completely covered by her hair. He thought that she was weeping behind it, and wished desperately that he could comfort her. Had she been his daughter, he could have put his arms round her,

11

and told her it didn't matter, everything would be all right. But he could think of nothing to say to this sad circus child.

'There it is!' She bent down suddenly and picked up a pink plastic slide from the ground, with which she then fastened back her hair from the undamaged side of her face. He could see the tear tracks still damp on her cheek, but her one visible eye was now dry.

'Did Charlie take his hat?' she asked.

'I don't know. I'm afraid I didn't notice. It doesn't seem to be here.'

'Must've done, then. Was there anything in it?'

'What?' He looked at her blankly.

'*Money!* Did you pay him, Mister?'

'Oh! No, I was just going to when . . .'

'You owe us, Mister,' she said. 'You saw the show. You tore Charlie's costume. And you're standing on my mask.'

He looked down guiltily and saw that the golden mask was under his toe. 'Sorry.' He picked it up and handed it to her; then said with awkward pity, 'You don't need a mask, my dear. You're a very pretty girl — '

'Sure. Like the fairy on top of the Christmas tree, — after the cat's got it.' Her voice was hard. He saw she did not want his sympathy, only his money, and got out his wallet. She watched his fingers hover over the one pound notes.

'It's for my face,' she confided, sounding suddenly different, her voice now soft, pathetically

12

childish. 'That's what we're doing this for, see? We're saving up so's I can have it fixed up proper. In Harley Street, where all the nobs go. Charlie says I'm to have the best,' she added proudly. Seeing his fingers had moved on to the fivers, she said, letting her voice tremble. 'Only it costs such a lot.' His fingers stopped.

'Don't!' he said sharply. 'Please don't!'

She looked puzzled. 'Don't what, Mister?'

'Don't ... Oh, it doesn't matter.' How could he tell her not to beg for pity, using her scar like a leper displaying his sores, or a freak in a sideshow? She was, after all, a circus child, trained to perform. Turning his back so that his wife could not see what he was doing, he extracted two fivers from his wallet, and dropped them into the waiting hand.

'What are you doing, Bill?' came his wife's suspicious voice from the car.

'Nothing, dear,' Mr Barker said, and saw the circus child smile.

'Thanks. Thanks a lot,' she whispered, and then urgently, 'you won't let her tell on us, will you? Only they'd be wild if they knew what we'd been up to. It's a secret, see? You don't want to get us into trouble, do you, Mister?'

'No,' he said, 'don't worry.'

'Thanks.'

He watched her run lightly across the road and vanish through the hedge.

'Bill!' his wife called. 'Bill!'

'Coming, dear,' he said.

Charlie had already changed when Belle came through the hedge, and was examining his costume ruefully.

'Let's see,' she said, 'is it torn bad?'

He showed it to her, putting his fingers through the long slit.

'Can you mend it for me, Belle?' he asked anxiously. His own large, staggering stitches would never escape notice. She nodded.

'Easy. It's only the seam gone,' she said. 'You'll have to wash it, though. It's filthy. What did you want to go rolling about in the dirt for? After I'd warned you, too.'

He had done it for her; but knew better than to say so. He had seen the look on her face before she had hidden it with her long hair, and just had to punch someone. Anyone. He had tried to count up to ten, as he'd promised the Guv'nor he would, after his last fight, but it was no use. His fists would not wait for his slow arithmetic: he had got no further than three before he had knocked the boy down.

'I'm not sorry,' he said stubbornly.

She turned her back on him and began taking off her yellow, sequined dress. She had lost weight since the accident, and her backbone showed up like a string of ivory beads.

Charlie folded up his dusty costume and put

14

it in the bottom of his bucket. It was Belle who had suggested using buckets. 'Walk off empty-handed and they'll catch us for some chore or other,' she had said. 'But if we carry buckets, they'll think someone else got us first. We can smuggle out our fancies easy.'

'Suppose they look inside?' he had asked, worried at the idea of using their best costumes for their private performances, knowing it would double their crime in the Guv'nor's eyes.

But Belle had only laughed. 'We'll put lids on the buckets and screw up our noses like they stink,' she had said. 'That'll keep them off.'

It had. So far, they had been lucky.

He looked back at Belle. She was fastening the buttons of her blue dress, her yellow costume lying in the grass at her feet like an enormous buttercup. He picked it up and began folding it.

'Leave that. I'll do it,' she said. 'Look in your hat, Charlie.'

He had left his hat, perched upside down on a clump of meadowsweet. When he reached for it, he saw the money she had put inside.

'Ten pounds! *Ten pounds*!' he said, astonished, 'I never expected . . . I thought I'd blown it!'

She said nothing.

'Belle, you're a marvel. Clever Belle,' he said, admiringly, wanting to please her. 'How on earth did you wangle it?'

'He was a soft touch,' she said: then burst into tears.

15

He did not know what to do. Belle never cried. Never! Not after the accident, with the blood streaming down her cheek. Not in hospital, with her face all wrapped in bandages, looking like the invisible man. Not once since he had first met her . . .

He had been five year's old then. He remembered standing, peeping through the tent door into the strange Big Top; bewildered, frightened and miserable. His parents had been killed in a road accident, and now his Uncle Bert and his Auntie Annie were going to look after him.

'You'll soon feel at home here, dear,' they had said, trying to comfort him. 'It's not as if you're leaving circus life. We're all one big family, aren't we? And there's our Belle, — she'll be a sister for you. You'll like that, won't you?'

He had nodded and sniffed, but he had not wanted a sister. He had wanted his mother and father back and their own circus; not this small shabby one, where they didn't even have big cats, only three elephants and a chimpanzee. He had peered sulkily through the tent door.

'There she is. On the Shetland,' they said.

She was dressed in a froth of silver lace, and had scarlet flowers in her golden hair. He thought he had never seen anything so beautiful. Not that she had done very much, being as young as he was. She had ridden once round the ring, kneeling on the back of her pony, and then had risen, very shakily, to her feet, with the catcher

16

running beside her, looking anxious until she sat down again with a bump. But the audience had loved her, and cheered her as she came riding out of the ring.

Her face was flushed with the pleasure of her success. She had jumped down from her pony and handed the ribbons to a ringman with all the assurance of a young princess. Then she had caught sight of Charlie and stopped. For a moment, she had stared at him curiously, while he gazed back at her, speechless. Then she had smiled and come running towards him, her hands outstretched.

'You're Charlie, ain't you?' she had said. 'You're my new brother.' And she had kissed him. But even then he had not wanted her for a sister.

'I'm going to marry you when I grow up,' he had told her, and everyone had laughed, while Belle had tossed her head, and said, 'You'll be lucky.' But he had known she was pleased.

He looked at her now, all these years later, a thin girl in a faded dress, weeping over her discarded finery, and his heart ached.

'Oh, stow it, Belle,' he said awkwardly. 'Stop snivelling. It isn't the end of the world.'

'It is!' she said, through her tears. 'I don't want to leave. I don't want to go to no new school where they'll all stare at me. I want to stay with the circus.'

'We'll think of something,' he said, but he knew it was no good. They would have to go.

3

There was no matinée that afternoon. Peachem's Circus was dozing in the sun. The artistes sat outside their trailers, their aproned laps filled with finery that needed a stitch, or props wanting a screw tightened or a leather strap adjusted. In the Box Office, Mrs Clarke yawned, frowned at the pile of unsold tickets, and then glanced, without much hope, at a group of children hanging about outside the entrance.

'Still a few seats left,' she called encouragingly. 'Book now to make sure of getting in.'

They smiled and shuffled their feet.

'Can we go and have a look at the animals?' one of them asked.

'Sorry, dear. Not this afternoon.'

Belle and Charlie came into sight. Belle was limping slightly. Charlie carried his bucket as though it were very heavy. They looked, quite convincingly, as if they had been running errands all afternoon and it would be unkind to expect them to do another thing.

'Excuse us. Mind your legs. Make way, please,' they said.

The loitering children turned to look at them.

'Do you work here?' a small boy asked, a look of wistful envy in his round eyes.

'Yes,' Belle said proudly, 'Cosmo and Christobel, the Star-Spinners, that's us.'

'Go on!'

'It's true. Come and see us tonight. I might blow you a kiss.'

She seemed in high spirits. There was no trace of tears left on her uncovered cheek. But as always, her hair concealed the left side of her face, hanging close to her nose like half a golden mask. Charlie sometimes wondered whether, if he pushed it back, he would find the hidden eye weeping for her lost beauty, even while she smiled.

'What's in them buckets?' another boy asked.

'Champagne for the elephants.'

'Carry it for you, Miss?' he offered hopefully. Belle laughed and shook her head.

As they passed the Box Office, Mrs Clarke looked at them benevolently.

'Still hard at work, I see,' she said.

'Just about finished,' said Charlie.

'That's good. Do with a rest, I expect.'

They smiled, and hurried on. But they were not safe yet. The fine day had brought too many people out. Three grooms, lying in the grass outside the stable tent, watched them pass.

'Hey, is that water?' said one, getting to his feet, 'Come on, 'and it over.'

'Fetch your own,' Charlie said, fending him off as the man reached for the bucket.

For water was in great demand. Their agent, perhaps because he had not been paid for some time, had had it laid on, not in the field itself, but halfway up the lane.

'It ain't water, anyhow. It's dirty washing,' Belle said. 'And you can have it over your head with pleasure.'

'Little spitfire,' the groom said, laughing.

They hurried on, wishing they were invisible. They had nearly reached the property wagons, when Belle's mother stepped out from behind a trailer.

'There you are,' she said, 'I've been looking for you everywhere.'

She was a plump, pretty woman, with rosy cheeks and bleached yellow hair, now hidden by a striped towel. She looked hot and rather cross. Then she noticed the buckets in their hands and her eyes brightened. 'Water! Bless you, my loves, just what . . .'

'Sorry, Mum,' Belle said hastily, holding her bucket out of her mother's reach, 'It's promised. It's for . . .' The warm, musky, familiar smell of elephants came from the tent beside her, 'It's for the elephants. Mr Murphy sent us f_r it.'

'Your mother comes first. He can make do

20

with one bucket.'

'It ain't water, it's — it's apples.'

'Vegetable scraps,' said Charlie at the same time.

Mrs Marriot looked from one to the other suspiciously.

'We'll get you some water later. Promise,' Belle said, and pulled Charlie into the tent, knowing her mother would not follow. Unlike Belle, Mrs Marriot was not overfond of elephants. It was no good everyone telling her they walked on their huge baggy legs as daintily as cats. The sight of a foot, big as a barrel, coming down anywhere near her painted toe-nails made her, she said, come over queer.

After the bright sunlight, it was dark inside the tent. They could see dimly the huge grey bulk of the three elephants, and the white patches on the Shetland pony from whom one of them, Stella, refused to be parted.

'No-one here,' Belle said, 'that's a bit of luck. We can hide till she's gone.'

There was a rustling in the straw, as the three great creatures shifted their feet. The largest, recognising Belle, stretched out her trunk in greeting. This was Tessie, an old animal with a ragged ear and a loving heart, whom Belle had known as long as she could remember. She often came to her, when she was in trouble, taking comfort from the enormous, gentle creature. As she walked up to her now, searching her pocket

21

for a titbit, a voice said,

'And who are you hiding from?'

Two men stepped out of the shadows and came towards them. One was Mr Murphy, the animal trainer. He wasn't so bad. Though it was well-known he liked elephants first, snakes second and boys not at all, he had a soft spot for Belle. The man who had spoken was another matter. Hugo Schneider was the star of the show, considered by some to be the finest wire-walker in the world. It was said he had only come to Peachem's because he was an old friend of the Guv'nor's, and already had a fine new job waiting. He was also the children's trainer, a stern, tall man, with sleek fair hair and eyes as sharp as pins.

'Well?' he said.

'We d-didn't see you,' Belle stammered.

'That is obvious. You haven't answered my question.'

But Mr Murphy had noticed their buckets.

'Water,' he said gratefully, 'now that was a kind thought.'

'We'll fetch you some water, Mr Murphy. Right away, Mr Murphy,' they said, edging towards the tent door.

Mr Schneider stretched out a long arm and blocked their way.

'You know, Danny, I think those buckets are empty,' he said to the animal trainer. Mr Murphy nodded.

'The bucket dodge,' he said.

'I have suspected it for a long time,' Mr Schneider said, 'I have never seen two children so attached to buckets. They carry them everywhere. I don't know who they think they are fooling.'

The animal trainer shook his head sadly,

'Shirkers, that's what they are. Never would've thought it of them. Little Belle now, always helping me with me fat friends. Shame on you, girl. Carrying around empty buckets, pretending to work and all the time sneaking off the tober.'

Belle hung her head. Don't let them ask to look in them, she prayed, glad that the lids were tightly on. Don't let them find our costumes!

Then to her astonishment, she heard the men laugh.

'Lord, we were on the bucket dodge long before you were born,' Mr Schneider said. 'Weren't we, Danny?'

The animal trainer nodded. 'Oldest trick in the world. Things don't change much. Or only for the worse,' he added, half under his breath, looking suddenly as grey and wrinkled as one of his beloved elephants. 'I never thought to see the end of Peachem's Circus. Thought it would last out our time, didn't we, Tessie, old girl?' The elephant reached out with her trunk and nuzzled him gently.

'I'll do what I can, Danny,' said Mr Schneider. 'But . . .'

'I know. I know. These are bad times, Hugo.

Not to worry. I hear your Mum and Dad are fixed up in America, Belle?' he said.

The children, thinking themselves forgotten, had been edging towards the tent door. They stopped.

'Well, sort of,' Belle said, 'Uncle Bob said he'd try and find them something in his show, but . . . it'll just be helping around at first. Not a proper billing.'

'Lucky to find anything these days,' said the old man. 'Are you going with them?'

Belle shook her head.

'Auntie Annie says they'll have to see how it works out,' Charlie explained. 'We're to stay with our Auntie May and go to school regular.'

'I don't know what for,' Belle muttered, 'I can read and write and do sums. But Dad says we got to be educated proper.'

Mr Schneider smiled at the bitterness in her voice. 'A terrible fate. You have my sympathy,' he said. 'Off with you now. Practice tomorrow. It'll be the last one, so see that you're there. *Both* of you.'

Belle looked guilty. She had often skipped practice since her accident, and thought no-one had noticed.

'Yes, you too, Belle. I have something I want to say to you all.'

'Wonder what?' she said, when she and Charlie had left the tent.

'Probably wants to say goodbye.'

24

'Goodbye,' she repeated, and shivered in the bright sunlight. She looked round at the circle of trailers and lorries and painted wagons, at the Big Top with its brave blue and white stripes, its yellow flags stirring idly in the soft wind. She could not believe it was all coming to an end.

4

The next morning was wet and windy again. Belle, sitting by herself in a ringside seat, could hear the rain beating on the canvas above her head, while all around her the Big Top shook, straining at its moorings as if impatient to be gone. She wished it would sail away, taking her with it. She was cold and bored.

In the ring, the Cosmic Kids were going through their routine on the trampoline, looking like Mexican jumping beans. She had been a Cosmic Kid once. Now, thank the Lord, she was too old for it. Poor Charlie, promoted to catcher, was hanging upside down from the low trapeze, his freckled face already as red as a strawberry.

'No! No! No!' Mr Schneider was saying to young Lily Reeves, 'Your timing is all out. On the *backward* swing, how many times must I tell you? Try again. Don't look at me, look at Charlie! Now, one and, two and, three . . .' he counted, as the little girl began her jumps, 'And *up*!' He

banged his hands down on the trampoline and
Lily shot up in the air. Charlie caught her neatly,
swung her backwards and then forwards into a
high somersault. She muffed it, twisting awkwardly in mid-air, coming down too near the edge
of the trampoline and bouncing off sideways.
Mr Schneider caught her before she hit the
sawdust, spun her round like a Catherine wheel
and set her on her feet.

'Smile!' he commanded. 'Hold your arms up
to the audience as if you're clever, instead of a
clumsy little dolt.'

The audience, that's me, Belle thought, and I
ain't going to clap. Bet she tries to blame it on
Charlie . . . yes, there she goes.

'It wasn't my fault,' Lily Reeves was saying,
in her high, whining voice, 'Charlie threw me
crooked.'

'I didn't!' Charlie sat up on his trapeze indig-
nantly. 'You messed it up like you always do.'

'I didn't!'

'Did!'

'That's enough,' Mr Schneider said, holding
up his hand. 'We will have no fighting, please.
You are supposed to be artistes, not monkeys.
All right, all of you. Get your jackets on and
then come and sit here. I have something I want
to say to you.'

He's forgotten our act, Belle thought joyfully.
She sat down quickly behind the other children,
trying to make herself as small and unnoticeable

27

as possible.

'Did you see that . . .' Charlie said, thumping down beside her, 'the stupid little . . .'

'Ssh!'

'I thought I would talk to you today,' Mr Schneider began, 'because tomorrow we will have no time. Tomorrow we have a matinée, an evening show; and then, the final pull-down. We go our separate ways . . .'

Charlie was right, a goodbye speech, Belle thought, bored. Why doesn't he get on with it — no need to make a big performance. We've heard it all before. Goodbye and thank you. You've been a pleasure to work with . . . real little troopers . . . a grand bunch of kids, etcetera and so on.' She yawned and looked into the ring.

Oh no! Two ringmen were spreading the blue and crimson carpet over the sawdust. She tried to catch their attention so that she could signal to them to take it away, but they did not look at her. Now they were bringing on the see-saw, and assembling the high ramp for the Star-Spinners act. Take it back! Quick, before he sees, she thought, wishing she could throw the silent words into their thick heads.

'Some of you, most of you, perhaps,' Mr Schneider was saying, 'must face the fact that you may never get another circus job.'

Belle turned to stare at him. *What?* This was no part of the usual goodbye speech.

'These are difficult times,' he went on,

'Peachem's is not the only circus to close down. Three went bust last year. Others are struggling. There will be fewer jobs, fiercer competition. Think about it. Decide now what you want to do. There are other careers, better paid, less demanding. Think about it.'

The children fidgeted and looked serious, trying to think as they had been directed, but finding their minds distracted by more immediate concerns. Lily Reeves was putting her tongue out at Charlie. Tim Clarke wanted to spend a penny. Mary Roget was scratching her head, worried in case she had got nits. Belle tried to think of nothing, a big round nothing that kept turning into a circus ring.

'Those of you who decide you do want to stay on in the circus, will have to work. Work, work, and more work,' Mr Schneider said. 'Most of you will be out for a time, but you can't afford to be idle. Practise. Practise at home, practise in gymnasiums . . .'

Just a pep talk, thought Belle, bored again, and looked away. The ringmen were now rolling in the two huge globes, blue and covered with yellow stars, like gigantic beachballs. Damn! Still, perhaps there would not be time, she thought, glancing at her watch. Madame Nanette and her Performing Poodles had booked the ring for eleven.

'That's all, children. You may go now,' said Mr Schneider. The children scrambled to their feet and crowded, chattering and laughing, towards the tent door. Belle had almost reached it when she heard Mr Schneider call,

'Not you, Charlie! Stay behind, please.'

She turned round. Surely he was not going to tell Charlie off for that catch? Any fool could tell him it had been Lily Reeves's fault. *She* would be that fool, if necessary.

Mr Schneider, catching sight of her, hesitated and then said,

'Yes. All right. You too Belle.'

They came up to him, a little nervously, wondering which of their various misdeeds had been found out. But though he looked serious, he did not seem to be angry.

'First you, Charlie,' he said, 'I'm quite pleased with you. I've been watching you. You've improved. In fact, you're not bad, not bad at all.' Charlie flushed with astonishment and delight. Mr Schneider went on, 'It would be a pity for you to give up now. So what I wanted to say is . . . well, I expect you've heard that I'm going to join Mayer's when I leave here. Remember, I shall be a new boy. My word will not count for much at first. But for what it's worth, it's yours. If you are looking for a holiday job at Christmas, come and see me. Mind, I promise nothing. There may be nothing. But it's worth a try, yes?' Seeing Charlie was speechless with pleasure, he smiled and said, 'O.K.?'

Charlie stammered his thanks, beaming. Then

he looked at Belle uncertainly, a little anxious now.

Belle was smiling too, a smile of pure, unselfish joy in another's success. It felt as if it was fastened to her face with nails, which made it difficult to speak. But she must say something. She did not want to spoil his pleasure.

'Good old Charlie,' she said, and listened to the sound of her own voice, bright, clear, no smudge of envy to be heard. Clap hands, everybody, she thought, that was my finest performance. She was rewarded when Charlie's smile widened again.

'Run along now, Charlie,' Mr Schneider said, 'and don't boast to the other children or they'll all be round my neck. Off with you! I want to speak to Belle alone.'

Charlie ran out, in great springing steps as if he were about to fly. They watched him go in silence. Then Mr Schneider sighed.

'Belle, I am sorry,' he said slowly, 'I have nothing good to say to you. When I first came here, I found you the young star, brilliant, born for the spotlight, everyone told me. Yes, you were good. You were also the vainest, most tiresome brat I'd ever met. But you had talent.'

Belle stared sulkily at her feet.

'What has happened to you?' Mr Schneider went on. 'I watch you now and you are nothing. Even Lily Reeves is better. Oh, it is not your scar,' he said, seeing her hand go up to the hair that concealed it, 'Your scar has done you a favour.

You are not so proud. What is a scar in the circus? Greasepaint, a few sequins stuck on, and it's gone. But courage, courage you need. We can't afford passengers in the ring.' Belle hung her head and said nothing. 'You've lost your nerve, Belle, haven't you?' he asked gently.

'No! No, I ain't! I just need time . . .'

'Time? Too much time is bad. Fall down, get up again, that's the only way.'

'How could I? I was in hospital.'

'And when you came out of hospital, what then? Did you go up the ramp? No. You were too tired, you had a headache, your tummy was upset. Excuses, always excuses. I was too soft with you, I think. No, leave that, please!' he added in a sharp voice.

Belle looked up, startled, and saw he was addressing the two ringmen, who had come back and were about to dismantle the ramp.

'It's five to eleven, Squire,' said one of them.

'So we have five minutes.'

'But Madame Nanette . . .'

'Must wait.'

The ringmen shrugged and left.

Mr Schneider turned back to Belle. 'It's not the high wire we are talking about,' he said. 'You had no business on the high wire, you know that now. I blame myself. I should've seen that it was taken down. But this is only the ramp. You have done it a hundred times before. Look at it! It is not so high, is it? What happens if you fall? I catch you. Don't you trust me?'

'Yes,' she said, sounding so doubtful that he shrugged and said,

'All right, say I miss you. What then? A few bruises, at worst a broken bone. Is that so bad?'

'No.'

'You say you need more time. There *is* no more time. Tomorrow we close. Now you must do it. Fasten back your hair. You must be able to see properly. Come on, I've seen your scar. I've seen worse scars than yours. That's better. Now, what's this?' he said as she still hung back, 'You are afraid? You are a little coward?'

'No!' she said, and took his outstretched hand.

He steadied her as she jumped up onto one of the globes, and set it moving with her feet. Then he let go and watched her as she circled the carpet, balancing easily on the spinning ball. She began to move towards the see-saw, but he stopped her, saying,

'I know you can still do that, and we're short of time. The ramp, please.'

She hesitated, the ball slowing beneath her feet.

'Now!' he shouted furiously.

She started up the first slope, looking down at her feet, seeing the yellow stars whirling beneath her bare toes, round and round . . . It was the stars, the stars were making her giddy. She glanced up and found she was reaching the first bend. Steady, steady! She let the ball slow, her feet fumbling as she changed direction, so that it hit the side of the ramp and nearly unbalanced her. Oh, please, please don't roll back! She thrust her legs down like pistons, forcing the ball forward and up. To think she'd once fooled about on the ramp, letting herself roll backwards deliberately towards Charlie, coming up behind her. Stopping just before the globes collided, making the flatties gasp. She'd *enjoyed* it then. Must've been mad!

How much further? She glanced up. Saw the Big Top spinning as if someone had set a whip to it. Her ball hit the side again and wobbled beneath her feet. Oh God, she was going to fall . . . Where was Mr Schneider? She looked down and saw him beneath her, his pale, upturned face blurring in the whirling shadows . . . There seemed to be several Mr Schneiders now, dancing in a ring, round and round, and shouting in her ears . . . Why were there so many Mr Schneiders?

'Charlie, help me!' she cried, and fell.

Mr Schneider caught her as she landed on him with a thud that knocked the breath out of her, and must have hurt him because he grunted. But he swung her over in a somersault and set her on her feet.

'Smile!' he said. 'Hold up your arms and smile!'

She smiled. She held her arms up to the rows of empty seats and smiled, and wanted to be sick.

'That's my girl,' he said, ruffling her hair.

'I tried!' she said, 'I did my best, honest.'

'I know you did, Belle. You were very brave.

You're a good girl,' he said gently. But he did not ask her to come to him for a job at Christmas. He did not ask her to try the ramp again. He knew she was finished.

Belle pulled the band out of her hair, letting it fall over her face, and rushed blindly out through the tent door.

Mr Schneider looked after her.

What have I done? he thought. There was a chance. I thought it might work, but . . . Poor child, what damage have I done?

'Mr Schneider,' said Madame Nanette, coming into the ring with a flurry of yelping, leaping poodles, 'Mr Schneider, you have stayed too long.'

5

The Big Top was down; only a discoloured circle showed where it had been. The painted buses, lorries and trailers had driven away in heavy rain, leaving in the gateway a weirdly-patterned moonscape of mud. Slowly as the weeks passed, the flattened grass recovered. Five cows now grazed where once the elephants had walked. Nothing was left of Peachem's World Famous Circus except a sodden paper rose, blooming improbably in a hedge. Belle and Charlie's world had ended.

Charlie was glad it was over. Since it had to end, he wished it could have ended more quickly; that he and Belle, after the last performance, could have been precipitated, like Cosmic Kids off the trampoline, into Aunt May's waiting hands. It was horrid having to go to their winter quarters, arriving so unseasonably in the summer rain. The farmer's wife, who usually welcomed them with warm smiles and hot supper, had seemed distinctly chilly. Perhaps she felt that failure was catching. Perhaps she was worried in case she would not get paid. The elephants especially, whom in the past she had professed to admire, now came in for cold glances, as if she was afraid Mr Murphy would sneak off in the night, leaving her with three mountainous, unpaying guests.

'Whatever will you do with them?' she said, 'I mean, if you can't get another job. Not that they're not welcome to stay here for a week or two, but you'll want to be making other arrangements.'

Even when the weather changed and became bright and warm, she remained as cool and sharp as one of her own kitchen knives. 'Mr Murphy, about them elephants . . .' she said yet again.

'Don't you worry, Mrs Thorpe,' he said, trying to sound cheerful and not altogether succeeding. 'Two of them have found good homes already. Going to a circus in Germany. They'll be off on Wednesday.'

'You ain't selling them?' Belle burst out, horrified. 'Mr Murphy, you ain't selling your friends?'

'Be quiet, Belle!' her father said.

'But — '

'That's enough!'

'It's all right, Bert. It's only natural she'll be upset,' Mr Murphy said kindly. 'She's always loved me elephants, haven't you, Belle?' He put his arm round her and explained, 'I can't help meself, lass, and that's the truth of it. I'll not be finding another job in a hurry, not at my age. And it's a good circus they're going to, else I'd not have done it, no matter what. They'll be well looked after. Don't make it harder for me, eh?'

She shook her head. 'Which two are going?' she asked in a small voice, 'Not — not Tessie?'

'No, bless you,' Mr Murphy said, smiling at her 'I'll not sell our fat darling, never you fear. She's been with me since I was a boy. We've grown old together, Tessie and me. I'll never be parting with her.'

Belle smiled at him, reassured.

But later, when she and Charlie went out into the yard, they were followed by the farmer's little boy, a sturdy child of six, with hair the colour of his father's hay. He was always hanging round them, as if he hoped they might suddenly jump through balloons, or do a high wire walk on his mother's washing line .

'Do you know why?' he said. 'Do you know why he won't be parting from the big 'un?'

'Because he loves her.'

'No, it isn't! T'isn't that at all. *I* know why. What'll you give me if I tell you?'

'A thump on your ear,' Charlie said, guessing uneasily that it was something they would rather not know. Belle told him to shut up.

'Tell me, Johnny. Come on, there's a sweetheart,' she wheedled, 'Tell me.' But he only grinned and looked knowing.

'Oh, you're silly. You're just making it up. You don't know nothing,' she said, changing her tactics.

He was young enough to fall for this.

'I do know! I do! I heard them,' he said, jumping up and down. 'He can't get rid of the big 'un. She's too old . . .'

'She's not.'

'And she's got them ugly scars on her ear. Nobody'd want her, not with them scars.'

He spoke in all innocence. He had not seen the circus children since last winter, and did not know about Belle's accident. So he could not understand why Charlie grabbed hold of him furiously, holding his arms so tight that it hurt.

'Shall I knock his head off, Belle?'

For a moment she was silent, and the little boy, thinking she was seriously considering it, began to whimper. Then she shook her head.

'No. Let's drown him in the duck pond.'

They carried him off between them, while he squealed and wriggled; and swung him backwards and forwards over the muddy water's edge. He was giggling now. He liked the circus children, even though they sometimes played rough, and did not believe they would throw him in. He was right. They set him down safely on the grass.

'Do it again! Drown me again,' he pleaded,

but they shook their heads and went off together, saying it was no good, they'd just remembered he could swim.

During the first two weeks at Goosebeak Farm, the various bits and pieces of their painted world were packed up, driven away, sold or burned. Two weeks of goodbyes, as the artistes departed in ones and twos, gloomily wishing each other luck. Two weeks of washing and ironing and packing, of having the backs of their necks scrubbed, their manners and their grammar examined, and found wanting . . .

'Don't say "ain't", Belle,' her mother said crossly, as they sat over their tea. 'How many times have I told you? You don't want your Auntie May to think you haven't been brought up proper, just because you're circus. Look at Charlie, now, you don't hear him saying "ain't".'

This earned Charlie a dark scowl from Belle. Mrs Marriot went on to make things worse. 'Perhaps if you'd worked as hard as he does, my girl, Mr Schneider would've offered *you* a job at Christmas.'

'He did, so there! He offered me a star billing!' Belle shouted. Seeing this lie was not believed, she added for good measure, 'I hate you!' and rushed from the room.

'I shouldn't have said that,' said Mrs Marriot. 'Shall I go after her?'

'No. Best leave it. She'll want to cry and she

won't like to be caught at it. She's a prickly little puss, is our Belle. Still, I shouldn't have said that.'

Charlie agreed with her, but silently. Auntie Annie had a biting tongue: she was always apologising for the wounds it inflicted, as if it were a fierce dog, quite beyond her control. Uncle Bert was different, a calm, easy-going man who walked away from arguments, saying it didn't do for a knife-throwing act to quarrel. 'Don't you provoke me, Annie,' he'd say, 'or my hand might slip tonight and you wouldn't like that. Don't want to end up like a sliced loaf, do you?' And she'd smile and catch her tongue between her teeth. They were very fond of each other, so close that sometimes Belle and Charlie felt left out.

'I wonder what Mr Schneider did say to her,' Mrs Marriot said now, 'Do you know, Charlie?'

'No.'

'She told me to mind my own business when I asked. My mother would've slapped me silly if I'd spoken to her like that. I thought of asking the Great Schneider himself, but then . . . She'd have told us soon enough if it had been anything nice. Poor Belle.' She sighed, looking gloomily at the bikini in her hands, on to which she was sewing scarlet sequins. 'She's a funny girl. D'you know what she said to me this morning, Charlie?'

'No.'

'She asked me if I wore red so the blood wouldn't show if anything went wrong. As if

41

Bert would ever miss! Never so much as grazed me in twenty years! Poor kid, she's lost her nerve, that's the trouble. Ever since the accident . . . Oh Charlie, I wish we didn't have to leave you both behind. But there, we were lucky to get the chance of a job, the way things are.'

She paused, looking so unhappy that Charlie said quickly,

'We'll be all right.'

She blinked and sniffed and smiled, all at the same time,

'Yes, of course. I'm just being silly. Where's my hanky? May's very nice, you know. She offered to have you when she heard Peachem's had gone bust. It wasn't me that asked. Well, I might've hinted a bit . . . Do you remember her, Charlie?'

'I think so.' He had a dim memory of a tall lady, thin, neat, dressed in grey. He had thought she was an inspector, come to check up on the number of hours the kids had worked, and had been surprised when she kissed him.

'Who's she?' he had whispered to Belle, when the lady had gone on, — she seemed to be kissing everyone. 'Our new auntie,' Belle had said, 'Uncle George has gone and married her. We're to have bubbly, kids and all.'

'Very much the lady, she was,' Mrs Marriot went on. 'Not one of us. Soon persuaded your poor Uncle George to leave the circus, said she couldn't bear to see him on that dangerous

42

trapeze. Bought a sweep shop in Worthing. And what happens? He goes and falls downstairs and breaks his neck! Not used to stairs, you see. Ladders, yes, and ropes, but not stairs. It just goes to show. You're better off where you belong . . .'
She caught sight of Charlie's face and added quickly, 'Charlie, I shouldn't have said that! I didn't mean . . . It's not as if you and Belle will be out for good. Just till you get yourself educated. And May's very kind. She used to send you presents, remember?'

He nodded. They had been terrible presents; fluffy pink rabbits and plastic ducks and picture books about elves, chosen for a baby he felt he had never been. Presents which, if opened carelessly in front of the other boys, had always led to jeers and fights.

'I'm sure you'll get on fine,' Mrs Marriot was saying, cheerful again. She was always an optimist, riding her troubles like horses. 'It's a hard life,' she was fond of saying. 'We all have to take a few knocks. Doesn't do us any harm.'

Charlie, watching her as she tried the effect of a silver sequin against the scarlet ones, thought, her head's full of America and her new job. She's forgotten us already.

So he was surprised when she told him she had arranged for them to have a holiday on the farm, after she and Uncle Bert had gone. Just for two weeks, before they went on to Auntie May's.

'It was Belle wanted it,' she said. 'Says you've

never had a proper holiday. I didn't like to refuse her, poor kid, when she's feeling so low. What do you think, Charlie? Would you like it?'

He hesitated, hating the idea. The farm depressed him now, with all their friends gone; the empty beds in his room, the yellow oblongs on the grass where the trailers had stood, the deserted stalls that had once held the circus horses, the Liberties, High School and Rosinbacks. Except for themselves and the farm people, there was only Mr Murphy left now, Mr Murphy and his Tessie, both looking greyer and more worried each day. Charlie longed to be gone. Then he thought of Belle. Belle hiding behind her hair, frightened of new people, an aunt she hardly remembered, neighbouring children who would point and whisper, 'What's that on her face?'

So he said loyally, 'Yes. That'd be great.'

Mrs Marriot smiled, and told him that he was a good boy, that she and Uncle Bert looked on him as their son . . .

'And you will take care of Belle, won't you, Charlie?'

'Yes,' he said, 'I'll always take care of Belle.'

His words rang in his head for some time after he had said them, a rash promise, one he should never have made.

6

That night, Charlie dreamed he was back in the
Big Top, smoothing footprints out of the sawdust with a rake. There were the small prints of
children, the big-booted ones of clowns, and
huge elephant tracks like cracked dinner plates.

'Look at me!' called a voice, high above him,
'Charlie, look at me!'

He tilted his head and saw Belle, standing on
the platform by the high wire, laughing down at
him. Little fool! Showing off again.

'No! Don't!' he shouted. 'Come down, Belle.
Don't be stupid.'

They were not allowed up there. A thousand
times they had been told: Never, never touch
the apparatus without permission. *Never*. It's as
much as your life is worth!

Belle tossed her head.

'I can do it! I can do anything,' she said, and
began walking out into space. He could see her
feet in their soft shoes curving round the wire,

her arms held out to balance her, the pale underside of her chin . . .

'Come down, Belle!' he cried, terrified. 'Come down at once!' And as if he had ill-wished her, she was falling, down . . . down . . . down . . .

He sat up with a jerk, his mind full of blood and sawdust, but there was only the dark room and the empty beds on either side of him. He shivered and hugged the blankets closer. Why did he always dream it that way? It had not ended like that. Belle was not dead.

He lay awake, staring into the dark, remembering . . . Belle's arms thrashing the air as if she were trying to fly. Belle falling, twisting her body in mid-air and catching hold of the wire with her hands. Swinging like a pendulum above his head while he watched in terror.

He could hardly remember climbing the ladder, his face wet with tears, expecting any moment to see her body rush past him to the sawdust below. No harness, no safety net.

But when he reached the platform, she was still there, hanging limply like washing on a line. She had been trying to swing herself up so that she could catch the wire with her feet, but could not manage it. Her hands must have been raw. Charlie had grasped the rail tightly, and leaned out from the platform as far as he dared, stretching out his arm.

She was too far away.

'I can't reach you!' he shouted desperately.

'You'll have to come nearer!'

'I can't move. I can't.'

'Yes, you can!' he screamed at her. 'You're the one who can do anything. Come on. Come on!'

And she'd moved her poor, bruised hands along the wire, one after another, until she was near enough for him to grab her wrist. Even then he was afraid, his hands were wet and slippery with sweat, no rosin, no chalk . . . he should have rubbed them in the sawdust, . . . too late now.

'I'm going to swing you towards me,' he said. 'Can you grab hold of something?'

She had nodded. Oh, she'd been brave enough. Even when the edge of the platform caught her cheek, ripping it open, she had bitten back her cry, and managed to catch hold of a strut, taking her weight off Charlie's arm. Then, when they were safe back in the ring, with her blood staining the sawdust at their feet, and a groom rushing in, exclaiming in horror, she had smiled and said faintly,

'Why, Charlie, you're a hero. You saved my life.'

He had been a hero for a whole week. People had kissed him, hugged him, shaken him by the hand and drunk his health. Then Belle had come back from the hospital, with a livid scar across her left cheek, and a new, uncertain look in her eyes. The other children had been kind to her, in their way.

'You poor thing. How can you bear it? You

47

were so pretty before, and now ... Poor old Belle!' Lily Reeves had kept saying, until Charlie had thumped her and had his ears boxed for hitting a girl.

Then he was back to being the old Charlie again, a boy more ready to use his fists than his tongue. People forgot he was a hero and treated him with the usual disrespect, making him fetch and carry, and cuffing him when they felt like it. True, Auntie Annie remembered, but only, he felt, when it suited her.

'I'll never forget you saved her life, Charlie,' she'd say, her eyes moist with sentiment. 'Never! My poor little Belle. It makes me feel better about leaving her. I know I can count on you to look after her.' As if, by saving Belle's life, Charlie was now responsible for her for ever.

'It's not fair,' he muttered, punching his pillow for want of a better target, 'Why should I? Belle's older than me.' (Only three weeks, but hadn't she let him know it, in the days before her accident, when she was still the young star. Vain, bossy, lording it over them all!)

But then he remembered how she had comforted him, in the early days, when he was small and clumsy, teased by the other children and shouted at by the trainer. One day she had found him crying, frightened that Auntie Annie and Uncle Bert would send him away, because he was no good.

'What's the matter?' she had asked. 'Is it the

other boys? Hit them if they're horrid. Hard. On the nose.' (Advice which he had later taken too much to heart.)

When he had confessed the shameful truth, that he was hopeless, that he'd never catch up with the other kids, she had hugged him and said, 'It ain't true. You can do it, Charlie. I'll show you. I'll help you. If you work at it, you can be as good as anyone. Well, except me, of course.'

And he knew he must always love her and look after her as best he could. But, tossing on his bed, he wished he were older, fearing uneasily, that his best would not be enough.

Three days later, Mr and Mrs Marriot left Goosebeak Farm. Belle had wanted to go to London with them, to see them off at the airport, but her mother had said that she hated long goodbyes.

'Hanging about for hours, having time to get miserable. It'd only make me cry, and spoil my mascara.' She blinked her eyes as if to show how thick and black her lashes were and what a pity it would be to spoil them. She did not look as sorry to go as she should have done. All dressed up for the journey in tight pink trousers and a white satin blouse, her bleached hair tied back with a scarlet ribbon, Mrs Marriot looked in a party rather than a departing mood. 'Goodbye, Belle darling,' she said, beaming. 'Be a good girl. Look after Charlie . . .' Above Belle's head, she caught Charlie's eye and winked, as if to say, 'You know who's really got to do the looking after, don't you?' Then she hugged Belle. 'There, give your mum a big kiss. Chin up and keep smiling, that's circus. Where's my bag gone? Charlie, have you seen ... oh, there it is! Come on, Bert, we don't want to miss the train. Bye, Belle! Bye, Charlie! Take care ...'

'Good luck! See you some time!' Belle called.

The car drove off down the muddy lane and they watched it out of sight, waving. Then it was gone. Twelve years, thought Belle, twelve years she had lived with her mum and dad, slept in the same trailer, listened to their snores through the thin partition when she woke at night. Twelve years of being kissed and cuffed by her mother, comforted by her father, — and now it was over. When they met again, she would be different; older, educated by a new school, turned by Auntie May into ... what? A young lady, perhaps, speaking in a mincing little voice, never saying 'ain't', wearing neat grey dresses and washing the back of her neck every day. They wouldn't recognise her. Come to that, she wouldn't recognise herself.

She didn't feel unhappy, exactly. She didn't know what she felt. Just blank. They were alone now, she and Charlie, alone in an inbetween time; the circus world gone, the suburbs and the sweetshop still to come. Oh well, might as well make the best of it while it lasted.

She glanced at Charlie and saw he was watching her uneasily. Wondering if I'm going to cry, she thought. For a moment she considered putting on a poor little orphan act, all wet and wistful, to embarrass Charlie and get Mrs Thorpe running round, offering hankies and buttered scones, with herself the centre of attention. But she decided against it. It wasn't her style: she was a secret weeper. She had done her crying last night, face pressed into a damp pillow. So she gave Charlie her widest smile and said cheerfully,

'That's that. What shall we do now?'

Mrs Thorpe, hearing her, thought, How heartless children are! You love them, work for them, worry about them, and then it's 'Goodbye, Mum. Goodbye, Dad. See you some time,' and they walk away laughing.

7

Mr Murphy was in the elephant shed.

'What are we going to do, Tessie, old girl?' he asked, popping a piece of apple into her soft mouth. 'Over three million out of work, they say. Time for old men and old elephants to retire, eh? Would you like that?'

The elephant rumbled softly, as if agreeing.

And for sure, they could both do with a rest, Mr Murphy thought. He hadn't been feeling himself lately. 'You don't look well, Danny,' his sister had said, last time they met. 'You need someone to look after you. Move in with me, I could do with a bit of company. Been a bit lonesome on me own.'

He was fond of Maureen. His sister, once at the top of a pyramid of acrobats, had retired five years ago to a council flat in Worthing. 'There's always room for you, Danny,' she had said. But not, of course, for his Tessie. 'We aren't allowed pets, not in our block. Not even a canary. Though

I won't say I haven't heard the odd cheep coming from behind closed doors. Nor the odd miaow, neither; though there's not a word I'd let slip about it to anyone but you. What's a few fleas compared to loneliness? But I'm sorry, there's limits, Danny. I can't do with an elephant in me kitchen. It's not a thing you can hide easy.'

True enough.

'Got to think of something, Tess,' he said, taking the elephant's trunk out of his pocket, where it had been searching hopefully for another titbit, 'Can't stay here for ever. Mrs Thorpe's got it in for you, lass. She don't like elephants no more, silly woman. Wants your shed to store turnips in, or something. You and me's got to move on . . .'

'Ain't you found nothing yet, Mr Murphy?'

It was Belle, coming silently into the shed. She moved like a shadow in her plimsolls. He never heard her coming nowadays. Getting a bit deaf, most likely. Talking to himself, too. Going to pieces.

He wondered how much she'd overheard. He didn't want to upset her, the poor little kid, with her face reflecting his own fears like a mirror. She loved that old elephant as much as he did.

'We was just talking, Tessie and me,' he said, smiling at her. 'And we've decided we're going to retire.'

'Retire?'

'We've got our plans fixed. A small zoo for Tessie, with me in a cottage at the gate, so I can visit easy. Maybe earn the odd penny helping to muck out. They'll be glad of a hand, no doubt, and that way Tessie won't get lonely.'

He did not tell her that he had already written to several zoos, with no success. With the price of feed and vet's bills rocketing, no-one wanted an old, scarred circus elephant, even as a gift. But the truth was too cold for children, you had to dress it up a little. How could he say that he often woke up, in the small dark hours, his heart on the trot, remembering his sister's words ... 'You've got to face it, Danny,' Maureen had said, 'you'll not get another job at your age. You'll have to have that poor old elephant put down. There's no way you can support her on a pension.'

No, he couldn't tell Belle that. So he told her instead about his dreams of a small zoo, with a cottage at the gate, till he almost came to believe in them himself. A garden where he could grow roses. Carrots and apples, too, to take to Tessie. His sister would come and live with him and cook his supper ... 'And when I'm back from visiting me fat friend, there'll be hot buttered crumpets and tea in a brown pot, and we'll yarn about old times. How does that sound, Belle?'

'Fantastic.'

Something in the way she said it made him look at her sharply, but she had turned away and was fondling the elephant's scarred ear. He could not see her face. They were too sharp, these kids. They grew up quickly nowadays, poor little devils.

He said, to change the subject, 'Heard from your mum and dad yet?'

'We got a cable, saying they'd arrived safely. It's too soon for a letter.'

'Of course, it's only three days. Enjoying your holiday, are you?'

'Not bad,' she said, shrugging, 'Mr Thorpe let us both have a turn driving the tractor yesterday. And today he showed us how to milk the cows. Me and Charlie had a cow each.' She laughed, glancing back at him, 'Charlie's kicked the bucket and there was milk all over. I never seen his feet so white before, — nor his face so red!'

'I thought it was all done electric?'

'Yes. But Mr Thorpe says you can't never tell when you're going to have a power cut. And it's something for us to do. Funny, ain't it? We was always having to work, never no time to ourselves, except when we . . .'

'When you sneaked off on the sly, eh? I know.'

'Yeh, well, — now we got all the time we want and . . .' she screwed up her face, 'I dunno. It don't seem so much fun, somehow.'

'And that's a fine thought for a man about to retire, I must say! Any more words of cheer for me, Belle? Anything else to hearten an old man who's hanging his cap up?'

She smiled, shaking her head. Her heavy yellow

hair swung back, showing the long ragged scar on her left cheek. He could not stop himself from glancing at it and though he looked immediately away again, she had noticed. Her hand went quickly up to pull her hair back into place, and she flushed.

Oh hell, poor kid! Should he say nothing? But someone ought to coax her out into the open. She couldn't go round with half a face for the rest of her life.

'Now, Belle me darling,' he began, but the pity showed in his voice and immediately she stiffened. Her one visible eye glared at him, and she sidled towards the open doors. Oh, he was grown old and clumsy. Losing his touch. There's times you can gentle a young lion, and times you'll get your head bitten off. Best change course . . .

'That's right, run away just when I'm after asking you a favour,' he said plaintively, as she reached the door.

She turned, looking doubtful.

'What favour?'

He'd offered to help Mr Thorpe repair some fencing tomorrow, he told her. Take all day, most likely, and there was poor old Tessie. He didn't like to leave her shut up by herself for so long, not when she was still missing her friends.

'No telling what mischief she'd get up to,' he said, looking round the large, dilapidated shed, with its high, cracked windows and chinks of light showing here and there through the boards, 'Wouldn't take much to have this place down about her ears. Only got to lean a little.'

'I'll look after her!' Belle said, her face brightening, as he had known it would. 'Me and Charlie. We'll take her for a walk. She'll like that.'

'No going down to the village to show off,' he warned her. 'Keep well away from the roads, we don't want her frightening some driver into the ditch.'

'No. I promise.'

'And not near the house, mind. I'd as soon Mrs Thorpe didn't catch sight of her, or she'll be after me again.'

'We'll be careful.'

'There's the bottom meadow, only check there's no cows in it first. Not that she'd hurt them, bless her, but if the milk comes out cheesy, it'll be our blame. We're not so welcome here any more, that's the sad truth.'

'We'll be careful, Mr Murphy, honest.' Belle said. 'We've looked after her before. You can trust us.'

'Yes,' he said, smiling, 'you've got a way with elephants, Belle. Tessie will do anything for you, I've noticed. I know she'll be all right. So I won't be fretting to come back early tomorrow.'

But he *was* back early. It was not yet twelve o'clock, with the sun high and hot in the sky, when they brought him back. Charlie and Belle

57

were leading Tessie back from the bottom meadow, where they had been playing in the stream, when they heard someone shouting. They looked round. Mr Thorpe and another man were coming slowly, heavily across the grass, carrying between them a wattle hurdle, on which lay something still and dark.

Mr Thorpe shouted again, and now they could make out the words,

'Run on ahead! Tell them to ring for an ambulance! Quick!'

Charlie turned and ran. Belle could hear his feet clattering as he reached the paved yard, and then his voice calling, high-pitched, and a door banging . . . She could see now whom they were carrying on the hurdle. It was Mr Murphy. She ran towards them.

Mr Murphy was lying on his back, his nose pointing to the sky, his eyes shut. From his mouth came odd, harsh, snoring noises that frightened her.

'Is he . . .' she began, but Mr Thorpe said sharply,

'Get that damn animal away!'

For Tessie had followed her, and was stretching out her trunk towards her old friend, as if puzzled by the strange sounds he was making.

'Back, Tessie, back,' Belle said, pushing against Tessie's cheek, trying to turn her. But the elephant had sensed something was wrong. Her ears came forward uneasily, and she began

58

swinging her trunk from side to side, her small, pouched eyes fixed with anxious love on the unconscious man.

'She won't do him no harm,' Belle said.

'For God's sake! She'll have him off the trestle in a minute!'

'Stand! Tessie, stand!' Belle commanded shrilly, pushing the elephant's trunk away from Mr Murphy, and getting between her and the trestle. For a moment she felt frightened, suddenly doubting her power over the great, grey colossus who loomed above her, three tons of worried elephant wanting to go forward, with only Belle in the way. Mustn't let fear show. Fear was catching. And it was only Tessie, whom she had known as long as she could remember.

'Steady, old girl,' she said, keeping her voice low and calm. 'Mustn't let Mr Murphy think you've forgotten all he's taught you. That's better. Now, right turn!' She put her hand behind Tessie's trunk and tried to lead her away. It was like trying to move a mountain. The elephant stood planted, her legs like trees, her heavy head turning to watch the men carrying Mr Murphy away. But she no longer tried to follow.

Belle felt her eyes blur with tears. 'Poor old Tess,' she said. 'You're worried, ain't you? But it'll be all right, you'll see. Mr Murphy ain't going to die. He *ain't*!'

She kept talking, soothing the great animal as they both watched their friend being carried into the house. Only when the door had shut, did Belle try again to lead the elephant back to the shed. Tessie came with her willingly now, though she was still uneasy, her ears moving like ragged leaves in the wind. Taking her into the shed, Belle fixed the leather-covered shackle onto her hind leg, that tethered her by a chain to an iron ring in the ground. Then she gave her water, and left her feed within easy reach.

'I'll be back, Tessie, don't worry,' she said, 'I must go and see how . . .'

She could not finish her sentence. She was shivering now and could no longer trust her voice. So she shut the door behind her, hearing as she did so, the wailing of an ambulance in the distance.

8

Mr Murphy had had a mild stroke, but there was every hope that, with good nursing and rest, he would make a complete recovery. So Mr Thorpe told them when he returned from the hospital, to eat his warmed-up, dried-up lunch at the kitchen table.

'Grandpa had a stroke last year,' Johnny Thorpe said. 'And now he walks funny, — hup bonk, hup bonk, hup bonk . . .' The small boy capered grotesquely round the table, crying, 'Watch me! I'm Grandpa!'

'Stop it, Johnny!' his mother said sharply.

'Can we go and see him?' Belle asked.

Not for the moment, Mr Thorpe told her, 'No visitors allowed, apart from family. His sister's coming up today.'

'That's nice,' Mrs Thorpe said. 'That'll be a comfort to him. There's nothing like your own family.'

'Does he talk funny?' Johnny asked. 'Grandpa

did. Grandpa went wah, wah, wah ... Ow!' he
finished shrilly as his mother slapped him.

'That's enough from you,' she said angrily,
and then turned to Belle: 'Don't worry, dear.
He'll be all right, I'm sure. It's wonderful how
they get over it. You should see Dad now, fit as
he's ever been, except for this little limp ...'

'Hup bonk, hup bonk.'

'Out!' she shouted furiously, and the small
boy fled.

The Thorpes smiled apologetically at Belle
and Charlie. Told them not to take any notice of
Johnny, ('You know what they're like at that
age.') No need to worry. Mr Murphy was going
to be all right ... Their voices poured over Belle
like golden syrup.

It was hot in the farmhouse kitchen. Sunlight
lay in yellow slices on the table, and the air
smelled richly of casserole and coalite. By the
window a fly was buzzing: it was the very sound
of summer. Belle looked across the table at
Charlie, who smiled at her, his mouth moustached
with milk. He was content, lapping up the
comforting words.

Perhaps there's something wrong with me,
Belle thought, I can't seem to believe anyone
no more. The kinder they sound, the more I
worry ...

Through the open window, she could hear
Johnny still chanting his verbal limping, though
quietly now, as if pride compelled him to

continue, but discretion warned him not to be heard. Hup bonk, hup bonk. Well, at least, she thought, comforted, his grandpa is able to walk, even though with a limp. She could trust Johnny. Johnny was too young to deceive her for her own good.

'How long will Mr Murphy be in hospital?' she asked.

It was too early to tell, they said. 'I expect Mrs O'Hara will ring us as soon as she has any news,' Mrs Thorpe added. 'She'll want to arrange to collect his things.'

'Won't he be coming back here?'

'I don't know, dear. I shouldn't think so. He'll probably go straight to his sister when he leaves hospital. He'll need looking after for a bit.'

'What about Tessie?' Belle asked.

The Thorpes exchanged a quick glance, but it was not quick enough. Belle might only have one eye uncovered, but that eye was sharp. They don't like Tessie, she thought, They want to get rid of her.

'We'll look after her,' she said quickly. 'She won't be no trouble to you. We can do it easy, can't we, Charlie?' He nodded.

'That's very kind of you, dear,' Mrs Thorpe said. Again she glanced briefly, warningly, at her husband. She might just as well have shouted, Keep it from the children. We don't want to upset them. There's no need for them to know.

'What is it? What's going to happen to Tessie?'

Belle demanded, her eyes going anxiously from one kindly-deceiving face to another.

'I don't know, dear. That's up to Mrs O'Hara now, not us. I'm sure she'll do what's best.'

Don't worry. Mr Murphy's comfortable. Mr Murphy's as well as can be expected. Everything's going to be all right. They were told this every day, when they asked, but Belle was uneasy.

'I think we should go and see him ourselves,' she said to Charlie, as they stood watching Tessie stuffing herself happily with hay. 'We could say we're relatives. Only I don't trust ... someone,' she ended, having caught sight of Johnny, sitting on the fence, his ears as large and red as poppies.

'Who?' the small boy asked.

'No-one you know.'

'I do, then! Bet I do!'

'Oh, go away, Johnny,' Belle said impatiently. 'Why do you always have to follow us around. We don't want you. Shove off!'

'Or we'll set Tessie on you,' said Charlie.

'And she'll squash you flat.'

'Then your mum will fold you up and keep you in a drawer.'

'All in the dark.'

The small boy's face crumpled, for there was an unkind note to the teasing. He climbed down from the fence, and said with childish dignity, trying not to cry:

'I was going to tell you something important,

but I won't now.'

Belle was immediately ashamed. 'I'm sorry, Johnny,' she said quickly. 'We didn't mean to be beastly. Only we're worried, see, and that makes people horrid. Would you like to feed Tessie an apple?'

'No.'

He was hurt. It took Belle all her charm and two toffees to appease him. Even then, she hesitated to ask him what he'd been about to tell them, in case he suspected the motives for her sudden kindness had been mixed.

Johnny had a gift for eavesdropping. Being small, he was often hidden by a table or behind an armchair. He could walk past a window and only the top tufts of his hair would be visible, easily mistaken for dried grass. If anyone could tell her what was going on, Johnny could. And did: he could never keep his illicit knowledge to himself for long.

'That woman's been and gone,' he said.

'What woman?'

'Mrs O' summat, — you know, his sister. She took his things away.'

'Mrs O'Hara? When? She hasn't left already?'

He nodded.

'But we wanted to see her! Why didn't you come and tell us she was here?'

'I was listening,' he said simply.

Belle pushed past him and raced back to the farmhouse, thundered into the kitchen, which was empty; shouted for Mrs Thorpe, who didn't answer.

Charlie and Johnny had followed her in. 'Where's your mum?' she asked the small boy.

'Dunno.'

She thumped the table angrily with her fist, making the tea cups rattle and a little milk slop out of a jug.

'I see she had time for tea,' she said bitterly. 'They might have sent for us. They knew we'd be with Tessie.'

'They said, better not,' Johnny explained, watching her curiously with his round blue eyes. 'They said you'd only make a fuss about the elephant.'

'What about her?'

'The slaughterhouse people are coming for her on Monday.' He giggled uneasily, looking at them from beneath his pale eyelashes. 'Won't she make a lot of cat's meat?'

9

When Charlie woke up, he was conscious of a shadow lying over the bright day like a bad dream. Then he remembered. Tessie! Not all their pleading last night had been any good; on Monday the slaughterhouse lorry was coming to take her away.

'It's murder!' Belle had shrieked. 'She can't do it! I won't let her! Tessie ain't hers. I'll go and tell Mr Murphy . . .'

Mr Murphy was very ill. Did she want to upset him? Did she want to spoil his recovery? Wasn't his life more important than any animal's? And had she no thought for Mrs O'Hara, frantic with worry about her brother, wanting to have him home with her so she could nurse him back to health . . .

'Be reasonable, Belle,' Mr Thorpe had said. 'How can they keep an elephant in a council flat?'

'Tessie's to go to a zoo! Mr Murphy told me!' It was then they learned that Mr Murphy had already written to several zoos, and been refused.

'What could he do? He had to agree. These are hard times,' Mr Thorpe had said. Everyone was always telling them that. These are hard times, bad times, you chose to be born at the wrong moment, you've missed out on the good old days ... As if they'd been careless, arriving too late for some party.

It was no use trying to go back to sleep. He had better go in and see if Belle was awake. Poor Belle, it was worse for her. She adored old Tessie; there was a bond between the scarred girl and the scarred elephant. He hated the thought of her unhappiness, dreaded finding her sunk into the deep misery that had made her say once, 'You shouldn't have saved my life, Charlie. You shouldn't have bothered.'

But when he opened her door, he found the room empty. She was already up. Where? Not in the kitchen, where Mrs Thorpe greeted him coldly, her patience having been strained by yesterday's scenes. The elephant shed? No. She had been there, for Tessie was outside, in the fenced-in patch of dried mud, peacefully eating some greens, and her tub was filled with fresh water. But there was no Belle. Charlie began to get worried.

'Belle!' he shouted, 'Belle!'

He looked out over the sunlit fields but he could not see her. The stream? Surely it was not deep enough to drown in?

He went racing over the grass towards the bottom meadow; and then he saw them, Belle and Johnny, sitting on the low branch of a tree, deep in talk. Belle was smiling. As he watched, she put out a hand and ruffled the small boy's hair.

'That's clever, Johnny,' she said. 'You *have* got a good memory. I bet you're top of the class at school.'

She was up to something. She was speaking in her buttering-up voice, the one she used to charm the money out of a flattie's pocket, after a private show. Puzzled, but not wanting to spoil her game, whatever it was, Charlie walked back to the elephant shed, and sat on the fence outside, waiting for her.

It was five minutes before she came, her face alight with triumph.

'Barstow's,' she said.

'What?'

'The slaughterhouse. Barstow's of Summaton. I can look them up in the directory. They ain't planning to do it here, — I suppose a live elephant's easier to move than a dead one. I'm going to ring them up and put them off. I'm good at doing voices. How's this?' She deepened her voice and it could have been the farmer's wife speaking, 'Is that Barstow's? This is Mrs Thorpe of Goosebeak Farm. I'm ringing to cancel the arrangements about the elephant.'

Charlie's heart sank. 'They'll only ring up to find out why the lorry didn't come,' he said, 'It

69

won't do any good.'

'I'm not thick, Charlie. I've got a plan.'

Her eye was shining, her face as bright as the summer morning. This was not the sad girl who had lost her nerve. This was Belle as she had once been, the young circus star, who had walked so lightly, so easily over the low wire, that she'd fixed her eyes on impossible heights, looking up to where the high wire, the forbidden wire, gleamed in the loft shadows of the Big Top. 'I can do anything,' she had said. But she had fallen.

'What plan?' Charlie asked, feeling horribly uneasy.

She hesitated, looking sly.

'Promise to help me?' she asked.

'Without knowing what I'm letting myself in for. Come off it, Belle! I'm not that daft!'

'Swear then,' she demanded. 'Swear on the Old Gent.' Her face grew solemn as she evoked the strange circus oath of secrecy, an oath heavy with time and usage, though its meaning was lost. Neither of them knew who the Old Gent was or why he should be so terrible. Some people said he was the devil, others that he was a man in evening dress who appeared in a ringside seat before every fatal accident. Whatever the truth, it was a vow no circus child would break lightly. But Charlie did not hesitate. He'd never sneak on Belle anyhow. She should have known that.

'May the Old Gent take me if I ever tell,' he said. Belle led him into the elephant shed, where none of the farm people would dare follow, being foolishly afraid of Tessie. They sat down on some straw in a dark corner, close as conspirators. Even then, she kept looking around uneasily, as if expecting to see the sun shining through a large red ear, pressed to one of the many chinks between the boards. When she spoke, her voice was so soft and breathy that Charlie hoped he was not hearing her aright.

For it was a crazy plan, as full of gaps as the shed they sat in. Kidnap Tessie? Oh sure! Sneak her out of the farm, and take her secretly, unseen, (an elephant, mind you,) through Yald Forest to Blanstock Safari Park on the other side. Some thirty miles as the crow flies, lucky bird; more like a hundred for two weary children and an elderly elephant, dodging the summer hikers and riders and campers round every tree.

'Blanstock's the first place Mr Murphy would have tried,' he objected. 'They've probably already turned her down.'

'It's easy to say no by letter. But once she's in there, once we've got her inside . . .'

'How? Do we wrap her up in brown paper, knock on their door and say we've brought them a big present?'

'Leave it to me,' Belle said, looking cross and stubborn. 'Just trust me, Charlie.'

He was silent, knowing it was no good trying to make her see reason when she was in this mood. 'Look after Belle,' his aunt had said. How?

Tie her up and lock her in a cupboard until Tuesday? Look at her now, her eye shining like a star, all excited about her silly plan. Didn't she know what it would mean? That it was no matter of being slapped and sent to bed without supper, when they were caught . . .

'You realise they'll have the whole police force after us?' he said.

But she shook her head: 'They won't know nothing about it. None of them. They'll all think we're somewhere else. I've got it worked out. Listen . . .'

So he listened, while she spun her thin, intricate web in his ear. No spider would have owned such a ramshackle affair, full of tangles and loose ends and holes big enough to put a camel through.

'But Belle,' he kept saying, and she would wave away his objections with a thin hand.

'We'll travel by night and hide up by day,' she said.

'It's impossible . . .'

'Everything sounds impossible till it's been done. Nobody'd ever have done the triple twist somersault, if they'd listened to you. Do you want poor Tessie to die?'

'No, but . . .'

'Just give it a try, that's all I'm asking. I'll *never* ask you for nothing again, I promise. I'll help you with your practice. I'll mend your beastly clothes when you've been fighting. I'll

tick up for you at that horrid new school. I'll
be an angel. *Please,* Charlie!'

He did not stand a chance. He could feel
himself weakening.

'We'd need money,' he said, on the edge on
his last ditch. 'We'd need a lot of things, sleeping
bags, groundsheets . . .'

'We got money. We got the fund.'

The fund. A hundred and seven pounds —
'But that was for your face,' he said, 'that was
for Harley Street.'

'This is more important.'

He was suddenly angry, thinking of the hours
they had worked at their private shows, the risks
they had taken, the hard dull slog of saving, going
without everything so that Belle could have a
pretty face again. And she could give it up just
like that.

'Oh, it's easy to say so now,' he said crossly.
'But what about later? Do you think they'll let
you wear your hair all over your face at our new
school? No chance! They'll make you tie it
back. How will you like that?'

'I don't care!'

'Tie it back then. Go on. Let's see your silly
scar.'

'If I do, then will you help me?'

He hesitated, seeing nothing but disaster in
her ridiculous plan, too many things to go wrong,
landing them in bad trouble with everyone.
Aunt May, the police, his aunt and uncle fetched

73

back from America, — and he himself losing his chance with Mr Schneider, for what circus would take on a boy who had pinched an elephant?

'Will you, Charlie?' she asked again.

'Yes,' he said helplessly.

'Got a piece of string?'

He fumbled in his pockets; two pennies, a dirty tissue, chewing gum, an old shoelace ... He handed it to her and watched her tie the long fair hair back from her face.

Then she turned to him, tilting her head so that the light from the small, high windows fell on her cheek. 'A penny for the peepshow,' she said bitterly.

He looked at her steadily. Her face still seemed cut in half, one side white, where it had been hidden from the sun, one brown. The scar had healed, its ugly, livid colour gone. It ran from the hairline, missing her eye, right down to her chin. The left side of her mouth was pulled up a little, so that she appeared to be smiling, though her eyes were miserable.

'It's not so bad,' he said. 'Dunno what you've been making such a fuss about. Now, this plan of ours ...'

He saw her face light up at the word 'ours' and felt guilty, knowing he was counting on things going wrong at the beginning, before they had gone too far. Oh, there'd still be a row, of course, but no worse than he and Belle had weathered in the past. But once in Yald Forest

— it was things going on behind his back he was afraid of. The police, the telephone calls, the headlines in the newspapers — HAVE YOU SEEN THESE CHILDREN OR THIS ELEPHANT? No, it mustn't come to that.

'But I won't cheat,' he told himself, soothing his conscience. 'I'll do my best. It won't be my fault then.'

10

Well, it was done now. The first step was taken and there was no going back. That afternoon, while Mr Thorpe was out mending his fences, and Mrs Thorpe was driving Johnny to a birthday party, the farmer's office was taken over. His chair was sat in, his telephone used, his wife's voice borrowed.

The man at Barstow's did not seem suspicious. 'Mrs Thorpe? Ah yes, good afternoon, Madam. That's the elephant, isn't it?' he said. 'We have it down on our books for collection on Monday . . . Oh. Oh, I see. You want to cancel it altogether?' He was obviously disappointed, sounding like an executioner who had been promised a queen, only to have her snatched away at the last moment, her head still on her shoulders. Barstow's would never make history now. It was back to the dull, bloody routine of sheep and cattle for them. 'I wish you could have let us know sooner, Madam,' he said coldly. 'We'd already arranged for the vet ... Yes. I see. I supposed it can't be helped. Very well, Madam.'

Belle's hand was trembling when she put down the telephone. She looked at Charlie, and they exchanged nervous smiles.

Outside in the yard again, they sat on a bench in the sun, rehearsing their next act until they were word perfect; then falling silent, with the familiar fluttering beginning in their stomachs. It was like waiting to go into the ring.

Belle's face felt naked. Her hand kept going up to her left cheek, her fingers touching the scar briefly.

'What's the matter? Does it itch?' Charlie asked, when she'd done it for the sixth time.

'No.'

'It wasn't so bad, was it? At lunch?'

She did not answer. He would never guess how she had felt, walking into the kitchen with her hair tied back, seeing Mrs Thorpe's eyes go to her cheek, then dart away again. Suppose I'll have to get used to it, she thought, people's eyes jumping away from my face like it was something nasty on the pavement. My eyes are all right, and my nose, even my mouth ain't too bad, but it don't make any difference. It's my scar they look at, and then wish they hadn't! Nobody'll ever look me straight in the face no more.

Except Johnny. Johnny was too young for tact. He had come right up to her and stared.

'Cor, what a big scar.' His voice had expressed

77

only interest, not pity. 'I've got a scar on my knee,' he'd said, showing it to her. 'I had to have three stitches. How many did you have?'

'Five hundred and fifty-five,' she said, exaggerating wildly.

He was impressed. 'How did you get it?' he'd asked, almost enviously, as if he'd have liked one just as large to show off at school.

'It was a tiger done it,' she invented. 'I was cleaning his cage, see, and I slipped on the soap. Never fall down in front of tigers, Johnny, or they'll do you. They can't help themselves, poor things, it's their nature.'

'Oh!' he'd breathed, his eyes and mouth round with wonder. At least there was one admirer she hadn't lost.

Then Charlie said suddenly, 'She's back!' and Belle saw the car coming through the farm gates.

They ran to meet Mrs Thorpe, putting on bright smiles like masks. They were practised performers. No-one listening to their excited voices would have guessed they were lying. Their aunt had just rung up, they told Mrs Thorpe. Auntie May was going to take them on a canal holiday, on a barge, — it would mean their leaving the farm early, but she didn't mind, did she? They did so want to go, they'd never been on a boat before . . .

'We told Auntie May it would be all right,' Belle said. 'We were sure you wouldn't mind.'

'Of course not, dear,' Mrs Thorpe said

comfortably. To tell the truth, she'd be glad to see the back of them. All that fuss about an elephant! 'I'll give your aunt a ring in a minute —'

But apparently that was not possible. Their aunt had already left, they told her. A friend was driving her up to fetch the barge, and there was no way of getting in touch with her now. But it was all arranged. Belle and Charlie were to meet the barge at Oxford on Monday. They were to catch the 2.35 from Summaton ...'

'*This* Monday?'

'Yes,' said Belle, and watched Mrs Thorpe from under her lashes. There was a funny look on the woman's face. Had she remembered Tessie was also going on Monday? Behind those blank blue eyes, was the image of a barge slowly turning into that of an elephant? Quick, say something. Don't give her time to get suspicious.

'Auntie May suggested Saturday at first, but ... but ...', Belle let her voice falter and hung her head to hide her tearless eyes, 'Poor old Tess, the least we can do is stay with her until ...' Her voice trailed away, and she sniffed loudly.

'Now don't you upset yourself again,' Mrs Thorpe said anxiously.

'You know, you'd never get Tessie on that truck without us,' Charlie said. 'Elephants can turn funny, if they take against someone. She's been acting sort of nervous lately, I dunno why. Seems to've gone off the men here. Probably blames them for taking Mr Murphy away.

79

Yesterday she was swinging her trunk like a sledge-hammer when Mr Thorpe went by. Scraping the ground with her foot, too. Reminded me of that time in Kent . . .'

'Shut up, Charlie! We're not supposed to talk about it. You know we promised.'

'About what? What happened?' Mrs Thorpe said sharply.

'Oh, nothing. Nothing much.'

'Just some man made a bit of a fuss. She didn't really hurt him.'

'He was only in hospital a week.'

Mrs Thorpe looked thoroughly alarmed. 'But Mr Murphy always said she was as gentle as a lamb . . .'

'Ah yes, with *him,* she is,' said Charlie.

'And with me,' said Belle.

'But she doesn't like strangers.'

'Nor lorries.'

'And you'd best keep Johnny away. She don't like small boys much.'

'Nor dogs.'

Mrs Thorpe looked suitably worried, and they thought they had better stop. They did not want to overdo it.

'Belle can handle her,' Charlie said. 'She'll do anything for Belle.'

'Yes.' Belle sounded sad. 'I'll load her up for you. She won't be frightened with me. But I wish it was over and we were on that barge.'

And she and Charlie started talking about

boats and canals and locks, until Mrs Thorpe's head spun, and there was no room for suspicion left inside it.

The expected letter from America came on Saturday, two pages for Belle and two for Charlie, on thin airmail paper that rustled in their fingers. The words were stilted and misspelt, (the Marriots seldom wrote letters,) but they were full of love.

'It's great here,' they said. 'They got it all, lions, tigers, a stagecoach, you ought to see the stagecoach galloping round the ring, with Indians after it and guns shooting, you'd love it. Puts dear old Peachem's in the shade. It's a bit big, not that we don't love it but we miss you both. Dad keeps saying Belle would like that, can't you see Charlie in that ten-gallon hat ...'

The pages were hemmed with kisses. Belle and Charlie were very quiet after they had finished reading. They folded the pages carefully and put them away, not looking at each other. 'Be good,' the letter had ended, 'Take care of yourselves. Don't do anything we wouldn't do.'

11

On Monday morning, at ten to eleven, an ill wind suddenly swept upon Goosebeak Farm. First Charlie came rushing in to say the cows were in the cornfield, — was that all right? Only they seemed to be making a mess of it. No, *he* hadn't left the gate open, he'd just found it like that. Perhaps it had blown open. Mr Thorpe and his cowman went off at a run, and Charlie vanished again.

Then Mrs Thorpe, coming into her kitchen, found her big glass jug on the floor, a hundred splinters in a sea of milk, spread before the feet of an astonished cat. She swore at the cat, who leaped onto the window sill, from where he gave her a look of affronted innocence, — *he* had nothing to do with it, he had just found it like that!

Before she had time to get a cloth, Johnny ran in, barefoot, to tell her the goat had somehow got loose from its tether and was now in the garden, munching pansies.

'Look out! There's broken glass everywhere!' she shouted at him. 'Go and put your shoes on this minute!'

'But, Mum, the goat . . .'

'Damn the goat!'

'Mrs Thorpe! Mrs Thorpe!' It was Charlie again, bursting in through the door in high excitement, 'Barstow's have come for Tessie.'

'Mind the milk!' she shrieked at him. He skidded to a halt, knocked into a chair and fell over with it.

'That's dangerous,' he said reproachfully, when he'd righted himself and the chair. 'You oughtn't to leave it, — look, there's glass all over! Someone could cut themselves.'

'I'm quite aware of that,' she said, tight-lipped. 'I was just going to clear it up. Tell the driver I'll be out in a minute . . .'

'Oh, he can't wait. He's in a hurry. He wouldn't even come up the lane.'

'What do you mean? Where is he?'

'Parked over there, on the main road,' Charlie said, pointing through the window, to where the top of a high truck was just visible above the distant hedge. 'Belle's taking Tessie down now. I'd keep Johnny in, if I were you, Mrs Thorpe. Tessie's playing up a bit.'

'But I want to watch! I want to watch!' said Johnny, making a dash for the door. His mother caught him back just before he stepped into the milk and dumped him on a chair, saying furiously,

'You stay there and don't move! Do you hear me? *Don't move.*'

'I just came to say goodbye,' Charlie said, 'and thanks for everything. I can't stop. The driver says he'll give us a lift to Summaton, if we hurry.'

'But Charlie, your train's not till . . .'

'By the way, I forgot to tell you. Did you know the goat's eating your roses?'

'*Not my Golden Glory?*'

'Dunno what they're called. Yellow ones. I must rush. We've already taken our luggage down. Goodbye, Mrs Thorpe. Bye, Johnny.'

'Charlie! Charlie, wait a minute!'

But he was gone. She could hear his feet thundering across the yard and down the lane.

She hesitated, her mind filled with goats and roses and broken glass . . . Why hadn't that stupid driver brought the lorry up to the farm? It was a long walk down the lane, and Johnny with no shoes on. Someone should supervise the loading of the elephant onto the lorry, — couldn't leave it all to the children. Still, the men from Barstow's would be there, it was their job. And what good would she be? That great lumbering creature frightened the life out of her, and they said animals could always tell. The smell of fear made them attack. Oh, why was William always out when he was needed? she thought unfairly, forgetting her husband was chasing the cows from the cornfield.

So she stood, with too many things to do,

doing none of them, but staring out of the window with the cloth in her hand, the milk on the floor, and her little boy whining on his chair because Belle had not said goodbye to him.

'And you shut up!' she told him crossly, 'If you'd got your shoes on, we could've gone after them. You've only yourself to blame.'

She felt uneasy, with an odd sense of having been blown off course ... But they were circus children, she comforted herself, brought up rough. They'd be all right.

It seemed ages since Belle had stopped the lorry. Why didn't Charlie come? Had something gone wrong? 'Give me fifteen minutes,' he'd said. 'You mustn't let it drive off too soon, or it'll give the show away. Wait for my signal.' It must be longer than fifteen minutes and she was running out of ideas. Already the driver was getting suspicious.

He had stopped with a hiss of brakes when she had flagged him down, waving her arms wildly, her hair flying, her mouth open in a childish cry for help. He was an Asian, a plump, youngish man, with kind dark eyes in a brown face. He had patted her shoulder gently, when she had leapt onto the step of the high cab, clutched hold of his arm through the open window and buried her face in his sleeve, sobbing noisily. He smelled of diesel and something sweetish, — was it chocolate? The advertisements must be true, she thought, swallowing an impulse to giggle, and lorry drivers really did eat chocolate all the time.

'What is the trouble? Try to tell me. You are safe now, my friend.'

She had taken her time, gulping and sniffing and whimpering, counting the slow seconds passing in her head. The more time she could waste the better. But she could not keep it up for ever. Lily Reeves could cry at will, real tears, simply by thinking of something sad. It was a talent Belle lacked, so she kept her face hidden, resisting the finger that tried gently to raise her chin. Half-opening one eye, she tried to squint at her watch, but it was too close. Out of focus, it looked like frog spawn, a black dot where the hands joined, in a round grey blurr.

'Are you hurt? Has someone frightened you?' the driver asked.

'No, I — uh, uh, uh! It's — uh, uh, uh!' she gulped, letting her voice rise as if climbing a ladder to hysteria.

He had moved his arm away from beneath her lowered head and clutching hands. Now she felt her chin being raised firmly and something hard being pressed against her lips. She expected brandy, but it was only luke-warm tea from a thermos, tasting of the plastic cup. By jerking her head, she managed to spill it, and while her kind Samaritan was mopping her up with his handkerchief, she risked a glance at her watch.

Oh Lord! Only three minutes gone.

The cup was filled again, and this time she drank, slowly, her eyes lowered.

'Good, good,' he said, taking the empty cup from her. 'Now you are feeling better, my friend. You can tell me your trouble, I think.'

'It's — it's little Tessie,' she mumbled, between sniffs. 'I think she's hurt bad. She won't answer me. She's just lying there, and — and I'm frightened!'

'Where is she?'

'Over there,' Belle said, waving her arm vaguely ahead. 'She fell into the ditch, and now . . . she won't *move*!'

It took them several minutes to search the ditch at the side of the road, going backwards and forwards, stinging their hands on nettles, parting the brambles to reveal nothing but mud and rusty tins and dirty bits of paper.

'Perhaps she crawled further up,' she suggested, but the driver was now looking at her doubtfully, his sympathy turned to suspicion.

'You will wait here, please,' he said, and went quickly back to his lorry, glancing sharply from side to side, at the high concealing hedges, the small copse on the other side of the road.

Belle ran after him. 'Please don't go! Please help me,' she cried.

He took no notice but walked right round his lorry, kicking his tyres, inspecting the lock at the back. Though by nature a friendly man, he had had to learn distrust the hard way, walking back through the cold grey streets of a new home town, in a new country, listening for the rush of plimsolled feet behind him, looking for the corner that might hide the mindless pack of thugs, waiting . . .

When he had satisfied himself that he had not been robbed, he came back to Belle.

'I think you are not truthful,' he said, his dark eyes moist with reproach.

'I am!'

'I have noticed, you look over your shoulder and at your watch, and your eyes do not look like they are crying. Who is it you expect? If it is to steal, tell your friends to keep away, please, or they will be regretting it.'

'I'm not a thief!' Belle said.

From the concealed entrance to the lane behind them, came the sound of an owl hooting, three times, hoo, hoo, hoo. An untimely sound in broad daylight.

'Look! There's Tessie!' Belle cried loudly, pointing in the opposite direction. 'There she is.'

'Where? I can see no-one.'

'Over there! In that field, d'you see her now. She's limping! She's hurt! Now she's fallen over!'

Behind the lorry driver's back, unnoticed, a freckled boy led out a huge grey shape, a vast wrinkled shadow that moved with swaying grace across the road and into the small wood. Its enormous feet made no sound on the tarmac.

Once in the wood, dead leaves muffled its tread, the small branches parting to make way for its bulk, rustled quietly as if in the wind.

And then the fat lump had to tread on a dead stick! There was a crack like a pistol shot and the driver swung round. He stared. Then he grasped Belle by the arm, and marched her across the road.

It was not a big wood. Defying the laws of perspective, it seemed to grow smaller as they approached it; the trees moving further apart, holes appearing in the thick green. Belle could see, quite plainly, slices of Tessie between the trees, like a jigsaw coming apart. She glanced sideways at her companion. Perhaps he would mistake that creased grey leg for a tree trunk, that gently swinging tail for a broken branch in the wind . . .

'There is an elephant in that wood,' he said.

'Oh, sure,' she said, laughing falsely. 'And I've got a tiger in my pocket. Want to see? Look out, there's a giraffe just behind you.'

'You are not fooling me,' he said. He smiled happily. 'It is a cow elephant, from India or Ceylon, perhaps. Not Africa, though she is very big, I know elephants, you see, so you cannot be fooling me. We had elephants at home when I was a small boy.' For a moment his dark eyes looked wistful; then he turned to Belle, 'Come, we will go to her, and you will tell me what naughty things you are up to, please.'

89

Belle felt her eyes sting. She'd mucked it up. She'd failed. Since the accident, nothing went right for her. *Nothing!* It was no use trying any more.

But the long years of training took over. She was circus. Artistes didn't snivel and give up when things went wrong. Remember what Mr Schneider was always saying —

To the driver's absolute amazement, the girl beside suddenly did three high, leaping somer-saults, one after another, held her skinny arms up in the air and smiled at him brilliantly.

'Tara boom!' she said. 'Meet Christabel, of Cosmo and Christabel, the Star Spinners. Come and see Tremendous Tessie, the largest and most lovable Indian Elephant in the world. All at Peachem's Circus next week. Tickets, £3, £2 or £1, cheap at the price.' A car horn, like a trumpet, blared loudly behind them, and she added earnestly, 'Best move your truck, Mister. It's blocking the road.'

12

The problem of kidnapping an elephant is its sheer size. Its colour is modest; a patchy grey merging into the leafy shadows, matching the asphalt of the roads, blending with the grey stone of the houses, but its size lets it down. Even a small elephant is large, and they go on growing all through their lives, unlike other animals which know when to stop. Tessie was both old and enormous.

Charlie, standing behind a tree in the inadequate wood, had heard the driver say, 'There is an elephant in that wood.'

His heart had jerked between dismay and relief. It was not his fault. Belle could not blame *him*, even though it was what he had secretly wanted, to be caught before they had gone too far. And yet, . . . poor Tessie.

He peered round the tree. Through the shifting curtain of leaves, he could see patches of Belle and the driver; now the pink of Belle's shirt, now a striped sleeve, rolled up to the elbow of a brown arm.

Ought he to go on? In front of him, there were glimpses of grass through the trees. Something black and white, — part of a cow. An invisible dog barked, a small dog by the sound of its shrill yapping — that might mean the owner close behind. He hesitated. 'Wait for me in the wood,' Belle had commanded. He shrugged and waited.

Belle was now doing a circus spiel. Why on earth . . .? he thought, puzzled. Unless she was trying to charm the driver, as she had once charmed audiences, in the days when she still had a pretty face and all the impudence in the world. She sounded nervous, he thought critically, no longer certain of her power to please. For some reason, it made him cross to hear her fawning, like one of Madame Nanette's poodles. At any moment she'd be sitting up and begging.

Then the voices were drowned out. Tessie, mistaking the leaves that tickled her rump for flies, broke a branch off the nearest tree and began swatting her flanks with it enthusiastically. Noisily. When it caught in other branches, she ripped them off too, until the little wood shook and tossed and crackled about them.

Charlie was too busy dodging the whipping twigs to think what to do. Besides, he doubted if he could quieten her. There was a mischievous look in the elephant's round brown eyes, as though she felt she had been standing in the wings too long, and was determined to reveal herself to the audience, even if it meant uprooting every tree.

'Charlie! Stop her, you fool! The whole wood's twitching like it's got fleas.'

It was Belle running up, her face flushed and excited.

'You stop her, if you think it's so easy,' he said furiously.

There was no need. Tessie, on hearing Belle's voice, had dropped the branch she was holding and was now standing still, trying to look innocent.

'You've just got to be firm,' Belle said. 'It ain't difficult.'

She and the elephant both looked smug: it infuriated Charlie. He had to bite his lip to prevent himself from saying the unforgivable words that crowded his tongue: Think yourself clever, don't you? But it's *me* Mr Schneider chose, not you, — and now you're going to muck it up for me.

He did not say these words, but they remained in his mind like poison.

Belle was too full of herself to notice his mood. She was telling him about the lorry driver.

'I couldn't think what to do. So I did a bit of an act, and it worked, Charlie! He said, "Oh, you're from a circus," as if that explained everything, as if he thought all circus people were mad, anyway. Then he laughed, and went back to his truck. I think he liked me,' she added, with a kind of humble wonder that almost softened Charlie's heart. Then he saw that her hair was loose on her shoulders again, with a few strands falling across her scarred cheek. She was cheating already.

Noticing his glance, she pushed her hair back from her face and said quickly, untruthfully, 'The shoelace must've fallen off.'

He looked at her in disbelief.

'Anyway, I always used to wear it like this. I only tied it back for practice, don't you remember?'

He said nothing.

'Charlie? Can't I wear it like this, Charlie? If I don't pull it forward?'

'Oh, suit yourself,' he said, feeling mean and cross. 'You always do.'

There was a short silence. Then she said in a subdued voice,

'Well, we'd best get on, hadn't we?'

They had two fields to cross before they reached the derelict barn where they planned to shelter until it was dark. Two large flat, exposed areas of grass, with nothing taller than a thistle to hide behind. 'We've got to take a few risks,' Belle had said.

Charlie climbed the gate between the two fields and looked round. No farmer, no dog walkers, no children picnicing, just his luck!

94

Nothing but a few cows, all staring at him as if trying to memorize his face in case anyone made inquiries later. Such as the police.

From here, Belle and Tessie were invisible in the wood. He waved his arm slowly from side to side, giving the signal. All clear.

They came out fast. Belle had to run to keep up with Tessie, whose lumbering, swaying walk covered the ground at an amazing speed. There was nothing comic in the sight, however, as there is when a fat woman scampers for a bus, or a hippopotamus teeters down a muddy bank on its too-small feet. The elephant looked hugely impressive as she charged across the grass, her ears standing out like maps of India and her trunk rolled up. The cows stared in amazement and backed away. A bird rose shrieking into the sky. And Charlie climbed down to put the gate between them, hoping Tessie would know when to stop.

She gave up long before she reached him, looking round at Belle as if to say, 'What's all the hurry about?' Then, taking hold of a clump of grass with her trunk, she sliced it off neatly at the roots with her toenails, beat it against her front leg to get rid of any earth, and stuffed it into her mouth. She obviously felt she had had enough exercise for the day.

Any minute someone might come, Charlie thought. Any minute a voice might shout, 'What the devil are you doing with that elephant in my field?'

But no-one came. They reached the barn undetected. Their luggage was still where they left it, behind a rusting bulk of farm machinery, long abandoned. Sacks of straw and greens and fruit for Tessie, tins of baked beans and tuna fish for themselves, ground sheets, torches, sleeping bags and a bucket, bought secretly in nearby villages and smuggled into the barn, had all been packed away in the huge pockets Belle had sewn on either side of Tessie's crimson and gold saddlecloth. They had found this still in the old tin trunk in the elephant shed. Either Mrs O'Hara had not known it was there, or she had deliberately left it behind.

Belle tethered Tessie in the darkest corner, by the tub of water they had filled before breakfast. Then she came and sat down beside Charlie. He glanced at her, and away again. She looked so pleased with herself. So smug. 'We've done it, Charlie!' she whispered. 'We've done it!'

'So far,' he said coldly.

There was a short silence. Then she shrugged and unpacked the sandwiches she had prepared. The bread was stale. The lettuce was limp and rusty-looking. He picked the cheese out, and pointedly threw the rest back into the paper bag.

'It's the heat,' she said apologetically. 'They've gone off a bit. But there's biscuits and cake.'

Another silence.

'How did things go at the farm?' she said at

last, showing a polite interest, as if she thought he was sulking because he wanted praise.

He was, in fact, rather proud of the way he'd managed. The goat had been a splendid touch. Good timing and good luck, that's what Mr Schneider always said an artiste needed . . . At the thought of Mr Schneider, he lost any desire to boast.

'Oh, all right,' he said shortly.

He knew he was behaving badly. He'd agreed to her silly plan and he ought to put a good face on it. It was mean to take it out on her because he was worried about the police and the headlines and Mr Schneider getting to hear about it. If only she'd have the sense to keep quiet and give him a chance to recover his temper. But she hadn't.

'Why are you so cross?' she asked. 'What's the matter?'

'Nothing.'

'I hate people who say "nothing", when they've got prickles sticking out a mile. You've been in a foul mood ever since we met in the wood. Did you think I didn't notice? I'm not thick, Charlie!'

'Aren't you?'

'I'll hit you in a minute!' she said furiously. 'Why are you being like this? D'you want to back out? Are you afraid of being caught, is that it? What if we are? They won't send us to prison, not kids of our age. We've got nothing to lose.'

That did it. 'You haven't anything to lose!' he shouted. 'You don't think of anyone else, do you? You don't care if I lose my chance . . .'

He broke off, furious with himself, and with her.

'I don't want to talk any more,' he said. 'I'm going to sleep. I've been up half the night, lugging those bleeding sacks, and I'm flat out. You'd better do the same. Did you pack the alarm clock?'

'Yes.'

'Best set it for eleven, then.'

He lay down and turned his back on her, ready to refuse to listen to her apologies and excuses. But she did not say anything. Angrily, without meaning to, he fell asleep.

When he woke up, it was dark in the barn, but he knew at once that he was alone. As he sat up, something rolled to the floor. He had to feel about to find it. It was a torch. He switched it on and its light confirmed what he had already sensed. Belle and Tessie had gone. The tub stood in the corner with half an inch of dirty water in the bottom. His holdall was standing beside it, with a note pinned to it. He unfastened it and read:

Dear Charlie,

I am sorry. I never thort. I am a pig. Tell them it was all me. Tell them you did not know nothing about it, and been looking for me. That way you will not get into trouble.

love Belle

P.S. Please do not tell where I am going.

He ran out of the barn into the cool dusk and gazed round. The fields were empty. Even the cows had vanished.

'Belle!' he called wildly, running towards the wood, 'Belle, where are you? Wait for me! *Please*!'

Where had she gone? It was only twilight. She wouldn't have started her journey yet. She must be hiding somewhere.

'Belle! Belle!'

No answer.

It was darker in the wood, and he crashed and stumbled about, scraping his elbows and knees. She was not there. Crying now, he ran along the verge of the Summaton road, passing the white gate with the For Sale sign beside it. The house itself was invisible behind tall fir trees. He did not know it was empty, and never even glanced at it. Belle, hiding with Tessie behind the trees, heard him go by.

13

It was midnight now. Belle stood by the gate of the empty house and watched the few, late cars go by, yellow-eyed as tigers in the night. She could see their headlights flickering through the hedges long before they came into sight. It was time to go.

If only she wasn't so tired! Her arms and legs ached. For ages, while Charlie slept, she had struggled in the barn, trying to drag the loaded saddlecloth on to the back of the kneeling elephant. It was too heavy for her. Hopeless. Then Tessie had taken over. Air whooshing up her trunk in great hopeful sniffs, the elephant had begun to unpack the pockets.

A tin of baked beans hit Belle on the knee. Apples rolled across the dirty floor of the barn and lost themselves in dark corners. A tube of toothpaste was trodden on, and split, whitening the great toes like mint-fresh frostbite. The elephant was enjoying herself.

It was the right idea. Unpack everything, fasten on the empty saddlecloth, put everything back. Easy. Or would have been, had not Tessie thought it was a game, throwing things out almost as fast as Belle could bundle them in, sneaking tomorrow's carrots into her mouth, tossing hay over her shoulder.

And still Charlie slept on.

Part of Belle was mean enough to want to prod him with her toe, as if by accident. To beg, 'Please come with me. I can't manage without you.'

She had never been alone. She had been born with the noise of the circus in her ears; shouts and laughter, whistling and hammering, dogs barking and the band playing. Now it was all gone, her mum and dad were gone, and that was bad enough. But parting with Charlie was the worst thing of all.

Still, it had to be done. He had saved her life: she could hardly repay him by spoiling his.

Good luck. See you sometime, she thought.

The old circus adieu. On a par with 'chin up and keep smiling', 'the show must go on', and all the other guff that had been pumped into her ears since she was a baby. Oddly enough, it helped her now.

To an invisible audience, to the sound of her heart drumming, she led the elephant out on parade; across the two fields, round the copse, and into the garden of the empty house by the back gate. She had had to trust to luck, for it was all she had left. It did not let her down. They reached the garden unobserved and hid behind the tall firs, waiting for the night.

No-one disturbed them. No exploring boy, no weary tramp came near them. No house agent called with a belated client. Only Charlie's footsteps, running through the gathering dark, his voice tolling dismally,

'Belle! Belle! Belle!'

She kept silent. Let him go. Let him have his chance to be a star.

This noble thought warmed her for all of two minutes. Then she was cold again, and frightened. There was no-one to clap. She had always needed an audience cheering her on. Alone, she felt very small and insignificant. A nobody. A nothing.

The elephant was standing patiently by her side; like a tame volcano, shaken occasionally by tiny eruptions. She had hiccups. Been drinking from the ornamental pool, probably swallowed a goldfish ... supposing she was sick? No good worrying now.

'Forward, Tess,' Belle said. 'Forward, old girl.' They crossed the road and started on their long journey.

Seven miles to Yald Forest by road. How many by field and footpath? Fifteen? Twenty? A hundred? At two o'clock in the moonlit morning, she was lost. She sat down on the dew-wet grass and cried.

She did not know where she was. She did not

know where her map was. She only knew that fields had gates in the stupidest places, had barbed wire woven into their hedges, and that no way, no way at all, could an elephant climb a stile. And the fat-faced moon was a deceiver; now flattening a pitted meadow so that she tripped and fell, now exaggerating each tiny irregularity so that she stepped too high over shadows and jarred every aching bone. It was no good.

'I can't ... I can't ... Somebody help me,' she whimpered.

The elephant stood motionless; silent, majestic, silvered by the moon. *She* had not suffered. The huge, cushioned circles of her feet had seemed to skim over the uneven ground like clouds. She had ambled forward when Belle told her to, stood still when Belle told her to; an old, patient, well-trained animal.

But every now and then, she would lift her great head and sniff the night air with her trunk. Then her pace had quickened ... Lord knew where she thought she was going, what ancient memories called her. Or perhaps she was merely looking for a warm shed or tent to sleep in.

Belle rubbed her eyes. 'What shall we do, Tess?' she asked.

As if in answer, the elephant swung her trunk towards Belle, and pulled at her gently. Get up? Why? What was the point? They could be going round in circles. For all Belle knew, Goosebeak

Farm might be hiding behind that clump of trees. She almost wished it were, with its warm kitchen. Where was Charlie now? she wondered. Snug in his bed, dreaming of the Big Top? Out searching for her with Mr Thorpe? Well, let them find her!

Now the elephant was prodding her.

'Stop it!' she said.

What did Tessie want? She couldn't be hungry again, not after all she'd eaten. Thirsty?

'Suck the grass, then. It's wet enough.'

Too wet to sleep on. A mist was creeping up, hugging the ground. Must be a river nearby. Belle got wearily to her feet.

'All right then. Drinkies.'

But which way? The black hedges barred her view. Perhaps Tessie could smell the water. 'Go on, then. Lead us to it.'

The elephant, puzzled, did not move. Belle looked up at the thick neck, the high shoulders half-covered by the bulging saddlecloth. Good view from up there.

All the time, walking, running, stumbling beside the elephant, she had known she ought to be riding her. Urging her on, instead of holding her back. Elephants, Mr Murphy had once told her, could walk ten miles in an hour. Or more. Even an old elephant, she thought, could probably do seven. It was not as if she had never ridden her before. Many times she had knelt on the looped trunk and allowed herself to be lifted up, until she could clutch the headband and scramble onto Tessie's neck. But that was before the accident. Before she lost her nerve.

And now? Without Mr Murphy standing by, sharp-eyed, ready to catch her if she slipped? With her knees weak and her head spinning? Supposing Tessie moved at the wrong time? Supposing she got impatient and shrugged Belle off like a fly? Trod on her in the dark!

No. She couldn't do it. She was a coward. Not circus any more, but the flattest of flatties. Dawn would come, and she and Tessie would be discovered cowering in this miserable field. At least, — Belle would be cowering, snivelling, waiting to be taken back in disgrace. Not Tessie. Gentle, patient, loving animal, she would be standing there, guarding her young friend. They would take her away, — how many tins of cat's meat would she make?

Four o'clock in the morning. Charlie got to his feet, yawning and stretching. Behind him, in the whispering, breathing, rustling darkness of the enclosed forest, something squealed. It was a pitiful, shivering sound. Hide, little creature, run back to your hole before the owl gets you, he thought. It must have been an animal. Couldn't possibly be Belle. But he could not rid himself of the feeling that, somewhere, she too was lost and frightened.

It was impossible that she could have got here

before him. A truck had given him a lift almost immediately, and he had been waiting ever since. For hours and hours, sitting on the ground with his back resting against the closed gate, he had stared from the shadows to the silvery road; at first hopefully, then anxiously, and now with the dull certainty that she would never come.

Had she changed her plan, not trusting him, and entered the forest another way? Or had she been caught already? Soon it would be dawn. Early risers would be waking. Milk trucks would go rattling over the cattlegrid on the road. It would be too late.

If I shut my eyes and count to a hundred, let her be there when I open them again ... But there were too many noises in the night for him to take the chance. Though he was guarding the gate to the bridle path, the road itself was protected only by a cattlegrid. This kept the wild ponies and donkeys and deer safe in the forest, but would it keep out an elephant? Tessie's huge feet could easily span the rungs, padded feet that might not even rattle the metal bars as she stole past him, while he sat with his eyes shut like an idiot. He dared not risk it.

So he went on staring up the empty road, jerking up his heavy eyelids every time he felt them falling. Now he seemed to see a grotesque shadow swaying silently up the grass verge. He looked at it sourly. He had been deceived before by wind-blown shadows, and this one was not even the right shape. Besides, there was no-one walking beside the shadow. No-one sitting on its neck. It was just another damn trick of the moonlight. Any moment it would dissolve into a thousand tossing leaves . . .

But the shadow kept on advancing, getting larger and more oddly-shaped by the moment, a monster growing out of the night. Three huge heads it had, and a single dim yellow eye . . . Then it stepped into a pool of moonlight and turned into Tessie, her figure distorted by the bulging pockets on her saddlecloth, and a bicycle lamp tied to her headband, the battery almost flat.

But where was Belle? What had happened?

He ran forward, shouting,

'Where is she? What have you done with her? I'll kill you if you've hurt her!'

'*Charlie*!'

Now he saw Belle. She was not so much riding the elephant, as glued to it, close as wallpaper. Her cheek was resting against the leathery skin, her hands clinging to the headband, and her feet thrust into the pockets among the apples and hay. She looked so strange lying there, a creature of moonlight, her eyes enormous in her silvery face, her hair spreading out like pale water over the elephant's massive head, that for a moment he could only stare at her, as if she were a stranger from another world.

Then she giggled, and the spell was broken.

'Where the devil have you been?' he demanded.

'Everywhere.'

'I've been waiting here all night.'

'I got lost.'

'You had the map —'

'Couldn't find it.'

'You're hopeless, aren't you? Useless. Just as well I came.'

She smiled down at him, and said cockily, 'I thought I might find you waiting here. Hogging my big act.' Then she said sharply, '*Car coming!*'

Charlie opened the gate to the bridle path and let them through. The three of them walked silently into the dark forest and vanished among the trees.

14

Black leaves blotted out the moon. The fading lamp on Tessie's headband, like a visible echo, lit their way briefly. Then it went out. Unperturbed, the elephant walked on.

'Stop!' Belle cried.

Too late. Twigs combed her hair spitefully and raked her shoulders. She flung her arms up in front of her face, and something hit her shoulder, pushing her off balance. A handful of leaves came away in her fingers. She was slipping, falling . . . the high wire, the circus ring far below her . . .

'Charlie!' she screamed.

It was not sawdust but a prickly bush that received her, breaking her fall and preserving her bones. Her nerve, however, the little remnant she'd had left, was shattered. She began to whimper.

A man's voice called out of the dark,

'Hullo? Who's there?'

She stuffed her knuckles into her mouth and was silent. The smell of elephant was strong in her nose. She felt it must be spreading through the trees, a give-away, a nasal advertisement, sharp as a circus trumpet.

A second voice mumbled sleepily, and the man said in reply,

'Something woke me. A scream, I think. Then I heard someone crying.'

'Oh hell, the boys . . .'

'A nightmare, I expect. I'll go and see.'

Splinters of light pricked the darkness. On Belle's left, leaves lit to a brilliant emerald. Then something blue . . . Tents! There were tents among the trees!

A hand touched hers and she jumped. Charlie's voice breathed in her ear,

'Come on. I've got Tess.'

They edged away from the light, arms outstretched to fend off the invisible trees. Dead twigs cracked beneath their feet.

The man said sharply, 'There's something moving over there!'

The light, broken up by the dark trees into a hundred golden arrows, was turning towards them . . .

'What's up?' It was a boy's voice now, young and shrill. 'Sir? Is that you, sir? What's happening?'

Belle whinnied loudly.

'A pony,' the man said, and laughed. 'Only

one of the forest ponies. Go back to sleep.'

The light turned away before it reached them. In the shadows, Belle felt Charlie pat her on the back, and she glowed with pleasure.

More boy's voices now.

'Sir, I want to go home. I don't like it here.'

'What's that horrible pong?'

'It's Roger. Sir, I want to change my tent. Roger stinks.'

'I don't! Anyway, you snore. Sir, he's been keeping me awake.'

Belle and Charlie crept away, leaving the voices behind them. They blundered deeper into the forest, which resisted them, scratching their faces and entangling their feet.

'Charlie,' Belle whispered, pulling her hair out of something prickly, 'Didn't you bring your torch.'

'They'd see the light. Best go on a bit.'

'It's so dark.'

'Feel your way.'

They went on and on. Unseen leaves slapped them, twigs poked them, branches brushed aside by the elephant whipped back in their faces. Now, not a yard away, an invisible creature sprang to its feet and crashed through the undergrowth.

Startled, the elephant raised her trunk and trumpeted into the night.

Birds exploded from the leaves above their heads. Small animals scuttled away in terror.

Belle felt Tessie move. She grabbed for her ear and missed. The warm, soft-crinkled skin — a leg, a stomach, another leg — brushed past her hands and the elephant was gone.

'*Stop! Tessie, stop!*'

She had a horrible vision of another camp, of a vast foot descending on a tent, of a small boy oozing between the great toes like jam.

There was a loud rustling, a splashing, then a steady gurgle.

Charlie switched on his torch. Tree trunks sprang out all around them, like great stone columns, greenish-grey in the light. Trees, bushes, ferns . . . No elephant.

'Tessie!' Belle yelled in panic. 'Tessie!'

A spray of water hit her face. She grabbed the torch from Charlie and shone it straight into a mischievous round eye, peering at her through a small gap in some thick holly. Getting down on her hands and knees, she wriggled beneath the low branches. She could hear Charlie following her, cursing under his breath.

The elephant was standing in a stream, cut deep in the floor of the forest. One of the high banks had crumbled, forming a small beach, half mud, half stones, and now heavily printed with elephant tracks.

It was much lighter. They were in a small clearing. On all sides, huge trees pushed through the undergrowth, elbowing each other for room. Here and there, they tilted at mad angles, dead and unable to lie down. Bushes filled the spaces between them and overhung the stream, so that it seemed to come from nowhere, swirl round the elephant's legs, and vanish again. Fallen branches spanned the hidden water, or lay piled together, as if for a bonfire, with ferns licking through them like green flames. High above their heads, a pale patch of sky shone through the leaves.

'It's almost day,' Charlie whispered. 'Listen, the birds are singing.'

'I'm so tired.'

'Shall we stay here? Seems safe enough. What d'you think?'

'Dunno.'

Belle sat down on the bank, half-asleep, barely conscious of Charlie leading the elephant out of the stream. In the dim light, the water looked discoloured, reddish from the iron in the ground.

'Oh, go to bed!' Charlie said kindly, throwing her sleeping-bag at her. 'You look half dead. I'll see to Tessie.'

'I must tether her . . .'

'I'll do it.'

'But . . .'

'Don't fuss. I can manage.'

She was too tired to argue. In her sleeping-bag in a nest of ferns, she was falling, falling, — only to wake with a jerk, seeming to hear her father's voice in her ears, 'Always check everything. Don't take risks. Life is dangerous enough.' Her mind was full of terrors; the dark forest, the sleeping boys, the great animal standing in a stream of blood ... She struggled against sleep, — wasn't there something she should have done? Told Charlie? What was it? The rope, use the rope ... It was no good. Her eyes closed again.

On the other side of the clearing, the elephant shifted her feet. She walked forward, felt the jerk of the tether on her hind leg, and swung her head round to look at it. Backing a little, she turned and pulled at the chain with her trunk. The stake to which it was attached slid gently out of the soft ground.

15

Someone was shaking Charlie and shouting his name. Go away. It can't be time to get up yet. Go away.

'Wake up! Charlie, *wake up!*'

He opened his eyes and saw Belle's face, freckled with sunlight and shadows. Her mouth was quivering.

'Tessie's gone,' she said.

'*What?*'

'She's gone.'

'She can't have gone,' he said stupidly.

She turned from him impatiently, and started running backwards and forwards in the clearing, calling, 'Tess! Tess!', her voice as high as a bird's.

There was confusion everywhere. Clothes and cabbage leaves, tins and torch batteries were scattered over the ground. Wisps of hay decorated the bushes like bleached tinsel. Belle's blue tee shirt floated in the stream.

'What happened?' he asked fearfully. 'Has

she gone crazy?'

'No, of course not. She just likes unpacking. And she's been at the food. Ain't got no table manners.' Belle's smile was shaky, but at least she had attempted a joke. Hadn't shouted at him, though it was his fault. *He* had tethered Tessie. 'Leave it to me,' he'd said ... Feeling guilty and miserable, he mumbled,

'She can't have gone far.' Another stupid remark, which Belle ignored. He didn't blame her. Tessie'd had all the time they had slept. She could be anywhere.

'Tessie! Tessie!' Now Belle was parting the branches on this side and that, trying to see through the crowding leaves.

Charlie scrambled to his feet, tripped over a hairbrush, trod on the recorder Uncle Bert had given him for Christmas. Automatically he picked it up. It seemed to be undamaged.

'I dunno where to start looking,' Belle said helplessly, and turned.

She caught sight of the recorder in his hands. Lost her temper. 'That's right! Don't worry about Tessie! Don't help me! Just stand there and play us a tune ...' She broke off. Her eyes widened and she said, 'Oh, Charlie, you're *clever!* That'll fetch her. Go on!'

He looked at her, pleased but bewildered by her sudden admiration, not liking to admit he had no idea what had caused it.

'Go on,' she said again; then, anxiously, 'Don't

116

say you've forgotten how it goes?'

What goes? Oh, of course! He put the recorder to his lips. Loud as he could, his cheeks blowing out like freckled balloons, he began to play the music for the entrance of the elephants.

There was a rustling of leaves, coming nearer, getting louder, a crackling of twigs, and the bushes parted.

But it was a man who walked into the clearing. He was tall, thin and somewhat untidy. Bits of bracken stuck to his crumpled trousers, a buttonless thread hung from his shirt, and he wore a lopsided haversack on his back. His fair, faded hair grew in long wisps all over his head and chin: he looked as if he needed mowing.

He smiled into their disappointed faces and said,

'Hullo. I thought you were Pan.'

'No,' Charlie muttered. 'Sorry.'

'We ain't seen no-one round here,' Belle said. 'Have we, Charlie?'

'No.'

'*Pan*,' the man repeated. 'You know, the merry, merry pipes of Pan.'

They stared at him. He smiled back at them so amiably that Charlie found himself apologising. 'Sorry. It was only me playing my recorder.'

The man tilted back his head and laughed.

Behind his back, making surprisingly little noise, the elephant loomed out of the bushes. The huge creature stood among the little, shaking

117

leaves, and gazed round. She seemed puzzled by so unusual a circus ring. And so small an audience. The man was still laughing. Hadn't heard her come. Had no idea she was standing behind him, like a house. Her eyes fixed with interest on his haversack.

She took a step towards him . . .

'*Stop!*' Belle shouted.

At one and the same time, the elephant stood still and the man stopped laughing. It was uncanny.

'I'm sorry. It was rude of me to laugh,' the man said. 'Unforgivable. Why should you have heard of Pan? Why in the world? No reason. I am a fool. *Mea culpa.*'

Behind his back the elephant stretched out a hopeful trunk towards his haversack.

'Sit down!' Belle cried.

Tessie sat obediently. The man looked surprised; then came forward and sat down too, on a log.

'Thank you,' he said.

There was a pause. The man just sat there, smiling, as if he thought they were going to offer him tea. Except that his nose kept wrinkling, he seemed quite unaware of the elephant sitting behind him.

Probably thinks it's us ponging, and is too polite to mention it, thought Charlie. Come to that, I expect we do a bit. Slept in our clothes, haven't washed since yesterday morning . . .

'Are you camping here?' he asked, and began to turn his head. At any moment he'd see Tessie! Couldn't miss her, sitting there, big as a bus, twiddling her trunk.

Belle stepped quickly in the way to block his view.

'I got to be excused. Don't watch! It's *rude!*'

She said this so sharply that the man went pink in the face, and looked away immediately.

'My dear child, I didn't intend . . . I'd no idea . . .'

'Well, don't turn round. I hate people staring at me!' she said and ran past him, across the clearing to Tessie.

'I assure you,' the man said, looking at Charlie in bewilderment, 'I had no idea of embarrassing your sister . . .'

'Cousin,' Charlie explained, 'she's shy.'

Behind the man's back, Belle had got Tessie to her feet and pushed her through the bushes. Then she held one hand up, the five fingers spread wide, before vanishing after the elephant.

Five minutes, Charlie translated. Five minutes to get rid of the man. How? Say straight out, 'Go away, you old goat. We don't want you here' . . .

But the man's face, sandwiched between his wispy hair and beard, looked so friendly. A friendly old goat; it would be like kicking an animal. While Charlie hesitated, he found he was being offered half a bar of chocolate.

'I'm afraid it's a bit sticky,' the man said, carefully wrapping the remaining half in its silver paper. 'I'll keep this for your cousin.'

'She won't come back while you're here,' Charlie said quickly. 'Like I said, she's shy. Hates being looked at.'

'Is it her scar?'

'Her scar's all right,' Charlie said shortly, 'I don't mind it.'

'No, indeed . . . In fact, I think it makes her look rather dashing, like a girl pirate. I only meant it was a pity if it worries her,' the man said gently. 'It's a difficult time, being a child . . . Was it a traffic accident?'

'No. She fell off something.' Charlie said, and then, because the man looked so kind and concerned, added impulsively, 'The thing is, — she's lost her head for heights.'

'That's very understandable.'

'D'you think she'll get over it?'

'I'm afraid I've no idea. You'd have to ask a doctor. Does it matter?'

'Yes,' said Charlie gloomily.

He had never dared ask anyone before. It mattered too much. He didn't quite know why, — there were other jobs in the circus. Belle's own mother never got her feet off the ground. She just stood in front of a painted board, while Uncle Bert outlined her plump, glittering figure with knives. And there was Mavis, the juggler's assistant, who handed him the props, and then pranced around, clicking her fingers and waggling her hips in time to the music. Belle could do that. Any fool could!

But what a come-down! He remembered how she used to swing high above his head, laughing down at him. He remembered her walking the low wire, light as thistledown, calling, 'Come on, Charlie! It's easy. You can do it! You can be as good as me — almost.'

He was better than Belle now. He ought to be pleased, but he wasn't. He was *miserable*. What good was it going up in the world, if he had to leave her behind on the sawdust, a skinny little bird with clipped wings?

The man, watching him, was puzzled. The boy looked so upset. How could it matter so much, — still it was none of his business.

'I must be getting on,' he said, rising to his feet, 'or I'll be late for lunch and my wife will be cross with me. She's not fond of walking. Rings on her fingers and corns on her toes, that's my fine lady.'

He had been hoping to make the boy smile, but Charlie just said dully,

'Goodbye, then.'

The man hesitated. Then he said, 'You know, it might be worth asking a doctor. I believe there's some sort of therapy that might work. Not that I know much about it. But I saw a programme on television ... actually, it was about people who are afraid of flying.'

Charlie's face brightened. In his mind he saw, not aeroplanes, but the Big Top, with the high flyers swooping and somersaulting above the safety net.

'Please, Mister, can you tell me about it?' he asked eagerly, 'I'll come with you part of the way. If you don't mind. Look, we can get through here. Careful, it's a bit prickly. Let me push back that branch . . .'

In the forest behind them, the elephant trumpeted.

'Good God, what was that?' the man said.

Charlie, startled, had let go the branch which swung back, its twigs getting entangled with his clothes and hair. He struggled wildly to free himself.

'Here, let me help you,' the man said. 'You're tearing your shirt.' He noticed the boy had gone quite white beneath his freckles, and added reassuringly, 'It must have been one of the wild donkeys. Horrible din, wasn't it? Quite enough to startle anyone.'

'Yes, a donkey,' Charlie babbled gratefully. 'It was a donkey.' He could have laughed with relief. People only heard what they expected to hear, he realised, and who would think of an elephant in Yald Forest?

The man smiled, glad to see the boy had recovered from his fright. They went off together, leaving the clearing empty.

16

Belle sat on the grassy bank, listening. Leaves whispered together. Water chattered with the pebbles in the stream. Birds above her head chirruped to one another. All the forest seemed to be conversing: she alone had no-one to talk to. Charlie was not back.

It was over two hours since she had heard him go off with the man. Two hours in which she had tidied away their belongings and repacked them neatly in the saddlebags. The map of Yald Forest had turned up among Charlie's shirts, and she left it out on the grass beside her. Then she had made baked beans and tuna fish sandwiches, wrapped them up in polythene; and waited.

And waited, growing more hungry and more anxious each minute.

'Silly fool's got lost,' she muttered.

The elephant, tethered by a long rope to a tree, was dreaming on her feet. She rumbled softly at the sound of Belle's voice, but did not open her eyes.

'If I go off to look for him, I'll get lost too, and then where will you be?'

The elephant did not answer.

'So what am I to do?'

The elephant had no ideas to offer. There was something very irritating about the way she stood, placidly snoozing while Belle fidgeted with worry.

'You're not much company, are you?'

The elephant opened her eyes and looked fondly and sleepily at Belle. Then she sat down and rolled over on to her side. Her great grey belly humped up from a sea of green ferns like a fissured rock. Dappled with sunlight and smudged with mud, it blended into the background, becoming part of the forest, a pattern of light and shade.

This is where she belongs, thought Belle, here in this wild nowhere. Not decked out in crimson and gold in a circus ring. Poor old Tess, she should've had a mate and calves of her own to love. Not just me and Charlie. Still, too late for that. It's us or the slaughterhouse now, old girl.

She picked up the map and spread it on the ground. Frowned. It was not an encouraging picture. Through the green hair of the forest, great bald patches showed; pink for heathland and yellow for downland. Grey scurfy villages hung in a net of roads, and there were red spots everywhere, for camping, fishing, horse riding and ancient monuments. Many of the green areas were divided up with dotted lines, and labelled: Canfield Enclosure, Cresswell Lawn Enclosure, Foxleap Enclosure . . .

Charlie had warned her. 'Look at it, Belle,' he had said. 'We'll never get through that lot unnoticed. It'll be crowded with trippers.'

And she had said, with the careless optimism that had so often got her into trouble, 'Oh, it'll be all right. We'll find somewhere to hide.'

Well, she supposed they had found somewhere, this little clearing in a tuft of trees. But already a man had come and walked off with Charlie. And now — now she could hear voices!

She jumped to her feet and stared through the leaves. Saw nothing but trees. She glanced back at the grey hump in the ferns. Would she know it was an elephant if she didn't know it was an elephant? Difficult to tell. Best leave Tessie sleeping, and go and meet trouble half way. Head it off, somehow. She parted the branches carefully, and wriggled through.

A figure rose out of the leaves and grabbed hold of her, crooking an elbow round her neck.

'Hey! I got another one!' it said.

She could not see who was holding her. She kicked backwards, but her soft sandals made no impression on a stout leg. The arm tightened round her neck, choking her. She could not scream.

Now her captor dragged her back into the

clearing. More figures stepped out from the trees. There were four of them, strange creatures, their faces painted with mud and half hidden by the leavy twigs attached to their hats. At first she thought they were soldiers. Then she noticed they were wearing faded denims below their patched khaki shirts, and one was a boy, no bigger than she was, holding a home-made bow and arrow.

A tall figure, who appeared to be their leader, strutted up and looked her over. In his mud-stained face, his grey eyes were as cold and pale as glass. He had a flick-knife in his hands and he pointed it at her, drawing patterns in the air as if planning how to cut her up. Then, as she stared at him in terror, he begun cleaning his nails with it.

'Bring in the prisoner,' he said.

Two more figures appeared, holding between them a struggling, squirming, cursing boy. It was Charlie. His face was patched with red, his lip split and bleeding, his shirt torn.

'Let her go!' he shouted. 'I'll kill you!'

'Shut up,' said the leader. 'You keep quiet, if you don't want your bird carved.' He looked back at Belle, then put out his hand and pushed the hair back from her cheek. 'Been done already, by the look of it. How d'you get that, eh?'

She could not speak. She could hardly breathe.

'Let go 'er neck, Jerry. You're strangling 'er. She won't scream. Will you, chick?'

The arm round her neck was taken away.

126

'What d'you want?' she croaked painfully. 'Who are you?'

She could see now that they were not men but youths, the oldest no more than sixteen or seventeen.

'We're outlaws,' said the one with the knife. 'Robin 'Ood and 'is merry men. Robbing the rich and giving to the poor. The rich, that's you. The poor, that's us.'

'I ain't got no money.'

'That's what 'e said,' the youth jerked his thumb at Charlie. 'And 'e were a dirty little liar, weren't 'e?' He patted his pocket, 'Thirty-five pound 'e 'ad on 'im. Not a bad haul.'

'I couldn't help it, Belle!' Charlie cried, close to tears. It was all they had left on their fund. They *needed* it.

'Turn your pockets out, — Belle, is it?' The youth said, 'Ding dong Belle, let's 'ear you chime. Come on, 'and it over like a good girl, or we'll 'ave to search you. Hey, what about it? Would you like that? Not ticklish, are you?'

'Leave her alone!' Charlie shouted, struggling helplessly.

But Belle had heard what none of them seemed to have noticed, a great heaving and rustling in the ferns behind her. She might not have a knife but perhaps she had something better; a tank, a juggernaut . . .

'*Don't move!*' she said.

Even as she spoke, she saw the leader's jaw

127

drop, as if a hinge had broken. The black stripes of mud now patterned a skin gone white, and from this zebra-face, his light eyes, fixed in terror, stared over her shoulder.

'She'll attack if you move!' Belle said fiercely. 'She'll mash you all into the mud. For God's sake, keep still.'

They stood like statues, except they trembled. They hardly seemed to breathe. The young boy whimpered once, then gagged his mouth with his hand. The two youths who had been holding Charlie, had let go, and were trying to inch back into the bushes.

'Don't move!' Belle said again, and they froze.

She looked at Charlie, trying not to laugh. To her astonishment, he too was staring past her, his eyes wide and frightened. Puzzled, she turned round.

The elephant, risen out of the ferns, no longer looked the gentle animal they had known. Her ragged ears stood rigidly out from her head. Her trunk swung like a truncheon. She was swaying backwards and forwards, her furious eyes fixed on the youth who had been holding Belle. Here, in this great green tangled world, old memories awoke. The elephant smelled fear. Her skinny little calf was frightened, and the great animal prepared to defend her. Raising her trunk aloft, she gave the trumpet scream of battle.

But now Belle was walking towards her, making soft noises, repeating the odd sound that the elephant knew meant she must not move her feet. Opposing instincts warred in her great head.

'Stand, Tess! Stand!'

The small, clear voice penetrated the dark confusions in her mind. She shook her head as if to clear it, and dust flew from her ears. Then, suddenly, she turned and vented her fury on an innocent bush. She smashed it with her trunk, pounded it into the earth and trampled on it, plucked the broken thing up by its roots and beat it against a tree. Only when it was a mangled corpse did she toss it away, and stand quietly, her sides heaving.

Belle laid a shaking hand on her trunk.

'Gently, old girl. Gently, my fat darling. Hush now. It's all right.'

She stood, soothing the elephant, and heard Charlie's voice behind her, rich with satisfaction.

'Get in line, you lot,' he was saying. 'I'll have my money back for a start, — and that knife! That's better. Anyone else got any weapons? Throw 'em down over there. You're *our* prisoners now.'

Prisoners! What on earth are we going to do with them? Belle wondered. Can't hand them over to the police, we're in hiding ourselves. Tie 'em up with rope . . . Rope!

She looked down at the long tether, lying like a snake in the ferns, hidden from all eyes but her own. Would it have held? She wondered. She went on stroking the elephant, whispering,

'What have we done to you, Tess? You're changing. The forest is changing you. Don't forget us. Don't forget you love me. Elephants aren't supposed to forget.'

17

It was odd that, after such a beginning, they should become friends. Well, friends of a sort. They did not trust one another, yet they sat, talking and laughing companionably, sharing their food. Charlie was not certain how it had come about.

First they had been his enemies, then his prisoners . . . perhaps that was the trouble. What can you do with prisoners if you don't have a handy gaol to put them in? No chance of shutting the door and forgetting them. There they were, six big sullen louts and a snivelling boy. So you start talking — well, you can't just stand staring at each other in silence, and the next thing you know you're swapping stories . . .

It began when the boy had started coughing, a dry, rapid cough that shook his shoulders and made him gasp for breath.

'Pat him on the back, can't you?' Charlie said, thinking he was choking. Then he saw, out of the corner of his eye, the leader slip his hand quickly into a pocket. 'Hey! Stop that!' he said sharply.

'Don't worry, kid. It ain't a gun,' the leader said, bringing out a crumpled paper bag and holding it up. Somebody sniggered. 'Fruit drops, see? For Billy. 'E don't like cough sweets. You ain't got no objections to 'im 'aving one, I 'ope.'

'No.'

' 'E's got a bit of a cold,' the leader explained, unwrapping a sweet and handing it to the coughing boy with an air of concern that seemed odd from such a sharp, dangerous-looking youth. He then held the bag out to Charlie.

'Like one?'

Charlie hesitated.

'They ain't poisoned, cross me 'eart,' the leader said, rather mockingly.

'All right, then. Thanks.'

It was as if he had accepted an olive branch. Immediately the outlaws relaxed.

' 'Ave a fag?' one of them offered.

'Mind if we sit dow?' another said. 'Me legs still 'urts. You didn't 'alf kick 'ard.'

'Yeh, you put up a good fight,' the leader said, admiringly. ' 'Ave to 'and it to you. Proper little scrapper, you are.'

''E may be a feather-weight, but 'e ain't chicken,' said a black youth, on whose ebony skin the mud smears looked sallow.

They all laughed at this. 'You can say that

132

again, Pete. 'E sure ain't chicken.'

Charlie could not help being pleased, even though he guessed they were deliberately flattering him. Behind his back, he could hear Belle still talking softly to the elephant, and was glad she could not see the silly smirk on his face.

'What's your name, kid?' the leader asked.

'Charlie.'

'I'm Flick, and Billy 'ere's me kid brother. Them's —' he waved his hand at the others and gabbled a list of names so quickly that it sounded like one word, 'Jobertdavejerripete'

Dazed by the excitements of the day, Charlie made no attempt to distinguish between them. It seemed right that the ring of faces, disguised with mud and shadowed by the leafy fronds on their hats, should have only one name. They were like a many-headed creature, a dragon of the forest, friendly now, but never quite to be trusted. Even when he got to know them better, something of this impression of them as a combined personality remained. He often could not tell who was speaking.

Now he smiled at them uncertainly, and said, 'What am I going to do with you?'

They looked at him reproachfully, saying, 'Why, we're friends now, ain't we?'

That's how it had begun. Now, hours later, he and Belle were sitting outside the outlaws' hide-out, drinking hot tea from enamel mugs; while the sun sank below the tree tops, and the forest closed in about them, dim, secret and safe.

Charlie still thought of them as the outlaws, though when he had asked them what they called themselves, they had said they didn't call themselves anything.

'We ain't a kid's gang,' Flick said. 'We're drop-outs. We don't want no part of their stinking civilisation. What's it ever done for us?'

The circus children did not know. They weren't even sure what civilisation was supposed to do for you. All the outlaws spoke of their world bitterly, as if it had cheated them of something. As if it would cheat anyone, given half a chance. Belle and Charlie exchanged uneasy glances: this was the world they were about to enter. No longer would the Big Top, with its brightly-striped canvas and sparkling lights, protect them from harsh winds. They felt young and ignorant.

'You mean, you've run away from home, then?' Belle asked.

''Ome? What's that?' Flick asked sourly. ''Aven't been in a 'Ome since I was fifteen. Then our mum took me back. Not Billy, 'e was too young to be useful. She only wanted me. Thought I was going to get a job and support 'er. What a laugh! I emptied 'er purse one afternoon, fetched Billy out of the dump, and came out 'ere. The forest is all right. We like it 'ere.'

'Won't they be looking for you?' Charlie asked.

'The police? Yeh. Bound to be. But not 'ere.

Laid a false trail, didn't we?' Flick said, 'I left a note for our mum, saying as 'ow we was going to Lunnon, and not to bother coming looking for us.'

'You gotta throw 'em off the scent,' said the black youth, whose name was Pete. 'We was in the same 'Ome, me and Bill and Jo. So when we was ready to go off, I looked round for the biggest blabbermouth and told 'im we was off up to the smoke. "It's a secret, mind," I said, knowing 'e couldn't keep 'is mouth shut in a sandstorm. Then we buzzed off quick and come down 'ere, where they'll never guess in an 'undred years. Think we're too soft to live wild, but we ain't. We're no tame cats, mewing for milk. We manage.'

'Yeh,' the others agreed. 'We manage all right.'

They seemed to have known each other for a long time, met in various Homes, remand centres, shared the same probation officer. Only Jerry, the one who had grabbed Belle, had no story to offer. He was a heavy, lumpish youth, big as a man, with a face like a dirty pudding, and small, blackcurrant eyes. He said very little, and smiled less. Occasionally Flick would glance at him, and Charlie thought his expression was uneasy.

The outlaws had lived in the forest for over three months, right under the noses of the forest authorities, and never once been caught. Nor even seen, unless they chose to be.

'We know our way around,' they boasted. 'It's

easy, if you know 'ow. We can crawl past a keeper so close 'e could touch us with 'is 'and, only 'e don't know we're there. We can snitch a purse out of picnic basket so quiet it don't disturb the flies. Oh, there ain't a fox can out-smart us! And we got our earths, too. What d'you think of our 'ide-out, eh? Not bad, is it? We 'ave them all over the forest.'

Belle and Charlie had been shown over the hide-out and had been impressed. Even close to, it was impossible to tell it was there. It looked like a bush, a living bush with green leaves. Only when you'd gone round the back and crawled under the low branches of a rhododendron, could you see that the bush was trained over a trapdoor. This trapdoor itself was stuck all over with dried grass and needed sharp eyes to discover it. Underneath, the ground had been hollowed out to make a low, small room, boarded with planks of wood, and roofed with old tarpaulins, ('It's shocking 'ow careless people are with their property'). They had a primus stove and a kettle and an old black frying pan. Their beds were of dried bracken, with a few grey blankets. Too few, thought Charlie, and was glad their sleeping bags were packed away from envious eyes. Still, it must have been hot in there, with all seven of them. Like a sardine-tin. He wouldn't fancy it himself. But you couldn't deny it was clever.

'You can't stay here for ever, though,' Belle

said. 'I mean, when winter comes . . .

It was as if she had said a dirty word, stubbed out a cigarette on a child's balloon. There was a shocked silence while they glared at her.

Then Flick said curtly, 'We'll manage. Some'ow.'

Belle looked doubtful, and Charlie was afraid she would argue and turn the outlaws against her. Since she had walked fearlessly up to the rampaging elephant, they had treated her with respect. She was their young queen, a right good 'un, a brave little chick. Belle had glowed under their open admiration, laughing and tossing back her hair, no longer ashamed of the scar that seemed, in this fierce company, like a badge of honour.

Well, she *had* been brave, though not quite as brave as they thought. And she'd been cunning too, saying innocently, 'I suppose I'd better tie her up now. Where's that rope gone?' — pretending to search in the ferns for a tether that (Charlie guessed) was already firmly attached to the elephant's ankle.

'It's an old rope,' she had warned them, untruthfully, 'Frayed. If she gets mad, it won't hold her, no more than a cobweb would. So don't get any ideas.'

No, they wouldn't, they had promised, looking uneasily at the elephant.

' 'Ow did you come by 'er, Miss?' Billy had asked. 'Is she yours?'

To Charlie's surprise, Belle had told them the truth, though not all of it. She had left out all names, except for their own, and did not say where they planned to end up. The outlaws' faces softened as they listened. One or two of them had murmured, 'Poor old elephant. What a shame. 'Ope you make it all right.'

Only Jerry had scowled and muttered that he'd prefer tins of cat's meat to that shoving monster any day.

Even now, he kept looking resentfully across the new clearing, to where Tessie was tethered.

'Do we 'ave to 'ave that stinking creature so near. Turns my stomach.'

'You don't smell so sweet yourself.'

'It ain't right to keep a dangerous animal.'

'Tessie's not dangerous. She's as gentle as a lamb,' Belle said, then added cautiously, 'unless she's provoked.'

'Some lamb!' Flick said, smiling at her.

'Honest! She's an old softie. Come and stroke her.'

Flick was taken aback. He looked suddenly uncertain, like a boy confronted with a dare he wanted to refuse, but could not. The other outlaws turned their mud-stained faces and stared silently at their leader, waiting. Jerry gave a grunting laugh, and sneered.

'Go on, Flick. Flick ain't scared, is 'e? Not our leader! Not Flick the Knife.'

Without meaning to, Belle had nudged the

balance of power and set it rocking. No leader of a pack could afford to show cowardice. Ordeal by elephant, thought Charlie, biting back a laugh.

Yet somehow, in the leafy half-light, with the forest stirring around them, it did not seem so ridiculous. The elephant was transformed. Like the vast stone goddess of an ancient religion, she stood under the trees and watched them impassively.

At last Flick got to his feet, and said, his voice strained,

'Yeah. Why not?'

He and Belle walked slowly up to the elephant, who stretched out her trunk to touch Belle briefly in greeting. Then she turned her attention to Flick. Across the clearing, they could hear the air whooshing through her trunk as she sniffed him all over. It made a strange sort of music, weird, primitive. He stood straight and still, like a young warrior undergoing an initiation ceremony, and the watchers held their breath. Then Flick reached up and touched the elephant's forehead, just once, before stepping back.

He laughed with relief, and turning to the others, said,

'Come on, you beggars. Pay your respects to the old lady.'

They went up one by one, slowly, nervously, to touch the elephant and move on. In the dim, fretted light, the figures with their mud-smeared faces and leafy hats looked like beings from a wilder planet, taking part in some dark ceremony. So strong and strange was the spell, that Charlie found himself following, to touch the elephant goddess in his turn. He was shocked when Belle winked at him. It was as if a priestess had stuck her tongue out.

When he had moved on to join the others, he heard her say sternly,

'No. Not you. Keep away.'

It was Jerry to whom she spoke. He stood there lumpishly, just out of reach of the elephant's trunk and glowered.

'What'cher mean? Why not me?'

'She hates you. You attacked me. She'll never forget. Never forgive. Look at her.'

And indeed the great animal was moving restlessly, pulling against her tether.

'Go back now,' Belle said, and they scattered to the far side of the clearing.

'Is she safe?' Billy asked, his voice high and afraid. 'She can't get loose, can she?'

'She'll be all right now,' Belle said, 'Only keep *him* away. The fat one.'

Charlie glanced at Jerry, and saw the black-currant eyes gleam with hate in the shadowed face. Belle had made an enemy. One who would never forget. Never forgive.

18

Somehow, the outlaws had taken charge of them.

'You'll never manage without us,' they said. 'Look 'ow easy we caught you. Babes in the wood, that's what you are. You'd end up in a campsite or a woodman's 'ut. 'Ere, let's 'ave a look at your map.'

They spread it on the ground. Already the light was so poor that they had to use a torch. The outlaws squatted round in a tight circle, all elbows and knees, like stick insects. Only Jerry stood back, looking over their shoulders; listening, watching, not saying anything.

'We thought we'd go this way tonight,' Belle said, tracing her finger over a large green area. 'Hide up somewhere here for the day. Then tomorrow night, we'll only have that open moor to cross.'

The outlaws leaned closer, so that the twigs on their hats met, forming a little forest of their own. Fingers jabbed at the map, voices excitedly

141

warned of the dangers; a bog here, a fence there, a car park, men digging ditches . . . Go this way, they said, No, that way. Hide here. Hide there. Their faces, lit from below by the torchlight, looked strange, unearthly. Behind them in the twilight, the tethered elephant shifted her great feet and looked down curiously at the little chattering creatures who were deciding her fate.

Finally Flick put down his finger firmly, brushing the other fingers aside. '*There*,' he said, 'I'll take you there. Good spot.'

Belle peered at the map.

'But it's an enclosure,' she objected.

'So what? There's gates.'

'Ain't they kept locked?'

'No. You can go in if you don't do no damage. It says so. No camping. No fires. Dogs to be kept on the lead.' He thought for a minute. 'Don't say nothing about elephants.'

Belle hesitated, not liking the thought of being fenced in.

'But . . .' she began doubtfully.

It was no good. They talked her down. Everyone agreed it was the best place, a smashing place; bracken higher than your head and branches down to your knees. What about people? No trouble. They kept to the paths.

'They won't see us,' Flick said. 'People are dead stupid. They don't know 'ow to look.'

'Kids are a nuisance, though,' Pete warned them.

'Kids didn't stay on the paths.'

'Sharp-eyed little beggars, some of them. You want to watch out for kids!'

'But don't worry. You leave them to us,' Flick said. 'We'll deal with them.' Belle looked at him sharply, and he laughed. 'Oh, we won't cut their throats or nothing like that. Just shove 'em around a bit. Send them back to their mums.'

'Doing them a favour, really,' said Pete. 'Stops them getting lost. We oughta charge for it.'

'We do,' said Flick slyly, and they all laughed.

Belle was silent, remembering Charlie's bruised and bleeding face, the stolen money, the arm crooked round her neck . . .

'It's a good place, honest,' Flick said, mistaking the reason for her silence, 'Trust us.'

They had to trust them, though it became more difficult as it grew darker, and the outlaws, their camouflaged faces melting into the shadows, became whispers in the night. Belle and Charlie kept close to Tessie, comforted by her huge bulk and warm, familiar smell. Every rustle in the leaves made them jump nervously, wondering if a new friend had become an enemy again, creeping up on them in the dark. They were relieved when Flick said it was time to go.

He led them along narrow roads, keeping a scout in front and one in the rear. The forest was not fenced here.

'When they give the signal, dive for cover,' he said.

'What's the signal?'

'This,' Flick said, and gave a high, warbling, bird-like call. His followers vanished. One moment they were on the road, and the next they were gone.

Flick laughed with pride, 'See 'ow it goes?' he said. He gave the call again, and the outlaws were back, seeming to rise out of the ground.

'You ought to be a general,' Charlie said admiringly, as they walked on.

'Me? Fight their bloody wars for them? Risk my life for *them*? What've they ever done for me?'

He spoke so bitterly that Charlie thought he meant particular enemies, with well-known and well-hated faces.

'Who?' he asked.

'*Them*,' Flick repeated, his voice harder than the road beneath their feet. 'Everybody. Everybody who ain't one of us.'

'Oh.' Charlie said; then, not to be outdone, added, 'We call them flatties.'

'What?'

'Everyone who's not circus, that's what we call them. Flatties. We don't hate them, though.' He smiled, 'I mean, someone's got to pay to see us.'

To his surprise, Flick said impatiently, 'Oh, you don't know nothing. You're just a kid,' and went off to walk with Pete.

It was cold now, with a wind blowing in the trees. The road stretched in front of them, striped like a tiger in the moonlight. Twice they heard the high, warbling signal. The first time, Charlie was half asleep. Taking it for a real bird, he would have gone on walking, had someone not grabbed his arm and dragged him into the trees. A car swept past, its headlights fanning the edge of the forest, seeming to seek them out. Then it was gone.

'They only look at the road ahead,' Flick said. 'They don't see nothing else. People are stupid.'

Charlie thought if you were driving, it was sensible to keep your eyes on the road; but he said nothing. He could not help being impressed by Flick's efficiency. When they reached the enclosure, Pete was told to walk ahead, shining a torch on the path in front of the elephant. The others walked behind, stopping occasionally to scuff their feet over the gravel, or brush a patch of earth with sticks.

'Try and keep 'er off the mud,' Flick said, ' 'er feet are too big. They'll never take that for no rabbit.'

After about ten minutes, Pete stopped and shone his torch briefly into the forest on one side. Water gleamed on the dead leaves in a wide ditch.

' 'Ere we are,' he said. 'Walk 'er along there. We don't want the bracken trampled. The water'll 'ide 'er tracks.'

The ditch ran straight into the forest. It was darker here, and the torchlight moved so quickly, they had to hurry to keep up with it. Twice Charlie stumbled over a hidden root and fell to his knees into a wet squelch of dead leaves. He was glad when Pete led them out of the ditch and on to dry ground. A dim figure brushed past him, and Flick's voice said, 'All right. This'll do.'

The outlaws flopped down on the ground, disappearing into the bracken between the tall trees. Pete switched off his torch. From the sudden darkness, a gruff voice said,

'What about that stinking brute? Don't want 'er near us. It ain't safe.'

There was a murmur of agreement.

Charlie said quickly, thankfully, 'It's all right. We'll take her further on. We can meet up in the morning.'

'I'll come with you,' Flick said, 'I ain't afraid of 'er. And we don't want you getting lost, do we?'

There was no way of refusing this kind offer. Charlie put his hand in his pocket and closed his fingers round Flick's knife, glad he had not given it back. I'd best stay awake, he thought; it isn't long till dawn. It's just the dark and not knowing . . .

For some time he lay, listening to the noises of the forest, the wind agitating the leaves, the sudden little scamperings in the undergrowth, an owl hooting its eternal question, who? who?

Nearby, Flick was breathing heavily, — was he really asleep? He had been nervous, worried about Tessie, insisting that they tethered her a long way off, inspecting the rope and the knots with his torch . . . 'You sure you done it right? I don't want to be mashed up in my sleep.'

Sleep. Tessie was asleep now. He could hear her snoring in the distance. It was a gentle, soothing sound, like surf on a beach, small waves stroking the shingle. When the tide was out, he and Belle danced on the sands, and the flatties loved them. They were filling his hat with silver coins, and gold . . . Five pound notes blew through the summer air, rustling like leaves on the trees . . . Charlie slept.

19

Tessie had got free again. She was standing over the saddlebags, with the tether trailing behind her, eating the last of the carrots.

'You ain't fit to look after 'er! Can't you even tie a knot proper?' It was Flick's voice that woke Belle. High and reproachful, it seemed to come from the bright sky itself.

She looked up and saw him sitting astride a branch, scowling down at her. In five other trees, youths hung like pale fruit. She hardly recognised them. They had washed the mud from their faces, and looked not so much clean as faded.

'I did!' she protested. 'I checked it twice. You saw me do it. We tied her to ... *Look!*' She pointed to a tree, around whose trunk part of the tether was still knotted. 'It must've broke.'

Charlie was already up. He ran over and picked up the rope. 'It's been *cut!*' he cried, staring. 'Someone's gone and cut it!'

The outlaws dropped down from their trees,

and came slowly towards them, keeping a wary eye on the elephant. Charlie held the rope up, showing the cut end. 'Who'd have done that?' he asked, bewildered.

'*Jerry*!' one of them said immediately, and the others agreed. 'Yeah, bet it was Jerry. Outa spite. 'E 'ad 'is knife all the time, 'idden in 'is sock.' One of them added reproachfully, 'You didn't ought to've said she 'ated 'im. 'Urt 'is feelings. Expect that's why 'e sloped off.'

'Must've made off early,' Pete said. 'There weren't no hollow in the bracken to show where 'e'd slept.'

'No,' the others agreed. 'We looked all over.'

'No sign of 'im.'

'I ain't worried,' Billy muttered, ' 'E weren't really one of us. Was 'e, Jo?'

'No. Just tagged along.'

Belle got the impression that none of them had liked him much. When she asked anxiously whether he would tell the police about Tessie, they all laughed, seeming to find the idea of Jerry's going anywhere near the police highly comic. 'Not 'im! 'E's on the run,' they said.

Jerry did not go to the police. He rang them from a call box.

'I got something to report,' he said in his hoarse voice. 'There's two circus kids 'iding out in the forest. They've stole a helephant.'

There was a muffled sound at the other end

of the wire; then a voice said politely, 'May I have your name and address, please, sir.'

'They're 'iding up in Foxleap Enclosure . . .'

'Just a minute, sir. May I have your name and address first. Then we can both get on to the elephant.'

Jerry put the telephone down and swore. Make fun of him, would they? He left the kiosk and walked moodily down the high street in the thin sunlight, pushing rudely past the early shoppers. Suddenly he stopped and stared in a window. Behind the glass, there were newspaper cuttings fastened to a board, and several glossy photographs; simpering children in fancy dress, a beaming man holding up a silver cup, some toffs in evening dress, grinning at the camera . . . Jerry stared at them, hating them all. He looked up. Above the window was a sign saying: RHINDHURST WEEKLY ADVERTISER.

He frowned at the lettering, his lips moving as he spelled out the words. Then he opened the door and went in.

''Ow much will you give me for a scoop?' he said.

The young reporter did not care for Jerry. Nobody ever had, that was his trouble. There was something very off-putting about his large, clumsy figure, and the podgy cheeks encrusted with acne. Though he had washed the mud from his face, it was not an improvement. Yet oddly enough, it was the spite in his small, dark eyes that made the young man take any notice of his story.

'You expect me to believe that?' he asked, half-believing it.

'It's true. I can show you where they're 'iding.'

'You're seriously telling me that an elephant was kidnapped two days ago, and nobody *noticed?*'

'They dunno it's gone, see? The farm people think it's at the slaughter'ouse, and the slaughter-'ouse think it's at the farm. I told you.'

'What's the farmer's name?'

'Dunno. They wouldn't say.'

'These circus children, Belle and Charlie, wasn't it you said? — what's their surname?'

'Dunno. They didn't say.'

'Name of the circus?'

'Dunno. They didn't say.'

'They don't seem to have trusted you much, do they?' asked the young man, looking at Jerry with distaste. 'What about the parents? Didn't they report the children as missing?'

'They gone off to America.'

'Just went off? Without making any arrangements for their children?'

Jerry looked at him blankly, seeing nothing unusual in that. In his world, children were often abandoned.

The young reporter hesitated. It seemed a fantastic story, — was it even worth checking? Then he looked back at Jerry and decided it was. That heavy, sullen face did not belong to a practical joker. After all, he had nothing much to do till four o'clock. And Foxleap Enclosure was only six miles from Rhindhurst.

Pete and Charlie were on look-out duty. They lay hidden in the tall bracken that edged the gravelled walk, talking idly in whispers. Charlie told Pete about life in the circus; about putting up the Big Top in a high wind, with the canvas fighting you and the ropes burning your hands. About hot tea and toast in the dawn, before the hard day's work; about the horses and the elephants, the trumpets and the drums.

Pete told him about the forest. 'Funny, ain't it?' he said, 'I was brought up in a town. Never thought much of the country before. We came 'ere with the school once. Nature trip. Never saw nothing, — too busy assing about with me mates. But living 'ere, it's different, some'ow. It gets you. Seen any deer yet?'

'No.'

'We 'ave. They 'ide up in the day. Come out early or when it's getting dark, stepping down the paths like they was wearing 'igh 'eels. Dainty walkers, they are. And we seen badgers, too, and fox cubs playing . . .' he smiled at Charlie, his teeth very white in his dark face. 'Think I've gone soft, doncha?'

'No,' Charlie said, 'I wish I could see them.'

'Ain't the right time now. But if you stay, I

could show you. Show you where to find marsh gentians and orchids, too. Know what that is?' He held out a small yellow flower.

'No.'

'Yellow pimpernel. And that's dog mercury. Betony. Wood spurge. I got their names outa a book. Snitched it from the back of a van,' he added, looking sideways at Charlie, with a sly grin.

'You ought to be a Forester,' Charlie said, referring to Pete's learning, rather than the way he'd picked it up.

'Who, me?' Pete said. 'Don't make me laugh.' But his face was nowhere near laughter. It looked for a moment bitterly unhappy.

'Why not?' Charlie asked, 'I bet you'd be good at it. Couldn't you . . .'

Pete interrupted him, saying angrily, as Flick had done,

'Oh, you don't know nothing! You're only a kid!' Then, seeing Charlie was offended, he explained, 'They wouldn't 'ave me. I ain't clean. Got a record, see? Most of us 'ave, except Billy. Dunno why. Daft, really.' He was silent for a moment, chewing a stalk of grass, his face bleak. 'It ain't what we want!' he burst out, 'living in concrete 'utches! Cooped up at school, watching the telly at night . . . We ain't like that! We need . . . oh, I dunno. Something different. We ain't thick, whatever they think. Flick's clever. And I ain't no dumbbell. You know, —' he laughed and looked at Charlie. 'You know, I bet I could've invented the wheel.'

'The *Wheel*?'

'Yeh. I know it's been done before. Everything's been done before. The 'ole stinking world's gone stale. It's all been parcelled out and there ain't nothing left for us. It ain't even human no more. Pressing buttons . . .'

He saw Charlie staring at him, and pushed him playfully, saying, 'Don't mind me, kid. Dunno what I'm talking about, do you?'

'Sort of,' Charlie said doubtfully.

'You're lucky. You got something.'

'What?'

'An elephant,' Pete said, and they both laughed.

It was warm and pleasant in the drowsy sunlight. Charlie forgot they were supposed to be look-outs and lay back, gazing up at the sky. But Pete had been well trained. His restless eyes, always moving backwards and forwards, always checking, saw the distant figures as soon as they came into view.

'Blimey, 'e's fetched the pigs!' he said, and crouching low, bolted through the bracken into the forest. Charlie followed. Once in the safety of the trees, they ran like hunted foxes, their hearts thundering, till they reached the outlaws' lair.

'Flick! Flick! Jerry's fetched the pigs. They'll be 'ere in a minute!'

There was an orderly confusion. The outlaws scurried about like ants, grabbing up their possessions. One of them, Bert it was, picked up the saddlebags, half-empty now, and slung them over his shoulder.

'Follow us,' Flick whispered.

They ran through the trees, leaping over fallen logs and arching roots. Tessie, with Belle running beside her, kept up with them easily, crashing through the obstructions as if they did not exist, leaving a trail behind them as wide as a bulldozer's. When they had run for about five minutes, Flick stopped them, and they stood poised, listening. They could hear voices faintly, in the distance.

'That's them,' Flick whispered. His sharp eyes looked round, noting the crushed bracken and trampled bushes behind them; and on one side, a wide stream, almost a river, flowing sluggishly between its banks. 'Get 'er in there,' he ordered. 'Pete, you take Jo and lay a false trail. Quick now! Meet up in Shortlands, the dead pine, — O.K.?'

The youths nodded, splashed their way across to the far bank and ran off, crushing the bracken and beating down the bushes with sticks as they went. Flick jumped into the stream and, beckoning the others to follow, ran swiftly through the water. Only when the stream narrowed a little, with dense bushes crowding the banks, did he slow down. 'Quiet now,' he whispered. 'Walk careful. Try not to splash.'

It was difficult not to make a noise. There

were stones and dead leaves in the mud at the bottom of the stream, and it was very slippery. The children lifted their feet high and slid them into the water like fish, but the elephant, of course, had not understood. She wallowed happily behind them, stopping now and again to suck water noisily up her trunk. Flick frowned angrily over his shoulder, but there was nothing Belle could do.

Now they came to a fallen tree spanning the water. The outlaws ducked underneath it, leaving the circus children and the elephant on the other side.

'Bleeding 'ell,' muttered Flick. He looked at the banks, but they were high and steep here, crowned with matted bushes. 'We'll 'ave to . . .'

'*Look out!*' Belle cried.

The elephant had lowered her great head and was pushing. The youths raced away, their feet transforming the brown water to flying diamonds. Now the fallen tree was shifting, tearing through the shrubs on either side. Branches cracked like pistol shots, the echoes ricocheting through the forest. Great rocks splashed into the stream. For two yards, the elephant drove the fallen tree before her, like a mudguard. Then its top branches met something immovable and it swung sideways, letting her through.

They hurried on, taking no care to be silent now, until they could go no further. To Charlie's surprise, the stream seemed to run straight into a short brick wall, with wire fences on either side. Then he saw it was a bridge, the shallow arch barely clearing the water. On the other side of the fences, there was a wide grass verge, a narrow road, and then the forest began again.

'Bill, Dave, look-outs!' Flick said, and the two youths climbed quickly over the fence and ran forward to take up positions at the roadside.

Then Flick turned and stared at the elephant, looking for the first time at a loss.

'What the 'ell we going to do with 'er?' he muttered.

'She can push that fence down easy,' Charlie suggested.

'Yeah? Get us all caught, that would! Nothing bugs the Foresters worse than broken fences. They'd be swarming all over, trying to find what done the damage. And *they* ain't blind.'

He stood frowning, while the children watched him. Then he shrugged. ''Ave to dump you. Sorry,' he said regretfully, a general abandoning three of his soldiers for the sake of his army. 'Once they got you, they won't look no further. Come on, Bert.'

He climbed over the fence. Bert, the saddle-cloth still over his shoulder, began to follow.

'That's ours!' Charlie protested, catching hold of it.

'*Was* yours, y'mean,' Bert grinned and jabbed him in the ribs, so hard that Charlie let go and staggered backwards.

'Flick!' Belle cried, 'Flick, *please!*'

Flick turned. Belle had led the elephant out of the stream and was standing by the fence, looking very small and fragile beside the huge creature.

'Oh, let 'em 'ave it, Bert,' he said, perhaps out of true generosity, or possibly because Bert, made nervous by Tessie's proximity, had already dropped the saddlecloth and was making off over the grass.

Flick hesitated, looking back at the children with a strange expression, half-sad, half-envious, as if they possessed something else he knew he could never have. Then he said, 'Bye, Circus. Been nice meeting you,' and was gone.

20

He'd deserted them! Left them out like titbits on a plate, for the police to gobble up while he and his gang made their escape.

'Get her to smash the fence,' Charlie said furiously. 'I hope they all get caught, rot 'em! Come on, Tessie, stamp on it, trample it down . . .'

But Belle stopped him. 'We'd be the ones caught,' she pointed out. 'We can't hide as easy as them. Not with Tess.'

'What else can we do? We've got to get out somehow.'

'I'll do it. I'll get her over. Easy. You be look-out. *Go on,* Charlie!'

'Look-out!' he thought angrily, as he climbed the fence and ran towards the road. She'd have said 'keep watch' before. Now it's all look-outs and scouts, — Flick and his phoney army! Bitterness rose in his throat, sour as vomit. He'd liked Flick, *admired* him . . .

Then he stopped, hearing Belle's voice

behind him.

'Hup! Hup! Hup!' she was saying, and he turned in time to see the elephant rear up on her hind legs, as she had been trained to do in the ring. But it was Belle, not Mr Murphy, who was facing her across the low fence. And it was bumpy, slippery grass, not sawdust, beneath her feet. Like a tottering mountain, she wobbled, her enormous forelegs like great rocks poised above Belle's head.

Belle was too near, Charlie thought. She hadn't allowed herself enough room . . . A muscle in his leg jumped, as if telling him to run and snatch her out of danger.

He did not move. Long training kept him from disturbing a performer's concentration. The elephant took a wavering step forwards . . .

'Down!' Belle shouted, and it was as if a mountain toppled.

Then the elephant was straddling the fence, her front legs on one side, her back legs on the other. All were safely planted in the grass, nowhere near Belle. She had not even had to jump out of the way.

Charlie let out his breath, — and heard, too late, the sound of a car coming.

'Hide!' he shouted, knowing there was no time. Belle did her best. Leaping up, she caught hold of a low branch and pulled it down to form a thin, leafy, inadequate screen.

Now the car was in plain sight. Through

its open windows, they could hear the radio warbling:

'Oo-oo-oo,
What a pretty bird,
Oo-oo-oo,
Is she gonna fly away?
Oo-oo-oo . . .'

The driver, a young man in a pink shirt, was looking straight ahead, whistling out of tune to the music. It seemed impossible that he should miss seeing Tessie, peeping over the leaves, like a large lady hiding behind too small a fan. But he never turned his head. Never slowed down. The car was there, before their eyes; then it had swept down the road, trailing its silly song behind it, 'Oo-oo-oo,' and it was gone.

'Sorry,' Charlie said guiltily. 'I didn't hear it in time. I was watching you.'

He could not have found a better excuse. Belle preened herself.

'Good, wasn't I?' she said, beaming. 'Mr Murphy couldn't have done no better. Now we've got to get her hind legs over.'

The wire was sagging under the elephant's belly, the two posts leaning inwards at a drunken angle.

'Come and hold her head a minute,' Belle said. 'We'll have to chance the cars. Got to take a few risks.'

So Charlie held Tessie's head, while Belle,

tapping each leg in turn, guided the huge feet as they lifted over the dipping wire. 'That's it. Anything coming?'

'Can't hear anything.'

'Best straighten up a bit.'

Quickly they pushed the posts upright, and fluffed up the crushed bracken with their hands. It didn't look too bad. Not from a distance.

'Anything coming?' Belle asked again.

Charlie ran down to the road. It was empty. About a hundred yards away, he saw a gateway into the forest on the other side.

'Quick! Follow me!' he shouted, and ran towards it, hearing Belle and Tessie behind him.

There was a notice on the gate. At the top, in large letters, it announced: SHORTLANDS ENCLOSURE. Charlie did not stop to read the small print, but swung the gate open to let Belle and Tessie through. They found themselves on another wide, gravelled path, with the forest pressing in on either side.

'Take her in this way,' Charlie said, pointing to a long drift of dead leaves. He had learned something from the outlaws. When Belle and Tessie were tucked among the trees, he raked over the leaves with a stick, before following. Flick would have been proud of him. Damn Flick!

They went on and on, deeper into the forest, wishing there were more bushes. Once they stopped dead, hearing voices horribly close.

'Beautiful, isn't it?' an invisible woman said

162

enthusiastically, and another replied, 'You should've seen it when the rhododendrons were out. You've missed the best of it.'

They crept away, not knowing where they were going, terrified of suddenly finding themselves in a picnic site, or surrounded by tents. The forest grew thicker and danker. The saddle-cloth, which they had thrown onto Tessie's back and fastened too loosely in their haste, kept catching in branches and slipping sideways. Now the ground squelched under their feet. Pale, bloated toadstools poked up like blind white eyes. They pushed through a dark-leafed shrub and came upon another stream, shallow and choked with debris, so that the dirty water slopped over the ground on either side. There was a foul, rotting stench, as if something had died nearby, and not been buried.

It seemed a secret, shunned place. A hiding place, for who would come here willingly? Except perhaps the police, beating down the undergrowth methodically, dogs smelling out an all too pungent trail . . .

'How many coppers were there?' Belle asked, and was astonished when Charlie said he had only seen one man with Jerry.

'*One*?'

'Yes. In plain clothes.'

'How did you know he was a policeman?'

'I didn't. Pete said . . .'

They stared at each other, and began to laugh

helplessly. They wouldn't try and find the outlaws, they decided. They would stay here.

The editor of *The Rhindhurst Weekly Advertiser* looked at his young reporter.

'Mmm — mm,' he said.

'What do you think?'

'Oh, it's a great story. I love it. "Kidnapped Elephant in Yald Forest." "We Couldn't Let Poor Jumbo Die, Say Circus Children." A great story. *But.*'

The young reporter looked anxious, 'But . . .?'

'But I'd be a lot happier if you'd actually seen the elephant. With your own two eyes. Or better still, through a camera lens. A vanishing elephant is a bit much to swallow, sonny.'

The young reporter looked crestfallen. He had had a horrible time. His face was scratched, his new jacket torn, his shoes ruined. Stumbling about in the unkempt forest with that lout, he had done everything except see the blasted elephant. He had heard it crashing through the undergrowth, — and fallen flat on his face when he gave chase. He had smelled it, — the whole place stank like a zoo. He had been shown droppings as large as footballs, branches torn off trees, carrots and wisps of hay lying on the ground . . .

Rabbits. Foxes. Deer, the editor kept suggesting, shrugging his shoulders.

But one thing could not be so easily explained

away. In a patch of damp ground by a stream, there had been a vast footprint, big as a hubcap.

'I took a tracing,' he said eagerly, holding out four pieces of lined paper, on each of which a wavering pencil line described part of a circle, 'I couldn't get it all on one page,' he explained, 'I only had my notebook with me.'

'A camera would have been better,' muttered the editor. He spread the four pages out on the desk. 'What's this meant to be? Oh, that way round, is it? Still doesn't look like anything,' he said. 'No, sonny, you need a bit more than this. A few hard facts. *One* would be better than nothing. All this is too airy-fairy.'

'I could find out what circuses have gone bankrupt this year,' the young man said eagerly.

The editor shook his head.

'Just look up the number of the Thorpes at Goosebeak Farm for me, son,' he said.

'Goosebeak Farm?'

'I should have taken on a local lad. Goosebeak Farm, sonny. On the Salisbury Road, some six or seven miles past Bradnam. The Thorpes let part of it to a circus for their winter quarters. Beecham's — no, Peachem's, that's it. Hadn't heard they were closing down. That's what comes of taking a month's holiday in Portugal. Everyone goes to sleep while I'm away. You should have picked that up. Local Circus Goes Bankrupt. The Big Top's Last Spin. Clowns on the Dole. Good grief, son, you want to smarten yourself up.'

The young reporter flushed miserably, and removed a frond of bracken from his sleeve.

'Your wits, I meant, not your flipping clothes ... Ah, Mrs Thorpe? Good afternoon. This is Jack Walker of the *Rhindhurst Weekly Advertiser*. What's this I hear about Peachem's going bust? Yes. Yes. They've packed up and gone already? You don't happen to know where I can get hold of two of the children. Belle and Charlie ... Marriot, did you say? Belle and Charlie Marriot. On a barge? Mmm. Mmm. If you can just let me have the aunt's address ... And there was one other thing, I heard they had to have an elephant put down ... When was this? Monday? That would be Barstow's, wouldn't it? No, I quite understand. Nothing else to be done in the circumstances. Mmm. Mmm.' He listened for some time, making occasional notes. Murphy, he wrote, Bradnam General Hospital.

When at last he rang off, he clicked his fingers at his young reporter,

'Quick. Get me Barstow's of Summaton on the line,' he said.

His call to the slaughterhouse was brief. When he put down the telephone, he was beaming. 'What a story we've got here, sonny,' he said, unblushingly claiming half of it, 'Too good to keep to ourselves. Now who will pay best? By the way, where's that young thug gone? I thought you said he'd be coming back.'

'He said he'd be back at two.'

'He's late. Didn't give him any money, did you?'

The young reporter blushed again, 'Only a fiver.'

'Never mind, sonny. You'll learn.' The editor turned to look at the map pinned to the wall behind his desk. 'Wonder where the devil they are?'

'I know which way they plan to go,' the young man said, and traced a line across the map with his finger. 'The girl showed them, apparently.'

'Over Black Ridge, eh? Towards . . . *Blanstock Safari Park!* That must be where they're making for. Probably planning to go down on their knees and beg the Duke to save their elephant. What a story! Here, let me arrange a reception committee for them.' He started to dial the number of the *Daily Planet* in London. As he waited for them to answer, he looked out of the window. The sky was dark, heavy with rain clouds. 'Poor little devils, I hope they look out for the bogs. "Children Brave Bogs to Save Beloved Pet. Elephant Lost in Black Bottom" . . .'

21

It was already dark, and wet. Wet sky, wet earth, wet woods, wet elephant. They had done what they could for Tessie. At seven, when the rain had started, they had spread one of their groundsheets on her back, where it looked like a pocket handkerchief. So they had given her the other one as well, and, putting up the hoods of their anoraks, crouched miserably under a dripping bush.

It did not help to think of the outlaws, sitting warm and dry in the cinema at Bradnam, or shooting down space-invaders in the amusement arcade. They had too much sense, Flick had said, to stay out in the rain. When the weather was bad, they went into the towns and only came back to the forest to sleep.

'Don't your hide-outs get damp?' Belle had asked, and Flick had laughed, saying, 'We don't sleep in them, chick. Too like a grave. We use them as storerooms. We got tents to sleep in.'

'Lucky devils,' she said enviously, wiping her

wet face with her wet hand, 'Perhaps I'll join them, Charlie, after we've settled Tessie.'

For they had liked her, she knew. They thought her brave, not knowing she had lost her nerve; and were impressed, not revolted, by her scar. Once Flick had said to her, when Charlie was not around, 'Come back in a few years, chick, when you've grown a bit. I think I could fancy you.' And what else did she have to look forward to? An unremembered aunt, a new school where she would be bottom of the class, her circus skills unwanted . . .

'They're *thieves*, Belle,' Charlie said.

She and Charlie had been brought up strictly, even if Mrs Marriot's morals were practical, rather than high-minded. 'What d'you think you're doing, girl?' she'd asked once when she'd found Belle going through her handbag; 'You want to watch it! You're an artiste, remember, not a thieving diddy. Travelling circuses *travel*. Abroad, sometimes. How'll you get a permit if you got a prison record as long as my arm? Eh?' It had been no good Belle saying she was just looking for a hanky. She'd had her bottom slapped.

Then, a year later, something had impressed her more than her mother's hard hand. On a wet, muddy Sunday, it was discovered that a tentboy had gone off with the week's takings. She would never forget the desolation, the cold wind blowing, the Guv'nor's wife in tears . . .

And then the whole circus had gathered round, patting the weeping woman on her shoulder; and holding out a hat into which they had put their hard-earned money. How proud she had felt to be one of them, an artiste, a worker, putting her fifty pence in with the rest.

The circus was over now, and her career all smashed up. But at least they had known it once, the belonging, and could hope for it again. She thought of Flick, saying, 'What have they ever done for me?' Meaning — nothing. Only the forest was kind to him. But then she remembered Billy coughing, pressing his thin hands to his chest, and Flick's anxious look. She remembered their faces, when she had asked, tactlessly about winter. Perhaps, cold and wet as they now were, she and Charlie were still the lucky ones.

'I ain't going to be no drop-out,' she said. 'I'm going right to the middle where it's warm.'

'What are you on about?'

'Dunno. I was thinking of the Big Top. All the trailers with their windows lit up. And rabbit stew.'

'Oh, shut up!'

At ten o'clock they could bear the leaking forest no longer, and decided to move. Because they did not know exactly where they were, they came out of the trees a good mile from the track Belle's finger had traced on the map, and did not see the waiting cars. They crossed the road silently and unobserved.

The rain had dwindled now. In the distance, sombre clouds swept down to the humped back of Black Ridge, so that it looked a mere reflection of other hills in the sky, as if the world were upside down. The heath itself was blurred, its contours disguised by a misty drizzle so that bushes might have been elephants, or elephants bushes, for all one could tell.

'Nobody'll see us in this muck,' Charlie said, 'I can hardly see myself.'

Belle looked back. The road was already invisible, but on the left a few hazy lights shone dimly through the mist. One of the forest villages, perhaps. Or a farm. She turned her back on the thought of a warm kitchen, and looked at the gloomy wilderness ahead.

'Which way?'

'Dunno. Straight ahead, I suppose.'

'Got your compass?'

'Too dark to see it, and we'd best not show a light yet. Let's go on.'

At first they led Tessie. The ground was rough and bumpy, bisected with narrow streams, and bristling with small bushes, seen too late. The elephant seemed unhappy at their slow, halting pace, and rumbled mournfully, pulling against Belle's restraining hand on her ear. Belle worried about her, frightened she would catch cold.

'If we rode her, she could go faster and keep warm,' Charlie suggested.

171

Belle was silent.

'We'll never get there if we don't. It's a long way.'

She hunched her shoulders and walked on, without answering.

'You won't fall off again. I'll hold onto you. Just pretend she's a double decker bus ...'

'I ain't afraid! Belle said furiously.

'Then why don't we ride her?' he asked, sweetly reasonable.

She scowled at him. He gave a re-assuring smile. Both expressions were wasted: their faces were dim blurs in the dark. After a weary pause, Charlie switched on his torch, shielding the beam with his fingers, which blossomed like red flowers in the night.

'What are you doing?'

'Looking at the compass,' he said. 'Which way do we want?'

'Left on the map.'

'West,' he translated.

'And a bit down.'

'West sou' west?'

'Dunno,' she said sulkily, not caring. 'Sounds all right.'

They stumbled on in silence for a while; then Belle gave in.

'All right. You win. We'll ride.'

'Not if you don't want to,' Charlie said airily. She could have hit him, and said so. For a moment, wet, hungry and exhausted, they hated each other. For two pins, they'd have walked off in different directions . . . except that it was too dark and desolate to be alone. So they mounted Tessie, and rode on in silence.

The elephant walked fearlessly over the dim heath, taking bushes and streams in her stride. Belle, sitting in front and clinging onto the head-band, was soon too tired to be frightened. She peered through the wet darkness until the blurred hills seemed to be swaying before her eyes. She was rocking, rocking in a boat. Waves slapped against the sides . . . She jerked awake, clutching the headband to stop herself slipping off.

The rain had stopped now, and a watery moon hung in the cloudy sky. The elephant was walking strangely, unevenly, dragging her feet. And still Belle could hear a sucking, splashing sound . . .

'It's a bog!' she screamed, 'Charlie, Tessie's gone into a bog!'

His arms jerked round her waist. 'Wha — what's the matter?' he mumbled.

'Stop! Tessie, stop!'

The elephant stood patiently. Charlie switched on his torch and shone it down. At first the ground looked firm enough, covered with low, small-leafed bushes and round hassocks of grass. Then they saw the gleam of dark water every-where. On the left, tall reeds grew thickly.

'What shall we do?'

'Turn her round. Go back.'

But Tessie, for the first time, was obstinate. She did not want to go back and ignored Belle's shouted orders. When Belle kicked her leg against the leathery neck, the elephant sucked up a trunkful of muddy water and tossed it over her shoulder, soaking the children.

'What's the matter with her?'

'Dunno.'

'Perhaps there's a deep hole behind her.'

'Can't be. She got here all right.'

'Why won't she turn round, then?'

'Prehaps she can't. Perhaps she's sinking!'

Terrified, with some idea of lightening the poor animal's weight, they slid off her back, landing in the soft, sodden bog myrtle, and stumbling to their feet, only ankle deep in thin mud. The elephant started to walk forwards again.

'Stop!' screamed Belle. The elephant stopped and sighed.

'Perhaps we ought to trust her,' Charlie said, 'Flick said the bogs weren't very deep.'

They looked at each other helplessly, not knowing what to do. They shone their torch round in a circle, but there was no telling where the bog began or ended. It all looked much the same, dark and dreary, stretching away into the mist. It might be safer to go on. The elephant's heavy weight might have disturbed the unstable ground behind them, setting it quaking like a black jelly.

'It doesn't seem very deep here,' Charlie said,

prodding the wet ground with his foot. 'I'll walk in front. Then if I start sinking, Tessie can pull me up, and we'll try another way.'

'No, Charlie! I don't want you to!'

'We can't stay here.'

So Charlie walked ahead, shining his torch on the ground, stepping from hassock to hassock, and testing the depths in between with his foot. Once he slipped and went up to the knee in thick water, feeling the mud beneath clutch his ankle. He could not help crying out, but before Belle and Tessie could reach him, he was safe again on a bush, only lacking one shoe.

'Don't bring her this way,' he shouted. 'There's a sort of hole. Take her round by those bushes.'

'Charlie, let's go back! It ain't safe.'

'It's not too bad. It's only deep in patches.'

'Let me go first, then.'

'No.'

'I want to!'

'You're better with Tessie. She wouldn't obey me.'

This was true, so Belle gave in, though she dreaded seeing Charlie vanish before her eyes, leaving only a few bubbles breaking in the mud. She was crying now, keeping so close behind Charlie that he kept shouting at her to keep back. She did not even notice the ground getting firmer beneath her feet until Charlie suddenly gave a whoop of triumph and started capering about, waving his torch like a mad fire-fly.

'We've done it! We've done it!' he shouted. 'It's solid!' He stamped on the ground. 'Well, almost.'

It was the only bog they came across. Now the ground began to rise steeply, and there were sharp stones between the bushes. They walked for a few miles, to give Tessie a rest. It helped to keep them warm. There was a cold wind blowing and their clothes were wet. But Charlie had put on his gumboots and his feet were soon sore, so they rode again. Up and up, they went, two children and an elephant, crossing the Black Ridge against the night sky, and vanishing out of sight.

22

It was a cool, moist morning, still damp from the night's rain. At six o'clock, the two children, carrying a spongebag, towels, a large scrubbing brush and a bucket, let the elephant out of a barn, and crossed a field to reach the stream on the other side.

'We'll have to do it early,' Charlie said. 'There's just nowhere to hide. Not unless we go back into the hills.'

'And we ain't doing that. Flipping map! Green for woodlands, it says. Ten trees and six bungalows, call that woodlands? This water ain't all that clean, Charlie.'

'Cleaner than us.'

'It's cold. I ain't stripping.'

'Just wash where it shows.'

Having done their faces and hands, they set to work on the elephant, dousing her with buckets of water and scrubbing everything they could reach. Back in the barn, they changed into

177

clean, though creased clothes, tucking their denim trousers neatly into their gumboots. They combed their hair carefully, and smoothed it down with their hands. Belle, glancing apologetically at Charlie, rubbed the damp soap over her scar and stuck a strand of hair over it.

'Got to look respectable,' she said. 'How's that, Charlie?'

'You'll do.'

But somehow, there was still a touch of the circus about them, a vagabond air. Perhaps it was the swagger in their walk, the slight exaggeration of their gestures. Or it might have been the rim of dirt round their shining faces.

'Do you think it will work?' Belle asked.

Charlie shrugged, then seeing her face, said, 'Of course it will!' 'It must. I couldn't bear it if . . . It *will* work.' she said, defying fate.

She gave Charlie a cheerful grin that cracked his heart. He did not think her plan stood a chance. Even if they got Tessie in, sooner or later the safari park would count their elephants, find they had one too many, and chuck her right out again. But he could not tell Belle this.

'Dunno why I'm so nervous,' she said uneasily, 'I wish . . . I wish I wasn't such a coward.'

It was the first time she had ever admitted being afraid. He said quickly, 'You're not! You're very brave. You've just lost your head for heights, that's all. It's nothing to do with being brave. It's sort of like being ill. You can be cured.'

But Belle was thinking of a dragonfly she had seen in the forest, glittering and dancing over the stream, with an easy, careless joy. Belonging in the air. 'I'll never be a high-flyer no more,' she said. 'Still, who cares? Not me. Only, I do want us to save Tessie . . .'

'We *will*,' Charlie said, feeling he'd kill anyone who stopped them.

At seven, they came out from behind a high hedge, about a quarter of a mile from Blanstock Safari Park, and began walking up the side of the road. They seemed angry and upset. Holding sticks in their hands, they drove the elephant in front of them, as if they were frightened of her. Every time she turned her head to look at them, they leapt back nervously, and said, 'Shoo! Go away! Shoo!'

A few minutes later, they had an audience. A farm truck came rattling round the corner, swerved wildly, narrowly missing the ditch on the other side, and stopped.

Charlie ran forward, shouting, 'An elephant's got loose from the safari park! We're trying to drive her back!'

The driver stared at him, at Belle, at the elephant.

'You're those . . .' he began.

Belle interrupted him. 'It frightened Star — '

'That's her pony,' Charlie said.

'I got thrown off! I'm bruised all over.'

'She might've been killed.'

179

'We're going to complain.'

'They should keep their elephants off the road.'

Under this barrage of indignation, the driver appeared bemused. He kept looking at the elephant, opening his mouth, shutting it again, and looking back at the elephant, as if he did not know the best thing to do. Only when Tessie, bored, began ambling towards the truck, did he make up his mind. He released the handbrake.

'You're going straight to Blanstock, then?' he asked, eyeing the approaching elephant uneasily.

'Yes. It ain't safe to leave her straying,' they said virtuously. 'You nearly had an accident.'

'I'll let them know you're coming,' the driver said. 'Keep her away from my truck, there's a good couple of kids. It's new.' And he drove off.

'Quick!' Belle said, and they began to hurry.

Timing, as Mr Schneider had so often told them, was the essence of a successful act. They wanted the gate-keeper flustered, half asleep, only too glad to fling open the gates and get the elephant off the road, before the park could be accused of negligence. They didn't want to give him time to think. They didn't want him to use his telephone.

They raced down the road, only slowing when they reached the corner. Now at least they saw the great gateway to Blanstock Safari Park before them. The farm truck was parked on the verge just past it, and there were other cars beyond. The driver was standing talking excitedly to a small group of men, and they all turned to look at the children as they herded the elephant down the last stretch of road.

The gates were opening! They'd done it! They were going to get Tessie in! It was all Belle could do to stop herself from leaping about with joy and triumph, as Tessie walked slowly and with enormous dignity through the tall, wrought-iron gates.

Then the world seemed to explode. Bright lights flashed in Belle's face. People crowded around her and Charlie. Men with cameras . . . *policemen!* . . .

'No!' she shouted, 'No!'

Pushing through them, she ran over to where the elephant was standing patiently, and flung her arms round Tessie's trunk.

'No! No!' she wept. 'Oh, Tessie, we did our best.'

And she felt Charlie's arm round her shoulder, and turning, saw that he was crying too.

23

It was this photograph that was to dog them for the rest of their lives; pinned to the notice board of their new school, turning up years later in old magazines, lining the drawer of a boarding house in Bognor, and found, framed and fly-blown, on the wall of a café in Brighton. There they were, caught for ever, crying like babies. There even seemed, by some trick of the light, to be a tear shining in Tessie's round, solemn eye.

The effect had been tremendous. Everyone wanted Tessie. The story of the two children, kidnapping their favourite elephant to save it from the knacker's yard, had gone to the hearts of the public, just as the editor of *The Rhindhurst Weekly Advertiser* had thought it would. People sent money. A Save Tessie Fund was started. Three circuses, suddenly warm-hearted, offered to take her. And so did the Duke of Blanstock. Unlike the many small children who wrote to offer homes for Tessie in garden sheds or spare bedrooms, *he* had a safari park.

So, with Mr Murphy's blessing, that was where Tessie stayed.

'She's old, like me,' Mr Murphy said. 'She deserves a rest. And the Duke's a gent. He won't turn her out when the public have forgotten her.'

He never had his cottage at the gate. Though out of hospital now, he still needed to be looked after. So he went to live with his sister in her council flat in Worthing, where he kept, strictly against the rules, a pet snake.

'You should call it Tessinose,' Belle said, eying its questing, greyish length.

Mr Murphy smiled and shook his head.

'Christabel,' he said, 'that's what she's called.'

Belle blushed at the compliment; even though she was not overfond of snakes.

They could hardly believe their luck. Instead of being punished, they were everyone's darlings. They felt very warm towards the world . . . even though they knew, in their heart of hearts, that had Tessie rioted, smashed property and people, they would have been, not darlings, but thoughtless little monsters. The difference had been the whereabouts of Tessie's feet.

Thanks to Tessie's gentleness and good sense, they were heroes. In public they behaved with becoming modesty. But it was too much to expect the same in private. In Aunt May's respectable sitting-room, they gave way to sudden fits of shrieking laughter and wild cartwheels.

Smilingly, Aunt May removed her more delicate ornaments.

She was no longer the thin, cool, grey lady of their memory. She had put on weight and a pink blouse, and become fat and jolly. Best of all, she obviously liked them.

A telephone call was made to Belle's parents in America. Aunt May had tracked them down to a small town in the Middle West. Their voices, squeezed through thousands of miles of wires, came out as small and excited as the children's. Aunt May smiled ruefully. Circus people never really grew up, she thought. It was only when her feckless sister and brother-in-law proposed that Belle and Charlie should take instant advantage of their temporary fame and come to America, that she put her foot down.

'School,' she said, taking the phone firmly from Belle. 'They've got to go to school, Annie. That's what we agreed.'

Belle's parents reluctantly gave in, comforting themselves with the thought that children, who had begun by kidnapping an elephant, would be sure to go on to even bigger things.

So they went to school. It was on the first day, walking through the windy streets, that Charlie noticed Belle's hand go up to her face in the old nervous gesture. She had not done this for weeks. Not since the forest.

'It hardly shows,' he said.

'No.'

They walked on in silence. They came to the school: it looked like a prison. On the pavement outside, there was a crowd of chattering children. On Belle and Charlie's approach, they stopped and stared. Uneasily, Belle reached for Charlie's hand.

'We've done it all before,' he said. 'In a week, we'll be old pros.'

'Yes.'

Charlie made a noise like a roll of drums. 'Positively the First Appearance before any Public! the Sensational Christabel and Cosmo! Remember?'

Belle smiled and nodded.

Now they had reached the other children.

'Hullo,' said Charlie boldly. 'We're new.'

'Hey, aren't you those circus kids?' a boy asked, inspecting them carefully. 'The ones in the papers?'

'That's us,' Belle said. She was stiff with fright. It made her look arrogant.

The watching faces turned hostile.

Then a gust of wind blew down the street, sending old bus tickets dancing down the pavement, and whipping aside Belle's carefully arranged hair. All eyes went to her scar. Charlie clenched his fists.

'Oh, snot! And I spent hours fixing it,' Belle said crossly, pulling at her hair, 'Old Scarface, that's me!' She made a rueful, clown's face, and laughed.

At once, the hostility vanished. Who could resist a clown? Belle, the practised performer, had won over her audience. She had them in the palm of her hand, thought Charlie. Admiringly, he watched as she disappeared in a crowd of girls, all eager for the privilege of her friendship.

They liked the school, maybe because the school liked them. Belle worked hard, having got it into her head that she'd like to be a zoologist. Or a vet.

'I'm good with animals,' she said, with her old, incurable boastfulness. 'The Duke says I'm amazing.'

Charlie was disconcerted.

'Aren't you going back into the circus?' he asked.

'Dunno.'

'Belle, you *must!* Mr Schneider said we could both have a job at Christmas. Not only me. You, too.'

'Big of him.' she tilted her nose and said grandly. 'The Duke said I could come and help at the safari park in the holidays. They like me there. The keepers say I'm a wonder.'

'Oh, Belle!' he said, laughing.

'It's true.'

'You've *got* to stay in the circus. Or I won't marry you when I grow up,' he said, looking at her slyly.

And she tossed her head, smiling, and said,

just as she had done so long ago, 'You'll be lucky.'

In the late autumn sunlight, two masked figures are dancing on the grass, like sequined dragonflies. The clown, it appears, is in love with the ballerina. He blows her kisses, walks upside down and somersaults before her. She does not seem to see him, but dances as if in a dream, serious and self-absorbed.

Now the clown holds up his hand, and a yellow rose blossoms from his fingers. He offers it to the ballerina, who takes it. Then she dances on. Round and round she goes, faster and faster, to sink at last into a deep curtsey. The clown bows.

There is a round of applause, and people shower coins into the clown's hat. 'It's them. It's Belle and Charlie,' they tell one another. Then they get back into their cars and drive off to see the baboons and the lions and, of course, the elephants. Especially their old favourite, Tessie of Yald Forest.

Blanstock Safari Park is doing well. The admissions have trebled since they took in the circus elephant. Everyone loves her. The Duke likes the children too, who amuse him. They are staying in Blanstock for their half-term holiday and coming in to help with the animals. Belle has a natural gift with them, and he hopes to persuade her to take a job at Blanstock when she leaves school. Charlie, he understands, is to be a circus star.

Sitting on the grass, wrapped up in their new winter coats, for it is cold in spite of the sun, Belle and Charlie are counting up their money.

'Not bad,' Charlie says. 'Eighty pence more than yesterday.'

They have started a new fund. They are saving up to buy a safari park, with a small circus in the grounds. They know it is only a dream, but they like dreaming.

'After all, the Duke's got a fairground here, so why not a circus?' Charlie says.

'We'll just have clowns and acrobats and high-flyers,' Belle suggests. She has become uneasy about performing animals.

'And Star-Spinners?'

'Yes,' she agrees, smiling. 'We'll get a couple of kids and train 'em.'

They are happy. They hardly ever think of the outlaws. Only sometimes on a cold night, when Belle hears the rain beating on her windows, she wonders about Flick and Pete and Billy, and what will happen to them when winter comes.